Doing Our 'Bit'

Doing Our 'Bit'

Two Classic Accounts of the Men of Kitchener's 'New Army' During the Great War

including

The First 100,000

& All In It

Ian Hay

Doing Our 'Bit': Two Classic Accounts of the Men of Kitchener's 'New Army' During the Great War including The First 100,000 & All In It
by Ian Hay

Published by Leonaur Ltd in 2007

ISBN: 978-1-84677-316-7 (hardcover)
ISBN: 978-1-84677-315-0 (softcover)

http://www.leonaur.com

Publisher's Notes

In the interests of authenticity, the spellings, grammar and place names used have been retained from the original edition.

The opinions expressed in this book are those of the author and are not necessarily those of the publisher.

Contents

The First 100,000

All In It

"K(1)"

We do not deem ourselves A 1,
We have no past: we cut no dash:
Nor hope, when launched against the Hun,
To raise a more than moderate splash.

But yesterday, we said farewell
To plough; to pit; to dock; to mill.
For glory? *Drop it!*
Why? Oh, well—
To have a slap at Kaiser Bill.

And now today has come along.
With rifle, haversack, and pack,
We're off, a hundred thousand strong.
And—some of us will not come back.

But all we ask, if that befall,
Is this. Within your hearts be writ
This single-line memorial:—
He did his duty—and his *BIT!*

Note

The reader is hereby cautioned against regarding this narrative as an official history of the Great War.

The following pages are merely a record of some of the personal adventures of a typical regiment of Kitchener's Army.

The chapters were written from day to day, and published from month to month. Consequently, prophecy is occasionally falsified, and opinions moderated, in subsequent pages.

The characters are entirely fictitious, but the incidents described all actually occurred.

Book 1
Blank Cartridges

Chapter 1
Ab Ovo

"Squoad—'*Shun*! Move to the right in fours. Forrm—*fourrrs*!"

The audience addressed looks up with languid curiosity, but makes no attempt to comply with the speaker's request.

"Come away now, come away!" urges the instructor, mopping his brow. "Mind me: on the command 'form fours,' odd numbers will stand fast; even numbers tak' a shairp pace to the rear and anither to the right. Now—forrm *fourrs*!"

The squad stands fast, to a man. Apparently—nay, verily—they are all odd numbers.

The instructor addresses a gentleman in a decayed Homburg hat, who is chewing tobacco in the front rank.

"Yous, what's your number?"

The ruminant ponders.

"Seeven fower ought seeven seeven," he announces, after a prolonged mental effort.

The instructor raises clenched hands to heaven.

"Man, I'm no askin' you your regimental number! Never heed that. It's your number in the squad I'm seeking. You numbered off frae the right five minutes syne."

Ultimately it transpires that the culprit's number is ten. He is pushed into his place, in company with the other even numbers, and the squad finds itself approximately in fours.

"Forrm—two *deep*!" barks the instructor.

The fours disentangle themselves reluctantly, Number Ten being the last to forsake his post.

"Now we'll dae it jist yince more, and have it right," announces the instructor, with quite unjustifiable optimism. "Forrm—*fourrs*!"

This time the result is better, but there is confusion on the left flank.

"Yon man, oot there on the left," shouts the instructor, "what's your number?"

Private Mucklewame, whose mind is slow but tenacious, answers—not without pride at knowing—

"Nineteen!"

(Thank goodness, he reflects, odd numbers stand fast upon all occasions.)

"Weel, mind this," says the sergeant—"Left files is always even numbers, even though they are odd numbers."

This revelation naturally clouds Private Mucklewame's intellect for the afternoon; and he wonders dimly, not for the first time, why he ever abandoned his well-paid and well-fed job as a butcher's assistant in distant Wishaw ten long days ago.

And so the drill goes on. All over the drab, dusty, gritty parade-ground, under the warm September sun, similar squads are being pounded into shape. They have no uniforms yet: even their instructors wear bowler hats or cloth caps. Some of the faces under the brims of these hats are not too prosperous. The junior officers are drilling squads too. They are a little shaky in what an actor would call their "patter," and they are inclined to lay stress on the wrong syllables; but they move their squads about somehow. Their seniors are dotted about the square, vigilant and helpful—here prompting a rusty sergeant instructor, there unravelling a squad which, in a spirited but misguided endeavour to obey an impossible order from Second Lieutenant Bobby Little, has wound itself up into a formation closely resembling the third figure of the Lancers.

Over there, by the officers' mess, stands the Colonel. He is in uniform, with a streak of parti-coloured ribbon running across above his left-hand breast-pocket. He is pleased to call himself a "dug-out." A fortnight ago he was fishing in the Garry, his fighting days avowedly behind him, and only the Special Reserve between him and *embonpoint.* Now he finds himself pitchforked back into the Active List, at the head of a battalion eleven hundred strong.

He surveys the scene. Well, his officers are all right. The Second in Command has seen almost as much service as himself. Of the four company commanders, two have been commandeered while home on leave from India, and the other two have practised the art of war in company with brother Boer. Of the rest, there are three subalterns from the Second Battalion—left behind, to their unspeakable woe—and four from the O.T.C. The juniors are very junior, but keen as mustard.

But the men! Is it possible? Can that awkward, shy, self-conscious mob, with scarcely an old soldier in their ranks, be pounded, within the space of a few months, into the Seventh (Service) Battalion of the Bruce and Wallace Highlanders—one of the most famous regiments in the British Army?

The Colonel's boyish figure stiffens.

"They're a rough crowd," he murmurs, "and a tough crowd: but they're a stout crowd. By gad! we'll make them a credit to the Old Regiment yet!"

Chapter 2
The Daily Grind

We have been in existence for more than three weeks now, and occasionally we are conscious of a throb of real life. Squad drill is almost a thing of the past, and we work by platoons of over fifty men. To-day our platoon once marched, in perfect step, for seven complete and giddy paces, before disintegrating into its usual formation—namely, an advance in irregular *echelon*, by individuals.

Four platoons form a company, and each platoon is (or should be) led by a subaltern, acting under his company commander. But we are very short of subalterns at present. (We are equally short of N.C.O.'s; but then you can always take a man out of the ranks and christen him sergeant, whereas there is no available source of Second Lieutenants save capricious Whitehall.) Consequently, three platoons out of four in our company are at present commanded by N.C.O.'s, two of whom appear to have retired from active service about the time that bows and arrows began to yield place to the arquebus, while the third has been picked out of the ranks simply because he possesses a loud voice and a cake of soap. None of them has yet mastered the new drill—it was all changed at the beginning of this year—and the majority of the officers are in no position to correct their anachronisms.

Still, we are getting on. Number Three Platoon (which boasts a subaltern) has just marched right round the barrack square, without—

(1) Marching through another platoon.

(2) Losing any part or parts of itself.

(3) Adopting a formation which brings it face to face with a blank wall, or piles it up in a tidal wave upon the veranda, of the married quarters.

They could not have done that a week ago.

But stay, what is this disturbance on the extreme left? The command "Right form" has been given, but six files on the outside flank have ignored the suggestion, and are now advancing (in skirmishing order) straight for the ashbin outside the cookhouse door, looking piteously round over their shoulders for some responsible person to give them an order which will turn them about and bring them back to the fold. Finally they are rounded up by the platoon sergeant, and restored to the strength.

"What went wrong, Sergeant?" inquires Second Lieutenant Bobby Little. He is a fresh-faced youth, with an engaging smile. Three months ago he was keeping wicket for his school eleven.

The sergeant comes briskly to attention.

"The order was not distinctly heard by the men, sir," he explains, "owing to the corporal that passed it on wanting a tooth. Corporal Blain, three paces forward—march!"

Corporal Blain steps forward, and after remembering to slap the small of his butt with his right hand, takes up his parable—

"I was sittin' doon tae ma dinner on Sabbath, sir, when my front teeth met upon a small piece bone that was stickit' in—"

Further details of this gastronomic tragedy are cut short by the blast of a whistle. The Colonel, at the other side of the square, has given the signal for the end of parade. Simultaneously a bugle rings out cheerfully from the direction of the orderly-room. Breakfast, blessed breakfast, is in sight. It is nearly eight, and we have been as busy as bees since six.

At a quarter to nine the battalion parades for a route-march. This, strange as it may appear, is a comparative rest. Once you have got your company safely decanted from column of platoons into column of route, your labours are at an end. All you have to do is to march; and that is no great hardship when you are as hard as nails, as we are fast becoming. On the march the mental gymnastics involved by the formation of an advanced guard or the disposition of a piquet line are removed to a safe distance. There is no need to wonder guiltily whether you have sent out a connecting-file between the vanguard and the main-guard, or if you remembered to instruct your sentry groups as to the position of the enemy and the extent of their own front.

Second Lieutenant Little heaves a contented sigh, and steps out manfully along the dusty road. Behind him tramp his men. We have no pipers as yet, but melody is supplied by "Tipperary," sung in ragged chorus, varied by martial interludes upon the mouth-organ. Despise not the mouth-organ. Ours has been a constant boon. It has kept sixty men in step for miles on end.

Fortunately the weather is glorious. Day after day, after a sharp and frosty dawn, the sun swings up into a cloudless sky; and the hundred thousand troops that swarm like ants upon, the undulating plains of Hampshire can march, sit, lie, or sleep on hard, sun-baked earth. A wet autumn would have thrown our training back months. The men, as yet, possess nothing but the fatigue uniforms they stand up in, so it is imperative to keep them dry.

Tramp, tramp, tramp. "Tipperary" has died away. The owner of the mouth-organ is temporarily deflated. Here is an opportunity for individual enterprise. It is soon seized. A husky soloist breaks into one of the deathless ditties of the new Scottish Laureate; his comrades take up the air with ready response; and presently we are all swinging along to the strains of "I Love a Lassie,"—"Roaming in the Gloaming" and "It's Just Like Being at Hame" being rendered as encores.

Then presently come snatches of a humorously amorous nature—"Hallo, Hallo, Who's Your Lady Friend?"; "You're my Baby"; and the ungrammatical "Who Were You With Last Night?" Another great favourite is an involved composition which always appears to begin in the middle. It deals severely with the precocity of a youthful lover who has been detected wooing his lady in the Park. Each verse ends, with enormous gusto—

"Hold your haand *oot*, you naughty boy!"

Tramp, tramp, tramp. Now we are passing through a village. The inhabitants line the pavement and smile cheerfully upon us—they are always kindly disposed toward "Scotchies"—but the united gaze of the rank and file wanders instinctively from the pavement towards upper windows and kitchen entrances, where the domestic staff may be discerned, bunched together and giggling. Now we are out on the road again, silent and dusty. Suddenly, far in the rear, a voice of singular sweetness strikes up "The Banks of Loch Lomond." Man after man joins in, until the swelling chorus runs from end to end of the long column. Half the battalion hail from the Loch Lomond district, and of the rest there is hardly a man who has not indulged, during some Trades' Holiday or other, in "a pleesure trup" upon its historic but inexpensive waters.

"You'll tak' the high road and I'll tak' the low road—"

On we swing, full-throated. An English battalion, halted at a cross-road to let us go by, gazes curiously upon us. "Tipperary" they know, Harry Lauder they have heard of; but this song has no meaning for them. It is ours, ours, ours. So we march on. The feet of Bobby Little, as he tramps at the head of his platoon, hardly touch the ground. His head is in the air. One day, he feels instinctively, he will hear that song again, amid sterner surroundings. When that day comes, the song, please God, for all its sorrowful wording, will reflect no sorrow from the hearts of those who sing it—only courage, and the joy of battle, and the knowledge of victory.

"—And I'll be in Scotland before ye. But me and my true love will never meet again On the bonny, bonny *baanks*—"

A shrill whistle sounds far ahead. It means "March at Attention." "Loch Lomond" dies away with uncanny suddenness—discipline is waxing stronger every day—and tunics are buttoned and rifles unslung. Three minutes later we swing demurely on to the barrack-square, across which a pleasant aroma of stewed onions is wafting, and deploy with creditable precision into the formation known as "mass." Then comes much dressing of ranks and adjusting of distances. The Colonel is very particular about a clean finish to any piece of work.

Presently the four companies are aligned: the N.C.O.'s retire to the supernumerary ranks. The battalion stands rigid, facing a motionless figure upon horseback. The figure stirs.

"Fall out, the officers!"

They come trooping, stand fast, and salute—very smartly. We must set an example to the men. Besides, we are hungry too.

"Battalion, slope *arms*! *Dis*-miss!"

Every man, with one or two incurable exceptions, turns sharply to his right and cheerfully smacks the butt of his rifle with his disengaged hand. The Colonel gravely returns the salute; and we stream away, all the thousand of us, in the direction of the savoury smell. Two o'clock will come round all too soon, and with it company drill and tiresome musketry exercises; but by that time we shall have *dined*, and Fate cannot touch us for another twenty-four hours.

Chapter 3
Growing Pains

We have our little worries, of course.

Last week we were all vaccinated, and we did not like it. Most of us have "taken" very severely, which is a sign that we badly needed vaccinating, but makes the discomfort no easier to endure. It is no joke handling a rifle when your left arm is swelled to the full compass of your sleeve; and the personal contact of your neighbour in the ranks is sheer agony. However, officers are considerate, and the work is made as light as possible. The faint-hearted report themselves sick; but the Medical Officer, an unsentimental man of coarse mental fibre, who was on a panel before he heard his country calling, merely recommends them to get well as soon as possible, as they are going to be inoculated for enteric next week. So we grouse—and bear it.

There are other rifts within the military lute. At home we are persons of some consequence, with very definite notions about the dignity of labour. We have employers who tremble at our frown; we have Trades Union officials who are at constant pains to impress upon us our own omnipotence in the industrial world in which we live. We have at our beck and call a Radical M.P. who, in return for our vote and suffrage, informs us that we are the backbone of the nation, and that we must on no account permit ourselves to be trampled upon by the effete and tyrannical upper classes. Finally, we are Scotsmen, with all a Scotsman's curious reserve and contempt for social airs and graces.

But in the Army we appear to be nobody. We are expected to stand stiffly at attention when addressed by an officer; even to call him "sir"—an honour to which our previous employer has been a stranger. At home, if we happened to meet the head of the firm in the street, and none of our colleagues was looking, we touched a cap, furtively. Now, we have no option in the matter. We are expected to degrade ourselves by meaningless and humiliating gestures. The N.C.O.'s are almost as bad. If you answer a sergeant as you would a foreman, you are impertinent; if you argue with him, as all good Scotsmen must, you are insubordinate; if you endeavour to drive a collective bargain with him, you are mutinous; and you are reminded that upon active service mutiny is punishable by death. It is all very unusual and upsetting.

You may not spit; neither may you smoke a cigarette in the ranks, nor keep the residue thereof behind your ear. You may not take beer to bed with you. You may not postpone your shave till Saturday: you must shave every day. You must keep your buttons, accoutrements, and rifle speckless, and have your hair cut in a style which is not becoming to your particular type of beauty. Even your feet are not your own. Every Sunday morning a young officer, whose leave has been specially stopped for the purpose, comes round the barrack-rooms after church and inspects your extremities, revelling in blackened nails and gloating over hammer-toes. For all practical purposes, decides Private Mucklewame, you might as well be in Siberia.

Still, one can get used to anything. Our lot is mitigated, too, by the knowledge that we are all in the same boat. The most olympian N.C.O. stands like a ramrod when addressing an officer, while lieutenants make obeisance to a company commander as humbly as any private. Even the Colonel was seen one day to salute an old gentleman who rode on to the parade-ground during morning drill, wearing a red band round his hat. Noting this, we realise that the Army is not, after all, as we first suspected, divided into two classes—oppressors and oppressed. We all have to "go through it."

Presently fresh air, hard training, and clean living begin to weave their spell. Incredulous at first, we find ourselves slowly recognising the fact that it is possible to treat an officer deferentially, or carry out an order smartly, without losing one's self-respect as a man and a Trades Unionist. The insidious habit of cleanliness, once acquired, takes despotic possession of its victims: we find ourselves looking askance at room-mates who have not yet yielded to such predilections. The swimming-bath, where once we flapped unwillingly and ingloriously at the shallow end, becomes quite a desirable resort, and we look forward to our weekly visit with something approaching eagerness. We begin, too, to take our profession seriously. Formerly we regarded outpost exercises, advanced guards, and the like, as a rather fatuous form of play-acting, designed to amuse those officers who carry maps and notebooks.

Now we begin to consider these diversions on their merits, and seriously criticise Second Lieutenant Little for having last night posted one of his sentry groups upon the skyline. Thus is the soul of a soldier born.

We are getting less individualistic, too. We are beginning to think more of our regiment and less of ourselves. At first this loyalty takes the form of criticising other regiments, because their marching is slovenly, or their accoutrements dirty, or—most significant sign of all—their discipline is bad. We are especially critical of our own Eighth Battalion, which is fully three weeks younger than we are, and is not in the First Hundred Thousand at all. In their presence we are war-worn veterans. We express it as our opinion that the officers of some of these battalions must be a poor lot. From this it suddenly comes home to us that our officers are a good lot, and we find ourselves taking a queer pride in our company commander's homely strictures and severe sentences the morning after pay-night. Here is another step in the quickening life of the regiment. *Esprit de corps* is raising its head, class prejudice and dour "independence" notwithstanding.

Again, a timely hint dropped by the Colonel on battalion parade this morning has set us thinking. We begin to wonder how we shall compare with the first-line regiments when we find ourselves "oot there." Silently we resolve that when we, the first of the Service Battalions, take our place in trench or firing line alongside the Old Regiment, no one shall be found to draw unfavourable comparisons between parent and offspring. We intend to show ourselves chips of the old block. No one who knows the Old Regiment can ask more of a young battalion than *that.*

CHAPTER 4
The Conversion of Private M'Slattery

One evening a rumour ran round the barracks. Most barrack rumours die a natural death, but this one was confirmed by the fact that next morning the whole battalion, instead of performing the usual platoon exercises, was told off for instruction in the art of presenting arms. "A" Company discussed the portent at breakfast.

"What kin' o' a thing is a Review?" inquired Private M'Slattery.

Private Mucklewame explained. Private M'Slattery was not impressed, and said so quite frankly. In the lower walks of the industrial world Royalty is too often a mere name. Personal enthusiasm for a Sovereign whom they have never seen, and who in their minds is inextricably mixed up with the House of Lords, and capitalism, and the police, is impossible to individuals of the stamp of Private M'Slattery. To such, Royalty is simply the head and corner-stone of a legal system which officiously prevents a man from being drunk and disorderly, and the British Empire an expensive luxury for which the working man pays while the idle rich draw the profits.

If M'Slattery's opinion of the Civil Code was low, his opinion of Military Law was at zero. In his previous existence in his native Clydebank, when weary of rivet-heating and desirous of change and rest, he had been accustomed to take a day off and become pleasantly intoxicated, being comfortably able to afford the loss of pay involved by his absence. On these occasions he was accustomed to sleep off his potations in some public place—usually upon the pavement outside his last house of call—and it was his boast that so long as nobody interfered with him he interfered with nobody. To this attitude the tolerant police force of Clydebank assented, having their hands full enough, as a rule, in dealing with more militant forms of alcoholism. But Private M'Slattery, No. 3891, soon realised that he and Mr. Matthew M'Slattery, rivet-heater and respected citizen of Clydebank, had nothing in common. Only last week, feeling pleasantly fatigued after five days of arduous military training, he had followed the invariable practice of his civil life, and taken a day off. The result had fairly staggered him. In the orderly-room upon Monday morning he was charged with—

(1) Being absent from Parade at 9 a.m. on Saturday.

(2) Being absent from Parade at 2 p.m. on Saturday.

(3) Being absent from Tattoo at 9.30 p.m. on Saturday.

(4) Being drunk in High Street about 9.40 p.m. on Saturday.

(5) Striking a Non-Commissioned Officer.

(6) Attempting to escape from his escort.

(7) Destroying Government property. (Three panes of glass in the guard-room.)

Private M'Slattery, asked for an explanation, had pointed out that if he had been treated as per his working arrangement with the police at Clydebank, there would have been no trouble whatever. As for his day off, he was willing to forgo his day's pay and call the thing square. However, a hidebound C.O. had fined him five shillings and sentenced him to seven days' C.B. Consequently he was in no mood for Royal Reviews. He stated his opinions upon the subject in a loud voice and at some length. No one contradicted him, for he possessed the straightest left in the company; and no dog barked even when M'Slattery said that black was white.

"I wunner ye jined the Airmy at all, M'Slattery," observed one bold spirit, when the orator paused for breath.

"I wunner myself," said M'Slattery simply. "If I had kent all aboot this 'attention,' and 'stan'-at-ease,' and needin' tae luft your hand tae your bunnet whenever you saw yin o' they gentry-pups of officers goin' by,—dagont if I'd hae done it, Germans or no! (But I had a dram in me at the time.) I'm weel kent in Clydebank, and they'll tell you there that I'm no the man to be wastin' my time presenting airms tae kings or any other bodies."

However, at the appointed hour M'Slattery, in the front rank of A Company, stood to attention because he had to, and presented arms very creditably. He now cherished a fresh grievance, for he objected upon principle to have to present arms to a motor-car standing two hundred yards away upon his right front.

"Wull we be gettin' hame to our dinners now?" he inquired gruffly of his neighbour.

"Maybe he'll tak' a closer look at us," suggested an optimist in the rear rank. "He micht walk doon the line."

"Walk? No him!" replied Private M'Slattery. "He'll be awa' hame in the motor. Hae ony o' you billies gotten a fag?"

There was a smothered laugh. The officers of the battalion were standing rigidly at attention in front of A Company. One of these turned his head sharply.

"No talking in the ranks there!" he said. "Sergeant, take that man's name."

Private M'Slattery, rumbling mutiny, subsided, and devoted his attention to the movements of the Royal motor-car.

Then the miracle happened.

The great car rolled smoothly from the saluting-base, over the undulating turf, and came to a standstill on the extreme right of the line, half a mile away. There descended a slight figure in khaki. It was the King—the King whom Private M'Slattery had never seen. Another figure followed, and another.

"Herself iss there too!" whinnied an excited Highlander on M'Slattery's right. "And the young leddy! Pless me, they are all for walking town the line on their feet. And the sun so hot in the sky! We shall see them close!"

Private M'Slattery gave a contemptuous sniff.

The excited battalion was called to a sense of duty by the voice of authority. Once more the long lines stood stiff and rigid—waiting, waiting, for their brief glimpse. It was a long time coming, for they were posted on the extreme left.

Suddenly a strangled voice was uplifted—"In God's name, what for can they no come tae *us*? Never heed the others!"

Yet Private M'Slattery was quite unaware that he had spoken.

At last the little procession arrived. There was a handshake for the Colonel, and a word with two or three of the officers; then a quick scrutiny of the rank and file. For a moment—yea, more than a moment—keen Royal eyes rested upon Private M'Slattery, standing like a graven image, with his great chest straining the buttons of his tunic.

Then a voice said, apparently in M'Slattery's ear—

"A magnificent body of men, Colonel. I congratulate you."

A minute later M'Slattery was aroused from his trance by the sound of the Colonel's ringing voice—

"Highlanders, three cheers for His Majesty the King!"

M'Slattery led the whole Battalion, his glengarry high in the air.

Suddenly his eye fell upon Private Mucklewame, blindly and woodenly yelling himself hoarse.

In three strides M'Slattery was standing face to face with the unconscious criminal. "Yous low, lousy puddock," he roared—"tak' off your bonnet!" He saved Mucklewame the trouble of complying, and strode back to his place in the ranks.

"Yin mair, chaps," he shouted—"for the young leddy!"

And yet there are people who tell us that the formula, O.H.M.S., is a mere relic of antiquity.

Chapter 5
"Crime"

"Bring in Private Dunshie, Sergeant-Major," says the Company Commander.

The Sergeant-Major throws open the door, and barks—"Private Dunshie's escort!"

The order is repeated *fortissimo* by some one outside. There is a clatter of ammunition boots getting into step, and a solemn procession of four files into the room. The leader thereof is a stumpy but enormously important-looking private. He is the escort. Number two is the prisoner. Numbers three and four are the accuser—counsel for the Crown, as it were—and a witness. The procession reaches the table at which the Captain is sitting. Beside him is a young officer, one Bobby Little, who is present for "instructional" purposes.

"Mark time!" commands the Sergeant-Major. "Halt! Right turn!"

This evolution brings the accused face to face with his judge. He has been deprived of his cap, and of everything else "which may be employed as, or contain, a missile." (They think of everything in the King's Regulations.)

"What is this man's crime, Sergeant-Major?" inquires the Captain.

"On this sheet, sir," replies the Sergeant-Major....

By a "crime" the ordinary civilian means something worth recording in a special edition of the evening papers—something with a meat-chopper in it. Others, more catholic in their views, will tell you that it is a crime to inflict corporal punishment on any human being; or to permit performing animals to appear upon the stage; or to subsist upon any food but nuts. Others, of still finer clay, will classify such things as Futurism, The Tango, Dickeys, and the Albert Memorial as crimes. The point to note is, that in the eyes of all these persons each of these things is a sin of the worst possible degree. That being so, they designate it a "crime." It is the strongest term they can employ.

But in the Army, "crime" is capable of infinite shades of intensity. It simply means "misdemeanour," and may range from being unshaven on parade, or making a frivolous complaint about the potatoes at dinner, to irrevocably perforating your rival in love with a bayonet. So let party politicians, when they discourse vaguely to their constituents about "the prevalence of crime in the Army under the present effete and undemocratic system," walk warily.

Every private in the Army possesses what is called a conduct-sheet, and upon this his crimes are recorded. To be precise, he has two such sheets. One is called his Company sheet, and the other his Regimental sheet. His Company sheet contains a record of every misdeed for which he has been brought before his Company Commander. His Regimental sheet is a more select document, and contains only the more noteworthy of his achievements—crimes so interesting that they have to be communicated to the Commanding Officer.

However, this morning we are concerned only with Company conduct-sheets. It is 7.30 A.M., and the Company Commander is sitting in judgment, with a little pile of yellow Army forms before him. He picks up the first of these, and reads—

"*Private Dunshie. While on active service, refusing to obey an order.* Lance-Corporal Ness!"

The figure upon the prisoner's right suddenly becomes animated. Lance-Corporal Ness, taking a deep breath, and fixing his eyes resolutely on the whitewashed wall above the Captain's head, recites—

"Sirr, at four P.M. on the fufth unst. I was in charge of a party told off for tae scrub the floor of Room Nummer Seeventeen. I ordered the prisoner tae scrub. He refused. I warned him. He again refused."

Click! Lance-Corporal Ness has run down. He has just managed the sentence in a breath.

"Corporal Mackay!"

The figure upon Lance-Corporal Ness's right stiffens, and inflates itself.

"Sirr, on the fufth unst. I was Orderly Sergeant. At aboot four-thirty P.M., Lance-Corporal Ness reported this man tae me for refusing for tae obey an order. I confined him."

The Captain turns to the prisoner.

"What have you to say, Private Dunshie?"

Private Dunshie, it appears, has a good deal to say.

"I jined the Airmy for tae fight they Germans, and no for tae be learned tae scrub floors—"

"Sirr!" suggests the Sergeant-Major in his ear.

"Sirr," amends Private Dunshie reluctantly. "I was no in the habit of scrubbin' the floor mysel' where I stay in Glesca'; and ma wife would be affronted—"

But the Captain looks up. He has heard enough.

"Look here, Dunshie," he says. "Glad to hear you want to fight the Germans. So do I. So do we all. All the same, we've got a lot of dull jobs to do first." (Captain Blaikie has the reputation of being the most monosyllabic man in the British Army.) "Coals, and floors, and fatigues like that: they are your job. I have mine too. Kept me up till two this morning. But the point is this. You have refused to obey an order. Very serious, that. Most serious crime a soldier can commit. If you start arguing now about small things, where will you be when the big orders come along—eh? Must learn to obey. Soldier now, whatever you were a month ago. So obey all orders like a shot. Watch me next time I get one. No disgrace, you know! Ought to be a soldier's pride, and all that. See?"

"Yes—sirr," replies Private Dunshie, with less truculence.

The Captain glances down at the paper before him.

"First time you have come before me. Admonished!"

"Right turn! Quick march!" thunders the Sergeant-Major.

The procession clumps out of the room. The Captain turns to his disciple.

"That's my homely and paternal tap," he observes. "For first offenders only. That chap's all right. Soon find out it's no good fussing about your rights as a true-born British elector in the Army. Sergeant-Major!"

"Sirr?"

"Private McNulty!"

After the usual formalities, enter Private McNulty and escort. Private McNulty is a small scared-looking man with a dirty face.

"Private McNulty, sirr!" announces the Sergeant-Major to the Company Commander, with the air of a popular lecturer on entomology placing a fresh insect under the microscope.

Captain Blaikie addresses the shivering culprit—

"*Private McNulty; charged with destroying Government property*. Corporal Mather!"

Corporal Mather clears his throat, and assuming the wooden expression and fish-like gaze common to all public speakers who have learned their oration by heart, begins—

"Sirr, on the night of the sixth inst. I was Orderly Sergeant. Going round the prisoner's room about the hour of nine-thirty I noticed that his three biscuits had been cut and slashed, apparently with a knife or other instrument."

"What did you do?"

"Sirr, I inquired of the men in the room who was it had gone for to do this. Sirr, they said it was the prisoner."

Two witnesses are called. Both, certify, casting grieved and virtuous glances at the prisoner, that this outrage upon the property of His Majesty was the work of Private McNulty.

To the unsophisticated Bobby Little this charge appears rather a frivolous one. If you may not cut or slash a biscuit, what *are* you to do with it? Swallow it whole?

"Private McNulty?" queries the Captain.

Private McNulty, in a voice which is shrill with righteous indignation, gives the somewhat unexpected answer—

"Sirr, I plead guilty!"

"Guilty—eh? You did it, then?"

"Yes, sir."

"Why?"

This is what Private McNulty is waiting for.

"The men in that room, sirr," he announces indignantly, "appear tae look on me as a sort of body that can be treated onyways. They go for tae aggravate me. I was sittin' on my bed, with my knife in my hand, cutting a piece bacca and interfering with naebody, when they all commenced tae fling biscuits at me. I was keepin' them off as weel as I could; but havin' a knife in my hand, I'll no deny but what I gave twa three of them a bit cut."

"Is this true?" asks the Captain of the first witness, curtly.

"Yes, sir."

"You saw the men throwing biscuits at the prisoner?"

"Yes, sir."

"He was daen' it himsel'!" proclaims Private McNulty.

"This true?"

"Yes, sir."

The Captain addresses the other witness.

"You doing it too?"

"Yes, sir."

The Captain turns again to the prisoner.

"Why didn't you lodge a complaint?" (The schoolboy code does not obtain in the Army.)

"I did, sir. I tellt"—indicating Corporal Mather with an elbow—"this genelman here."

Corporal Mather cannot help it. He swells perceptibly. But swift puncture awaits him.

"Corporal Mather, why didn't you mention this?"

"I didna think it affected the crime, sir."

"Not your business to think. Only to make a straightforward charge. Be very careful in future. You other two"—the witnesses come guiltily to attention—"I shall talk to your platoon sergeant about you. Not going to have Government property knocked about!"

Bobby Little's eyebrows, willy-nilly, have been steadily rising during the last five minutes. He knows the meaning of red tape now!

Then comes sentence.

"Private McNulty, you have pleaded guilty to a charge of destroying Government property, so you go before the Commanding Officer. Don't suppose you'll be punished, beyond paying for the damage."

"Right turn! Quick march!" chants the Sergeant-Major.

The downtrodden McNulty disappears, with his traducers. But Bobby Little's eyebrows have not been altogether thrown away upon his Company Commander.

"Got the biscuits here, Sergeant-Major?"

"Yes, sirr."

"Show them."

The Sergeant-Major dives into a pile of brown blankets, and presently extracts three small brown mattresses, each two feet square. These appear to have been stabbed in several places with a knife.

Captain Blaikie's eyes twinkle, and he chuckles to his now scarlet-faced junior—

"More biscuits in heaven and earth than ever came out of Huntley and Palmer's, my son! Private Robb!"

Presently Private Robb stands at the table. He is a fresh-faced, well-set-up youth, with a slightly receding chin and a most dejected manner.

"*Private Robb*," reads the Captain. "*While on active service, drunk and singing in Wellington Street about nine p.m. on Saturday, the sixth*. Sergeant Garrett!"

The proceedings follow their usual course, except that in this case some of the evidence is "documentary"—put in in the form of a report from the sergeant of the Military Police who escorted the melodious Robb home to bed.

The Captain addresses the prisoner.

"Private Robb, this is the second time. Sorry—very sorry. In all other ways you are doing well. Very keen and promising soldier. Why is it—eh?"

The contrite Robb hangs his head. His judge continues—

"I'll tell you. You haven't found out yet how much you can hold. That it?"

The prisoner nods assent.

"Well—find out! See? It's one of the first things a young man ought to learn. Very valuable piece of information. I know myself, so I'm safe. Want you to do the same. Every man has a different limit. What did you have on Saturday?"

Private Robb reflects.

"Five pints, sirr," he announces.

"Well, next time try three, and then you won't go serenading policemen. As it is, you will have to go before the Commanding Officer and get punished. Want to go to the front, don't you?"

"Yes, sirr." Private Robb's dismal features flush.

"Well, mind this. We all want to go, but we can't go till every man in the battalion is efficient. You want to be the man who kept the rest from going to the front—eh?"

"No, sirr, I do not."

"All right, then. Next Saturday night say to yourself: 'Another pint, and I keep the Battalion back!' If you do that, you'll come back to barracks sober, like a decent chap. That'll do. Don't salute with your cap off. Next man, Sergeant-Major!"

"Good boy, that," remarks the Captain to Bobby Little, as the contrite Robb is removed. "Keen as mustard. But his high-water mark for beer is somewhere in his boots. All right, now I've scared him."

"Last prisoner, sirr," announces the Sergeant-Major.

"Glad to hear it. H'm! Private M'Queen again!"

Private M'Queen is an unpleasant-looking creature, with a drooping red moustache and a cheese-coloured complexion. His misdeeds are recited. Having been punished for misconduct early in the week, he has piled Pelion on Ossa by appearing fighting drunk at defaulters' parade. From all accounts he has livened up that usually decorous assemblage considerably.

After the corroborative evidence, the Captain asks his usual question of the prisoner—

"Anything to say?"

"No," growls Private M'Queen.

The Captain takes up the prisoner's conduct-sheet, reads it through, and folds it up deliberately.

"I am going to ask the Commanding Officer to discharge you," he says; and there is nothing homely or paternal in his speech now.

"Can't make out why men like you join the Army—especially *this* Army. Been a nuisance ever since you came here. Drunk—beastly drunk—four times in three weeks. Always dirty and insubordinate. Always trying to stir up trouble among the young soldiers. Been in the army before, haven't you?"

"No."

"That's not true. Can always tell an old soldier on parade. Fact is, you have either deserted or been discharged as incorrigible. Going to be discharged as incorrigible again. Keeping the regiment back, that's why: that's a real crime. Go home, and explain that you were turned out of the King's Army because you weren't worthy of the honour of staying in. When decent men see that people like you have no place in this regiment, perhaps they will see that this regiment is just the place for them. Take him away."

Private M'Queen shambles out of the room for the last time in his life. Captain Blaikie, a little exhausted by his own unusual loquacity, turns to Bobby Little with a contented sigh.

"That's the last of the shysters," he says. "Been weeding them out for six weeks. Now I have got rid of that nobleman I can look the rest of the Company in the face. Come to breakfast!"

Chapter 6

The Laws of the Medes and Persians

One's first days as a newly-joined subaltern are very like one's first days at school. The feeling is just the same. There is the same natural shyness, the same reverence for people who afterwards turn out to be of no consequence whatsoever, and the same fear of transgressing the Laws of the Medes and Persians—regimental traditions and conventions—which alter not.

Dress, for instance. "Does one wear a sword on parade?" asks the tyro of himself his first morning. "I'll put it on, and chance it." He invests himself in a monstrous claymore and steps on to the barrack square. Not an officer in sight is carrying anything more lethal than a light cane. There is just time to scuttle back to quarters and disarm.

Again, where should one sit at meal-times? We had supposed that the C.O. would be enthroned at the head of the table, with a major sitting on his right and left, like Cherubim and Seraphim; while the rest disposed themselves in a descending scale of greatness until it came down to persons like ourselves at the very foot. But the C.O. has a disconcerting habit of sitting absolutely anywhere. He appears to be just as happy between two Second Lieutenants as between Cherubim and Seraphim. Again, we note that at breakfast each officer upon entering sits down and shouts loudly, to a being concealed behind a screen, for food, which is speedily forthcoming. Are we entitled to clamour in this peremptory fashion too? Or should we creep round behind the screen and take what we can get? Or should we sit still, and wait till we are served? We try the last expedient first, and get nothing. Then we try the second, and are speedily convinced, by the demeanour of the gentleman behind the screen, that we have committed the worst error of which we have yet been guilty.

There are other problems—saluting, for instance. On the parade ground this is a simple matter enough; for there the golden rule appears to be—When in doubt, salute! The Colonel calls up his four Company Commanders. They salute. He instructs them to carry on this morning with coal fatigues and floor-scrubbing. The Company Commanders salute, and retire to their Companies, and call up their subalterns, who salute. They instruct these to carry on this morning with coal fatigues and floor-scrubbing. The sixteen subalterns salute, and retire to their platoons. Here they call up their Platoon Sergeants, who salute. They instruct these to carry on this morning with coal fatigues and floor-scrubbing. The Platoon Sergeants salute, and issue commands to the rank and file. The rank and file, having no instructions to salute sergeants, are compelled, as a last resort, to carry on with the coal fatigues and floor-scrubbing themselves. You see, on parade saluting is simplicity itself.

But we are not always on parade; and then more subtle problems arise. Some of those were discussed one day by four junior officers, who sat upon a damp and slippery bank by a muddy roadside during a "fall-out" in a route-march. The four ("reading from left to right," as they say in high journalistic society) were Second Lieutenant Little, Second Lieutenant Waddell, Second Lieutenant Cockerell, and Lieutenant Struthers, surnamed "Highbrow." Bobby we know. Waddell was a slow-moving but pertinacious student of the science of war from the kingdom of Fife. Cockerell came straight from a crack public-school corps, where he had been a cadet officer; so nothing in the heaven above or the earth beneath was hid from him. Struthers owed his superior rank to the fact that in the far back ages, before the days of the O.T.C., he had held a commission in a University Corps. He was a scholar of his College, and was an expert in the art of accumulating masses of knowledge in quick time for examination purposes. He knew all the little red manuals by heart, was an infallible authority on buttons and badges, and would dip into the King's Regulations or the Field Service Pocket-book as another man might dip into the "Sporting Times." Strange to say, he was not very good at drilling a platoon. We all know him.

"What do you do when you are leading a party along a road and meet a Staff Officer?" asked Bobby Little.

"Make a point," replied Cockerell patronisingly, "of saluting all persons wearing red bands round their hats. They may not be entitled to it, but it tickles their ribs and gets you the reputation, of being an intelligent young officer."

"But I say," announced Waddell plaintively, "*I* saluted a man with a red hat the other day, and he turned out to be a Military Policeman!"

"As a matter of fact," announced the pundit Struthers, after the laughter had subsided, "you need not salute anybody. No compliments are paid on active service, and we are on active service now."

"Yes, but suppose some one salutes *you*?" objected the conscientious Bobby Little. "You must salute back again, and sometimes you don't know how to do it. The other day I was bringing the company back from the ranges and we met a company from another battalion—the Mid Mudshires, I think. Before I knew where I was the fellow in charge called them to attention and then gave 'Eyes right!'"

"What did you do?" asked Struthers anxiously.

"I hadn't time to do anything except grin, and say, 'Good morning!'" confessed Bobby Little.

"You were perfectly right," announced Struthers, and Cockerell murmured assent.

"Are you sure?" persisted Bobby Little. "As I passed the tail of their company one of their subs turned to another and said quite loud, 'My God, what swine!'"

"Showed his rotten ignorance," commented Cockerell.

At this moment Mr. Waddell, whose thoughts were never disturbed by conversation around him, broke in with a question.

"What does a Tommy do," he inquired, "if he meets an officer wheeling a wheelbarrow?"

"Who is wheeling the barrow," inquired the meticulous Struthers—"the officer or the Tommy?"

"The Tommy, of course!" replied Waddell in quite a shocked voice. "What is he to do? If he tries to salute he will upset the barrow, you know."

"He turns his head sharply towards the officer for six paces," explained the ever-ready Struthers. "When a soldier is not in a position to salute in the ordinary way—"

"I say," inquired Bobby Little rather shyly, "do you ever look the other way when you meet a Tommy?"

"How do you mean?" asked everybody.

"Well, the other day I met one walking out with his girl along the road, and I felt so blooming *de trop* that—"

Here the "fall-in" sounded, and this delicate problem was left unsolved. But Mr. Waddell, who liked to get to the bottom of things, continued to ponder these matters as he marched. He mistrusted the omniscience of Struthers and the superficial infallibility of the self-satisfied Cockerell. Accordingly, after consultation with that eager searcher after knowledge, Second Lieutenant Little, he took the laudable but fatal step of carrying his difficulties to one Captain Wagstaffe, the humorist of the Battalion.

Wagstaffe listened with an appearance of absorbed interest. Finally he said—

"These are very important questions, Mr. Waddell, and you acted quite rightly in laying them before me. I will consult the Deputy Assistant Instructor in Military Etiquette, and will obtain a written answer to your inquiries."

"Oh, thanks awfully, sir!" exclaimed Waddell.

The result of Captain Wagstaffe's application to the mysterious official just designated was forthcoming next day in the form of a neatly typed document. It was posted in the Ante-room (the C.O. being out at dinner), and ran as follows:

SALUTES

YOUNG OFFICERS, HINTS FOR THE GUIDANCE OF

The following is the correct procedure for a young officer in charge of an armed party upon meeting—

(a) A Staff Officer riding a bicycle.

Correct Procedure.—If marching at attention, order your men to march at ease and to light cigarettes and eat bananas. Then, having fixed bayonets, give the order: *Across the road—straggle!*

(b) A funeral.

Correct Procedure.—Strike up *Tipperary*, and look the other way.

(c) A General Officer, who strolls across your Barrack Square precisely at the moment when you and your Platoon have got into mutual difficulties.

Correct Procedure.—Lie down flat upon your face (directing your platoon to do the same), cover your head with gravel, and pretend you are not there.

SPECIAL CASES

(a) A soldier, wheeling a wheelbarrow and balancing a swill-tub on his head, meets an officer walking out in review dress.

Correct Procedure.—The soldier will immediately cant the swill-tub to an angle of forty-five degrees at a distance of one and a half inches above his right eyebrow. (In the case of Rifle Regiments the soldier will balance the swill-tub on his nose.) He will then invite the officer, by a smart movement of the left ear, to seat himself on the wheelbarrow.

Correct Acknowledgment.—The officer will comply, placing his feet upon the right and left hubs of the wheel respectively, with the ball of the toe in each case at a distance of one inch (when serving abroad, 2½ centimetres) from the centre of gravity of the wheelbarrow. (In the case of Rifle Regiments the officer will tie his feet in a knot at the back of his neck.) The soldier will then advance six paces, after which the officer will dismount and go home and have a bath.

(b) A soldier, with his arm round a lady's waist in the gloaming, encounters an officer.

Correct Procedure.—The soldier will salute with his disengaged arm. The lady will administer a sharp tap with the end of her umbrella to the officer's tunic, at point one inch above the lowest button.

Correct Acknowledgment.—The officer will take the end of the umbrella firmly in his right hand, and will require the soldier to introduce him to the lady. He will then direct the soldier to double back to barracks.

(c) A party of soldiers, seated upon the top of a transport wagon, see an officer passing at the side of the road.

Correct Procedure.—The senior N.C.O. (or if no N.C.O. be present, the oldest soldier) will call the men to attention, and the party, taking their time from the right, will spit upon the officer's head in a soldier-like manner.

Correct Acknowledgment.—The officer will break into a smart trot.

(d) A soldier, driving an officer's motor-car without the knowledge of the officer, encounters the officer in a narrow country lane.

Correct Procedure.—The soldier will open the throttle to its full extent and run the officer over.

Correct Acknowledgment.—No acknowledgment is required.

NOTE.—*None of the above compliments will be paid upon active service.*

Unfortunately the Colonel came home from dining out sooner than was expected, and found this outrageous document still upon the notice-board. But he was a good Colonel. He merely remarked approvingly—

"H'm. Quite so! *Non semper arcum tendit Apollo*. It's just as well to keep smiling these days."

Nevertheless, Mr. Waddell made a point in future, when in need of information, of seeking the same from a less inspired source than Captain Wagstaffe.

****

There was another Law of the Medes and Persians with which our four friends soon became familiar—that which governs the relations of the various ranks to one another. Great Britain is essentially the home of the chaperon. We pride ourselves, as a nation, upon the extreme care with which we protect our young gentlewomen from contaminating influences. But the fastidious attention which we bestow upon our national maidenhood is as nothing in comparison with the protective commotion with which we surround that shrinking sensitive plant, Mr. Thomas Atkins.

Take etiquette and deportment. If a soldier wishes to speak to an officer, an introduction must be effected by a sergeant. Let us suppose that Private M'Splae, in the course of a route-march, develops a blister upon his great toe. He begins by intimating the fact to the nearest lance-corporal. The lance-corporal takes the news to the platoon sergeant, who informs the platoon commander, who may or may not decide to take the opinion of his company commander in the matter. Anyhow, when the hobbling warrior finally obtains permission to fall out and alleviate his distress, a corporal goes with him, for fear he should lose himself, or his boot—it is wonderful what Thomas *can* lose when he sets his mind to it—or, worst crime of all, his rifle.

Again, if two privates are detailed to empty the regimental ash-bin, a junior N.C.O. ranges them in line, calls them to attention, and marches them off to the scene of their labours, decently and in order. If a soldier obtains leave to go home on furlough for the week-end, he is collected into a party, and, after being inspected to see that his buttons are clean, his hair properly cut, and his nose correctly blown, is marched off to the station, where a ticket is provided for him, and he and his fellow-wayfarers are safely tucked into a third-smoker labelled "Military Party." (No wonder he sometimes gets lost on arriving at Waterloo!) In short, if there is a job to be done, the senior soldier present chaperons somebody else while he does it.

This system has been attacked on the ground that it breeds loss of self-reliance and initiative. As a matter of fact, the result is almost exactly the opposite. Under its operation a soldier rapidly acquires the art of placing himself under the command of his nearest superior in rank; but at the same time he learns with equal rapidity to take command himself if no superior be present—no bad thing in times of battle and sudden death, when shrapnel is whistling, and promotion is taking place with grim and unceasing automaticity.

This principle is extended, too, to the enforcement of law and order. If Private M'Sumph is insubordinate or riotous, there is never any question of informal correction or summary justice. News of the incident wends its way upward, by a series of properly regulated channels, to the officer in command. Presently, by the same route, an order comes back, and in a twinkling the offender finds himself taken under arrest and marched off to the guard-room by two of his own immediate associates. (One of them may be his own rear-rank man.) But no officer or non-commissioned officer ever lays a finger on him. The penalty for striking a superior officer is so severe that the law decrees, very wisely, that a soldier must on no account ever be arrested by any save men of his own rank. If Private M'Sumph, while being removed in custody, strikes Private Tosh upon the nose and kicks Private Cosh upon the shin, to the effusion of blood, no great harm is done—except to the lacerated Cosh and Tosh; but if he had smitten an intruding officer in the eye, his punishment would have been dire and grim. So, though we may call military law cumbrous and grandmotherly, there is sound sense and real mercy at the root of it.

* * * * * * * *

But there is one Law of the Medes and Persians which is sensibly relaxed these days. We, the newly joined, have always been given to understand that whatever else you do, you must never, never betray any interest in your profession—in short, talk shop—at Mess. But in our Mess no one ever talks anything else. At luncheon, we relate droll anecdotes concerning our infant platoons; at tea, we explain, to any one who will listen, exactly how we placed our sentry line in last night's operations; at dinner, we brag about our Company musketry returns, and quote untruthful extracts from our butt registers. At breakfast, every one has a newspaper, which he props before him and reads, generally aloud. We exchange observations upon the war news. We criticise von Kluck, and speak kindly of Joffre. We note, daily, that there is nothing to report on the Allies' right, and wonder regularly how the Russians are really getting on in the Eastern theatre.

Then, after observing that the only sportsman in the combined forces of the German Empire is—or was—the captain of the *Emden*, we come to the casualty lists—and there is silence.

Englishmen are fond of saying, with the satisfied air of men letting off a really excellent joke, that every one in Scotland knows every one else. As we study the morning's Roll of Honour, we realise that never was a more truthful jest uttered. There is not a name in the list of those who have died for Scotland which is not familiar to us. If we did not know the man—too often the boy—himself, we knew his people, or at least where his home was. In England, if you live in Kent, and you read that the Northumberland Fusiliers have been cut up or the Duke of Cornwall's Light Infantry badly knocked about, you merely sigh that so many more good men should have fallen. Their names are glorious names, but they are only names. But never a Scottish regiment comes under fire but the whole of Scotland feels it. Scotland is small enough to know all her sons by heart. You may live in Berwickshire, and the man who has died may have come from Skye; but his name is quite familiar to you. Big England's sorrow is national; little Scotland's is personal.

Then we pass on to our letters. Many of us—particularly the senior officers—have news direct from the trenches—scribbled scraps torn out of field-message books. We get constant tidings of the Old Regiment. They marched thirty-five miles on such a day; they captured a position after being under continuous shell fire for eight hours on another; they were personally thanked by the Field-Marshal on another. Oh, we shall have to work hard to get up to that standard!

"They want more officers," announces the Colonel. "Naturally, after the time they've been having! But they must go to the Third Battalion for them: that's the proper place. I will not have them coming here: I've told them so at Headquarters. The Service Battalions simply *must* be led by the officers who have trained them if they are to have a Chinaman's chance when we go out. I shall threaten to resign if they try any more of their tricks. That'll frighten 'em! Even dug-outs like me are rare and valuable objects at present."

The Company Commanders murmur assent—on the whole sympathetically. Anxious though they are to get upon business terms with the Kaiser, they are loath to abandon the unkempt but sturdy companies over which they have toiled so hard, and which now, though destitute of blossom, are rich in promise of fruit. But the senior subalterns look up hopefully. Their lot is hard. Some of them have been in the Service for ten years, yet they have been left behind. They command no companies. "Here," their faces say, "we are merely marking time while others learn. Send *us*!"

* * * * * * * *

However, though they have taken no officers yet, signs are not wanting that they will take some soon. Today each of us was presented with a small metal disc.

Bobby Little examined his curiously. Upon the face thereof was stamped, in ragged, irregular capitals—

LITTLE, R.,
2ND LT., B. & W. HIGHRS.
C. OF E.

"What is this for?" he asked.

Captain Wagstaffe answered.

"You wear it round your neck," he said.

Our four friends, once bitten, regarded the humorist suspiciously.

"Are you rotting us?" asked Waddell cautiously.

"No, my son," replied Wagstaffe, "I am not."

"What is it for, then?"

"It's called an Identity Disc. Every soldier on active service wears one."

"Why should the idiots put one's religion on the thing?" inquired Master Cockerell, scornfully regarding the letters "C. of E." upon his disc.

Wagstaffe regarded him curiously.

"Think it over," he suggested.

CHAPTER 7
Shooting Straight

"What for is the wee felly gaun' tae show us puctures?"

Second Lieutenant Bobby Little, assisted by a sergeant and two unhandy privates, is engaged in propping a large and highly-coloured work of art, mounted on a rough wooden frame and supported on two unsteady legs, against the wall of the barrack square. A half-platoon of A Company, seated upon an adjacent bank, chewing grass and enjoying the mellow autumn sunshine, regard the swaying masterpiece with frank curiosity. For the last fortnight they have been engaged in imbibing the science of musketry. They have learned to hold their rifles correctly, sitting, kneeling, standing, or lying; to bring their backsights and foresights into an undeviating straight line with the base of the bull's-eye; and to press the trigger in the manner laid down in the Musketry Regulations—without wriggling the body or "pulling-off."

They have also learned to adjust their sights, to perform the loading motions rapidly and correctly, and to obey such simple commands as—

"*At them two, weemen*"—officers' wives, probably—"*proceeding from left tae right across the square, at five hundred yairds*"

—they are really about fifteen yards away, covered with confusion—"*five roonds, fire!*"

But as yet they have discharged no shots from their rifles. It has all been make-believe, with dummy cartridges, and fictitious ranges, and snapping triggers. To be quite frank, they are getting just a little tired of musketry training—forgetting for the moment that a soldier who cannot use his rifle is merely an expense to his country and a free gift to the enemy. But the sight of Bobby Little's art gallery cheers them up. They contemplate the picture with childlike interest. It resembles nothing so much as one of those pleasing but imaginative posters by the display of which our Railway Companies seek to attract the tourist to the less remunerative portions of their systems.

"What for is the wee felly gaun' tae show us puctures?"

Thus Private Mucklewame. A pundit in the rear rank answers him.

"Yon's Gairmany."

"Gairmany ma auntie!" retorts Mucklewame. "There's no chumney-stalks in Gairmany."

"Maybe no; but there's wundmulls. See the wundmull there—on yon wee knowe!"

"There a pit-held!" exclaims another voice. This homely spectacle is received with an affectionate sigh. Until two months ago more than half the platoon had never been out of sight of at least half a dozen.

"See the kirk, in ablow the brae!" says some one else, in a pleased voice. "It has a nock in the steeple."

"I hear they Gairmans send signals wi' their kirk-nocks," remarks Private M'Micking, who, as one of the Battalion signallers—or "buzzers," as the vernacular has it, in imitation of the buzzing of the Morse instrument—regards himself as a sort of junior Staff Officer. "They jist semaphore with the haunds of the nock—"

"I wonder," remarks the dreamy voice of Private M'Leary, the humorist of the platoon, "did ever a Gairman buzzer pit the ba' through his ain goal in a fitba' match?"

This irrelevant reference to a regrettable incident of the previous Saturday afternoon is greeted with so much laughter that Bobby Little, who has at length fixed his picture in position, whips round.

"Less talking there!" he announces severely, "or I shall have to stand you all at attention!"

There is immediate silence—there is nothing the matter with Bobby's discipline—and the outraged M'Micking has to content himself with a homicidal glare in the direction of M'Leary, who is now hanging virtuously upon his officer's lips.

"This," proceeds Bobby Little, "is what is known as a landscape target."

He indicates the picture, which, apparently overcome by so much public notice, promptly falls flat upon its face. A fatigue party under the sergeant hurries to its assistance.

"It is intended," resumes Bobby presently, "to teach you—us—to become familiar with various kinds of country, and to get into the habit of picking out conspicuous features of the landscape, and getting them by heart, and—er—so on. I want you all to study this picture for three minutes. Then I shall face you about and ask you to describe it to me."

After three minutes of puckered brows and hard breathing the squad is turned to its rear and the examination proceeds.

"Lance-Corporal Ness, what did you notice in the foreground of the picture?"

Lance-Corporal Ness gazes fiercely before him. He has noticed a good deal, but can remember nothing. Moreover, he has no very clear idea what a foreground may be.

"Private Mucklewame?"

Again silence, while the rotund Mucklewame perspires in the throes of mental exertion.

"Private Wemyss?"

No answer.

"Private M'Micking!"

The "buzzer" smiles feebly, but says nothing.

"Well,"—desperately—"Sergeant Angus! Tell them what you noticed in the foreground."

Sergeant Angus (*floruit* A.D. 1895) springs smartly to attention, and replies, with the instant obedience of the old soldier—

"The sky, sirr."

"Not in the foreground, as a rule," replies Bobby Little gently. "About turn again, all of you, and we'll have another try."

In his next attempt Bobby abandons individual catechism.

"Now," he begins, "what conspicuous objects do we notice on this target? In the foreground I can see a low knoll. To the left I see a windmill. In the distance is a tall chimney. Half-right is a church. How would that church be marked on a map?"

No reply.

"Well," explains Bobby, anxious to parade a piece of knowledge which he only acquired himself a day or two ago, "churches are denoted in maps by a cross, mounted on a square or circle, according as the church has a square tower or a steeple. What has this church got?"

"A nock!" bellow the platoon, with stunning enthusiasm. (All but Private M'Micking, that is.)

"A clock, sir," translates the sergeant, *sotto voce.*

"A clock? All right: but what I wanted was a steeple. Then, farther away, we can see a mine, a winding brook, and a house, with a wall in front of it. Who can see them?"

To judge by the collective expression of the audience, no one does. Bobby ploughs on.

"Upon the skyline we notice—Squad, '*shun*!"

Captain Wagstaffe has strolled up. He is second in command of A Company. Bobby explains to him modestly what he has been trying to do.

"Yes, I heard you," says Wagstaffe. "You take a breather, while I carry on for a bit. Squad, stand easy, and tell me what you can see on that target. Lance-Corporal Ness, show me a pit-head."

Lance-Corporal Ness steps briskly forward and lays a grubby forefinger on Bobby's "mine."

"Private Mucklewame, show me a burn."

The brook is at once identified.

"Private M'Leary, shut your eyes and tell me what there is just to the right of the windmill."

"A wee knowe, sirr," replies M'Leary at once. Bobby recognises his "low knoll"—also the fact that it is no use endeavouring to instruct the unlettered until you have learned their language.

"Very good!" says Captain Wagstaffe. "Now we will go on to what is known as Description and Recognition of Targets. Supposing I had sent one of you forward into that landscape as a scout.—By the way, what is a scout?"

Dead silence, as usual.

"Come along! Tell me, somebody! Private Mucklewame?"

"They gang oot in a procession on Setter-day efternoons, sirr, in short breeks," replies Mucklewame promptly.

"A procession is the very last thing a scout goes out in!" raps Wagstaffe. (It is plain to Mucklewame that the Captain has never been in Wishaw, but he does not argue the point.) "Private M'Micking, what is a scout?"

"A spy, sirr," replies the omniscient one.

"Well, that's better; but there's a big difference between the two. What is it?"

This is a poser. Several men know the difference, but feel quite incapable of explaining it. The question runs down the front rank. Finally it is held up and disposed of by one Mearns (from Aberdeen).

"A spy, sirr, gets mair money than a scout."

"Does he?" asks Captain Wagstaffe, smiling. "Well, I am not in a position to say. But if he does, he earns it! Why?"

"Because if he gets catched he gets shot," volunteers a rear-rank man.

"Right. Why is he shot?"

This conundrum is too deep for the squad. The Captain has to answer it himself.

"Because he is not in uniform, and cannot therefore be treated as an ordinary prisoner of war. So never go scouting in your nightshirt, Mucklewame!"

The respectable Mucklewame blushes deeply at this outrageous suggestion, but Wagstaffe proceeds—

"Now, supposing I sent you out scouting, and you discovered that over there—somewhere in the middle of this field"—he lays a finger on the field in question—"there was a fold in the ground where a machine-gun section was concealed: what would you do when you got back?"

"I would tell you, sirr," replied Private M'Micking politely.

"Tell me what?"

"That they was there, sirr."

"Where?"

"In yon place."

"How would you indicate the position of the place?"

"I would pint it oot with ma finger, sirr."

"Invisible objects half a mile away are not easily pointed out with the finger," Captain Wagstaffe mentions. "Lance-Corporal Ness, how would you describe it?"

"I would tak' you there, sirr."

"Thanks! But I doubt if either of us would come back! Private Wemyss?"

"I would say, sirr, that the place was west of the mansion-hoose."

"There's a good deal of land west of that mansion-house, you know," expostulates the Captain gently; "but we are getting on. Thompson?"

"I would say, sir," replies Thompson, puckering his brow, "that it was in ablow they trees."

"It would be hard to indicate the exact trees you meant. Trees are too common. You try, Corporal King."

But Corporal King, who earned his stripes by reason of physical rather than intellectual attributes, can only contribute a lame reference to "a bit hedge by yon dyke, where there's a kin' o' hole in the tairget." Wagstaffe breaks in—

"Now, everybody, take some conspicuous and unmistakable object about the middle of that landscape—something which no one can mistake. The mansion-house will do—the near end. Now then—*mansion-house, near end*! Got that?"

There is a general chorus of assent.

"Very well. I want you to imagine that the base of the mansion-house is the centre of a great clock-face. Where would twelve o'clock be?"

The platoon are plainly tickled by this new round-game. They reply—

"Straught up!"

"Right. Where is nine o'clock?"

"Over tae the left."

"Very good. And so on with all the other hours. Now, supposing I were to say, *End of mansion-house—six o'clock—white gate*—you would carry your eye straight *downward*, through the garden, until it encountered the gate. I would thus have enabled you to recognise a very small object in a wide landscape in the quickest possible time. See the idea?"

"Yes, sirr."

"All right. Now for our fold in the ground. *End of mansion-house—eight o'clock*—got that?"

There is an interested murmur of assent.

"That gives you the direction from the house. Now for the distance! *End of mansion-house—eight o 'clock—two finger-breadths*—what does that give you, Lance-Corporal Ness?"

"The corrner of a field, sirr."

"Right. This is *our* field. We have picked it correctly out of about twenty fields, you see. *Corner of field. In the middle of the field, a fold in the ground. At nine hundred—at the fold in the ground—five rounds—fire*! You see the idea now?"

"Yes, sirr."

"Very good. Let the platoon practise describing targets to one another, Mr. Little. Don't be too elaborate. Never employ either the clock or finger method if you can describe your target without. For instance: *Left of windmill—triangular cornfield. At the nearest corner—six hundred—rapid fire*! is all you want. Carry on, Mr. Little."

And leaving Bobby and his infant class to practise this new and amusing pastime, Captain Wagstaffe strolls away across the square to where the painstaking Waddell is contending with another squad.

They, too, have a landscape target—a different one. Before it half a dozen rifles stand, set in rests. Waddell has given the order: *Four hundred—at the road, where it passes under the viaduct—fire!* and six privates have laid the six rifles upon the point indicated. Waddell and Captain Wagstaffe walk down the line, peering along the sights of the rifles. Five are correctly aligned: the sixth points to the spacious firmament above the viaduct.

"Hallo!" observes Wagstaffe.

"This is the man's third try, sir," explains the harassed Waddell. "He doesn't seem to be able to distinguish anything at all."

"Eyesight wrong?"

"So he says, sir." "Been a long time finding out, hasn't he?"

"The sergeant told me, sir," confides Waddell, "that in his opinion the man is 'working for his ticket.'"

"Umph!"

"I did not quite understand the expression, sir," continues the honest youth, "so I thought I would consult you."

"It means that he is trying to get his discharge. Bring him along: I'll soon find out whether he is skrim-shanking or not."

Private M'Sweir is introduced, and led off to the lair of that hardened cynic, the Medical Officer. Here he is put through some simple visual tests. He soon finds himself out of his depth. It is extremely difficult to feign either myopia, hypermetria, or astigmatism if you are not acquainted with the necessary symptoms, and have not decided beforehand which (if any) of these diseases you are suffering from. In five minutes the afflicted M'Sweir is informed, to his unutterable indignation, that he has passed a severe ocular examination with flying colours, and is forthwith marched back to his squad, with instructions to recognise all targets in future, under pain of special instruction in the laws of optics during his leisure hours. Verily, in K (1)—that is the tabloid title of the First Hundred Thousand—the way of the malingerer is hard. Still, the seed does not always fall upon stony ground. On his way to inspect a third platoon Captain Wagstaffe passes Bobby Little and his merry men. They are in pairs, indicating targets to one another.

Says Private Walker (oblivious of Captain Wagstaffe's proximity) to his friend, Private M'Leary—in an affected parody of his instructor's staccato utterance—

"*At yon three Gairman spies, gaun' up a close for tae despatch some wireless telegraphy—fufty roonds—fire!*"

To which Private M'Leary, not to be outdone, responds—

"*Public hoose—in the baur—back o' seeven o'clock—twa drams—fower fingers—rapid!*"

II

From this it is a mere step to—

"Butt Pairty, '*shun*! Forrm fourrs! Right! By your left, quick *marrch*!"

—on a bleak and cheerless morning in late October. It is not yet light; but a depressed party of about twenty-five are falling into line at the acrid invitation of two sergeants, who have apparently decided that the pen is mightier than the Lee-Enfield rifle; for each wears one stuck in his glengarry like an eagle's feather, and carries a rabbinical-looking inkhorn slung to his bosom. This literary pose is due to the fact that records are about to be taken of the performances of the Company on the shooting-range.

A half-awakened subaltern, who breakfasted at the grisly hour of a quarter-to-six, takes command, and the dolorous procession disappears into the gloom.

Half an hour later the Battalion parades, and sets off, to the sound of music, in pursuit. (It is perhaps needless to state that although we are deficient in rifles, possess neither belts, pouches, nor greatcoats, and are compelled to attach, our scanty accoutrements to our persons with ingenious contrivances of string, we boast a fully equipped and highly efficient pipe band, complete with pipers, big drummer, side drummers, and corybantic drum-major.)

By eight o'clock, after a muddy tramp of four miles, we are assembled at the two-hundred-yards firing point upon Number Three Range. The range itself is little more than a drive cut through, a pinewood. It is nearly half a mile long. Across the far end runs a high sandy embankment, decorated just below the ridge with, a row of numberboards—one for each target. Of the targets themselves nothing as yet is to be seen.

"Now then, let's get a move on!" suggests the Senior Captain briskly. "Cockerell, ring up the butts, and ask Captain Wagstaffe to put up the targets."

The alert Mr. Cockerell hurries to the telephone, which lives in a small white-painted structure like a gramophone-stand. (It has been left at the firing-point by the all-providing butt-party.) He turns the call-handle smartly, takes the receiver out of the box, and begins....

There is no need to describe the performance which ensues. All telephone-users are familiar with it. It consists entirely of the word "Hallo!" repeated *crescendo* and *furioso* until exhaustion supervenes.

Presently Mr. Cockerell reports to the Captain—

"Telephone out of order, sir."

"I never knew a range telephone that wasn't," replies the Captain, inspecting the instrument. "Still, you might give this one a sporting chance, anyhow. It isn't a *wireless* telephone, you know! Corporal Kemp, connect that telephone for Mr. Cockerell."

A marble-faced N.C.O. kneels solemnly upon the turf and raises a small iron trapdoor—hitherto overlooked by the omniscient Cockerell—revealing a cavity some six inches deep, containing an electric plug-hole. Into this he thrusts the terminal of the telephone wire. Cockerell, scarlet in the face, watches him indignantly.

Telephonic communication between firing-point and butts is now established. That is to say, whenever Mr. Cockerell rings the bell some one in the butts courteously rings back. Overtures of a more intimate nature are greeted either with stony silence or another fantasia on the bell.

Meanwhile the captain is superintending firing arrangements.

"Are the first details ready to begin?" he shouts.

"Quite ready, sir," runs the reply down the firing line.

The Captain now comes to the telephone himself. He takes the receiver from Cockerell with masterful assurance.

"Hallo, there!" he calls. "I want to speak to Captain Wagstaffe."

"Honkle yang-yang?" inquires a ghostly voice.

"Captain Wagstaffe! Hurry up!"

Presently the bell rings, and the Captain gets to business.

"That you, Wagstaffe?" he inquires cheerily. "Look here, we're going to fire Practice Seven, Table B,—snap-shooting. I want you to raise all the targets for six seconds, just for sighting purposes. Do you understand?"

Here the bell rings continuously for ten seconds. Nothing daunted, the Captain tries again.

"That you, Wagstaffe? Practice Seven, Table B!"

"T'chk, t'chk!" replies Captain Wagstaffe.

"Begin by raising all the targets for six seconds. Then raise them six times for five seconds each.—no, as you were! Raise them five times for six seconds each. Got that? I say, are you *there*? What's that?"

"*Przemysl*" replies the telephone—or something to that effect. "*Czestochowa! Krsyszkowice! Plock!*"

The Captain, now on his mettle, continues:—

"I want you to signal the results on the rear targets as the front ones go down. After that we will fire—oh, *curse* the thing!"

He hastily removes the receiver, which is emitting sounds suggestive of the buckling of biscuit-tins, from his ear, and lays it on its rest. The bell promptly begins to ring again.

"Mr. Cockerell," he says resignedly, "double up to the butts and ask Captain Wagstaffe—"

"I'm here, old son," replies a gentle voice, as Captain Wagstaffe touches him upon the shoulder. "Been here some time!"

After mutual asperities, it is decided by the two Captains to dispense with the aid of the telephone proper, and communicate by bell alone. Captain Wagstaffe's tall figure strides back across the heather; the red flag on the butts flutters down; and we get to work.

Upon a long row of waterproof sheets—some thirty in all—lie the firers. Beside each is extended the form of a sergeant or officer, tickling his charge's ear with incoherent counsel, and imploring him, almost tearfully, not to get excited.

Suddenly thirty targets spring out of the earth in front of us, only to disappear again just as we have got over our surprise. They are not of the usual bull's-eye pattern, but are what is known as "figure" targets. The lower half is sea-green, the upper, white. In the centre, half on the green and half on the white, is a curious brown smudge. It might be anything, from a splash of mud to one of those mysterious brown-paper patterns which fall out of ladies' papers, but it really is intended to represent the head and shoulders of a man in khaki lying on grass and aiming at us. However, the British private, with his usual genius for misapprehension, has christened this effigy "the beggar in the boat."

With equal suddenness the targets swing up again. Crack! An uncontrolled spirit has loosed off his rifle before it has reached his shoulder. Blistering reproof follows. Then, after three or four seconds, comes a perfect salvo all down the line. The conscientious Mucklewame, slowly raising his foresight as he has been taught to do, from the base of the target to the centre, has just covered the beggar in the boat between wind and water, and is lingering lovingly over the second pull, when the inconsiderate beggar (and his boat) sink unostentatiously into the abyss, leaving the open-mouthed marksman with his finger on the trigger and an unfired cartridge still in the chamber. At the dentist's Time crawls; in snap-shooting contests he sprints.

Another set of targets slide up as the first go down, and upon these the hits are recorded by a forest of black or white discs, waving vigorously in the air. Here and there a red-and-white flag flaps derisively. Mucklewame gets one of these.

The marking-targets go down to half-mast again, and then comes another tense pause. Then, as the firing-targets reappear, there is another volley. This time Private Mucklewame leads the field, and decapitates a dandelion. The third time he has learned wisdom, and the beggar in the boat gets the bullet where all mocking foes should get it—in the neck!

Snap-shooting over, the combatants retire to the five-hundred-yards firing-point, taking with them that modern hair-shirt, the telephone.

Presently a fresh set of targets swing up—of the bull's-eye variety this time—and the markers are busy once more.

The interior of the butts is an unexpectedly spacious place. From the nearest firing-point you would not suspect their existence, except when the targets are up. Imagine a sort of miniature railway station—or rather, half a railway station—sunk into the ground, with a very long platform and a very low roof—eight feet high at the most. Upon the opposite side of this station, instead of the other platform, rises the sandy ridge previously mentioned—the stop-butt—crowned with its row of number-boards. Along the permanent way, in place of sleepers and metals, runs a long and narrow trough, in which, instead of railway carriages, some thirty great iron frames are standing side by side. These frames are double, and hold the targets. They are so arranged that if one is pushed up the other comes down. The markers stand along the platform, like railway porters.

There are two markers to each target. They, stand with their backs to the firers, comfortably conscious of several feet of earth and a stout brick wall, between them and low shooters. Number one squats down, paste-pot in hand, and repairs the bullet-holes in the unemployed target with patches of black or white paper. Number two, brandishing a pole to which is attached a disc, black on one side and white on the other, is acquiring a permanent crick in the neck through gaping upwards at the target in search of hits. He has to be sharp-eyed, for the bullet-hole is a small one, and springs into existence without any other intimation than a spurt of sand on the bank twenty yards behind. He must be alert, too, and signal the shots as they are made; otherwise the telephone will begin to interest itself on his behalf. The bell will ring, and a sarcastic voice will intimate—assuming that you can hear what it says—that C Company are sending a wreath and message of condolence as their contribution to the funeral of the marker at Number Seven target, who appears to have died at his post within the last ten minutes; coupled with a polite request that his successor may be appointed as rapidly as possible, as the war is not likely to last more than three years. To this the butt-officer replies that C Company had better come a bit closer to the target and try, try again.

There are practically no restrictions as to the length to which one may go in insulting butt-markers. The Geneva Convention is silent upon the subject, partly because it is almost impossible to say anything which can really hurt a marker's feelings, and partly because the butt-officer always has the last word in any unpleasantness which may arise. That is to say, when defeated over the telephone, he can always lower his targets, and with his myrmidons feign abstraction or insensibility until an overheated subaltern arrives at the double from the five-hundred-yards firing-point, conveying news of surrender.

Captain Wagstaffe was an admitted master of this game. He was a difficult subject to handle, for he was accustomed to return an eye for an eye when repartees were being exchanged; and when overborne by heavier metal—say, a peripatetic "brass-hat" from Hythe—he was accustomed to haul up the red butt-flag (which automatically brings all firing to a standstill), and stroll down the range to refute the intruder at close quarters. We must add that he was a most efficient butt-officer. When he was on duty, markers were most assiduous in their attention to theirs, which is not always the case.

Thomas Atkins rather enjoys marking. For one thing, he is permitted to remove as much clothing as he pleases, and to cover himself with stickiness and grime to his heart's content—always a highly prized privilege. He is also allowed to smoke, to exchange full-flavoured persiflage with his neighbours, and to refresh himself from time to time with mysterious items of provender wrapped in scraps of newspaper. Given an easy-going butt-officer and some timid subalterns, he can spend a very agreeable morning. Even when discipline is strict, marking is preferable to most other fatigues.

Crack! Crack! Crack! The fusillade has begun. Privates Ogg and Hogg are in charge of Number Thirteen target. They are beguiling the tedium of their task by a friendly gamble with the markers on Number Fourteen—Privates Cosh and Tosh. The rules of the game are simplicity itself. After each detail has fired, the target with the higher score receives the sum of one penny from its opponents. At the present moment, after a long run of adversity, Privates Cosh and Tosh are one penny to the good. Once again fortune smiles upon them. The first two shots go right through the bull—eight points straight away. The third is an inner; the fourth another bull; the fifth just grazes the line separating inners from outers. Private Tosh, who is scoring, promptly signals an inner. Meanwhile, target Number Thirteen is also being liberally marked—but by nothing of a remunerative nature. The gentleman at the firing-point is taking what is known as "a fine sight"—so fine, indeed, that each successive bullet either buries itself in the turf fifty yards short, or ricochets joyously from off the bank in front, hurling itself sideways through the target, accompanied by a storm of gravel, and tearing holes therein which even the biased Ogg cannot class as clean hits.

"We hae gotten eighteen that time," announces Mr. Tosh to his rival, swinging his disc and inwardly blessing his unknown benefactor. (For obvious reasons the firer is known only to the marker by a number.) "Hoo's a' wi' you, Jock?"

"There's a [adjective] body here," replies Ogg, with gloomy sarcasm, "flingin' bricks through this yin!" He picks up the red-and-white flag for the fourth time, and unfurls it indignantly to the breeze.

"Here the officer!" says the warning voice of Hogg. "I doot he'll no allow your last yin, Peter."

He is right. The subaltern in charge of targets Thirteen to Sixteen, after a pained glance at the battered countenance of Number Thirteen, pauses before Fourteen, and jots down a figure on his butt-register.

"Fower, fower, fower, three, three, sirr," announces Tosh politely.

"Three bulls, one inner, and an ahter, sir," proclaims the Cockney sergeant simultaneously.

"Now, suppose *I* try," suggests the subaltern gently.

He examines the target, promptly disallows Tosh's last inner, and passes on.

"Seventeen *only!*" remarks Private Ogg severely. "I thocht sae!"

Private Cosh speaks—for the first time—removing a paste-brush, and some patching-paper from his mouth—

"Still, it's better nor a wash-oot! And onyway, you're due us tippence the noo!"

By way of contrast to the frivolous game of chance in the butts, the proceedings at the firing-point resolve themselves into a desperately earnest test of skill. The fortnight's range-practice is drawing to a close. Each evening registers have been made up, and firing averages adjusted, with the result that A and D Companies are found to have entirely outdistanced B and C, and to be running neck and neck for the championship of the battalion. Up till this morning D's average worked out at something under fifteen (out of a possible twenty), and A's at something over fourteen points. Both are quite amazing and incredible averages for a recruits' course; but then nearly everything about "K(1)" is amazing and incredible. Up till half an hour ago D had, if anything, increased their lead: then dire calamity overtook them.

One Pumpherston, Sergeant-Major and crack shot of the Company, solemnly blows down the barrel of his rifle and prostrates himself majestically upon his more than considerable stomach, for the purpose of firing his five rounds at five hundred yards. His average score so far has been one under "possible." Three officers and a couple of stray corporals gather behind him in eulogistic attitudes.

"How are the Company doing generally, Sergeant-Major?" inquires the Captain of D Company.

"Very well, sirr, except for some carelessness," replies the great man impressively. "That man there"—he indicates a shrinking figure hurrying rearwards—"has just spoilt his own score and another man's by putting two shots on the wrong target."

There is a horrified hum at this, for to fire upon some one else's target is the gravest crime in musketry. In the first place, it counts a miss for yourself. In the second, it may do a grievous wrong to your neighbour; for the law ordains that, in the event of more than five shots being found upon any target, only the worst five shall count. Therefore, if your unsolicited contribution takes the form of an outer, it must be counted, to the exclusion, possibly, of a bull. The culprit broke into a double.

Having delivered himself, Sergeant-Major Pumpherston graciously accepted the charger of cartridges which an obsequious acolyte was proffering, rammed it into the magazine, adjusted the sights, spread out his legs to an obtuse angle, and fired his first shot.

All eyes were turned upon target Number Seven. But there was no signal. All the other markers were busy flourishing discs or flags; only Number Seven remained cold and aloof.

The Captain of D Company laughed satirically.

"Number Seven gone to have his hair cut!" he observed.

"Third time this morning, sir," added a sycophantic subaltern.

The sergeant-major smiled indulgently,

"I can do without signals, sir," he said "I know where the shot went all right. I must get the next a *little* more to the left. That last one was a bit too near to three o'clock to be a certainty."

He fired again—with precisely the same result.

Every one was quite apologetic to the sergeant-major this time.

"This must be stopped," announced the Captain. "Mr. Simson, ring up Captain Wagstaffe on the telephone."

But the sergeant-major would not hear of this.

"The butt-registers are good enough for me, sir," he said with a paternal smile. He fired again. Once more the target stared back, blank and unresponsive.

This time the audience were too disgusted to speak. They merely shrugged their shoulders and glanced at one another with sarcastic smiles. The Captain, who had suffered a heavy reverse at the hands of Captain Wagstaffe earlier in the morning, began to rehearse the wording of his address over the telephone.

The sergeant-major fired his last two shots with impressive aplomb—only to be absolutely ignored twice more by Number Seven. Then he rose to his feet and saluted with ostentatious respectfulness.

"Four bulls and one inner, I *think*, sir. I'm afraid I pulled that last one off a bit."

The Captain is already at the telephone. For the moment this most feminine of instruments is found to be in an accommodating frame of mind. Captain Wagstaffe's voice is quickly heard.

"That you, Wagstaffe?" inquires the Captain. "I'm so sorry to bother you, but could you make inquiries and ascertain when the marker on Number Seven is likely to come out of the chloroform?"

"He has been sitting up and taking nourishment for some hours," replies the voice of Wagstaffe. "What message can I deliver to him?"

"None in particular, except that he has not signalled a single one of Sergeant-Major Pumpherston's shots!" replies the Captain of D, with crushing simplicity.

"Half a mo'!" replies Wagstaffe.... Then, presently—

"Hallo! Are you there, Whitson?"

"Yes. We are still here," Captain Whitson assures him frigidly.

"Right. Well, I have examined Number Seven target, and there are no shots on it of any kind whatever. But there are ten shots on Number Eight, if that's any help. Buck up with the next lot, will you? We are getting rather bored here. So long!"

There was nothing in it now. D Company had finished. The last two representatives of A were firing, and subalterns with note-books were performing prodigies of arithmetic. Bobby Little calculated that if these two scored eighteen points each they would pull the Company's total average up to fifteen precisely, beating D by a decimal.

The two slender threads upon which the success of this enterprise hung were named Lindsay and Budge. Lindsay was a phlegmatic youth with watery eyes. Nothing disturbed him, which was fortunate, for the commotion which surrounded him was considerable. A stout sergeant lay beside him on a waterproof sheet, whispering excited counsels of perfection, while Bobby Little danced in the rear, beseeching him to fire upon the proper target.

"Now, Lindsay," said Captain Whitson, in a trembling voice, "you are going to get into a good comfortable position, take your time, and score five bulls."

The amazing part of it all was that Lindsay very nearly did score five bulls. He actually got four, and would have had a fifth had not the stout sergeant, in excess of solicitude, tenderly wiped his watery eye for him with a grubby handkerchief just as he took the first pull for his third shot.

Altogether he scored nineteen; and the gallery, full of congratulations, moved on to inspect the performance of Private Budge, an extremely nervous subject: who, thanks to the fact that public attention had been concentrated so far upon Lindsay, and that his ministering sergeant was a matter-of-fact individual of few words, had put on two bulls—eight points. He now required to score only nine points in three shots.

Suddenly the hapless youth became aware of the breathless group in his rear. He promptly pulled his trigger, and just nicked the outside edge of the target—two points.

"I doot I'm gettin' a thing nairvous," he muttered apologetically to the sergeant.

"Havers! Shut your held and give the bull a bash!" responded that admirable person.

The twitching Budge, bracing himself, scored an inner—three points.

"A bull, and we do it!" murmured Bobby Little. Fortunately Budge did not hear.

"Ye're no daen badly," admitted the sergeant grudgingly.

Budge, a little piqued, determined to do better. He raised his foresight slowly; took the first pull; touched "six o'clock" on the distant bull—luckily the light was perfect—and took the second pull for the last time.

Next moment a white disc rose slowly out of the earth and covered the bull's-eye.

So Bobby Little was able next morning to congratulate his disciples upon being "the best-shooting platoon in the best-shooting Company in the best-shooting Battalion in the Brigade."

Not less than fifty other subalterns within a radius of five miles were saying the same thing to their platoons. It is right to foster a spirit of emulation in young troops.

Chapter 8

Billets

Scene, a village street, deserted. Rain falls. (It has been falling for about three weeks.) *A tucket sounds. Enter, reluctantly, soldiery. They grouse. There appear severally, in doorways, children. They stare. And at chamber-windows, serving-maids. They make eyes. The soldiery make friendly signs.*

Such is the stage setting for our daily morning parade. We have been here for some weeks now, and the populace is getting used to us. But when we first burst upon this peaceful township I think we may say, without undue egoism, that we created a profound sensation. In this sleepy corner of Hampshire His Majesty's uniform, enclosing a casual soldier or sailor on furlough, is a common enough sight, but a whole regiment on the march is the rarest of spectacles. As for this tatterdemalion northern horde, which swept down the street a few Sundays ago, with kilts swinging, bonnets cocked, and Pipes skirling, as if they were actually returning from a triumphant campaign instead of only rehearsing for one—well, as I say, the inhabitants had never seen anything like us in the world before. We achieved a *succes fou*. In fact, we were quite embarrassed by the attention bestowed upon us. During our first few parades the audience could with difficulty be kept off the stage. It was impossible to get the children into school, or the maids to come in and make the beds. Whenever a small boy spied an officer, he stood in his way and saluted him. Dogs enlisted in large numbers, sitting down with an air of pleased expectancy in the supernumerary rank, and waiting for this new and delightful pastime to take a fresh turn. When we marched out to our training area, later in the day, infant schools were decanted on to the road under a beaming vicar, to utter what we took to be patriotic sounds and wave handkerchiefs.

Off duty, we fraternised with the inhabitants. The language was a difficulty, of course; but a great deal can be done by mutual goodwill and a few gestures. It would have warmed the heart of a philologist to note the success with which a couple of kilted heroes from the banks of Loch Lomond would sidle up to two giggling damosels of Hampshire at the corner of the High Street, by the post office, and invite them to come for a walk. Though it was obvious that neither party could understand a single word that the other was saying, they never failed to arrive at an understanding; and the quartette, having formed two-deep, would disappear into a gloaming as black as ink, to inhale the evening air and take sweet counsel together—at a temperature of about twenty-five degrees Fahrenheit.

You ought to see us change guard. A similar ceremony takes place, we believe, outside Buckingham Palace every morning, and draws a considerable crowd; but you simply cannot compare it with ours. How often does the guard at Buckingham Palace fix bayonets? Once! and the thing is over. It is hardly worth while turning out to see. *We* sometimes do it as much as seven or eight times before we get it right, and even then we only stop because the sergeant-in-charge is threatened with clergyman's sore throat. The morning Private Mucklewame fixed his bayonet for the first time, two small boys stayed away from school all day in order to see him unfix it when he came off guard in the afternoon. Has any one ever done that at Buckingham Palace?

However, as I say, they have got used to us now. We fall in for our diurnal labours in comparative solitude, usually in heavy rain and without pomp. We are fairly into the collar by this time. We have been worked desperately hard for more than four months; we are grunting doggedly away at our job, not because we like it, but because we know it is the only thing to do. To march, to dig, to extend, to close; to practise advance-guards and rear-guards, and pickets, in fair weather or foul, often with empty stomachs—that is our daily and sometimes our nightly programme. We are growing more and more efficient, and our powers of endurance are increasing. But, as already stated, we no longer go about our task like singing birds.

It is a quarter to nine in the morning. All down the street doors are opening, and men appear, tugging at their equipment. (Yes, we are partially equipped now.) Most of B Company live in this street. They are fortunate, for only two or three are billeted in each little house, where they are quite domestic pets by this time. Their billeting includes "subsistence," which means that they are catered for by an experienced female instead of a male cooking-class still in the elementary stages of its art.

"A" are not so fortunate. They are living in barns or hay-lofts, sleeping on the floor, eating on the floor, existing on the floor generally. Their food is cooked (by the earnest band of students aforementioned) in open-air camp-kitchens; and in this weather it is sometimes difficult to keep the fires alight, and not always possible to kindle them.

"D" are a shade better off. They occupy a large empty mansion at the end of the street. It does not contain a stick of furniture; but there are fireplaces (with Adam mantelpieces), and the one thing of which the War Office never seems to stint us is coal. So "D" are warm, anyhow. Thirty men live in the drawing-room. Its late tenant would probably be impressed with its new scheme of upholstery. On the floor, straw palliasses and gravy. On the walls, "cigarette photties"—by the way, the children down here call them "fag picters." Across the room run clothes-lines, bearing steaming garments (and tell it not in Gath!) an occasional hare skin.

"C" are billeted in a village two miles away, and we see them but rarely.

The rain has ceased for a brief space—it always does about parade time—and we accordingly fall in. The men are carrying picks and shovels, and make no attempt to look pleased at the circumstance. They realise that they are in for a morning's hard digging, and very likely for an evening's field operations as well. When we began, company training a few weeks ago, entrenching was rather popular. More than half of us are miners or tillers of the soil, and the pick and shovel gave us a home-like sensation. Here was a chance, too, of showing regular soldiers how a job should be properly accomplished. So we dug with great enthusiasm.

But A Company have got over that now. They have developed into sufficiently old soldiers to have acquired the correct military attitude towards manual labour. Trench-digging is a "fatigue," to be classed with, coal-carrying, floor-scrubbing, and other civilian pursuits. The word "fatigue" is a shibboleth with, the British private. Persuade him that a task is part of his duty as a soldier, and he will perform it with tolerable cheerfulness; but once allow him to regard that task as a "fatigue," and he will shirk it whenever possible, and regard himself as a deeply injured individual when called upon to undertake it. Our battalion has now reached a sufficient state of maturity to be constantly on the *qui vive* for cunningly disguised fatigues. The other day, when kilts were issued for the first time, Private Tosh, gloomily surveying his newly unveiled extremities, was heard to remark with a sigh—

"Anither fatigue! Knees tae wash, noo!"

Presently Captain Blaikie arrives upon the scene; the senior subaltern reports all present, and we tramp off through the mud to our training area.

We are more or less in possession of our proper equipment now. That is to say, our wearing apparel and the appurtenances thereof are no longer held in position with string. The men have belts, pouches, and slings in which to carry their greatcoats. The greatcoats were the last to materialise. Since their arrival we have lost in decorative effect what we have gained in martial appearance. For a month or two each man wore over his uniform during wet weather—in other words, all day—a garment which the Army Ordnance Department described as—"Greatcoat, Civilian, one." An Old Testament writer would have termed it "a coat of many colours." A tailor would have said that it was a "superb vicuna raglan sack." You and I would have called it, quite simply, a reach-me-down. Anyhow, the combined effect was unique. As we plodded patiently along the road in our tarnished finery, with our eye-arresting checks and imitation velvet collars, caked with mud and wrinkled with rain, we looked like nothing so much on earth as a gang of weighers returning from an unsuccessful day at a suburban race-meeting.

But now the khaki-mills have ground out another million yards or so, and we have regulation greatcoats. Water-bottles, haversacks, mess-tins, and waterproof sheets have been slowly filtering into our possession; and whenever we "mobilise," which we do as a rule about once a fortnight—whether owing to invasion scares or as a test of efficiency we do not know—we fall in on our alarm-posts in something distinctly resembling 'the full "Christmas-tree" rig. Sam Browne belts have been wisely discarded by the officers in favour of web-equipment; and although Bobby Little's shoulders ache with the weight of his pack, he is comfortably conscious of two things—firstly, that even when separated from his baggage he can still subsist in fair comfort on what he carries upon his person; and secondly, that his "expectation of life," as the insurance offices say, has increased about a hundred per cent. now that the German sharpshooters will no longer be able to pick him out from his men.

Presently we approach the scene of our day's work, Area Number Fourteen. We are now far advanced in company training. The barrack square is a thing of the past. Commands are no longer preceded by cautions and explanations. A note on a whistle, followed by a brusque word or gesture, is sufficient to set us smartly on the move.

Suddenly we are called upon to give a test of our quality. A rotund figure upon horseback appears at a bend in the road. Captain Blaikie recognises General Freeman.

(We may note that the General's name is not really Freeman. We are much harried by generals at present. They roam about the country on horseback, and ask company commanders what they are doing; and no company commander has ever yet succeeded in framing an answer which sounds in the least degree credible. There are three generals; we call them Freeman, Hardy, and Willis, because we suspect that they are all—to judge from their fondness for keeping us on the run—financially interested in the consumption of shoe-leather. In other respects they differ, and a wise company commander will carefully bear their idiosyncrasies in mind and act accordingly, if he wishes to be regarded as an intelligent officer.)

Freeman is a man of action. He likes to see people running about. When he appears upon the horizon whole battalions break into a double.

Hardy is one of the old school: he likes things done decently and in order. He worships bright buttons, and exact words of command, and a perfectly wheeling line. He mistrusts unconventional movements and individual tactics. "No use trying to run," he says, "before you can walk." When we see him, we dress the company and advance in review order.

Willis gives little trouble. He seldom criticises, but when he does his criticism is always of a valuable nature; and he is particularly courteous and helpful to young officers. But, like lesser men, he has his fads. These are two—feet and cookery. He has been known to call a private out of the ranks on a route-march and request him to take his boots off for purposes of public display. "A soldier marches on two things," he announces—"his feet and his stomach." Then he calls up another man and asks him if he knows how to make a sea-pie. The man never does know, which is fortunate, for otherwise General Willis would not be able to tell him. After that he trots happily away, to ask some one else.

However, here we are face to face with General Freeman. Immediate action is called for. Captain Blaikie flings an order over his shoulder to the subaltern in command of the leading platoon—

"Pass back word that this road is under shell fire. Move!"—and rides forward to meet the General.

In ten seconds the road behind him is absolutely clear, and the men are streaming out to right and left in half-platoons. Waddell's platoon has the hardest time, for they were passing a quickset hedge when the order came. However, they hurl themselves blasphemously through, and double on, scratched and panting.

"Good morning, sir!" says Captain Blaikie, saluting.

"Good morning!" says General Freeman. "What was that last movement?"

"The men are taking 'artillery' formation, sir. I have just passed the word down that the road is under shell fire."

"Quite so. But don't you think you ought to keep some of your company in rear, as a supporting line? I see you have got them all up on one front."

By this time A Company is advancing in its original direction, but split up into eight half-platoons in single file—four on each side of the road, at intervals of thirty yards. The movement has been quite smartly carried out. Still, a critic must criticise or go out of business. However, Captain Blaikie is an old hand.

"I was assuming that my company formed part of a battalion, sir," he explained. "There are supposed to be three other companies in rear of mine."

"I see. Still, tell two of your sections to fall back and form a supporting line."

Captain Blaikie, remembering that generals have little time for study of such works as the new drill-book, and that when General Freeman says "section" he probably means "platoon," orders Numbers Two and Four to fall back. This manoeuvre is safely accomplished.

"Now, let me see them close on the road."

Captain Blaikie blows a whistle, and slaps himself on the top of the head. In three minutes the long-suffering platoons are back on the road, extracting thorns from their flesh and assuaging the agony of their abrasions by clandestine massage.

General Freeman rides away, and the column moves on. Two minutes later Captain Wagstaffe doubles up from the rear to announce that General Hardy is only two hundred yards behind.

"Pass back word to the men," groans Captain Blaikie, "to march at attention, put their caps straight, and slope their shovels properly. And send an orderly to that hilltop to look out for General Willis. Tell him to unlace his boots when he gets there, and on no account to admit that he knows how to make a sea-pie!"

CHAPTER 9

Mid-Channel

The Great War has been terribly hard on the text-books.

When we began to dig trenches, many weeks ago, we always selected a site with a good field of fire.

"No good putting your trenches," said the text-book, "where you can't see the enemy."

This seemed only common-sense; so we dug our trenches in open plains, or on the forward slope of a hill, where we could command the enemy's movements up to two thousand yards.

Another maxim which we were urged to take to heart was—When not entrenched, always take advantage of *natural* cover of any kind; such as farm buildings, plantations, and railway embankments.

We were also given practice in describing and recognising inconspicuous targets at long range, in order to be able to harass the enemy the moment he showed himself.

Well, recently generals and staff officers have been coming home from the front and giving us lectures. We regard most lectures as a "fatigue"—but not these. We have learned more from these quiet-mannered, tired-looking men in a brief hour than from all the manuals that ever came out of Gale and Poldens'. We have heard the history of the War from the inside. We know why our Army retreated from Mons; we know what prevented the relief of Antwerp. But above all, we have learned to revise some of our most cherished theories.

Briefly, the amended version of the law and the prophets comes to this:—

Never, under any circumstances, place your trenches where you can see the enemy a long way off. If you do, he will inevitably see you too, and will shell you out of them in no time. You need not be afraid of being rushed; a field of fire of two hundred yards or so will be sufficient to wipe him off the face of the earth.

Never, under any circumstances, take cover in farm buildings, or plantations, or behind railway embankments, or in any place likely to be marked on a large-scale map. Their position and range are known to a yard. Your safest place is the middle of an open plain or ploughed field. There it will be more difficult for the enemy's range-takers to gauge your exact distance.

In musketry, concentrate all your energies on taking care of your rifle and practising "rapid." You will seldom have to fire over a greater distance than two hundred yards; and at that range British rapid fire is the most dreadful medium of destruction yet devised in warfare.

All this scraps a good deal of laboriously acquired learning, but it rings true. So we site our trenches now according to the lessons taught us by the bitter experience of others.

Having arrived at our allotted area, we get to work. The firing-trench proper is outlined on the turf a hundred yards or so down the reverse slope of a low hill. When it is finished it will be a mere crack in the ground, with no front cover to speak of; for that would make it conspicuous. Number One Platoon gets to work on this. To Number Two is assigned a more subtle task—namely, the construction of a dummy trench a comfortable distance ahead, dug out to the depth of a few inches, to delude inquisitive aeroplanes, and rendered easily visible to the enemy's observing stations by a parapet of newly-turned earth. Numbers Three and Four concentrate their energies upon the supporting trench and its approaches.

The firing-trench is our place of business—our office in the city, so to speak. The supporting trench is our suburban residence, whither the weary toiler may betake himself periodically (or, more correctly, in relays) for purposes of refreshment and repose. The firing-trench, like most business premises, is severe in design and destitute of ornament. But the suburban trench lends itself to more imaginative treatment. An auctioneer's catalogue would describe it as *A commodious bijou residence, on* (or of) *chalky soil; three feet wide and six feet deep; in the style of the best troglodyte period. Thirty seconds brisk crawl* (or per stretcher) *from the firing line. Gas laid on—*

But only once, in a field near Aldershot, where Private Mucklewame first laid bare, and then perforated, the town main with his pick.

—With own water supply—ankle-deep at times—*telephone, and the usual offices.*

We may note that the telephone communicates with the observing-station, lying well forward, in line with the dummy trench. The most important of the usual offices is the hospital—a cavern excavated at the back of the trench, and roofed over with hurdles, earth, and turf.

It is hardly necessary to add that we do not possess a real field-telephone. But when you have spent four months in firing dummy cartridges, performing bayonet exercises without bayonets, taking hasty cover from non-existent shell fire, capturing positions held by no enemy, and enacting the part of a "casualty" without having received a scratch, telephoning without a telephone is a comparatively simple operation. All you require is a ball of string and no sense of humour. Second Lieutenant Waddell manages our telephone.

Meanwhile we possess our souls in patience. We know that the factories are humming night and day on our behalf; and that if, upon a certain day in a certain month, the contractors do not deliver our equipment down to the last water-bottle cork, "K" will want to know the reason why; and we cannot imagine any contractor being so foolhardy as to provoke that terrible man into an inquiring attitude of mind.

Now we are at work. We almost wish that Freeman, Hardy, and Willis could see us. Our buttons may occasionally lack lustre; we may cherish unorthodox notions as to the correct method of presenting arms; we may not always present an unbroken front on the parade-ground—but we *can* dig! Even the fact that we do not want to, cannot altogether eradicate a truly human desire to "show off." "Each man to his art," we say. We are quite content to excel in ours, the oldest in the world. We know enough now about the conditions of the present war to be aware that when we go out on service only three things will really count—to march; to dig; and to fire, upon occasion, fifteen rounds a minute. Our rapid fire is already fair; we can march more than a little; and if men who have been excavating the bowels of the earth for eight hours a day ever since they were old enough to swing a pick cannot make short work of a Hampshire chalk down, they are no true members of their Trades Union or the First Hundred Thousand.

We have stuck to the phraseology of our old calling.

"Whaur's ma drawer?" inquires Private Hogg, a thick-set young man with bandy legs, wiping his countenance with a much-tattooed arm. He has just completed five strenuous minutes with a pick. "Come away, Geordie, wi' yon shovel!"

The shovel is preceded by an adjective. It is the only adjective that A Company knows. (No, not that one. The second on the list!)

Mr. George Ogg steps down into the breach, and sets to work. He is a small man, strongly resembling the Emperor of China in a third-rate provincial pantomime. His weapon is the spade. In civil life he would have shovelled the broken coal into a "hutch," and "hurled" it away to the shaft. That was why Private Hogg referred to him as a "drawer." In his military capacity he now removes the chalky soil from the trench with great dexterity, and builds it up into a neat parapet behind, as a precaution against the back-blast of a "Black Maria."

There are not enough, picks and shovels to go round—*cela va sans dire*. However, Private Mucklewame and others, who are not of the delving persuasion, exhibit no resentment. Digging is not their department. If you hand them a pick and shovel and invite them to set to work, they lay the pick upon the ground beside the trench and proceed to shovel earth over it until they have lost it. At a later stage in this great war-game they will fight for these picks and shovels like wild beasts. Shrapnel is a sure solvent of professional etiquette.

However, today the pickless squad are lined up a short distance away by the relentless Captain Wagstaffe, and informed—

"You are under fire from that wood. Dig yourselves in!"

Digging oneself in is another highly unpopular fatigue. First of all you produce your portable entrenching-tool—it looks like a combination of a modern tack-hammer and a medieval back-scratcher—and fit it to its haft. Then you lie flat upon your face on the wet grass, and having scratched up some small lumps of turf, proceed to build these into a parapet. Into the hole formed by the excavation of the turf you then put your head, and in this ostrich-like posture await further instructions. Private Mucklewame is of opinion that it would be equally effective, and infinitely less fatiguing, simply to lie down prone and close the eyes.

After Captain Wagstaffe has criticised the preliminary parapets—most of them are condemned as not being bullet-proof—the work is continued. It is not easy, and never comfortable, to dig lying down; but we must all learn to do it; so we proceed painfully to construct a shallow trough for our bodies and an annexe for our boots. Gradually we sink out of sight, and Captain Wagstaffe, standing fifty yards to our front, is able to assure us that he can now see nothing—except Private Mucklewame's lower dorsal curve.

By this time the rain has returned for good, and the short winter day is drawing to a gloomy close. It is after three, and we have been working, with one brief interval, for nearly five hours. The signal is given to take shelter. We huddle together under the leafless trees, and get wetter.

Next comes the order to unroll greatcoats. Five minutes later comes another—to fall in. Tools are counted; there is the usual maddening wait while search is made for a missing pick. But at last the final word of command rings out, and the sodden, leaden-footed procession sets out on its four-mile tramp home.

We are not in good spirits. One's frame of mind at all times depends largely upon what the immediate future has to offer; and, frankly, we have little to inspire us in that direction at present. When we joined, four long months ago, there loomed largely and splendidly before our eyes only two alternatives—victory in battle or death with honour. We might live, or we might die; but life, while it lasted, would not lack great moments. In our haste we had overlooked the long dreary waste which lay—which always lies—between dream and fulfilment. The glorious splash of patriotic fervour which launched us on our way has subsided; we have reached mid-channel; and the haven where we would be is still afar off. The brave future of which we dreamed in our dour and uncommunicative souls seems as remote as ever, and the present has settled down into a permanency.

To-day, for instance, we have tramped a certain number of miles; we have worked for a certain number of hours; and we have got wet through for the hundredth time. We are now tramping home to a dinner which will probably not be ready, because, as yesterday, it has been cooked in the open air under weeping skies. While waiting for it, we shall clean the same old rifle. When night falls, we shall sleep uneasily upon a comfortless floor, in an atmosphere of stale food and damp humanity. In the morning we shall rise up reluctantly, and go forth, probably in heavy rain, to our labour until the evening—the same labour and the same evening. We admit that it can't be helped: the officers and the authorities do their best for us under discouraging circumstances: but there it is. Out at the front, we hear, men actually get as much as three days off at a time—three days of hot baths and abundant food and dry beds. To us, in our present frame of mind, that seems worth any number of bullets and frost-bites.

And—bitterest thought of all—New Year's Day, with all its convivial associations, is only a few weeks away. When it comes, the folk at home will celebrate it, doubtless with many a kindly toast to the lads "oot there," and the lads "doon there." But what will that profit us? In this barbarous country we understand that they take no notice of the sacred festival at all. There will probably be a route-march, to keep us out of the public-houses.

Et patiti, et patita. Are we fed up? YES!

As we swing down the village street, slightly cheered by a faint aroma of Irish stew—the cooks have got the fires alight after all—the adjutant rides up, and reins in his horse beside our company commander.

Battalion orders of some kind! Probably a full-dress parade, to trace a missing bayonet!

Presently he rides away; and Captain Blaikie, instead of halting and dismissing us in the street as usual, leads us down an alley into the backyard which serves as our apology for a parade-ground. We form close column of platoons, stand at ease, and wait resignedly.

Then Captain Blaikie's voice falls upon our ears.

"A Company, I have an announcement to make to you. His Majesty the King—"

So that is it. Another Royal Review! Well, it will be a break in the general monotony.

"—who has noted your hard work, good discipline, and steady progress with the keenest satisfaction and pride—"

We are not utterly forgotten, then.

"—has commanded that every man in the battalion is to have seven days' full leave of absence."

"A-a-ah!" We strain our tingling ears.

"We are to go by companies, a week at a time. 'C' will go first."

"C" indeed! Who are "C," to—?

"A Company's leave—*our* leave—will begin on the twenty-eighth of December, and extend to the third of January."

The staccato words sink slowly in, and then thoughts come tumbling.

"Free—free on New Year's Day! Almichty! Free to gang hame! Free tae—"

Then comes an icy chill upon our hearts. How are we to get home? Scotland is hundreds of miles away. The fare, even on a "soldier's" ticket—

But the Captain has not quite finished.

"Every man will receive a week's pay in advance; and his fare, home and back, will be paid by Government. That is all."

And quite enough too! We rock upon our squelching feet. But the Captain adds, without any suspicion of his parade-ground manner—

"If I may say so, I think that if ever men deserved a good holiday, you do. Company, slope arms! Dis-*miss*!"

* * * * * * * *

We do not cheer: we are not built that way. But as we stream off to our Irish stew, the dourest of us says in his heart—

"God Save the King!"

CHAPTER 10

Deeds of Darkness

A moonlit, wintry night. Four hundred men are clumping along the frost-bound road, under the pleasing illusion that because they are neither whistling nor talking they are making no noise.

At the head of the column march Captains Mackintosh and Shand, the respective commanders of C and D Companies. Occasionally Mackintosh, the senior, interpolates a remark of a casual or professional nature. To all these his colleague replies in a low and reproachful whisper. The pair represent two schools of military thought—a fact of which their respective subalterns are well aware,—and act accordingly.

"In preparing troops for active service, you must make the conditions as *real* as possible from the very outset," postulates Shand. "Perform all your exercises just as you would in war. When you dig trenches, let every man work with his weather-eye open and his rifle handy, in case of sudden attack. If you go out on night operations don't advertise your position by stopping to give your men a recitation. No talking—no smoking—no unnecessary delay or exposure! Just go straight to your point of deployment, and do what you came out to do."

To this Mackintosh replies,—

"That's all right for trained troops. But ours aren't half-trained yet; all our work just now is purely educational. It's no use expecting a gang of rivet-heaters from Clydebank to form an elaborate outpost line, just because you whispered a few sweet nothings in the dark to your leading section of fours! You simply *must* explain every step you take, at present."

But Shand shakes his head.

"It's not soldierly," he sighs.

Hence the present one-sided—or apparently one-sided—dialogue. To the men marching immediately behind, it sounds like something between a soliloquy and a chat over the telephone.

Presently Captain Mackintosh announces,—

"We might send the scouts ahead now I think."

Shand gives an inaudible assent. The column is halted, and the scouts called up. A brief command, and they disappear into the darkness, at the double. C and D Companies give them five minutes start, and move on. The road at this point runs past a low mossy wall, surmounted by a venerable yew hedge, clipped at intervals into the semblance of some heraldic monster. Beyond the hedge, in the middle distance, looms a square and stately Georgian mansion, whose lights twinkle hospitably.

"I think, Shand," suggests Mackintosh with more formality, now that he is approaching the scene of action, "that we might attack at two different points, each of us with his own company. What is your opinion?"

The officer addressed makes no immediate reply. His gaze is fixed upon the yew hedge, as if searching for gun positions or vulnerable points. Presently, however, he turns away, and coming close to Captain Mackintosh, puts his lips to his left ear. Mackintosh prepares his intellect for the reception of a pearl of strategy.

But Captain Shand merely announces, in his regulation whisper,—

"Dam pretty girl lives in that house, old man!"

* * * * * * * *

Private Peter Dunshie, scout, groping painfully and profanely through a close-growing wood, paused to unwind a clinging tendril from his bare knees. As he bent down, his face came into sudden contact with a cold, wet, prickly bramble-bush, which promptly drew a loving but excoriating finger across his right cheek.

He started back, with a muffled exclamation. Instantly there arose at his very feet the sound as of a motor-engine being wound up, and a flustered and protesting cock-pheasant hoisted itself tumultuously clear of the undergrowth and sailed away, shrieking, over the trees.

Finally, a hare, which had sat cowering in the bracken, hare-like, when it might have loped away, selected this, the one moment when it ought to have sat still, to bolt frantically between Peter's bandy legs and speed away down a long moon-dappled avenue.

Private Dunshie, a prey to nervous shock, said what naturally rose to his lips. To be frank, he said it several times. He had spent the greater part of his life selling evening papers in the streets of Glasgow: and the profession of journalism, though it breeds many virtues in its votaries, is entirely useless as a preparation for conditions either of silence or solitude. Private Dunshie had no experience of either of these things, and consequently feared them both. He was acutely afraid. What he understood and appreciated was Argyle Street on a Saturday night. That was life! That was light! That was civilisation! As for creeping about in this uncanny wood, filled with noxious animals and adhesive vegetation—well, Dunshie was heartily sorry that he had ever volunteered for service as a scout. He had only done so, of course, because the post seemed to offer certain relaxations from the austerity of company routine—a little more freedom of movement, a little less trench-digging, and a minimum of supervision. He would have been thankful for a supervisor now!

That evening, when the scouts doubled ahead, Lieutenant Simson had halted them upon the skirts of a dark, *dreich* plantation, and said—

"A and B Companies represent the enemy. They are beyond that crest, finishing the trenches which were begun the 'other day. They intend to hold these against our attack. Our only chance is to take them by surprise. As they will probably have thrown out a line of outposts, you scouts will now scatter and endeavour to get through that line, or at least obtain exact knowledge of its composition. My belief is that the enemy will content themselves with placing a piquet on each of the two roads which run through their position; but it is possible that they will also post sentry-groups in the wood which lies between. However, that is what you have to find out. Don't go and get captured. Move!"

The scouts silently scattered, and each man set out to pierce his allotted section of the enemy's position. Private Dunshie, who had hoped for a road, or at least a cart-track, to follow, found himself, by the worst of luck, assigned to a portion of the thick belt of wood which stretched between the two roads. Nature had not intended him for a pioneer: he was essentially a city man. However, he toiled on, rending the undergrowth, putting up game, falling over tree-roots, and generally acting as advertising agent for the approaching attack.

By way of contrast, two hundred yards to his right, picking his way with cat-like care and rare enjoyment, was Private M'Snape. He was of the true scout breed. In the dim and distant days before the call of the blood had swept him into "K(1)," he had been a Boy Scout of no mean repute. He was clean in person and courteous in manner. He could be trusted to deliver a message promptly. He could light a fire in a high wind with two matches, and provide himself with a meal of sorts where another would have starved. He could distinguish an oak from an elm, and was sufficiently familiar with the movements of the heavenly bodies to be able to find his way across country by night. He was truthful, and amenable to discipline. In short, he was the embodiment of a system which in times of peace had served as a text for innumerable well-meaning but muddle-headed politicians of a certain type, who made a specialty of keeping the nation upon the alert against the insidious encroachments of—Heaven help us!—Militarism!

To-night all M'Snape's soul was set on getting through the enemy's outpost line, and discovering a way of ingress for the host behind him. He had no map, but he had the Plough and a fitful moon to guide him, and he held a clear notion of the disposition of the trenches in his retentive brain. On his left he could hear the distressing sounds of Dunshie's dolorous progress; but these were growing fainter. The reason was that Dunshie, like most persons who follow the line of least resistance, was walking in a circle. In fact, a few minutes later his circuitous path brought him out upon the long straight road which ran up over the hill towards the trenches.

With a sigh of relief Dunshie stepped out upon the good hard macadam, and proceeded with the merest show of stealth up the gentle gradient. But he was not yet at ease. The over-arching trees formed a tunnel in which his footsteps reverberated uncomfortably. The moon had retired behind a cloud. Dunshie, gregarious and urban, quaked anew. Reflecting longingly upon his bright and cosy billet, with the "subsistence" which was doubtless being prepared against his return, he saw no occasion to reconsider his opinion that in the country no decent body should over be called up to go out after dark unaccompanied. At that moment Dunshie would have bartered his soul for the sight of an electric tram.

The darkness grew more intense. Something stirred in the wood beside him, and his skin tingled. An owl hooted suddenly, and he jumped. Next, the gross darkness was illuminated by a pale and ghostly radiance, coming up from behind; and something brushed past him—something which squeaked and panted. His hair rose upon his scalp. A friendly "Good-night!" uttered in a strong Hampshire accent into his left ear, accentuated rather than soothed his terrors. He sat down suddenly upon a bank by the roadside, and feebly mopped his moist brow.

The bicycle, having passed him, wobbled on up the hill, shedding a fitful ray upon alternate sides of the road. Suddenly—raucous and stunning, but oh, how sweet!—rang out the voice of Dunshie's lifelong friend, Private Mucklewame.

"Halt! Wha goes there!"

The cyclist made no reply, but kept his devious course. Private Mucklewame, who liked to do things decently and in order, stepped heavily out of the hedge into the middle of the road, and repeated his question in a reproving voice. There was no answer.

This was most irregular. According to the text of the spirited little dialogue in which Mucklewame had been recently rehearsed by his piquet commander, the man on the bicycle ought to have said "Friend!" This cue received, Mucklewame was prepared to continue. Without it he was gravelled. He tried once more.

"Halt! Wha goes—"

"On His Majesty's Service, my lad!" responded a hearty voice; and the postman, supplementing this information with a friendly goodnight, wobbled up the hill and disappeared from sight.

The punctilious Mucklewame was still glaring severely after this unseemly "gagger," when he became aware of footsteps upon the road. A pedestrian was plodding up the hill in the wake of the postman. He would stand no nonsense this time.

"Halt!" he commanded. "Wha goes there?"

"Hey, Jock," inquired a husky voice, "is that you?"

This was another most irregular answer. Declining to be drawn into impromptu irrelevancies, Mucklewame stuck to his text.

"Advance yin," he continued, "and give the coontersign, if any!"

Private Dunshie drew nearer.

"Jock," he inquired wistfully, "hae ye gotten a fag?"

"Aye," replied Mucklewame, friendship getting the better of conscience.

"Wull ye give a body yin?"

"Aye. But ye canna smoke on ootpost duty," explained Mucklewame sternly. "Forbye, the officer has no been roond yet," he added.

"Onyway," urged Dunshie eagerly, "let nae be your prisoner! Let me bide with the other boys in here ahint the dyke!"

The hospitable Mucklewame agreed, and Scout Dunshie, overjoyed at the prospect of human companionship, promptly climbed over the low wall and attached himself, in the *role* of languishing captive, to Number Two Sentry-Group of Number Three Piquet.

Meanwhile M'Snape had reached the forward edge of the wood, and was cautiously reconnoitring the open ground in front of him. The moon had disappeared altogether now, but M'Snape was able to calculate, by reason of the misdirected exuberance of the vigilant Mucklewame, the exact position of the sentry-group on the left-hand road. About the road on his right he was not so certain; so he set out cautiously towards it, keeping to the edge of the wood, and pausing every few yards to listen. There must be a sentry-group somewhere here, he calculated—say midway between the roads. He must walk warily.

Easier said than done. At this very moment a twig snapped beneath his foot with a noise like a pistol-shot, and a covey of partridges, lying out upon the stubble beside him, made an indignant evacuation of their bedroom. The mishap seemed fatal: M'Snape stood like a stone. But no alarm followed, and presently all was still again—so still, indeed, that presently, out on the right, two hundred yards away, M'Snape heard a man cough and then spit. Another sentry was located!

Having decided that there was no sentry-group between the two roads, M'Snape turned his back upon the wood and proceeded cautiously forward. He was not quite satisfied in his mind about things. He knew that Captain Wagstaffe was in command of this section of the defence. He cherished a wholesome respect for that efficient officer, and doubted very much if he would really leave so much of his front entirely unguarded.

Next moment the solution of the puzzle was in his very hand—in the form of a stout cord stretching from right to left. He was just in time to avoid tripping over it. It was suspended about six inches above the ground.

You cannot follow a clue in two directions at once; so after a little consideration M'Snape turned and crawled along to his right, being careful to avoid touching the cord. Presently a black mass loomed before him, acting apparently as terminus to the cord. Lying flat on his stomach, in order to get as much as possible of this obstacle between his eyes and the sky, M'Snape was presently able to descry, plainly silhouetted against the starry landscape, the profile of one Bain, a scout of A Company, leaning comfortably against a small bush, and presumably holding the end of the cord in his hand.

M'Snape wriggled silently away, and paused to reflect. Then he began to creep forward once more.

Having covered fifty yards, he turned to his right again, and presently found himself exactly between Bain and the trenches. As he expected, his hand now descended upon another cord, lying loosely on the ground, and running at right angles to the first. Plainly Bain was holding one end of this, and some one in the trenches—Captain Wagstaffe himself, as like as not—was holding the other. If an enemy stumbled over the trip-cord, Bain would warn the defence by twitching the alarm-cord.

Five minutes later M'Snape was back at the rendezvous, describing to Simson what he had seen. That wise subaltern promptly conducted him to Captain Mackintosh, who was waiting with his Company for something to go upon. Shand had departed with his own following to make an independent attack on the right flank. Seven of the twelve scouts were there. Of the missing, Dunshie, as we know, was sunning his lonely soul in the society of his foes; two had lost themselves, and the remaining two had been captured by a reconnoitring patrol. Of the seven which strayed not, four had discovered the trip-cord; so it was evident that that ingenious contrivance extended along the whole line. Only M'Snape, however, had penetrated farther. The general report was that the position was closely guarded from end to end.

"You say you found a cord running back from Bain to the trenches, M'Snape," asked Captain Mackintosh, "and a sentry holding on to it?"

"Yess, sirr," replied the scout, standing stiffly to attention in the dark.

"If we could creep out of the wood and rush *him*, we might be able to slip our attack in at that point," said the Captain. "You say there is cover to within twenty yards of where he is sitting?"

"Yes, sirr."

"Still, I'm afraid he'll pull that cord a bit too soon for us."

"He'll no, sirr," remarked M'Snape confidently.

"Why not?" asked the Captain.

M'Snape told him.

Captain Mackintosh surveyed the small wizened figure before him almost affectionately.

"M'Snape," he said, "to-morrow I shall send in your name for lance-corporal!"

The defenders were ready. The trenches were finished: "A" and "B" had adjusted their elbow-rests to their liking, and blank ammunition had been served out. Orders upon the subject of firing were strict.

"We won't loose off a single shot until we actually *see* you," Captain Blaikie had said to Captain Mackintosh. "That will teach your men to crawl upon their little tummies, and ours to keep their eyes skinned."

(Captain Wagstaffe's string alarm had been an afterthought. At least, it was not mentioned to the commander of the attack.)

Orders were given that the men were to take things easily for half an hour or so, as the attack could not possibly be developed within that time. The officers established themselves in a splinter-proof shelter at the back of the supporting trench, and partook of provender from their haversacks.

"I don't suppose they'll attack much before nine," said the voice of a stout major named Kemp. "My word, it is dark in here! *And* dull! Curse the Kaiser!"

"I don't know," said Wagstaffe thoughtfully. "War is hell, and all that, but it has a good deal to recommend it. It wipes out all the small nuisances of peace-time."

"Such as—!"

"Well, Suffragettes, and Futurism, and—and—"

"Bernard Shaw," suggested another voice. "Hall Caine—"

"Yes, and the Tango, and party politics, and golf-maniacs. Life and Death, and the things that really are big, get viewed in their proper perspective for once in a way."

"And look how the War has bucked up the nation," said Bobby Little, all on fire at once. "Look at the way girls have given up fussing over clothes and things, and taken to nursing."

"My poor young friend," said the voice of the middle-aged Kemp, "tell me honestly, would you like to be attended to by some of the young women who have recently taken up the nursing profession?"

"Rather!" said Bobby, with thoughtless fervour.

"I didn't say *one*," Kemp pointed out, amid laughter, "but *some*. Of course we all know of one. Even I do. It's the rule, not the exception, that we are dealing with just now."

Bobby, realising that he had been unfairly surprised in a secret, felt glad that the darkness covered his blushes.

"Well, take my tip," continued Kemp, "and avoid amateur ministering angels, my son. I studied the species in South Africa. For twenty-four hours they nurse you to death, and after that they leave you to perish of starvation. Women in war-time are best left at home."

A youthful paladin in the gloom timidly mentioned the name of Florence Nightingale.

"One Nightingale doesn't make a base hospital," replied Kemp. "I take off my hat—we all do—to women who are willing to undergo the drudgery and discomfort which hospital training involves. But I'm not talking about Florence Nightingales. The young person whom I am referring to is just intelligent enough to understand that the only possible thing to do this season is to nurse. She qualifies herself for her new profession by dressing up like one of the chorus of 'The Quaker Girl,' and getting her portrait, thus attired, into the 'Tatler.' Having achieved this, she has graduated. She then proceeds to invade any hospital that is available, where she flirts with everything in pyjamas, and freezes you with a look if you ask her to empty a basin or change your sheets. I know her! I've had some, and I know her! She is one of the minor horrors of war. In peace-time she goes out on Alexandra Day, and stands on the steps of men's clubs and pesters the members to let her put a rose in their button-holes. What such a girl wants is a good old-fashioned mother who knows how to put a slipper to its right use!"

"I don't think," observed Wagstaffe, since Kemp had apparently concluded his philippic, "that young girls are the only people who lose their heads. Consider all the poisonous young blighters that one sees about town just now. Their uplift is enormous, and their manners in public horrid; and they hardly know enough about their new job to stand at attention when they hear 'God Save the King.' In fact, they deserve to be nursed by your little friends, Bobby!"

"They are all that you say," conceded Kemp. "But after all, they do have a fairly stiff time of it on duty, and they are going to have a much stiffer time later on. And they are not going to back out when the romance of the new uniform wears off, remember. Now these girls will play the angel-of-mercy game for a week or two, and then jack up and confine their efforts to getting hold of a wounded officer and taking him to the theatre. It is *dernier cri* to take a wounded officer about with you at present. Wounded officers have quite superseded Pekinese, I am told."

"Women certainly are the most extraordinary creatures," mused Ayling, a platoon commander of "B." "In private life I am a beak at a public school—"

"What school?" inquired several voices. Ayling gave the name, found that there were two of the school's old boys present, and continued—

"Just as I was leaving to join this battalion, the Head received a letter from a boy's mother intimating that she was obliged to withdraw her son, as he had received a commission in the army for the duration of the war. She wanted to know if the Head would keep her son's place open for him until he came back! What do you think of that?"

"Sense of proportion wasn't invented when women were made," commented Kemp. "But we are wandering from the subject, which is: what advantages are we, personally, deriving from the war? Wagger, what are you getting out of it?"

"Half-a-crown a day extra pay as Assistant Adjutant," replied Wagstaffe laconically. "Ainslie, wake up and tell us what the war has done for you, since you abandoned the Stock Exchange and took to foot-slogging."

"Certainly," replied Ainslie. "A year ago I spent my days trying to digest my food, and my nights trying to sleep. I was not at all successful in either enterprise. I can now sit down to a supper of roast pork and bottled stout, go to bed directly afterwards, sleep all night, and wake up in the morning without thinking unkind things of anybody—not even my relations-in-law! Bless the Kaiser, say I! Borrodaile, what about you? Any complaints?"

"Thank you," replied Borrodaile's dry voice; "there are no complaints. In civil life I am what is known as a 'prospective candidate.' For several years I have been exercising this, the only, method of advertising permitted to a barrister, by nursing a constituency. That is, I go down to the country once a week, and there reduce myself to speechlessness soliciting the votes of the people who put my opponent in twenty years ago, and will keep him in by a two thousand majority as long as he cares to stand. I have been at it five years, but so far the old gentleman has never so much as betrayed any knowledge of my existence."

"That must be rather galling," said Wagstaffe.

"Ah! but listen! Of course party politics have now been merged in the common cause—see local organs, *passim*—and both sides are working shoulder to shoulder for the maintenance of our national existence."

"*Applause!*" murmured Kemp.

"That is to say," continued Borrodaile with calm relish, "my opponent, whose strong suit for the last twenty years has been to cry down the horrors of militarism, and the madness of national service, and the unwieldy size of the British Empire, is now compelled to spend his evenings taking the chair at mass meetings for the encouragement of recruiting. I believe the way in which he eats up his own previous utterances on the subject is quite superb. On these occasions I always send him a telegram, containing a kindly pat on the back for him and a sort of semi-official message for the audience. He has to read this out on the platform!"

"What sort of message?" asked a delighted voice.

"Oh—*Send along some more of our boys. Lord Kitchener says there are none to touch them. Borrodaile, Bruce and Wallace Highlanders.* Or—*All success to the meeting, and best thanks to you personally for carrying on in my absence. Borrodaile, Bruce and Wallace Highlanders.* I have a lot of quiet fun," said Borrodaile meditatively, "composing those telegrams. I rather fancy"—he examined the luminous watch on his wrist—"it's five minutes past eight: I rather fancy the old thing is reading one now!"

The prospective candidate leaned back against the damp wall of the dug-out with a happy sigh. "What have you got out of the war, Ayling?" he inquired.

"Change," said Ayling.

"For better or worse?"

"If you had spent seven years in a big public school," said Ayling, "teaching exactly the same thing, at exactly the same hour, to exactly the same kind of boy, for weeks on end, what sort of change would you welcome most?"

"Death," said several voices.

"Nothing of the kind!" said Ayling warmly. "It's a great life, if you are cut out for it. But there is no doubt that the regularity of the hours, and the absolute certainty of the future, make a man a bit groovy. Now in this life we are living we have to do lots of dull or unpleasant things, but they are never quite the same things. They are progressive, and not circular, if you know what I mean; and the immediate future is absolutely unknown, which is an untold blessing. What about you, Sketchley?"

A fat voice replied—

"War is good for adipose Special Reservists. I have decreased four inches round the waist since October. Next?"

So the talk ran on. Young Lochgair, heir to untold acres in the far north and master of unlimited pocket-money, admitted frankly that the sum of eight-and-sixpence per day, which he was now earning by the sweat of his brow and the expenditure of shoe-leather, was sweeter to him than honey in the honeycomb. Hattrick, who had recently put up a plate in Harley Street, said it was good to be earning a living wage at last. Mr. Waddell, pressed to say a few words of encouragement of the present campaign, delivered himself of a guarded but illuminating eulogy of war as a cure for indecision of mind; from which, coupled with a coy reference to "some one" in distant St. Andrews, the company were enabled to gather that Mr. Waddell had carried a position with his new sword which had proved impregnable to civilian assault.

Only Bobby Little was silent. In all this genial symposium there had been no word of the spur which was inciting him—and doubtless the others—along the present weary and monotonous path; and on the whole he was glad that it should be so. None of us care to talk, even privately, about the Dream of Honour and the Hope of Glory. The only difference between Bobby and the others was that while they could cover up their aspirations with a jest, Bobby must say all that was in his heart, or keep silent. So he held his peace.

A tall figure loomed against the starlit sky, and Captain Wagstaffe, who had been out in the trench, spoke quickly to Major Kemp:—

"I thing we had better get to our places, sir. Some criminal has cut my alarm-cord!"

****

Five minutes previously, Private Bain, lulled to a sense of false security by the stillness of the night, had opened his eyes, which had been closed for purposes of philosophic reflection, to find himself surrounded by four ghostly figures in greatcoats. With creditable presence of mind he jerked his alarm-cord. But, alas! the cord came with his hand.

He was now a prisoner, and his place in the scout-line was being used as a point of deployment for the attacking force.

"We're extended right along the line now," said Captain Mackintosh to Simson. "I can't wait any longer for Shand: he has probably lost himself. The sentries are all behind us. Pass the word along to crawl forward. Every man to keep as low as he can, and dress by the right. No one to charge unless he hears my whistle, or is fired on."

The whispered word—Captain Mackintosh knows when to whisper quite as well as Captain Shand—runs down the line, and presently we begin to creep forward, stooping low. Sometimes we halt; sometimes we swing back a little; but on the whole we progress. Once there is a sudden exclamation. A highly-strung youth, crouching in a field drain, has laid his hand upon what looks and feels like a clammy human face, lying recumbent and staring heavenward. Too late, he recognises a derelict scarecrow with a turnip head. Again, there is a pause while the extreme right of the line negotiates an unexpected barbed-wire fence. Still, we move on, with enormous caution. We are not certain where the trenches are, but they must be near. At any moment a crackling volley may leap out upon us. Pulses begin to beat.

In the trench itself eyes are strained and ears cocked. It is an eerie sensation to know that men are near you, and creeping nearer, yet remain inaudible and invisible. It is a very dark night. The moon appears to have gone to bed for good, and the stars are mostly covered. Men unconsciously endeavour to fan the darkness away with their hands, like mist. The broken ground in front, with the black woods beyond, might be concealing an army corps for all the watchers in the trenches can tell. Far away to the south a bright finger of light occasionally stabs the murky heavens. It is the searchlight of a British cruiser, keeping ceaseless vigil in the English Channel, fifteen miles away. If she were not there we should not be making-believe here with such comfortable deliberation. It would be the real thing.

Bobby Little, who by this time can almost discern spiked German helmets in the gloom, stands tingling. On either side of him are ranged the men of his platoon—some eager, some sleepy, but all silent. For the first time he notices that in the distant woods ahead of him there is a small break—a mere gap—through which one or two stars are twinkling. If only he could contrive to get a line of sight direct to that patch of sky—

He moves a few yards along the trench, and brings his eye to the ground-level. No good: a bush intervenes, fifteen yards away. He moves further and tries again.

Suddenly, for a brief moment, against the dimly illuminated scrap of horizon, he descries a human form, clad in a kilt, advancing stealthily. . . .

"*Number one Platoon—at the enemy in front—rapid fire!*"

He is just in time. There comes an overwrought roar of musketry all down the line of trenches. Simultaneously, a solid wall of men rises out of the earth not fifty yards away, and makes for the trenches with a long-drawn battle yell.

Make-believe has its thrills as well as the genuine article.

And so home to bed. M'Snape duly became a lance-corporal, while Dunshie resigned his post as a scout and returned to duty with the company.

Chapter 11
Olympus

Under this designation it is convenient to lump the whole heavenly host which at present orders our goings and shapes our ends. It includes—

(1) The War Office

(2) The Treasury

(3) The Army Ordnance Office

(4) Our Divisional Office

—and other more local and immediate homes of mystery.

The Olympus which controls the destinies of "K(1)" differs in many respects from the Olympus of antiquity, but its celestial inhabitants appear to have at least two points in common with the original body—namely, a childish delight in upsetting one another's arrangements, and an untimely sense of humour when dealing with mortals.

So far as our researches have gone, we have been able to classify Olympus, roughly, into three departments—

(1) Round Game Department (including Dockets, Indents, and all official correspondence).

(2) Fairy Godmother Department.

(3) Practical Joke Department.

The outstanding feature of the Round Game Department is its craving for irrelevant information and its passion for detail. "Open your hearts to us," say the officials of the Department; "unburden your souls; keep nothing from us—and you will find us most accommodating. But stand on your dignity; decline to particularise; hold back one irrelevant detail—and it will go hard with you! Listen, and we will explain the rules of the game. Think of something you want immediately—say the command of a brigade, or a couple of washers for the lock of a machine-gun—and apply to us. The application must be made in writing, upon the Army Form provided for the purpose, and in triplicate. *And*—you must put in all the details you can possibly think of."

For instance, in the case of the machine-gun washers—by the way, in applying for them, you must call them *Gun, Machine, Light Vickers, Washers for lock of, two.* That is the way we always talk at the Ordnance Office. An Ordnance officer refers to his wife's mother as *Law, Mother-in-, one*—you should state when the old washers were lost, and by whom; also why they were lost, and where they are now. Then write a short history of the machine-gun from which they were lost, giving date and place of birth, together with, a statement of the exact number of rounds which it has fired—a machine-gun fires about five hundred rounds a minute—adding the name and military record of the pack-animal which usually carries it. When you have filled up this document you forward it to the proper quarter and await results.

The game then proceeds on simple and automatic lines. If your application is referred back to you not more than five times, and if you get your washers within three months of the date of application, you are the winner. If you get something else instead—say an aeroplane, or a hundred wash-hand basins—it is a draw. But the chances are that you lose.

Consider. By the rules of the game, if Olympus can think of a single detail which has not been thought of by you—for instance, if you omit to mention that the lost washers were circular in shape and had holes through the middle—you are *ipso facto* disqualified, under Rule One. Rule Two, also, is liable to trip you up. Possibly you may have written the pack-mule's name in small block capitals, instead of ordinary italics underlined in red ink, or put the date in Roman figures instead of Arabic numerals. If you do this, your application is referred back to you, and you lose a life. And even if you survive Rules One and Two, Rule Three will probably get you in the end. Under its provision your application must be framed in such language and addressed in such a manner that it passes through every department and sub-department of Olympus before it reaches the right one. The rule has its origin in the principle which governs the passing of wine at well-regulated British dinner-tables. That is, if you wish to offer a glass of port to your neighbour on your right, you hand the decanter to the neighbour on your left, so that the original object of your hospitality receives it, probably empty, only after a complete circuit of the table. In the present instance, the gentleman upon your right is the President of the Washer Department, situated somewhere in the Army Ordnance Office, the remaining guests representing the other centres of Olympian activity. For every department your application misses, you lose a life, three lost lives amounting to disqualification.

When the washers are issued, however, the port-wine rule is abandoned; and the washers are despatched to you, in defiance of all the laws of superstition and tradition, "widdershins," or counter-clockwise. No wonder articles thus jeopardised often fail to reach their destination!

Your last fence comes when you receive a document from Olympus announcing that your washers are now prepared for you, and that if you will sign and return the enclosed receipt they will be sent off upon their last journey. You are now in the worst dilemma of all. Olympus will not disgorge your washers until it has your receipt. On the other hand, if you send the receipt, Olympus can always win the game by losing the washers, and saying that *you* have got them. In the face of your own receipt you cannot very well deny this. So you lose your washers, and the game, and are also made liable for the misappropriation of two washers, for which Olympus holds your receipt.

Truly, the gods play with loaded dice.

On the whole, the simplest (and almost universal) plan is to convey a couple of washers from some one else's gun.

The game just described is played chiefly by officers; but this is a democratic age, and the rank and file are now occasionally permitted to take part.

For example, boots. Private M'Splae is the possessor, we will say, of a pair of flat feet, or arched insteps, or other military incommodities, and his regulation boots do not fit him. More than that, they hurt him exceedingly, and as he is compelled to wear them through daily marches of several miles, they gradually wear a hole in his heel, or a groove in his instep, or a gathering on his great toe. So he makes the first move in the game, and reports sick—"sair feet."

The Medical Officer, a terribly efficient individual, keenly—sometimes too keenly—alert for signs of malingering, takes a cursory glance at M'Splae's feet, and directs the patient's attention to the healing properties of soap and water. M'Splae departs, grumbling, and reappears on sick parade a few days later, palpably worse. This time, the M.O. being a little less pressed with work, M'Splae is given a dressing for his feet, coupled with a recommendation to procure a new pair of boots without delay. If M'Splae is a novice in regimental diplomacy, he will thereupon address himself to his platoon sergeant, who will consign him, eloquently, to a destination where only boots with asbestos soles will be of any use. If he is an old hand, he will simply cut his next parade, and will thus, rather ingeniously, obtain access to his company commander, being brought up before him at orderly-room next morning as a defaulter. To his captain he explains, with simple dignity, that he absented himself from parade because he found himself unable to "rise up" from his bed. He then endeavours, by hurriedly unlacing his boots, to produce his feet as evidence; but is frustrated, and awarded three extra fatigues for not formally reporting himself sick to the orderly sergeant. The real point of issue, namely, the unsuitability of M'Splae's boots, again escapes attention.

There the matter rests until, a few days later, M'Splae falls out on a long regimental route-march, and hobbles home, chaperoned by a not ungrateful lance-corporal, in a state of semi-collapse. This time the M.O. reports to the captain that Private M'Splae will be unfit for further duty until he is provided with a proper pair of boots. Are there no boots in the quartermaster's store?

The captain explains that there are plenty of boots, but that under the rules of the present round game no one has any power to issue them. (This rule was put in to prevent the game from becoming too easy, like the spot-barred rule in billiards.) It is a fact well known to Olympus that no regimental officer can be trusted with boots. Not even the colonel can gain access to the regimental boot store. For all Olympus can tell, he might draw a pair of boots and wear them himself, or dress his children up in them, or bribe the brigadier with them, instead of issuing them to Private M'Splae. No, Olympus thinks it wiser not to put temptation in the way of underpaid officers. So the boots remain locked up, and the taxpayer is protected.

But to be just, there is always a solution to an Olympian enigma, if you have the patience to go on looking for it. In this case the proper proceeding is for all concerned, including the prostrate M'Splae, to wait patiently for a Board to sit. No date is assigned for this event, but it is bound to occur sooner or later, like a railway accident or an eclipse of the moon. So one day, out of a cloudless sky, a Board materialises, and sits on M'Splae's boots. If M'Splae's company commander happens to be president of the Board the boots are condemned, and the portals of the quarter-master's store swing open for a brief moment to emit a new pair.

When M'Splae comes out of hospital, the boots, provided no one has appropriated them during the term, of his indisposition, are his. He puts them on, to find that they pinch him in the same place as the old pair.

* * * * * * * *

Then there is the Fairy Godmother Department, which supplies us with unexpected treats. It is the smallest department on Olympus, and, like most philanthropic institutions, is rather unaccountable in the manner in which it distributes its favours. It is somewhat hampered in its efforts, too, by the Practical Joke Department, which appears to exercise a sort of general right of interference all over Olympus. For instance, the Fairy Godmother Department decrees that officers from Indian regiments, who were home on leave when the War broke out and were commandeered for service with the Expeditionary Force, shall continue to draw pay on the Indian scale, which is considerably higher than that which prevails at home. So far, so good. But the Practical Joke Department hears of this, and scents an opportunity, in the form of "deductions." It promptly bleeds the *beneficiaire* of certain sums per day, for quarters, horse allowance, forage, and the like. It is credibly reported that one of these warriors, on emerging from a week's purgatory in a Belgian trench, found that his accommodation therein had been charged against him, under the head of "lodgings," at the rate of two shillings and threepence a night!

But sometimes the Fairy Godmother Department gets a free hand. Like a benevolent maiden aunt, she unexpectedly drops a twenty-pound note into your account at Cox's Bank, murmuring something vague about "additional outfit allowance"; and as Mr. Cox makes a point of backing her up in her little secret, you receive a delightful surprise next time you open your pass-book.

She has the family instinct for detail, too, this Fairy Godmother. Perhaps the electric light in your bedroom fails, and for three days you have to sit in the dark or purchase candles. An invisible but observant little cherub notes this fact; and long afterwards a postal order for tenpence flutters down upon you from Olympus, marked "light allowance." Once Bobby Little received a mysterious postal order for one-and-fivepence. It was in the early days of his novitiate, before he had ceased to question the workings of Providence. So he made inquiries, and after prolonged investigation discovered the source of the windfall. On field service an officer is entitled to a certain sum per day as "field allowance." In barracks, however, possessing a bedroom and other indoor comforts, he receives no such gratuity. Now Bobby had once been compelled to share his room for a few nights with a newly-joined and homeless subaltern. He was thus temporarily rendered the owner of only half a bedroom. Or, to put it another way, only half of him was able to sleep in barracks. Obviously, then, the other half was on field service, and Bobby was therefore entitled to half field allowance. Hence the one-and-fivepence. I tell you, little escapes them on Olympus. So does much, but that is another story.

* * * * * * * *

Last of all comes the Practical Joke Department. It covers practically all of one side of Olympus—the shady side.

The jokes usually take the form of an order, followed by a counter-order. For example—

In his magisterial days Ayling, of whom we have previously heard, was detailed by his Headmaster to undertake the organisation of a school corps to serve as a unit of the Officers' Training Corps—then one of the spoilt bantlings of the War Office. Being a vigorous and efficient young man, Ayling devoted four weeks of his summer holiday to a course of training with a battalion of regulars at Aldershot. During that period, as the prospective commander of a company, he was granted the pay and provisional rank of captain, which all will admit was handsome enough treatment. Three months later, when after superhuman struggles he had pounded his youthful legionaries into something like efficiency, his appointment to a commission was duly confirmed, and he found himself gazetted—Second Lieutenant. In addition to this, he was required to refund to the Practical Joke Department the difference between second lieutenant's pay and the captain's pay which he had received during his month's training at Aldershot!

But in these strenuous days the Department has no time for baiting individuals. It has two or three millions of men to sharpen its wit upon. Its favourite pastime at present is a sort of giant's game of chess, the fair face of England serving as board, and the various units of the K. armies as pieces. The object of the players is to get each piece through as many squares as possible in a given time, it being clearly understood that no move shall count unless another piece is evicted in the process. For instance, we, the *x*th Brigade of the *y*th Division, are suddenly uprooted from billets at A and planted down in barracks at B, displacing the *p*th Brigade of the *q*th Division in the operation. We have barely cleaned tip after the *p*th—an Augean task—and officers have just concluded messing, furnishing, and laundry arrangements with the local *banditti*, when the Practical Joke Department, with its tongue in its cheek, bids us prepare to go under canvas at C. Married officers hurriedly despatch advance parties, composed of their wives, to secure houses or lodgings in the bleak and inhospitable environs of their new station; while a rapidly ageing Mess President concludes yet another demoralising bargain with a ruthless and omnipotent caterer. Then—this is the cream of the joke—the day before we expect to move, the Practical Joke Department puts out a playful hand and sweeps us all into some half-completed huts at D, somewhere at the other end of the Ordnance map, and leaves us there, with a happy chuckle, to sink or swim in an Atlantic of mud.

So far as one is able to follow the scoring of the game, some of the squares in the chessboard are of higher value than others. For instance, if you are dumped down into comparatively modern barracks at Aldershot, which, although they contain no furniture, are at least weatherproof and within reach of shops, the Practical Joke Department scores one point. Barracks condemned as unsafe and unsanitary before the war, but now reckoned highly eligible, count three points; rat-ridden billets count five. But if you can manoeuvre your helpless pawns into Mudsplosh Camp, you receive ten whole points, with a bonus of two points thrown in if you can effect the move without previous notice of any kind.

We are in Mudsplosh Camp to-day. In transferring us here the Department secured full points, including bonus.

Let it not be supposed, however, that we are decrying our present quarters. Mudsplosh Camp is—or is going to be—a nobly planned and admirably equipped military centre. At present it consists of some three hundred wooden huts, in all stages of construction, covering about twenty acres of high moorland. The huts are heated with stoves, and will be delightfully warm when we get some coal. They are lit by—or rather wired for—electric light. Meanwhile a candle-end does well enough for a room only a hundred feet long. There are numerous other adjuncts to our comfort—wash-houses, for instance. These will be invaluable, when the water is laid on. For the present, there is a capital standpipe not a hundred yards away; and all you have to do, if you want an invigorating scrub, is to wait your turn for one of the two tin basins supplied to each fifty men, and then splash to your heart's content. There is a spacious dining-hall; and as soon as the roof is on, our successors, or their successors, will make merry therein. Meanwhile, there are worse places to eat one's dinner than the floor—the mud outside, for instance.

The stables are lofty and well ventilated. At least, we are sure they will be. Pending their completion the horses and mules are very comfortable, picketed on the edge of the moor.... After all, there are only sixty of them; and most of them have rugs; and it can't possibly go on snowing for ever.

The only other architectural feature of the camp is the steriliser, which has been working night and day ever since we arrived. No, it does not sterilise water or milk, or anything of that kind—only blankets. Those men standing in a *queue* at its door are carrying their bedding. (Yes, quite so. When blankets are passed from regiment to regiment for months on end, in a camp where opportunities for ablution are not lavish, these little things will happen.)

You put the blankets in at one end of the steriliser, turn the necessary handles, and wait. In due course the blankets emerge, steamed, dried, and thoroughly purged. At least, that is the idea. But listen to Privates Ogg and Hogg, in one of their celebrated cross-talk duologues.

Ogg (examining his blanket). "They're a' there yet. See!"

Hogg (an optimist). "Aye; but they must have gotten an awfu' fricht!"

But then people like Ogg are never satisfied with anything.

However, *the* feature of this camp is the mud. That is why it counts ten points. There was no mud, of course, before the camp was constructed—only dry turf, and wild yellow gorse, and fragrant heather. But the Practical Joke Department were not to be discouraged by the superficial beauties of nature. They knew that if you crowd a large number of human dwellings close together, and refrain from constructing any roads or drains as a preliminary, and fill these buildings with troops in the rainy season, you will soon have as much mud as ever you require. And they were quite right. The depth varies from a few inches to about a foot. On the outskirts of the camp, however, especially by the horse lines or going through a gate, you may find yourself up to your knees. But, after all, what is mud! Most of the officers have gum-boots, and the men will probably get used to it. Life in K(1) is largely composed of getting used to things.

In the more exclusive and fashionable districts—round about the Orderly-room, and the Canteen, and the Guard-room—elevated "duck-walks" are laid down, along which we delicately pick our way. It would warm the heart of a democrat to observe the ready—nay, hasty—courtesy with which an officer, on meeting a private carrying two overflowing buckets of kitchen refuse, steps down into the mud to let his humble brother-in-arms pass. Where there are no duck-walks, we employ planks laid across the mud. In comparatively dry weather these planks lie some two or three inches below the mud, and much innocent amusement may be derived from trying to locate them. In wet weather, however, the planks float to the surface, and then of course everything is plain sailing. When it snows, we feel for the planks with our feet. If we find them we perform an involuntary and unpremeditated skiing act: if we fail, we wade to our quarters through a sort of Neapolitan ice—snow on the top, mud underneath.

Our parade-ground is a mud-flat in front of the huts. Here we take our stand each morning, sinking steadily deeper until the order is given to move off. Then the battalion extricates itself with one tremendous squelch, and we proceed to the labours of the day.

Seriously, though—supposing the commanding officer were to be delayed one morning at orderly-room, and were to ride on to the parade-ground twenty minutes late, what would he find? Nothing! Nothing but a great *parterre* of glengarries, perched upon the mud in long parallel rows, each glengarry flanked on the left-hand side by the muzzle of a rifle at the slope. (That detached patch over there on the left front, surrounded by air-bubbles, is the band. That cavity like the crater of an extinct volcano, in Number one Platoon of A Company, was once Private Mucklewame.)

And yet people talk about the sinking of the *Birkenhead*!

****

This morning some one in the Department has scored another ten points. Word has just been received that we are to move again to-morrow—to a precisely similar set of huts about a hundred yards away!

They are mad wags on Olympus.

Chapter 12
And Some Fell by the Wayside

"*Firing parrty, revairse arrms!*"

Thus the platoon sergeant—a little anxiously; for we are new to this feat, and only rehearsed it for a few minutes this morning.

It is a sunny afternoon in late February. The winter of our discontent is past. (At least, we hope so.) Comfortless months of training are safely behind us, and lo! we have grown from a fortuitous concourse of atoms to a cohesive unit of fighting men. Spring is coming; spring is coming; our blood runs quicker; active service is within measurable distance; and the future beckons to us with both hands to step down at last into the arena, and try our fortune amid the uncertain but illimitable chances of the greatest game in the World.

To all of us, that is, save one.

The road running up the hill from the little mortuary is lined on either side by members of our company, specklessly turned out and standing to attention. At the foot of the slope a gun-carriage is waiting, drawn by two great dray horses and controlled by a private of the Royal Artillery, who looks incongruously perky and cockney amid that silent, kilted assemblage. The firing party form a short lane from the gun-carriage to the door of the mortuary. In response to the sergeant's command, each man turns over his rifle, and setting the muzzle carefully upon his right boot—after all, it argues no extra respect to the dead to get your barrel filled with mud—rests his hands upon the butt-plate and bows his head, as laid down in the King's Regulations.

The bearers move slowly down the path from the mortuary, and place the coffin upon the gun-carriage. Upon the lid lie a very dingy glengarry, a stained leather belt, and a bayonet. They are humble trophies, but we pay them as much reverence as we would to the *baton* and cocked hat of a field-marshal, for they are the insignia of a man who has given his life for his country.

On the hill-top above us, where the great military hospital rears its clock-tower foursquare to the sky, a line of convalescents, in natty blue uniforms with white facings and red ties, lean over the railings deeply interested. Some of them are bandaged, others are in slings, and all are more or less maimed. They follow the obsequies below with critical approval. They have been present at enough hurried and promiscuous interments of late—more than one of them has only just escaped being the central figure at one of these functions—that they are capable of appreciating a properly conducted funeral at its true value.

"They're putting away a bloomin' Jock," remarks a gentleman with an empty sleeve.

"And very nice, too!" responds another on crutches, as the firing party present arms with creditable precision. "Not 'arf a bad bit of eyewash at all for a bandy-legged lot of coal-shovellers."

"That lot's out of K(1)," explains a well-informed invalid with his head in bandages. "Pretty 'ot stuff they're gettin'. *Tres moutarde*! Now we're off."

The signal is passed up the road to the band, who are waiting at the head of the procession, and the pipes break into a lament. Corporals step forward and lay four wreaths upon the coffin—one from each company. Not a man in the battalion has failed to contribute his penny to those wreaths; and pennies are not too common with us, especially on a Thursday, which comes just before payday. The British private is commonly reputed to spend all, or most of, his pocket-money upon beer. But I can tell you this, that if you give him his choice between buying himself a pint of beer and subscribing to a wreath, he will most decidedly go thirsty.

The serio-comic charioteer gives his reins a twitch, the horses wake up, and the gun-carriage begins to move slowly along the lane of mourners. As the dead private passes on his way the walls of the lane melt, and his comrades fall into their usual fours behind the gun-carriage.

So we pass up the hill towards the military cemetery, with the pipes wailing their hearts out, and the muffled drums marking the time of our regulation slow step. Each foot seems to hang in the air before the drums bid us put it down.

In the very rear of the procession you may see the company commander and three subalterns. They give no orders, and exact no attention. To employ a colloquialism, this is not their funeral.

Just behind the gun-carriage stalks a solitary figure in civilian clothes—the unmistakable "blacks" of an Elder of the Kirk. At first sight, you have a feeling that some one has strayed into the procession who has no right there. But no one has a better. The sturdy old man behind the coffin is named Adam Carmichael, and he is here, having travelled south from Dumbarton by the night train, to attend the funeral of his only son.

Peter Carmichael was one of the first to enlist in the regiment. There was another Carmichael in the same company, so Peter at roll-call was usually addressed by the sergeant as "Twenty-seven fufty-fower Carmichael," 2754 being his regimental number. The army does not encourage Christian names. When his attestation paper was filled up, he gave his age as nineteen; his address, vaguely, as Renfrewshire; and his trade, not without an air, as a "holder-on." To the mystified Bobby Little he entered upon a lengthy explanation of the term in a language composed almost entirely of vowels, from which that officer gathered, dimly, that holding-on had something to do with shipbuilding.

Upon the barrack square his platoon commander's attention was again drawn to Peter, owing to the passionate enthusiasm with which he performed the simplest evolutions, such as forming fours and sloping arms—military exercises which do not intrigue the average private to any great extent. Unfortunately, desire frequently outran performance. Peter was undersized, unmuscular, and extraordinarily clumsy. For a long time Bobby Little thought that Peter, like one or two of his comrades, was left-handed, so made allowances. Ultimately he discovered that his indulgence was misplaced: Peter was equally incompetent with either hand. He took longer in learning to fix bayonets or present arms than any other man in the platoon. To be fair, Nature had done little to help him. He was thirty-three inches round the chest, five feet four in height, and weighed possibly nine stone. His complexion was pasty, and, as Captain Wagstaffe remarked, you could hang your hat on any bone in his body. His eyesight was not all that the Regulations require, and on the musketry-range he was "put back," to his deep distress, "for further instruction." Altogether, if you had not known the doctor who passed him, you would have said it was a mystery how he passed the doctor.

But he possessed the one essential attribute of the soldier. He had a big heart. He was keen. He allowed nothing to come between him and his beloved duties. ("He was aye daft for to go sogerin'," his father explained to Captain Blaikie; "but his mother would never let him away. He was ower wee, and ower young.") His rifle, buttons, and boots were always without blemish. Further, he was of the opinion that a merry heart goes all the way. He never sulked when the platoon were kept on parade five minutes after the breakfast bugle had sounded. He made no bones about obeying orders and saluting officers—acts of abasement which grated sorely at times upon his colleagues, who reverenced no one except themselves and their Union. He appeared to revel in muddy route-marches, and invariably provoked and led the choruses. The men called him "Wee Pe'er," and ultimately adopted him as a sort of company mascot. Whereat Pe'er's heart glowed; for when your associates attach a diminutive to your Christian name, you possess something which millionaires would gladly give half their fortune to purchase.

And certainly he required all the social success he could win, for professionally Peter found life a rigorous affair. Sometimes, as he staggered into barracks after a long day, carrying a rifle made of lead and wearing a pair of boots weighing a hundredweight apiece, he dropped dead asleep on his bedding before he could eat his dinner. But he always hotly denied the imputation that he was "sick."

Time passed. The regiment was shaking down. Seven of Peter's particular cronies were raised to the rank of lance-corporal—but not Peter. He was "off the square" now—that is to say, he was done with recruit drill for ever. He possessed a sound knowledge of advance-guard and outpost work; his conduct-sheet was a blank page. But he was not promoted. He was "ower wee for a stripe," he told himself. For the present he must expect to be passed over. His chance would come later, when he had filled out a little and got rid of his cough.

The winter dragged on: the weather was appalling: the grousers gave tongue with no uncertain voice, each streaming field-day. But Wee Pe'er enjoyed it all. He did not care if it snowed ink. He was a "sojer."

One day, to his great delight, he was "warned for guard"—a particularly unpopular branch of a soldier's duties, for it means sitting in the guard-room for twenty-four hours at a stretch, fully dressed and accoutred, with intervals of sentry-go, usually in heavy rain, by way of exercise. When Peter's turn for sentry-go came on he splashed up and down his muddy beat—the battalion was in billets now, and the usual sentry's veranda was lacking—as proud as a peacock, saluting officers according to their rank, challenging stray civilians with great severity, and turning out the guard on the slightest provocation. He was at his post, soaked right through his greatcoat, when the orderly officer made his night round. Peter summoned his colleagues; the usual inspection of the guard took place; and the sleepy men were then dismissed to their fireside. Peter remained; the officer hesitated. He was supposed to examine the sentry in his knowledge of his duties. It was a profitless task as a rule. The tongue-tied youth merely gaped like a stranded fish, until the sergeant mercifully intervened, in some such words as these—

"This man, sirr, is liable to get over-excited when addressed by an officer."

Then, soothingly—

"Now, Jimmy, tell the officer what would ye dae in case of fire?"

"Present airrms!" announces the desperate James. Or else, almost tearfully, "I canna mind. I had it all fine just noo, but it's awa' oot o' ma heid!"

Therefore it was with no great sense of anticipation that the orderly officer said to Private Carmichael—

"Now, sentry, can you repeat any of your duties?"

Peter saluted, took a full breath, closed both eyes, and replied rapidly,—

"For tae tak' chairge of all Government property within sicht of this guairdhoose tae turrn out the guaird for all arrmed pairties approaching also the commanding officer once a day tae salute all officers tae challenge all pairsons approaching this post tae—"

His recital was interrupted by a fit of coughing.

"Thank you," said the officer hastily; "that will do. Good night!"

Peter, not sure whether it would be correct to say "good night" too, saluted again, and returned to his cough.

"I say," said the officer, turning back, "you have a shocking cold."

"Och, never heed it, sirr," gasped Peter politely.

"Call the sergeant," said the officer.

The fat sergeant came out of the guardhouse again, buttoning his tunic.

"Sirr?"

"Take this man off sentry-duty and roast him at the guard-room fire."

"I will, sirr," replied the sergeant; and added paternally, "this man has no right for to be here at all. He should have reported sick when warned for guard; but he would not. He is very attentive to his duties, sirr."

"Good boy!" said the officer to Peter. "I wish we had more like you."

Wee Pe'er blushed, his teeth momentarily ceased chattering, his heart swelled. Appearances to the contrary, he felt warm all through. The sergeant laid a fatherly hand upon his shoulder.

"Go you your ways intil the guard-room, boy," he commanded, "and send oot Dunshie. He'll no hurt. Get close in ahint the stove, or you'll be for Cambridge!"

(The last phrase carries no academic significance. It simply means that you are likely to become an inmate of the great Cambridge Hospital at Aldershot.)

Peter, feeling thoroughly disgraced, cast an appealing look at the officer.

"In you go!" said that martinet.

Peter silently obeyed. It was the only time in his life that he ever felt mutinous.

A month later Brigade Training set in with customary severity. The life of company officers became a burden. They spent hours in thick woods with their followers, taking cover, ostensibly from the enemy, in reality from brigade-majors and staff officers. A subaltern never tied his platoon in a knot but a general came trotting round the corner. The wet weather had ceased, and a biting east wind reigned in its stead.

On one occasion an elaborate night operation was arranged. Four battalions were to assemble at a given point five miles from camp, and then advance in column across country by the light of the stars to a position indicated on the map, where they were to deploy and dig themselves in! It sounded simple enough in operation orders; but when you try to move four thousand troops—even well-trained troops—across three miles of broken country on a pitch-dark night, there is always a possibility that some one will get mislaid. On this particular occasion a whole battalion lost itself without any delay or difficulty whatsoever. The other three were compelled to wait for two hours and a half, stamping their feet and blowing on their fingers, while overheated staff officers scoured the country for the truants. They were discovered at last waiting virtuously at the wrong rendezvous, three-quarters of a mile away. The brazen-hatted strategist who drew up the operation orders had given the point of assembly for the brigade as: ... *the field* S.W. *of* WELLINGTON WOOD *and due* E. *of* HANGMAN'S COPSE, *immediately below the first* O *in* GHOSTLY BOTTOM,—but omitted to underline the O indicated. The result was that three battalion commanders assembled at the O in "ghostly," while the fourth, ignoring the adjective in favour of the noun, took up his station at the first O in "bottom."

The operations had been somewhat optimistically timed to end at 11 p.m., but by the time that the four battalions had effected a most unloverly tryst, it was close on ten, and beginning to rain. The consequence was that the men got home to bed, soaked to the skin, and asking the Powers Above rhetorical questions, at three o'clock in the morning.

Next day Brigade Orders announced that the movement would be continued at nightfall, by the occupation of the hastily-dug trenches, followed by a night attack upon the hill in front. The captured position would then be retrenched.

When the tidings went round, fourteen of the more quick-witted spirits of "A" Company hurriedly paraded before the Medical Officer and announced that they were "sick in the stomach." Seven more discovered abrasions upon their feet, and proffered their sores for inspection, after the manner of Oriental mendicants. One skrimshanker, despairing of producing any bodily ailment, rather ingeniously assaulted a comrade-in-arms, and was led away, deeply grateful, to the guard-room. Wee Peter, who in the course of last night's operations had stumbled into an old trench half-filled with ice-cold water, and whose temperature to-day, had he known it, was a hundred and two, paraded with his company at the appointed time. The company, he reflected, would get a bad name if too many men reported sick at once.

Next day he was absent from parade. He was "for Cambridge" at last.

Before he died, he sent for the officer who had befriended him, and supplemented, or rather corrected, some of the information contained in his attestation paper.

He lived in Dumbarton, not Renfrewshire. He was just sixteen. He was not—this confession cost him a great effort—a full-blown "holder-on" at all; only an apprentice. His father was "weel kent" in the town of Dumbarton, being a chief engineer, employed by a great firm of shipbuilders to extend new machinery on trial trips.

Needless to say, he made a great fight. But though his heart was big enough, his body was too frail. As they say on the sea, he was over-engined for his beam.

And so, three days later, the simple soul of Twenty-seven fifty-four Carmichael, "A" Company, was transferred, on promotion, to another company—the great Company of Happy Warriors who walk the Elysian Fields.

"*Firing parrty, one round blank—load!*"

There is a rattle of bolts, and a dozen barrels are pointed heavenwards. The company stands rigid, except the buglers, who are beginning to finger their instruments.

"*Fire!*"

There is a crackling volley, and the pipes break into a brief, sobbing wail. Wayfarers upon the road below look up curiously. One or two young females with perambulators come hurrying across the grass, exhorting apathetic babies to sit up and admire the pretty funeral.

Twice more the rifles ring out. The pipes cease their wailing, and there is an expectant silence.

The drum-major crooks his little finger, and eight bugles come to the "ready." Then "Last Post," the requiem of every soldier of the King, swells out, sweet and true.

The echoes lose themselves among the dripping pines. The chaplain closes his book, takes off his spectacles, and departs.

Old Carmichael permits himself one brief look into his son's grave, resumes his crape-bound tall hat, and turns heavily away. He finds Captain Blaikie's hand waiting for him. He grips it, and says—

"Weel, the laddie has had a grand sojer's funeral. His mother will be pleased to hear that."

He passes on, and shakes hands with the platoon sergeant and one or two of Peter's cronies. He declines an invitation to the Sergeants' Mess.

"I hae a trial-trup the morn," he explains. "I must be steppin'. God keep ye all, brave lads!"

The old gentleman sets off down the station road. The company falls in, and we march back to barracks, leaving Wee Pe'er—the first name on our Roll of Honour—alone in his glory beneath, the Hampshire pines.

CHAPTER 13
Concert Pitch

We have only two topics of conversation now—the date of our departure, and our destination. Both are wrapped in mystery so profound that our range of speculation is practically unlimited.

Conjecture rages most fiercely in the Officers' Mess, which is in touch with sources of unreliable information not accessible to the rank and file. The humblest subaltern appears to be possessed of a friend at court, or a cousin in the Foreign Office, or an aunt in the Intelligence Department, from whom he can derive fresh and entirely different information each week-end leave.

Master Cockerell, for instance, has it straight from the Horse Guards that we are going out next week—as a single unit, to be brigaded with two seasoned regiments in Flanders. He has a considerable following.

Then comes Waddell, who has been informed by the Assistant sub-Editor of an evening journal widely read in his native Dundee, that The First Hundred Thousand are to sit here, eating the bread of impatience, until The First Half Million are ready. Thereupon we shall break through our foeman's line at a point hitherto unassailed and known only to the scribe of Dundee, and proceed to roll up the German Empire as if it were a carpet, into some obscure corner of the continent of Europe.

Bobby Little, not the least of whose gifts is a soaring imagination, has mapped out a sort of strategical Cook's Tour for us, beginning with the sack of Constantinople, and ending, after a glorified route-march up the Danube and down the Rhine, which shall include a pitched battle once a week and a successful siege once a month, with a "circus" entry into Potsdam.

Captain Wagstaffe offers no opinion, but darkly recommends us to order pith helmets. However, we are rather suspicious of Captain Wagstaffe these days. He suffers from an over-developed sense of humour.

The rank and file keep closer to earth in their prognostications. In fact, some of them cleave to the dust. With them it is a case of hope deferred. Quite half of them enlisted under the firm belief that they would forthwith be furnished with a rifle and ammunition and despatched to a vague place called "the front," there to take pot-shots at the Kaiser. That was in early August. It is now early April, and they are still here, performing monotonous evolutions and chafing under the bonds of discipline. Small wonder that they have begun to doubt, these simple souls, if they are ever going out at all. Private M'Slattery put the general opinion in a nutshell.

"This regiment," he announced, "is no' for the front at all. We're jist tae bide here, for tae be inspeckit by Chinese Ministers and other heathen bodies!"

This withering summary of the situation was evoked by the fact that we had once been called out, and kept on parade for two hours in a north-east wind, for the edification of a bevy of spectacled dignitaries from the Far East. For the Scottish, artisan the word "minister," however, has only one significance; so it is probable that M'Slattery's strictures were occasioned by sectarian, rather than racial, prejudice.

Still, whatever our ultimate destination and fate may be, the fact remains that we are now as fit for active service as seven months' relentless schooling, under make-believe conditions, can render us. We shall have to begin all over again, we know, when we find ourselves up against the real thing, but we have at least been thoroughly grounded in the rudiments of our profession. We can endure hail, rain, snow, and vapour; we can march and dig with the best; we have mastered the first principles of musketry; we can advance in an extended line without losing touch or bunching; and we have ceased to regard an order as an insult, or obedience as a degradation. We eat when we can and what we get, and we sleep wherever we happen to find ourselves lying. That is something. But there are certain military accomplishments which can only be taught us by the enemy. Taking cover, for instance. When the thin, intermittent crackle of blank ammunition shall have been replaced by the whistle of real bullets, we shall get over our predilection for sitting up and taking notice. The conversation of our neighbour, or the deplorable antics of B Company on the neighbouring skyline, will interest us not at all. We shall get down, and stay down.

We shall also be relieved of the necessity of respecting the property of those exalted persons who surround their estates with barbed wire, and put up notices, even now, warning off troops. At present we either crawl painfully through that wire, tearing our kilts and lacerating our legs, or go round another way. "Oot there," such unwholesome deference will be a thing of the past. Would that the wire-setters were going out with us. We would give them the place of honour in the forefront of battle!

We have fired a second musketry course, and are now undergoing Divisional Training, with the result that we take our walks abroad several thousand strong, greatly to the derangement of local traffic.

Considered all round, Divisional Training is the pleasantest form of soldiering that we have yet encountered. We parade bright and early, at full battalion strength, accompanied by our scouts, signallers, machine-guns, and transport, and march off at the appointed minute to the starting-point. Here we slip into our place in an already moving column, with three thousand troops in front of us and another two thousand behind, and tramp to our point of deployment. We feel pleasantly thrilled. We are no longer a battalion out on a route-march: we are members of a White Army, or a Brown Army, hastening to frustrate the designs of a Blue Army, or a Pink Army, which has landed (according to the General Idea issued from Headquarters) at Portsmouth, and is reported to have slept at Great Snoreham, only ten miles away, last night.

Meanwhile our Headquarters Staff is engaged in the not always easy task of "getting into touch" with the enemy—*anglice*, finding him. It is extraordinary how elusive a force of several thousand troops can be, especially when you are picking your way across a defective half-inch map, and the commanders of the opposing forces cherish dissimilar views as to where the point of encounter is supposed to be. However, contact is at length established; and if it is not time to go home, we have a battle.

Various things may now happen to you. You may find yourself detailed for the Firing-line. In that case your battalion will take open order; and you will advance, principally upon your stomach, over hill and dale until you encounter the enemy, doing likewise. Both sides then proceed to discharge blank ammunition into one another's faces at a range, if possible, of about five yards, until the "cease fire" sounds.

Or you may find yourself in Support. In that case you are held back until the battle has progressed a stage or two, when you advance with fixed bayonets to prod your own firing line into a further display of valour and agility.

Or you may be detailed as Reserve. Membership of Brigade Reserve should be avoided. You are liable to be called upon at any moment to forsake the sheltered wood or lee of a barn under which you are huddling, and double madly up a hill or along a side road, tripping heavily over ingenious entanglements composed of the telephone wires of your own signallers, to enfilade some unwary detachment of the enemy or repel a flank attack. On the other hand, if you are ordered to act as Divisional Reserve, you may select the softest spot on the hillside behind which you are sheltering, get out your haversack ration, and prepare to spend an extremely peaceful (or extremely dull) day. Mimic warfare enjoys one enormous advantage over the genuine article: battles—provided you are not out for the night—*must always* end in time for the men to get back to their dinners at five o'clock. Under this inexorable law it follows that, by the time the General has got into touch with the enemy and brought his firing line, supports, and local reserves into action, it is time to go home. So about three o'clock the bugles sound, and the combatants, hot and grimy, fall back into close order at the point of deployment, where they are presently joined by the Divisional Reserve, blue-faced and watery-eyed with cold. This done, principals and understudies, casting envious glances at one another, form one long column of route and set out for home, in charge of the subalterns. The senior officers trot off to the "pow-wow," there, with the utmost humility and deference, to extol their own tactical dispositions, belittle the achievements of the enemy, and impugn the veracity of one another.

Thus the day's work ends. Our divisional column, with its trim, sturdy, infantry battalions, its jingling cavalry and artillery, its real live staff, and its imposing transport train, sets us thinking, by sheer force of contrast, of that dim and distant time seven months ago, when we wrestled perspiringly all through long and hot September days, on a dusty barrack square, with squad upon squad of dazed and refractory barbarians, who only ceased shuffling their feet in order to expectorate. And these are the self-same men! Never was there a more complete vindication of the policy of pegging away.

So much for the effect of its training upon the regiment as a whole. But when you come to individuals, certain of whom we have encountered and studied in this rambling narrative, you find it impossible to generalise. Your one unshakable conclusion is that it takes all sorts to make a type.

There are happy, careless souls like McLeary and Hogg. There are conscientious but slow-moving worthies like Mucklewame and Budge. There are drunken wasters like—well, we need name no names. We have got rid of most of these, thank heaven! There are simple-minded enthusiasts of the breed of Wee Pe'er, for whom the sheer joy of "sojering" still invests dull routine and hard work with a glamour of their own. There are the old hands, versed in every labour-saving (and duty-shirking) device. There are the feckless and muddle-headed, making heavy weather of the simplest tasks. There is another class, which divides its time between rising to the position of sergeant and being reduced to the ranks, for causes which need not be specified. There is yet another, which knows its drill-book backwards, and can grasp the details of a tactical scheme as quickly as a seasoned officer, but remains in the ruck because it has not sufficient force of character to handle so much as a sentry-group. There are men, again, with initiative but no endurance, and others with endurance but no initiative. Lastly, there are men, and a great many of them, who appear to be quite incapable of coherent thought, yet can handle machinery or any mechanical device to a marvel. Yes, we are a motley organisation.

But the great sifting and sorting machine into which we have been cast is shaking us all out into our appointed places. The efficient and authoritative rise to non-commissioned rank. The quick-witted and well-educated find employment on the Orderly Room staff, or among the scouts and signallers. The handy are absorbed into the transport, or become machine-gunners. The sedentary take post as cooks, or tailors, or officers' servants. The waster hews wood and draws water and empties swill-tubs. The great, mediocre, undistinguished majority merely go to stiffen the rank and file, and right nobly they do it. Each has his niche.

To take a few examples, we may begin with a typical member of the undistinguished majority. Such an one is that esteemed citizen of Wishaw, John Mucklewame. He is a rank-and-file man by training and instinct, but he forms a rare backbone for K(1). There are others, of more parts—Killick, for instance. Not long ago he was living softly, and driving a Rolls-Royce for a Duke. He is now a machine-gun sergeant, and a very good one. There is Dobie. He is a good mechanic, but short-legged and shorter-winded. He makes an excellent armourer.

Then there is Private Mellish. In his company roll he is described as "an actor." But his orbit in the theatrical firmament has never carried him outside his native Dunoon, where he follows the blameless but monotonous calling of a cinematograph operator. On enlistment he invited the attention of his platoon, from the start by referring to his rear-rank man as "this young gentleman"; and despite all the dissuading influences of barrack-room society, his manners never fell below this standard. In a company where practically every man is addressed either as "Jock" or "Jimmy," he created a profound and lasting sensation one day, by saying in a winning voice to Private Ogg,—

"Do not stand on ceremony with me, Mr. Ogg. Call me Cyril!"

For such an exotic there could only be one destination, and in due course Cyril became an officer's servant. He now polishes the buttons and washes the hose-tops of Captain Wagstaffe; and his elegant extracts amuse that student of human nature exceedingly.

Then comes a dour, silent, earnest specimen, whose name, incredible as it may appear, is M'Ostrich. He keeps himself to himself. He never smiles. He is not an old soldier, yet he performed like a veteran the very first day he appeared on parade. He carries out all orders with solemn thoroughness. He does not drink; he does not swear. His nearest approach to animation comes at church, where he sings the hymns—especially *O God, our help in ages past!*—as if he were author and composer combined. His harsh, rasping accent is certainly not that of a Highlander, nor does it smack altogether of the Clydeside. As a matter of fact he is not a Scotsman at all, though five out of six of us would put him down as such. Altogether he is a man of mystery; but the regiment could do with many more such.

Once, and only once, did he give us a peep behind the scenes. Private Burke, of D Company, a cheery soul, who possesses the entirely Hibernian faculty of being able to combine a most fanatical and seditious brand of Nationalism with a genuine and ardent enthusiasm for the British Empire, one day made a contemptuous and ribald reference to the Ulster Volunteers and their leader. M'Ostrich, who was sitting on his bedding at the other side of the hut, promptly rose to his feet, crossed the floor in three strides, and silently felled the humorist to the earth. Plainly, if M'Ostrich comes safe through the war, he is prepared for another and grimmer campaign.

Lastly, that jack-of-all trades and master of none, Private Dunshie. As already recorded, Dunshie's original calling had been that of a street news-vendor. Like all literary men, he was a Bohemian at heart. Routine wearied him; discipline galled him; the sight of work made him feel faint. After a month or two in the ranks he seized the first opportunity of escaping from the toils of his company, by volunteering for service as a Scout. A single experience of night operations in a dark wood, previously described, decided him to seek some milder employment. Observing that the regimental cooks appeared to be absolved, by virtue of their office, not only from all regimental parades, but from all obligations on the subject of correct attire and personal cleanliness, he volunteered for service in the kitchen. Here for a space—clad in shirt, trousers, and canvas shoes, unutterably greasy and waxing fat—he prospered exceedingly.

But one sad day he was detected by the cook-sergeant, having just finished cleaning a flue, in the act of washing his hands in ten gallons of B Company's soup. Once more our versatile hero found himself turned adrift with brutal and agonising suddenness, and bidden to exercise his talents elsewhere.

After a fortnight's uneventful dreariness with his platoon, Dunshie joined the machine-gunners, because he had heard rumours that these were conveyed to and from their labours in limbered wagons. But he had been misinformed. It was the guns that were carried; the gunners invariably walked, sometimes carrying the guns and the appurtenances thereof. His very first day Dunshie was compelled to double across half a mile of boggy heath-land carrying two large stones, meant to represent ammunition-boxes, from an imaginary wagon to a dummy gun. It is true that as soon as he was out of sight of the corporal he deposited the stones upon the ground, and ultimately proffered two others, picked up on nearing his destination, to the sergeant in charge of the proceedings; but even thus the work struck him as unreasonably exacting, and he resigned, by the simple process of cutting his next parade and being ignominiously returned to his company.

After an unsuccessful application for employment as a "buzzer," or signaller, Dunshie made trial of the regimental transport, where there was a shortage of drivers. He had strong hopes that in this way he would attain to permanent carriage exercise. But he was quickly undeceived. Instead of being offered a seat upon the box of a G.S. wagon, he was bidden to walk behind the same, applying the brake when necessary, for fourteen miles. The next day he spent cleaning stables, under a particularly officious corporal. On the third, he was instructed in the art of grooming a mule. On the fourth, he was left to perform this feat unaided, and the mule, acting under extreme provocation, kicked him in the stomach. On the fifth day he was returned to his company.

But Mecca was at hand. That very morning Dunshie's company commander received the following ukase from headquarters:—

Officers commanding Companies will render to the Orderly Room without fail, by 9 a.m. to-morrow, the name of one man qualified to act as chiropodist to the Company.

Major Kemp scratched his nose in a dazed fashion, and looked over his spectacles at his Quartermaster-Sergeant.

"What in thunder will they ask for next?" he growled. "Have we got any tame chiropodists in the company, Rae?"

Quartermaster-Sergeant Rae turned over the Company roll.

"There is no—no—no man of that profession here, sirr," he reported, after scanning the document. "But," he added optimistically, "there is a machine-fitter and a glass-blower. Will I warn one of them?"

"I think we had better call for a volunteer first," said Major Kemp tactfully.

Accordingly, that afternoon upon parade, Platoon commanders were bidden to hold a witch hunt, and smell out a chiropodist. But the enterprise terminated almost immediately; for Private Dunshie, caressing his injured abdomen in Number Three Platoon, heard the invitation, and quickly stepped forward.

"So you are a chiropodist as well as everything else, Dunshie!" said Ayling incredulously.

"That's right, sirr," assented Dunshie politely.

"Are you a professional?"

"No exactly that, sirr," was the modest reply.

"You just make a hobby of it?"

"Just that, sirr."

"Have you had much experience?"

"No that much."

"But you feel capable of taking on the job?"

"I do, sirr."

"You seem quite eager about it."

"Yes, sirr," said Dunshie, with gusto.

A sudden thought occurred to Ayling.

"Do you know what a chiropodist is?" he asked.

"No, sirr," replied Dunshie, with unabated aplomb.

* * * * * * * *

To do him justice, the revelation of the nature of his prospective labours made no difference whatever to Dunshie's willingness to undertake them. Now, upon Saturday mornings, when men stand stiffly at attention beside their beds to have their feet inspected, you may behold, sweeping majestically in the wake of the Medical Officer as he makes his rounds, the swelling figure of Private Dunshie, carrying the implements of his gruesome trade. He has found his vocation at last, and his bearing in consequence is something between that of a Court Physician and a Staff Officer.

So much for the rank and file. Of the officers we need only say that the old hands have been a godsend to our young regiment; while the juniors, to quote their own Colonel, have learned as much in six months as the average subaltern learns in three years; and whereas in the old days a young officer could always depend on his platoon sergeant to give him the right word of command or instruct him in company routine, the positions are now in many cases reversed. But that by the way. The outstanding feature of the relationship between officers and men during all this long, laborious, sometimes heartbreaking winter has been this—that, despite the rawness of our material and the novelty of our surroundings, in the face of difficulties which are now happily growing dim in our memory, the various ranks have never quite given up trying, never altogether lost faith, never entirely forgotten the Cause which has brought us together. And the result—the joint result—of it all is a real live regiment, with a *morale* and soul of its own.

But so far everything has been purely suppositious. We have no knowledge as to what our real strength or weakness may be. We have run our trial trips over a landlocked stretch of smooth water. To-morrow, when we steam out to face the tempest which is shaking the foundations of the world, we shall see what we shall see. Some of us, who at present are exalted for our smartness and efficiency, will indubitably be found wanting—wanting in stamina of body or soul—while others, hitherto undistinguished, will come to their own. Only War itself can discover the qualities which count in War. But we silently pray, in our dour and inarticulate hearts, that the supreme British virtue—the virtue of holding on, and holding on, and holding on, until our end is accomplished—may not be found wanting in a single one of us.

To take a last survey of the regiment which we have created—one little drop in the incredible wave which has rolled with gathering strength from, end to end of this island of ours during the past six months, and now hangs ready to crash upon the gates of our enemies—what manner of man has it produced? What is he like, this impromptu Thomas Atkins?

Well, when he joined, his outstanding feature was a sort of surly independence, the surliness being largely based upon the fear of losing the independence. He has got over that now. He is no longer morbidly sensitive about his rights as a free and independent citizen and the backbone of the British electorate. He has bigger things to think of. He no longer regards sergeants as upstart slave-drivers—frequently he is a sergeant himself—nor officers as grinding capitalists. He is undergoing the experience of the rivets in Mr. Kipling's story of "The Ship that Found Herself." He is adjusting his perspectives. He is beginning to merge himself in the Regiment.

He no longer gets drunk from habit. When he does so now, it is because there were no potatoes at dinner, or because there has been a leak in the roof of his hut for a week and no one is attending to it, or because his wife is not receiving her separation allowance. Being an inarticulate person, he finds getting drunk the simplest and most effective expedient for acquainting the powers that be with the fact that he has a grievance. Formerly, the morning list of "drunks" merely reflected the nearness or remoteness of payday. Now, it is a most reliable and invaluable barometer of the regimental atmosphere.

He has developed—quite spontaneously, for he has had few opportunities for imitation—many of the characteristics of the regular soldier. He is quick to discover himself aggrieved, but is readily appeased if he feels that his officer is really doing his best for him, and that both of them are the victims of a higher power. On the other hand, he is often amazingly cheerful under uncomfortable and depressing surroundings. He is growing quite fastidious, too, about his personal appearance when off duty. (You should see our quiffs on Saturdays!) He is quite incapable of keeping possession of his clothing, his boots, his rifle, his health, or anything that is his, without constant supervision and nurse-maiding. And that he is developing a strong bent towards the sentimental is evinced by the choruses that he sings in the gloaming and his taste in picture post-cards.

So far he may follow the professional model, but in other respects he is quite *sui generis*. No sergeant in a Highland regiment of the line would ever refer to a Cockney private, with all humility, as "a young English gentleman"; neither would an ordinary soldier salute an officer quite correctly with one hand while employing the other to light his pipe. In "K(1)" we do these things and many others, which, give us a *cachet* of our own of which we are very rightly and properly proud.

So we pin our faith to the man who has been at once our despair and our joy since the month of August. He has character; he has grit; and now that he is getting discipline as well, he is going to be an everlasting credit to the cause which roused his manhood and the land which gave him birth.

* * * * * * * *

That is the tale of The First Hundred Thousand—*Part One*. Whether *Part Two* will be forthcoming, and how much of it there will be, depends upon two things—the course of history, and the present historian's eye for cover.

Book Two

Live Rounds

CHAPTER 14
The Back of the Front

The last few days have afforded us an excellent opportunity of studying the habits of that ubiquitous attendant of our movements, the Staff Officer.

He is not always a real Staff Officer—the kind that wears a red hatband. Sometimes he is an obvious "dug-out," with a pronounced *embonpoint* or a game leg. Sometimes he is a mere stripling, with a rapidly increasing size in hats. Sometimes he is an ordinary human being. But whoever he is, and whatever his age or rank, one thing is certain. He has no mean: he is either very good or very bad. When he is good he is very good indeed, and when he is bad he is horrid. He is either Jekyll or Hyde.

Thrice blessed, then, is that unit which, upon its journey to the seat of war, encounters only the good of the species. To transfer a thousand men, with secrecy and despatch, from camp to train, from train to ship, from ship to train, and from train to a spot near the battle line, is a task which calls for the finest organisation and the most skilful administration. Let it be said at once that our path to our present address has been almost universally lined with Jekylls. The few Hydes whom we have encountered are by this time merely a subject for amusing anecdote.

As for the organisation of our journey—well, it was formulated upon Olympus, and was marked by those Olympian touches of which mention has been previously made. For instance, immense pains were taken, by means of printed rules and official memoranda, to acquaint us with the procedure to be followed at each point of entrainment or embarkation. Consequently we set out upon our complicated pilgrimage primed with explicit instructions and ready for any emergency. We filled up forms with countless details of our equipment and personnel, which we knew would delight the heart of the Round

Game Department. We divided our followers, as directed, into Loading Parties, and Ration Parties, and Hold Parties, and many other interesting subdivisions, as required by the rules of the game. But we had reckoned without the Practical Joke Department. The Round Game Department having furnished us with one set of rules, the Practical Joke Department prepared another, entirely different, and issued them to the officers who superintended such things as entrainment and embarkation. At least, that is the most charitable explanation of the course of action adopted by the few Mr. Hydes whom we encountered.

Two of these humorists linger in the memory. The first was of the type which is admiringly referred to in commercial circles as a hustler. His hustling took the form of beginning to shout incomprehensible orders almost before the train had drawn up at the platform. After that he passed from party to party, each of which was working strenuously under its own sergeant, and commanded them (not the sergeant) to do something else, somewhere else—a course of action naturally calculated to promote unity and celerity of action all round. A perspiring sergeant who ventured to point out that his party were working under the direct orders of their Company Commander, was promptly placed under arrest, and his flock enjoyed a welcome and protracted breathing-space until an officer of sufficient standing to cope with Mr. Hyde—unfortunately he was Major Hyde—could be discovered and informed.

The second required more tactful handling. As our train-load drew up at the platform, the officer in charge—it was Captain Blaikie, supported by Bobby Little—stepped out, saluted the somewhat rotund Colonel Hyde whom he saw before him, and proffered a sheaf of papers.

"Good-morning, sir," he said. "Here is my train statement. Shall I carry on with the unloading? I have all my parties detailed."

The great man waved away the papers magnificently. (To be just, even the Jekylls used to wave away our papers.)

"Take those things away," he commanded, in a voice which made it plain that we had encountered another hustler. "Burn them, if you like! Now listen to me. Tell off an officer and seventy men at once."

"I have all the necessary parties detailed already, sir."

"Will you listen to me?" roared the Colonel. He turned to where Captain Blaikie's detachment were drawn up on the platform, "Take the first seventy men of that lot, and tell them to stand over there, under an officer."

Captain Blaikie gave the necessary order.

"Now," continued Colonel Hyde, "tell them to get the horses out and on board that steamer at once. The rest of your party are to go by another steamer. See?"

"Yes, sir, perfectly. But—"

"Do you understand my order?" thundered the Colonel, with increasing choler.

"I do, sir," replied Blaikie politely, "but—"

"Then, for heaven's sake, carry on!"

Blaikie saluted.

"Very good, sir," he answered. "Mr. Little, come with me."

He turned upon his heel and disappeared rapidly round a corner, followed by the mystified Bobby.

Once out of the sight of the Colonel, Captain Blaikie halted, leaned against a convenient pillar, and lit a cigarette.

"And what do you think of that?" he inquired.

Bobby told him.

"Quite so," agreed Blaikie. "But what you say helps nobody, though doubtless soothing to the feelings. Now listen, Bobby, and I will give you your first lesson in the Tactical Handling of Brass Hats. Of course we might do as that dear old gentleman suggests, and send seventy horses and mules on a sea voyage in charge of a party of cooks, signallers, and machine-gunners, and let the grooms and drivers go with the bicycles and machine-guns and field kitchens. But I don't think we will. Nobody would enjoy the experiment much—except perhaps the mules. No: we will follow the golden rule, which is: When given an impossible job by a Brass Hat, salute smartly, turn about, and go and wait round a corner for five minutes. Then come back and do the job in a proper manner. Our five minutes are up: the coast should be clear. Come along, Bobby, and help me to exchange those two parties."

But we encountered surprisingly few Hydes. Nearly all were Jekylls—Jekylls of the most competent and courteous type. True, they were inclined to treat our laboriously completed returns with frivolity.

"Never mind those things, old man," they would say. "Just tell me who you are, and how many. That's right: now I know all about you. Got your working parties fixed up? Good! They ought to have everything cleared in a couple of hours. I'll see that a ration of hot tea is served out for them. Your train starts at a quarter past seven this evening—remember to call it nineteen-fifteen, by the way, in this country—and you ought to be at the station an hour before the time. I'll send you a guide. What a fine-looking lot these chaps of yours are! Best lot I've seen here for a very long time. Working like niggers, too! Now come along with me for ten minutes and I'll show you where to get a bite of breakfast. Expect you can do with a bit!"

That is Brass-Hat Jekyll—officer and gentleman; and, to the eternal credit of the British Army, be it said that he abounds in this well-conducted campaign. As an instance of his efficiency, let the case of our own regiment be quoted. The main body travelled here by one route, the transport, horses, and other details by another. The main body duly landed, and were conveyed to the rendezvous—a distant railway junction in Northern France. There they sat down to await the arrival of the train containing the other party; which had left England many hours before them, had landed at a different port, and had not been seen or heard of since.

They had to wait exactly ten minutes!

"Some Staff—what?" as the Adjutant observed, as the train lumbered into view.

Most of us, in our travels abroad, have observed the closed trucks which are employed upon French railways, and which bear the legend—

Hommes.... 40 *Chevaux*.... 8

Doubtless we have wondered, idly enough, what it must feel like to be one of the forty *hommes*. Well, now we know.

When we landed, we were packed into a train composed of fifty such trucks, and were drawn by a mighty engine for a day and a night across the pleasant land of France. Every six hours or so we were indulged with a *Halte Repas*. That is to say, the train drew up in a siding, where an officer with R.T.O. upon his arm made us welcome, and informed us that hot water was available for taking tea. Everybody had two days' rations in his haversack, so a large-scale picnic followed. From the horse-trucks emerged stolid individuals with canvas buckets—you require to be fairly stolid to pass the night in a closed box, moving at twenty miles an hour, in company with eight riotous and insecurely tethered mules—to draw water from the hydrant which supplied the locomotives. The infant population gathered round, and besought us for "souvenirs," the most popular taking the form of "*biskeet*" or "bully-*boeuf*." Both were given freely: with but little persuasion our open-handed warriors would have fain squandered their sacred "emergency ration" upon these rapacious infants.

After refreshment we proceeded to inspect the station. The centre of attraction was the French soldier on guard over the water-tank. Behold this same sentry confronted by Private Mucklewame, anxious to comply with Divisional Orders and "lose no opportunity of cultivating the friendliest relations with those of our Allies whom you may chance to encounter." So Mucklewame and the sentry (who is evidently burdened with similar instructions) regard one another with shy smiles, after the fashion of two children who have been introduced by their nurses at a party.

Presently the sentry, by a happy inspiration, proffers his bayonet for inspection, as it were a new doll. Mucklewame bows solemnly, and fingers the blade. Then he produces his own bayonet, and the two weapons are compared—still in constrained silence. Then Mucklewame nods approvingly.

"Verra goody!" he remarks, profoundly convinced that he is speaking the French language.

"Olrigh! Tipperary!" replies the sentry, not to be outdone in international courtesy.

Unfortunately, the further cementing of the Entente Cordiale is frustrated by the blast of a whistle. We hurl ourselves into our trucks; the R.T.O. waves his hand in benediction; and the regiment proceeds upon its way, packed like herrings, but "all jubilant with song."

We have been "oot here" for a week now, and although we have had no personal encounter with the foe, our time has not been wasted. We are filling up gaps in our education, and we are tolerably busy. Some things, of course, we have not had to learn. We are fairly well inured, for instance, to hard work and irregular meals. What we have chiefly to acquire at present is the art of adaptability. When we are able to settle down into strange billets in half an hour, and pack up, ready for departure, within the same period, we shall have made a great stride in efficiency, and added enormously to our own personal comfort.

Even now we are making progress. Observe the platoon who are marching into this farmyard. They are dead tired, and the sight of the straw-filled barn is too much for some of them. They throw themselves down anywhere, and are asleep in a moment. When they wake up—or more likely, are wakened up—in an hour or two, they will be sorry. They will be stiff and sore, and their feet will be a torment. Others, more sensible, crowd round the pump, or dabble their abraded extremities in one of the countless ditches with which this country is intersected. Others again, of the more enterprising kind, repair to the house-door, and inquire politely for "the wife." (They have long given up inquiring for "the master." There is no master on this farm, or indeed on any farm throughout the length and breadth of this great-hearted land. Father and sons are all away, restoring the Bosche to his proper place in the animal kingdom. We have seen no young or middle-aged man out of uniform since we entered this district, save an occasional imbecile or cripple.)

Presently "the wife" comes to the door, with a smile. She can afford to smile now, for not so long ago her guests were Uhlans. Then begins an elaborate pantomime. Private Tosh says *"Bonjourr!"* in husky tones—last week he would have said "Hey, Bella!"—and proceeds to wash his hands in invisible soap and water. As a reward for his ingenuity he receives a basin of water: sometimes the water is even warm. Meanwhile Private Cosh, the linguist of the platoon, proffers twopence, and says: "Doolay—ye unnerstand?" He gets a drink of milk, which is a far, far better thing than the appalling green scum-covered water with which his less adaptable brethren are wont to refresh themselves from wayside ditches. Thomas Atkins, however mature, is quite incorrigible in this respect.

Yes, we are getting on. And when every man in the platoon, instead of merely some, can find a place to sleep, draw his blanket from the wagon, clean his rifle and himself, and get to his dinner within the half-hour already specified, we shall be able justly to call ourselves seasoned.

We have covered some distance this week, and we have learned one thing at least, and that is, not to be uppish about our sleeping quarters. We have slept in chateaux, convents, farm-houses, and under the open sky. The chateaux are usually empty. An aged retainer, the sole inhabitant, explains that M. le Comte is at Paris; M. Armand at Arras; and M. Guy in Alsace,—all doing their bit. M. Victor is in hospital, with Madame and Mademoiselle in constant attendance.

So we settle down in the chateaux, and unroll our sleeping-bags upon its dusty parquet. Occasionally we find a bed available. Then two officers take the mattress, upon the floor, and two more take what is left of the bed. French chateaux do not appear to differ much as a class. They are distinguished by great elegance of design, infinite variety in furniture, and entire absence of drains. The same rule applies to convents, except that there is no furniture.

Given fine weather, by far the most luxurious form of lodging is in the open air. Here one may slumber at ease, fanned by the wings of cockchafers and soothed by an unseen choir of frogs. There are drawbacks, of course. Mr. Waddell one evening spread his ground-sheet and bedding in the grassy meadow, beside a murmuring stream. It was an idyllic resting-place for a person of romantic or contemplative disposition. Unfortunately it is almost impossible nowadays to keep one's favourite haunts select. This was evidently the opinion of the large water-rat which Waddell found sitting upon his air-pillow when he returned from supper. Although French, the animal exhibited no disposition to fraternise, but withdrew in the most pointed fashion, taking an Abernethy biscuit with him.

Accommodation in farms is best described by the word "promiscuous." There are twelve officers and two hundred men billeted here. The farm is exactly the same as any other French farm. It consists of a hollow square of buildings—dwelling-house, barns, pigstyes, and stables—with a commodious manure-heap, occupying the whole yard except a narrow strip round the edge, in the middle, the happy hunting-ground of innumerable cocks and hens and an occasional pig. The men sleep in the barns. The senior officers sleep in a stone-floored boudoir of their own. The juniors sleep where they can, and experience little difficulty in accomplishing the feat. A hard day's marching and a truss of straw—these two combined form an irresistible inducement to slumber.

Only a few miles away big guns thunder until the building shakes. To-morrow a select party of officers is to pay a visit to the trenches. Thereafter our whole flock is to go, in its official capacity. The War is with us at last. Early this morning a Zeppelin rose into view on the skyline. Shell fire pursued it, and it sank again—rumour says in the British lines. Rumour is our only war correspondent at present. It is far easier to follow the course of events from home, where newspapers are more plentiful than here.

But the grim realities of war are coming home to us. Outside this farm stands a tall tree. Not many months ago a party of Uhlans arrived here, bringing with them a wounded British prisoner. They crucified him to that self-same tree, and stood round him till he died. He was a long time dying.

Some of us had not heard of Uhlans before. These have now noted the name, for future reference—and action.

Chapter 15

In the Trenches—An Off-Day

This town is under constant shell fire. It goes on day after day: it has been going on for months. Sometimes a single shell comes: sometimes half a dozen. Sometimes whole batteries get to work. The effect is terrible. You who live at home in ease have no conception of what it is like to live in a town which is under intermittent shell fire.

I say this advisedly. You have no conception whatsoever.

We get no rest. There is a distant boom, followed by a crash overhead. Cries are heard—the cries of women and children. They are running frantically—running to observe the explosion, and if possible pick up a piece of the shell as a souvenir. Sometimes there are not enough souvenirs to go round, and then the clamour increases.

We get no rest, I say—only frightfulness. British officers, walking peaceably along the pavement, are frequently hustled and knocked aside by these persons. Only the other day, a full colonel was compelled to turn up a side-street, to avoid disturbing a ring of excited children who were dancing round a beautiful new hole in the ground in the middle of a narrow lane.

If you enter into a cafe or estaminet, a total stranger sidles to your table, and, having sat down beside you, produces from the recesses of his person a fragment of shrapnel. This he lays before you, and explains that if he had been standing at the spot where the shell burst, it would have killed him. You express polite regret, and pass on elsewhere, seeking peace and finding none. The whole thing is a public scandal.

Seriously, though, it is astonishing what contempt familiarity can breed, even in the case of high-explosive shells. This little town lies close behind the trenches. All day long the big guns boom. By night the rifles and machine-guns take up the tale. One is frequently aroused from slumber, especially towards dawn, by a perfect tornado of firing. The machine-guns make a noise like a giant tearing calico. Periodically, too, as already stated, we are subjected to an hour's intimidation in the shape of bombardment. Shrapnel bursts over our heads; shells explode in the streets, especially in open spaces, or where two important streets cross. (With modern artillery you can shell a town quite methodically by map and compass.)

Brother Bosche's motto appears to be: "It is a fine morning. There is nothing in the trenches doing. We abundant ammunition have. Let us a little frightfulness into the town pump!" So he pumps.

But nobody seems to mind. Of course there is a casualty now and then. Occasionally a hole is blown in a road, or the side of a house is knocked in. Yet the general attitude of the population is one of rather interested expectancy. There is always the cellar to retire to if things get really serious. The gratings are sandbagged to that end. At other times—well, there is always the pleasing possibility of witnessing the sudden removal of your neighbour's landmark.

Officers breakfasting in their billets look up from their porridge, and say,—

"That's a dud! *That's* a better one! Stick to it, Bill!"

It really is most discouraging, to a sensitive and conscientious Hun.

The same unconcern reigns in the trenches. Let us imagine that we are members of a distinguished party from Headquarters, about to make a tour of inspection.

We leave the town, and after a short walk along the inevitable poplar-lined road turn into a field. The country all round us is flat—flat as Cheshire; and, like Cheshire, has a pond in every field. But in the hazy distance stands a low ridge.

"Better keep close to the hedge," suggests the officer in charge. "There are eighty guns on that ridge. It's a misty morning; but they've got all the ranges about here to a yard; so they *might*—"

We keep close to the hedge.

Presently we find ourselves entering upon a wide but sticky path cut in the clay. At the entrance stands a neat notice-board, which announces, somewhat unexpectedly—OLD KENT ROAD.

The field is flat, but the path runs downhill. Consequently we soon find ourselves tramping along below the ground-level, with a stout parapet of clay on either side of us. Overhead there is nothing—nothing but the blue sky, with the larks singing, quite regardless of the War.

"Communication trench," explains the guide.

We tramp along this sunken lane for the best part of a mile. It winds a good deal. Every hundred yards or so comes a great promontory of sandbags, necessitating four right-angle turns. Once we pass under the shadow of trees, and apple-blossom flutters down upon our upturned faces. We are walking through an orchard. Despite the efforts of ten million armed men, brown old Mother Earth has made it plain that seedtime and harvest shall still prevail.

Now we are crossing a stream, which cuts the trench at right angles. The stream is spanned by a structure of planks—labelled, it is hardly necessary to say, LONDON BRIDGE. The side-street, so to speak, by which the stream runs away, is called JOCK'S JOY. We ask why?

"It's the place where the Highlanders wash their knees," is the explanation.

Presently we arrive at PICCADILLY CIRCUS, a muddy excavation in the earth, from which several passages branch. These thoroughfares are not all labelled with strict regard for London geography. We note THE HAYMARKET, also PICCADILLY; but ARTILLERY LANE seems out of place, somehow. On the site, too, of the Criterion, we observe a subterranean cavern containing three recumbent figures, snoring lustily. This bears the sign CYCLISTS' REST.

We, however, take the turning marked SHAFTESBURY AVENUE, and after passing (quite wrongly, don't you think?) through TRAFALGAR SQUARE—six feet by eight—find ourselves in the actual firing trench.

It is an unexpectedly spacious place. We, who have spent the winter constructing slits in the ground two feet wide, feel quite lost in this roomy thoroughfare. For a thoroughfare it is, with little toy houses on either side. They are hewn out of the solid earth, lined with planks, painted, furnished, and decorated. These are, so to speak, permanent trenches, which have been occupied for more than six months.

Observe this eligible residence on your left. It has a little door, nearly six feet high, and a real glass window, with a little curtain. Inside, there is a bunk, six feet long, together with an ingenious folding washhand-stand, of the nautical variety, and a flap-table. The walls, which are painted pale green, are decorated with elegant extracts from the "Sketch" and "La Vie Parisienne." Outside, the name of the villa is painted up. It is in Welsh—that notorious railway station in Anglesey which runs to thirty-three syllables or so—and extends from one end of the facade to the other. A small placard announces that Hawkers, Organs, and Street-cries are prohibited.

"This is my shanty," explains a machine-gun officer standing by. "It was built by a Welsh Fusilier, who has since moved on. He was here all winter, and made everything himself, including the washhand-stand. Some carpenter—what? of course I am not here continuously. We have six days in the trenches and six out; so I take turns with a man in the Midland Mudcrushers, who take turns with us. Come in and have some tea."

It is only ten o'clock in the morning, but tea—strong and sweet, with condensed milk—is instantly forthcoming. Refreshed by this, and a slice of cake, we proceed upon our excursion.

The trench is full of men, mostly asleep; for the night cometh, when no man may sleep. They lie in low-roofed rectangular caves, like the interior of great cucumber-frames, lined with planks and supported by props. The cave is really a homogeneous affair, for it is constructed in the R.E. workshops and then brought bodily to the trenches and fitted into its appointed excavation. Each cave holds three men. They lie side by side, like three dogs in a triple kennel, with their heads outward and easily accessible to the individual who performs the functions of "knocker-up."

Others are cooking, others are cleaning their rifles. The proceedings are superintended by a contemplative tabby cat, coiled up in a niche, like a feline flower in a crannied wall.

"She used ter sit on top of the parapet," explains a friendly lance-corporal; "but became a casualty, owin' to a sniper mistakin' 'er for a Guardsman's bearskin. Show the officer your back, Christabel!"

We inspect the healed scar, and pass on. Next moment we round a traverse—and walk straight into the arms of Privates Ogg and Hogg!

No need now to remain with the distinguished party from Headquarters. For the next half-mile of trench you will find yourselves among friends. "K(1)" and Brother Bosche are face to face at last, and here you behold our own particular band of warriors taking their first spell in the trenches.

Let us open the door of this spacious dug-out—the image of an up-river bungalow, decorated with window-boxes and labelled Potsdam View—and join the party of four which sits round the table.

"How did your fellows get on last night, Wagstaffe?" inquires Major Kemp.

"Very well, on the whole. It was a really happy thought on the part of the authorities—almost human, in fact—to put us in alongside the old regiment."

"Or what's left of them."

Wagstaffe nods gravely.

"Yes. There are some changes in the Mess since I last dined there," he says. "Anyhow, the old hands took our boys to their bosoms at once, and showed them the ropes."

"The men did not altogether fancy look-out work in the dark, sir," says Bobby Little to Major Kemp.

"Neither should I, very much," said Kemp. "To take one's stand on a ledge fixed at a height which brings one's head and shoulders well above the parapet, and stand there for an hour on end, knowing that a machine-gun may start a spell of rapid traversing fire at any moment—well, it takes a bit of doing, you know, until you are used to it. How did you persuade 'em, Bobby?"

"Oh, I just climbed up on the top of the parapet and sat there for a bit," says Bobby Little modestly. "They were all right after that."

"Had you any excitement, Ayling?" asks Kemp. "I hear rumours that you had two casualties."

"Yes," says Ayling. "Four of us went out patrolling in front of the trench—"

"Who?"

"Myself, two men, and old Sergeant Carfrae."

"Carfrae?" Wagstaffe laughs. "That old fire-eater? I remember him at Paardeberg. You were lucky to get back alive. Proceed, my son!"

"We went out," continues Ayling, "and patrolled."

"How?"

"Well, there you rather have me. I have always been a bit foggy as to what a patrol really does—what risks it takes, and so on. However, Carfrae had no doubts on the subject whatever. His idea was to trot over to the German trenches and look inside."

"Quite so!" agreed Wagstaffe, and Kemp chuckled.

"Well, we were standing by the barbed wire entanglement, arguing the point, when suddenly some infernal imbecile in our own trenches—"

"Cockerell, for a dollar!" murmurs Wagstaffe. "Don't say he fired at you!"

"No, he did worse. He let off a fireball."

"Whew! And there you stood in the limelight!"

"Exactly."

"What did you do?"

"I had sufficient presence of mind to do what Carfrae did. I threw myself on my face, and shouted to the two men to do the same."

"Did they?"

"No. They started to run back towards the trenches. Half a dozen German rifles opened on them at once."

"Were they badly hit?"

"Nothing to speak of, considering. The shots mostly went high.

Preston got his elbow smashed, and Burke had a bullet through his cap and another in the region of the waistband. Then they tumbled into the trench like rabbits. Carfrae and I crawled after them."

At this moment the doorway of the dugout is darkened by a massive figure, and Major Kemp's colour-sergeant announces—

"There's a parrty of Gairmans gotten oot o' their trenches, sirr. Will we open fire?"

"Go and have a look at 'em, like a good chap, Wagger," says the Major. "I want to finish this letter."

Wagstaffe and Bobby Little make their way along the trench until they come to a low opening marked MAXIM VILLA. They crawl inside, and find themselves in a semicircular recess, chiefly occupied by an earthen platform, upon which a machine-gun is mounted. The recess is roofed over, heavily protected with sandbags, and lined with iron plates; for a machine-gun emplacement is the object of frequent and pressing attention from high-explosive shells. There are loopholes to right and left, but not in front. These deadly weapons prefer diagonal or enfilade fire. It is not worth while to fire them frontally.

Wagstaffe draws back a strip of sacking which covers one loophole, and peers out. There, a hundred and fifty yards away, across a sunlit field, he beholds some twenty grey figures, engaged in the most pastoral of pursuits, in front of the German trenches.

"They are cutting the grass," he says. "Let 'em, by all means! If they don't, we must. We don't want their bomb-throwers crawling over here through a hay-field. Let us encourage them by every means in our power. It might almost be worth our while to send them a message. Walk along the trench, Bobby, and see that no excitable person looses off at them."

Bobby obeys; and peace still broods over the sleepy trench. The only sound which breaks the summer stillness is the everlasting crack, crack! of the snipers' rifles. On an off-day like this the sniper is a very necessary person. He serves to remind us that we are at war. Concealed in his own particular eyrie, with his eyes for ever laid along his telescopic sight, he keeps ceaseless vigil over the ragged outline of the enemy's trenches. Wherever a head, or anything resembling a head, shows itself, he fires. Were it not for his enthusiasm, both sides would be sitting in their shirt-sleeves upon their respective parapets, regarding one another with frank curiosity; and that would never do. So the day wears on.

Suddenly, from far in our rear, comes a boom, then another. Wagstaffe sighs resignedly.

"Why can't they let well alone?" he complains. "What's the trouble now?"

"I expect it's our Divisional Artillery having a little target practice," says Captain Blaikie. He peers into a neighbouring trench-periscope. "Yes, they are shelling that farm behind the German second-line trench. Making good shooting too, for beginners," as a column of dust and smoke rises from behind the enemy's lines. "But brother Bosche will be very peevish about it. We don't usually fire at this time of the afternoon. Yes, there is the haymaking party going home. There will be a beastly noise for the next half-hour. Pass the word along for every man to get into his dug-out."

The warning comes none too soon. In five minutes the incensed Hun is retaliating for the disturbance of his afternoon siesta. A hail of bullets passes over our trench. Shrapnel bursts overhead. High-explosive shells rain upon and around the parapet. One drops into the trench, and explodes, with surprisingly little effect. (Bobby Little found the head afterwards, and sent it home as a memento of his first encounter with reality.)

Our trench makes no reply. There is no need. This outburst heralds no grand assault. It is a mere display of "frightfulness," calculated to cow the impressionable Briton. We sit close, and make tea. Only the look-out men, crouching behind their periscopes and loopholes, keep their posts. The wind is the wrong way for gas, and in any case we all have respirators. Private M'Leary, the humorist of "A" Company, puts his on, and pretends to drink his tea through it.

Altogether, the British soldier appears sadly unappreciative either of "frightfulness" or practical chemistry. He is a hopeless case.

The firing ceases as suddenly as it began. Silence reigns again, broken only by a solitary shot from a trench-mortar—a sort of explosive postscript to a half hour's Hymn of Hate.

"And that's that!" observes Captain Blaikie cheerfully, emerging from Potsdam View. "The Hun is a harmless little creature, but noisy when roused. Now, what about getting home? It will be dark in half an hour or so. Platoon commanders, warn your men!"

It should be noted that upon this occasion we are not doing our full spell of duty—that is, six days. We have merely come in for a spell of instruction, of twenty-four hours' duration, under the chaperonage of our elder and more seasoned brethren.

Bobby Little, having given the necessary orders to his sergeant, proceeded to Trafalgar Square, there to await the mustering of his platoon.

But the first arrival took the form of a slow-moving procession—a corporal, followed by two men carrying a stretcher. On the stretcher lay something covered with a ground-sheet. At one end projected a pair of regulation boots, very still and rigid.

Bobby caught his breath. He was just nineteen, and this was his first encounter with sudden death.

"Who is it?" he asked unsteadily.

The corporal saluted.

"Private M'Leary, sirr. That last shot from the trench-mortar got him. It came in kin' o' sideways. He was sittin' at the end of his dug-oot, gettin' his tea. Stretcher party, advance!"

The procession moved off again, and disappeared round the curve of Shaftesbury Avenue. The off-day was over.

CHAPTER 16
"Dirty Work at the Cross-Roads Tonight"

Last week we abandoned the rural billets in which we had been remodelling some of our methods (on the experiences gained by our first visit to the trenches), and paraded at full strength for a march which we knew would bring us right into the heart of things. No more trial trips; no more chaperoning! This time, we decided, we were "for it."

During our three weeks of active service we have learned two things—the art of shaking down quickly into our habitation of the moment, as already noted; and the art of reducing our personal effects to a portable minimum.

To the private soldier the latter problem presents no difficulties. Everything is arranged for him. His outfit is provided by the Government, and he carries it himself. It consists of a rifle, bayonet, and a hundred and twenty rounds of ammunition. On one side of him hangs his water-bottle, containing a quart of water, on the other, a haversack, occupied by his "iron ration"—an emergency meal of the tinned variety, which must never on any account be opened except by order of the C.O.—and such private effects as his smoking outfit and an entirely mythical item of refreshment officially known as "the unexpended portion of the day's ration." On his back he carries a "pack," containing his greatcoat, waterproof sheet, and such changes of raiment as a paternal Government allows him. He also has to find room therein for a towel, housewife, and a modest allowance of cutlery. (He frequently wears the spoon in his stocking, as a *skean-dhu*.) Round his neck he wears his identity disc. In his breast-pocket he carries a respirator, to be donned in the event of his encountering the twin misfortunes of an east wind and a gaseous Hun. He also carries a bottle of liquid for damping the respirator. In the flap of his jacket is sewn a field dressing.

Slung behind him is an entrenching tool.

Any other space upon his person is at his own disposal, and he may carry what he likes, except "unsoldierly trinkets"—whatever these may be. However, if the passion for self-adornment proves too strong, he may wear "the French National Colours"—a compliment to our gallant ally which is slightly discounted by the fact that her national colours are the same as our own.

However, once he has attached this outfit to his suffering person, and has said what he thinks about its weight, the private has no more baggage worries. Except for his blanket, which is carried on a wagon, he is his own arsenal, wardrobe, and pantry.

Not so the officer. He suffers from *embarras de choix*. He is the victim of his female relatives, who are themselves the victims of those enterprising tradesmen who have adopted the most obvious method of getting rid of otherwise unsaleable goods by labelling everything *For Active Service*—a really happy thought when you are trying to sell a pipe of port or a manicure set. Have you seen Our Active Service Trouser-Press?

By the end of April Bobby Little had accumulated, with a view to facilitating the destruction of the foe—

An automatic Mauser pistol, with two thousand rounds of ammunition.

A regulation Service revolver.

A camp bed.

A camp table.

A camp chair.

A pneumatic mattress.

(This ingenious contrivance was meant to be blown up, like an air-cushion, and Bobby's servant expended most of the day and much valuable breath in performing the feat. Ultimately, in a misguided attempt to save his lungs from rupture, he employed a bicycle pump, and burst the bed.)

A sleeping (or "flea") bag.

A portable bath.

A portable washhand-stand.

A dressing-case, heavily ballasted with cut-glass bottles.

A primus stove.

A despatch case.

The "Service" Kipling (about forty volumes.)

Innumerable socks and shirts.

A box of soap.

Fifty boxes of matches.

A small medicine chest.

About a dozen first-aid outfits.

A case of pipes, and cigarettes innumerable.

[Bobby's aunts regarded cigars as not quite ascetic enough for active service. Besides, they might make him sick.]

About a cubic foot of chocolate (various).

Numerous compressed foods and concentrated drinks.

An "active service" cooking outfit.

An electric lamp, with several refills.

A pair of binoculars.

A telescope.

A prismatic compass.

A sparklet siphon.

A luminous watch.

A pair of insulated wire-cutters.

"There's only one thing you've forgotten," remarked Captain Wagstaffe, when introduced to this unique collection of curios.

"What is that?" inquired Bobby, always eager to learn.

"A pantechnicon! Do you known how much personal baggage an officer is allowed, in addition to what he carries himself?"

"Thirty-five pounds."

"Correct."

"It sounds a lot," said Bobby.

"It looks precious little!" was Wagstaffe's reply.

"I suppose they won't be particular to a pound or so," said Bobby optimistically.

"Listen," commanded Wagstaffe. "When we go abroad, your Wolseley valise, containing this"—he swept his hand round the crowded hut—"this military museum, will be handed to the Quartermaster. He is a man of singularly rigid mind, with an exasperating habit of interpreting rules and regulations quite literally. If you persist in this scheme of asking him to pass half a ton of assorted lumber as a package weighing thirty-five pounds, he will cast you forth and remain your enemy for life. And personally," concluded Wagstaffe, "I would rather keep on the right side of my Regimental Quartermaster than of the Commander-in-Chief himself. Now, send all this stuff home—you can use it on manoeuvres in peace-time—and I will give you a little list which will not break the baggage-wagon's back."

The methodical Bobby produced a notebook.

"You will require to wash occasionally. Take a canvas bucket, some carbolic soap, and a good big towel. Also your toothbrush, and—excuse the question, but do you shave?"

"Twice a week," admitted the blushing Bobby.

"Happy man! Well, take a safety-razor. That will do for cleanliness. Now for clothing. Lots of socks, but only one change of other things, unless you care to take a third shirt in your greatcoat pocket. Two good pairs of boots, and a pair of slacks. Then, as regards sleeping. Your flea-bag and your three Government blankets, with your valise underneath, will keep you (and your little bedfellows) as warm as toast. You may get separated from your valise, though, so take a groundsheet in your pack. Then you will be ready to dine and sleep simply anywhere, at a moment's notice. As regards comforts generally, take a 'Tommy's cooker,' if you can find room for it, and scrap all the rest of your cuisine except your canteen. Take a few meat lozenges and some chocolate in one of your ammunition-pouches, in case you ever have to go without your breakfast. Rotten work, marching or fighting on a hollow tummy!"

"What about revolvers?" inquired Bobby, displaying his arsenal, a little nervously.

"If the Germans catch you with that Mauser, they will hang you. Take the Webley. Then you can always draw Service ammunition." Wagstaffe ran his eye over the rest of Bobby's outfit. "Smokes? Take your pipe and a tinder-box: you will get baccy and cigarettes to burn out there. Keep that electric torch; and your binoculars, of course. Also that small map-case: it's a good one. Also wire-cutters. You can write letters in your field-message-book. Your compass is all right. Add a pair of canvas shoes—they're a godsend after a long day,—an air-pillow, some candle-ends, a tin of Vaseline, and a ball of string, and I think you will do. If you find you still have a pound or so in hand, add a few books—something to fall back on, in case supplies fail. Personally, I'm taking 'Vanity Fair' and 'Pickwick.' But then, I'm old-fashioned."

* * * * * * * *

Bobby took Wagstaffe's advice, with the result that that genial obstructionist, the Quartermaster, smiled quite benignly upon him when he presented his valise; while his brother officers, sternly bidden to revise their equipment, were compelled at the last moment to discriminate frantically between the claims of necessity and luxury—often disastrously.

However, we had all found our feet, and developed into seasoned vagabonds when we set out for the trenches last week. A few days previously we had been inspected by Sir John French himself.

"And that," explained Major Kemp to his subalterns, "usually means dirty work at the cross-roads at no very distant period!"

* * * * * * * *

Major Kemp was right—quite literally right.

Our march took us back to Armentieres, whose sufferings under intermittent shell fire have already been described. We marched by night, and arrived at breakfast-time. The same evening two companies and a section of machine-gunners were bidden to equip themselves with picks and shovels and parade at dusk. An hour later we found ourselves proceeding cautiously along a murky road close behind the trenches.

The big guns were silent, but the snipers were busy on both sides. A German searchlight was combing out the heavens above: a constant succession of star-shells illumined the earth beneath.

"What are we going to do to-night, sir?" inquired Bobby Little, heroically resisting an inclination to duck, as a Mauser bullet spat viciously over his head.

"I believe we are going to dig a redoubt behind the trenches," replied Captain Blaikie. "I expect to meet an R.E. officer somewhere about here, and he will tell us the worst. That was a fairly close one, Bobby! Pass the word down quietly that the men are to keep in to each side of the road, and walk as low as they can. Ah, there is our sportsman, I fancy. Good evening!"

A subaltern of that wonderful corps, the Royal Engineers, loomed out of the darkness, removed a cigarette from his mouth, and saluted politely.

"Good evening, sir," he said to Blaikie. "Will you follow me, please? I have marked out each man's digging position with white tape, so they ought to find no difficulty in getting to work. Brought your machine-gun officer?"

The machine-gun officer, Ayling, was called up.

"We are digging a sort of square fort," explained the Engineer, "to hold a battalion. That will mean four guns to mount. I don't know much about machine-guns myself; so perhaps you"—to Ayling—"will walk round with me outside the position, and you can select your own emplacements."

"I shall be charmed," replied Ayling, and Blaikie chuckled.

"I'll just get your infantry to work first," continued the phlegmatic youth. "This way, sir!"

The road at this point ran through a hollow square of trees, and it was explained to the working-party that the trees, roughly, followed the outlines of the redoubt.

"The trenches are about half-finished," added the Engineer. "We had a party from the Seaforths working here last night. Your men have only to carry on where they left off. It's chiefly a matter of filling sandbags and placing them on the parapet." He pointed to a blurred heap in a corner of the wood. "There are fifty thousand there. Leave what you don't want!"

"Where do we get the earth to fill the sandbags?" asked Blaikie. "The trenches, or the middle of the redoubt?"

"Oh, pretty well anywhere," replied the Engineer. "Only, warn your men to be careful not to dig too deep!"

And with this dark saying he lounged off to take Ayling for his promised walk.

"I'll take you along the road a bit, first," he said, "and then we will turn off into the field where the corner of the redoubt is, and you can look at things from the outside."

Ayling thanked him, and stepped somewhat higher than usual, as a bullet struck the ground at his feet.

"Extraordinary how few casualties one gets," continued the Sapper chattily. "Their snipers go potting away all night, but they don't often get anybody. By the way, they have a machine-gun trained on this road, but they only loose it off every second night. Methodical beggars!"

"Did they loose it off last night?"

"No. To-night's the night. Have you finished here!"

"Yes, thanks!"

"Right-o! We'll go to the next corner. You'll get a first-class field of fire there, I should say."

The second position was duly inspected, the only incident of interest being the bursting of a star-shell directly overhead.

"Better lie down for a minute," suggested the Engineer.

Ayling, who had been struggling with a strong inclination to do so for some time, promptly complied.

"Just like the Crystal Palace on a benefit night!" observed his guide admiringly, as the landscape was lit up with a white glare. "Now you can see your position beautifully. You can fire obliquely in this direction, and then do a first-class enfilade if the trenches get rushed."

"I see," said Ayling, surveying the position with real interest. He was beginning to enjoy selecting gun-emplacements which really mattered. It was a change from nine months of "eye-wash."

When the German star-shell had spent itself they crossed the road, to the rear of the redoubt, and marked the other two emplacements—in comparative safety now.

"The only trouble about this place," said Ayling, as he surveyed the last position, "is that my fire will be masked by that house with the clump of trees beside it."

The Engineer produced a small note-book, and wrote in it by the light of a convenient star-shell.

"Right-o!" he said. "I'll have the whole caboodle pushed over for you by to-morrow night. Anything else?"

Ayling began to enjoy himself. After you have spent nine months in an unprofitable attempt to combine practical machine-gun tactics with a scrupulous respect for private property, the realisation that you may now gratify your destructive instincts to the full comes as a welcome and luxurious shock.

"Thanks," he said. "You might flatten out that haystack, too."

* * * * * * * *

They found the others hard at work when they returned. Captain Blaikie was directing operations from the centre of the redoubt.

"I say," he said, as the Engineer sat down beside him, "I'm afraid we're doing a good deal of body-snatching. This place is absolutely full of little wooden crosses."

"Germans," replied the Engineer laconically.

"How long have they been—here?"

"Since October."

"So I should imagine," said Blaikie, with feeling.

"The crosses aren't much guide, either," continued the Engineer. "The deceased are simply all over the place. The best plan is to dig until you come to a blanket. (There are usually two or three to a blanket.) Then tell off a man to flatten down clay over the place at once, and try somewhere else. It is a rotten job, though, however you look at it."

"Have you been here long?" inquired Bobby Little, who had come across the road for a change of air.

"Long enough! But I'm not on duty continuously. I am Box. Cox takes over to-morrow." He rose to his feet and looked at his watch.

"You ought to move off by half-past one, sir," he said to Blaikie. "It begins to get light after that, and the Bosches have three shells for that cross-road over there down in their time-table at two-fifteen. They're a hide-bound lot, but punctual!"

"Thanks," said Blaikie. "I shall not neglect your advice. It is half-past eleven now. Come along, Bobby, and we'll see how old Ayling is getting on."

* * * * * * * *

Steadily, hour by hour, in absolute silence, the work went on. There was no talking, but (under extenuating circumstances) smoking was permitted. Periodically, as the star-shells burst into brilliance overhead, the workers sank down behind a parapet, or, if there was no time, stood rigid—the one thing to avoid upon these occasions is movement of any kind—and gave the snipers a chance. It was not pleasant, but it was duty; and the word duty has become a mighty force in "K(1)" these days. No one was hit, which was remarkable, when you consider what an artist a German sniper is. Possibly the light of the star-shells was deceptive, or possibly there is some truth in the general rumour that the Saxons, who hold this part of the line, are well-disposed towards us, and conduct their offensive operations with a tactful blend of constant firing and bad shooting, which, while it satisfies the Prussians, causes no serious inconvenience to Thomas Atkins.

At a quarter-past one a subdued order ran round the trenches; the men fell in on the sheltered side of the plantation; picks and shovels were checked; rifles and equipment were resumed; and the party stole silently away to the cross-road, where the three shells were timed to arrive at two-fifteen. When they did so, with true Teutonic punctuality, an hour later, our friends were well on their way home to billets and bed—with the dawn breaking behind them, the larks getting to work overhead, and all the infected air of the German graveyard swept out of their lungs by the dew of the morning.

As for that imperturbable philosopher, Box, he sat down with a cigarette, and waited for Cox.

CHAPTER 17
The New Warfare

The trench system has one thing to recommend it. It tidies things up a bit.

For the first few months after the war broke out confusion reigned supreme. Belgium and the north of France were one huge jumbled battlefield, rather like a public park on a Saturday afternoon—one of those parks where promiscuous football is permitted. Friend and foe were inextricably mingled, and the direction of the goal was uncertain. If you rode into a village, you might find it occupied by a Highland regiment or a squadron of Uhlans. If you dimly discerned troops marching side by side with you in the dawning, it was by no means certain that they would prove to be your friends. On the other hand, it was never safe to assume that a battalion which you saw hastily entrenching itself against your approach was German. It might belong to your own brigade. There was no front and no rear, so direction counted for nothing. The country swarmed with troops which had been left "in the air," owing to their own too rapid advance, or the equally rapid retirement of their supporters; with scattered details trying to rejoin their units; or with despatch riders hunting for a peripatetic Divisional Headquarters. Snipers shot both sides impartially. It was all most upsetting.

Well, as already indicated, the trench system has put all that right. The trenches now run continuously—a long, irregular, but perfectly definite line of cleavage—from the North Sea to the Vosges. Everybody has been carefully sorted out—human beings on one side, Germans on the other. ("Like the Zoo," observes Captain Wagstaffe.) Nothing could be more suitable. *You're there, and I'm here, so what do we care?* in fact.

The result is an agreeable blend of war and peace. This week, for instance, our battalion has been undergoing a sort of rest-cure a few miles from the hottest part of the firing line. (We had a fairly heavy spell of work last week.) In the morning we wash our clothes, and perform a few mild martial exercises. In the afternoon we sleep, in all degrees of *deshabille*, under the trees in an orchard. In the evening we play football, or bathe in the canal, or lie on our backs on the grass, watching our aeroplanes buzzing home to roost, attended by German shrapnel. We could not have done this in the autumn. Now, thanks to our trenches, a few miles away, we are as safe here as in the wilds of Argyllshire or West Kensington.

But there are drawbacks to everything. The fact is, a trench is that most uninteresting of human devices, a compromise. It is neither satisfactory as a domicile nor efficient as a weapon of offence. The most luxuriant dug-out; the most artistic window-box—these, in spite of all biased assertions to the contrary, compare unfavourably with a flat in Knightsbridge. On the other hand, the knowledge that you are keeping yourself tolerably immune from the assaults of your enemy is heavily discounted by the fact that the enemy is equally immune from yours. In other words, you "get no forrarder" with a trench; and the one thing which we are all anxious to do out here is to bring this war to a speedy and gory conclusion, and get home to hot baths and regular meals.

So a few days ago we were not at all surprised to be informed, officially, that trench life is to be definitely abandoned, and Hun-hustling to begin in earnest.

(To be just, this decision was made months ago: the difficulty was to put it into execution. The winter weather was dreadful. The enemy were many and we were few. In Germany, the devil's forge at Essen was roaring night and day: in Great Britain Trades Union bosses were carefully adjusting the respective claims of patriotism and personal dignity before taking their coats off. So we cannot lay our want of progress to the charge of that dogged band of Greathearts which has been holding on, and holding on, and holding on—while the people at home were making up for lost time—ever since the barbarian was hurled back from the Marne to the Aisne and confined behind his earthen barrier. We shall win this war one day, and most of the credit will go, as usual, to those who are in at the finish. But—when we assign the glory and the praise, let us not forget those who stood up to the first rush. The new armies which are pouring across the Channel this month will bring us victory in the end. Let us bare our heads, then, in all reverence, to the memory of those battered, decimated, indomitable legions which saved us from utter extinction at the beginning.)

The situation appears to be that if we get through—and no one seems to doubt that we shall: the difficulty lies in staying there when you have got through—we shall be committed at once to an endless campaign of village-fighting. This country is as flat as Cambridgeshire. Every yard of it is under cultivation. The landscape is dotted with farm-steadings. There is a group of cottages or an *estaminet* at every cross-roads. When our great invading line sweeps forward, each one of these buildings will be held by the enemy, and must be captured, house by house, room by room, and used as a base for another rush.

And how is this to be done?

Well, it will be no military secret by the time these lines appear. It is no secret now. The answer to the conundrum is—Bombs!

To-day, out here, bombs are absolutely *dernier cri*. We talk of nothing else. We speak about rifles and bayonets as if they were so many bows and arrows. It is true that the modern Lee-Enfield and Mauser claim to be the most precise and deadly weapons of destruction ever devised. But they were intended for proper, gentlemanly warfare, with the opposing sides set out in straight lines, a convenient distance apart. In the hand-to-hand butchery which calls itself war to-day, the rifle is rapidly becoming *demode*. For long ranges you require machine-guns; for short, bombs and hand-grenades. Can you empty a cottage by firing a single rifle-shot in at the door? Can you exterminate twenty Germans in a fortified back-parlour by a single thrust with a bayonet? Never! But you can do both these things with a jam-tin stuffed with dynamite and scrap-iron.

So the bomb has come to its own, and has brought with it certain changes—tactical, organic, and domestic. To take the last first, the bomb-officer, hitherto a despised underling, popularly (but maliciously) reputed to have been appointed to his present post through inability to handle a platoon, has suddenly attained a position of dazzling eminence. From being a mere super, he has become a star. In fact, he threatens to dispute the pre-eminence of that other regimental parvenu, the Machine-Gun Officer. He is now the confidant of Colonels, and consorts upon terms of easy familiarity with Brigade Majors. He holds himself coldly aloof from the rest of us, brooding over the greatness of his responsibilities; and when he speaks, it is to refer darkly to "detonators," and "primers," and "time-fuses." And we, who once addressed him derisively as "Anarchist," crowd round him and hang upon his lips.

The reason is that in future it is to be a case of—"For every man, a bomb or two"; and it is incumbent upon us, if we desire to prevent these infernal machines from exploding while yet in our custody, to attain the necessary details as to their construction and tender spots by the humiliating process of conciliating the Bomb Officer.

So far as we have mastered the mysteries of the craft, there appear to be four types of bomb in store for us—or rather, for Brother Bosche. They are:—

(1) The hair-brush.

(2) The cricket-ball.

(3) The policeman's truncheon.

(4) The jam-tin.

The hair-brush is very like the ordinary hair-brush, except that the bristles are replaced by a solid block of high-explosive. The policeman's truncheon has gay streamers of tape tied to its tail, to ensure that it falls to the ground nose downwards. Both these bombs explode on impact, and it is unadvisable to knock them against anything—say the back of the trench—when throwing them. The cricket-ball works by a time-fuse. Its manipulation is simplicity itself. The removal of a certain pin releases a spring which lights an internal fuse, timed to explode the bomb in five seconds. You take the bomb in your right hand, remove the pin, and cast the thing madly from you. The jam-tin variety appeals more particularly to the sportsman, as the element of chance enters largely into its successful use. It is timed to explode about ten seconds after the lighting of the fuse. It is therefore unwise to throw it too soon, as there will be ample time for your opponent to pick it up and throw it back. On the other hand, it is unwise to hold on too long, as the fuse is uncertain in its action, and is given to short cuts.

Such is the tactical revolution promised by the advent of the bomb and other new engines of war. As for its effect upon regimental and company organisation, listen to the plaintive voice of Major Kemp:—

"I was once—only a few months ago—commander of a company of two hundred and fifty disciplined soldiers. I still nominally command that company, but they have developed into a heterogeneous mob of specialists. If I detail one of my subalterns to do a job of work, he reminds me that he is a bomb-expert, or a professor of sandbagging, or director of the knuckle-duster section, or Lord High Thrower of Stink-pots, and as such has no time to play about with such a common thing as a platoon. As for the men, they simply laugh in the sergeant-major's face. They are 'experts,' if you please, and are struck off all fatigues and company duty! It was bad enough when Ayling pinched fourteen of my best men for his filthy machine-guns; now, the company has practically degenerated into an academy of variety artists. The only occasion upon which I ever see them all together is payday!"

* * * * * * * *

Meanwhile, the word has just gone forth, quietly and without fuss, that we are to uproot ourselves from our present billets, and be ready to move at 5 A.M. to-morrow morning.

Is this the Big Push at last?

II

We have been waiting for the best part of two days and nights listening to the thunder of the big guns, but as yet we have received no invitation to "butt in."

"Plenty of time yet," explains Captain Blaikie to his subalterns, in reply to Bobby Little's expressions of impatience. "It's this way. We start by 'isolating' a section of the enemy's line, and pound it with artillery for about forty-eight hours. Then the guns knock off, and the people in front rush the German first-line trenches. After that they push on to their second and third lines; and if they can capture and *hold them*—well, that's where the fun comes in. We go for all we are worth through the gaps the others have made, and carry on the big push, and keep the Bosches on the run until they drop in their tracks! That's the situation. If we are called up to-night or to-morrow, it will mean that things are going well. If not, it means that the attack has failed—or, very likely, has succeeded, but it has been found impossible to secure the position—and a lot of good chaps have been scuppered, all for nothing."

Next morning has arrived, and with it the news that our services will not be required. The attack, it appears, was duly launched, and succeeded beyond all expectations. The German line was broken, and report says that four Divisions poured through the gap. They captured the second-line trenches, then the third, and penetrated far into the enemy's rear.

Then—from their front and flanks, artillery and machine-guns opened fire upon them. They were terribly exposed; possibly they had been lured into a trap. At any rate, the process of "isolation" had not been carried far enough. One thing, and only one thing, could have saved them from destruction and their enterprise from disaster—the support of big guns, and big guns, and more big guns. These could have silenced the hostile tornado of shrapnel and bullets, and the position could have been made good.

But—apparently the supply of big-gun ammunition is not quite so copious as it might be. We have only been at war ten months, and people at home are still a little dazed with the novelty of their situation. Out here, we are reasonable men, and we realise that it requires some time to devise a system for supplying munitions which shall hurt the feelings of no pacifist, which shall interfere with no man's holiday or glass of beer, which shall insult no honest toiler by compelling him to work side by side with those who are not of his industrial tabernacle, and which shall imperil no statesman's seat in Parliament. Things will be all right presently.

Meanwhile, the attacking party fell back whence they came—but no longer four full Divisions.

CHAPTER 18

The Front of the Front

We took over these trenches a few days ago; and as the Germans are barely two hundred yards away, this chapter seems to justify its title.

For reasons foreshadowed last month, we find that we are committed to an indefinite period of trench life, like every one else.

Certainly we are starting at the bottom of the ladder. These trenches are badly sited, badly constructed, difficult of access from the rear, and swarming with large, fat, unpleasant flies, of the bluebottle variety. They go to sleep, chiefly upon the ceiling of one's dug-out, during the short hours of darkness, but for twenty hours out of twenty-four they are very busy indeed. They divide their attentions between stray carrion—there is a good deal hereabout—and our rations. If you sit still for five minutes they also settle upon *you*, like pins in a pin-cushion. Then, when face, hands, and knees can endure no more, and the inevitable convulsive wriggle occurs, they rise in a vociferous swarm, only to settle again when the victim becomes quiescent. To these, high-explosives are a welcome relief.

The trenches themselves are no garden city, like those at Armentieres. They were sited and dug in the dark, not many weeks ago, to secure two hundred yards of French territory recovered from the Bosche by bomb and bayonet. (The captured trench lies behind us now, and serves as our second line.) They are muddy—you come to water at three feet—and at one end, owing to their concave formation, are open to enfilade. The parapet in many places is too low. If you make it higher with sandbags you offer the enemy a comfortable target: if you deepen the trench you turn it into a running stream. Therefore long-legged subalterns crawl painfully past these danger-spots on all-fours, envying Little Tich.

Then there is Zacchaeus. We call him by this name because he lives up a tree. There is a row of pollarded willows standing parallel to our front, a hundred and fifty yards away. Up, or in, one of these lives Zacchaeus. We have never seen him, but we know he is there; because if you look over the top of the parapet he shoots you through the head. We do not even know which of the trees he lives in. There are nine of them, and every morning we comb them out, one by one, with a machine-gun. But all in vain. Zacchaeus merely crawls away into the standing corn behind his trees, and waits till we have finished. Then he comes back and tries to shoot the machine-gun officer. He has not succeeded yet, but he sticks to his task with gentle persistence. He is evidently of a persevering rather than vindictive disposition.

Then there is Unter den Linden. This celebrated thoroughfare is an old communication-trench. It runs, half-ruined, from the old German trench in our rear, right through our own front line, to the present German trenches. It constitutes such a bogey as the Channel Tunnel scheme once was: each side sits jealously at its own end, anticipating hostile enterprises from the other. It is also the residence of "Minnie." But we will return to Minnie later.

The artillery of both sides, too, contributes its mite. There is a dull roar far in the rear of the German trenches, followed by a whirring squeak overhead. Then comes an earth-shaking crash a mile behind us. We whip round, and there, in the failing evening light, against the sunset, there springs up the silhouette of a mighty tree in full foliage. Presently the silhouette disperses, drifts away, and—

"The coals is hame, right enough!" comments Private Tosh.

Instantly our guns reply, and we become the humble spectators of an artillery duel. Of course, if the enemy gets tired of "searching" the countryside for our guns and takes to "searching" our trenches instead, we lose all interest in the proceedings, and retire to our dug-outs, hoping that no direct hits will come our way.

But guns are notoriously erratic in their time-tables, and fickle in their attentions. It is upon Zacchaeus and Unter den Linden—including Minnie—that we mainly rely for excitement.

As already recorded, we took over these trenches a few days ago, in the small hours of the morning. In the ordinary course of events, relieving parties are usually able to march up under cover of darkness to the reserve trench, half a mile in rear of the firing line, and so proceed to their appointed place. But on this occasion the German artillery happened to be "distributing coal" among the billets behind. This made it necessary to approach our new home by tortuous ways, and to take to subterranean courses at a very early stage of the journey. For more than two hours we toiled along a trench just wide enough to permit a man to wear his equipment, sometimes bent double to avoid the bullets of snipers, sometimes knee-deep in glutinous mud.

Ayling, leading a machine-gun section who were burdened with their weapons and seven thousand rounds of ammunition, mopped his steaming brow and inquired of his guide how much farther there was to go.

"Abart two miles, sir," replied the youth with gloomy satisfaction. He was a private of the Cockney regiment whom we were relieving; and after the manner of his kind, would infinitely have preferred to conduct us down half a mile of a shell-swept road, leading straight to the heart of things, than waste time upon an uninteresting but safe *detour.*

At this Ayling's Number One, who was carrying a machine-gun tripod weighing forty-eight pounds, said something—something distressingly audible—and groaned deeply.

"If we'd come the way I wanted," continued the guide, much pleased with the effect of his words upon his audience, "we'd a' been there be now. But the Adjutant, 'e says to me—"

"If we had come the way you wanted," interrupted Ayling brutally, "we should probably have been in Kingdom Come by now. Hurry up!" Ayling, in common with the rest of those present, was not in the best of tempers, and the loquacity of the guide had been jarring upon him for some time.

The Cockney private, with the air of a deeply-wronged man, sulkily led on, followed by the dolorous procession. Another ten minutes' laboured progress brought them to a place where several ways met.

"This is the beginning of the reserve trenches, sir," announced the guide. "If we'd come the way I—"

"Lead on!" said Ayling, and his perspiring followers murmured threatening applause.

The guide, now in his own territory, selected the muddiest opening and plunged down it. For two hundred yards or so he continued serenely upon his way, with the air of one exhibiting the metropolis to a party of country cousins. He passed numerous turnings. Then, once or twice, he paused irresolutely; then moved on. Finally he halted, and proceeded to climb out of the trench.

"What are you doing?" demanded Ayling suspiciously.

"We got to cut across the open 'ere, sir," said the youth glibly. "Trench don't go no farther. Keep as low as you can."

With resigned grunts the weary pilgrims hoisted themselves and their numerous burdens out of their slimy thoroughfare, and followed their conductor through the long grass in single file, feeling painfully conspicuous against the whitening sky. Presently they discovered, and descended into, another trench—all but the man with the tripod, who descended into it before he discovered it—and proceeded upon their dolorous way. Once more the guide, who had been refreshingly but ominously silent for some time, paused irresolutely.

"Look here, my man," said Ayling, "do you, or do you not, know where you are?"

The paragon replied hesitatingly:—

"Well, sir, if we'd come by the way I—"

Ayling took a deep breath, and though conscious of the presence of formidable competitors, was about to make the best of an officer's vocabulary, when a kilted figure loomed out of the darkness.

"Hallo! Who are you?" inquired Ayling.

"This iss the Camerons' trenches, sirr," replied a polite West Highland voice. "What trenches wass you seeking?"

Ayling told him.

"They are behind you, sirr."

"I was just goin' to say, sir," chanted the guide, making one last effort to redeem his prestige, "as 'ow—"

"Party," commanded Ayling, "about turn!"

Having received details of the route from the friendly Cameron, he scrambled out of the trench and crawled along to what was now the head of the procession. A plaintive voice followed him.

"Beg pardon, sir, where shall *I* go now?"

Ayling answered the question explicitly, and moved off, feeling much better. The late conductor of the party trailed disconsolately in the rear.

"I should like to know wot I'm 'ere for," he murmured indignantly.

He got his answer, like a lightning-flash.

"For tae carry *this*," said the man with the tripod, turning round. "Here, caatch!"

The day's work in trenches begins about nine o'clock the night before. Darkness having fallen, various parties steal out into the no-man's-land beyond the parapet. There are numerous things to be done. The barbed wire has been broken up by shrapnel, and must be repaired. The whole position in front of the wire must be patrolled, to prevent the enemy from creeping forward in the dark. The corn has grown to an uncomfortable height in places, so a fatigue party is told off to cut it—surely the strangest species of harvesting that the annals of agriculture can record. On the left front the muffled clinking of picks and shovels announces that a "sap" is in course of construction: those incorrigible night-birds, the Royal Engineers, are making it for the machine-gunners, who in the fullness of time will convey their voluble weapon to its forward extremity, and "loose off a belt or two" in the direction of a rather dangerous hollow midway between the trenches, from which of late mysterious sounds of digging and guttural talking have been detected by the officer who lies in the listening-post, in front of our barbed-wire entanglement, drawing secrets from the bowels of the earth by means of a microphone.

Behind the firing trench even greater activity prevails. Damage done to the parapet by shell fire is being repaired. Positions and emplacements are being constantly improved, communication trenches widened or made more secure. Down these trenches fatigue parties are filing, to draw rations and water and ammunition from the limbered wagons which are waiting in the shadow of a wood, perhaps a mile back. It is at this hour, too, that the wounded, who have been lying pathetically cheerful and patient in the dressing-station in the reserve trench, are smuggled to the Field Ambulance—probably to find themselves safe in a London hospital within twenty-four hours. Lastly, under the kindly cloak of night, we bury our dead.

Meanwhile, within various stifling dug-outs, in the firing trench or support-trench, overheated company commanders are dictating reports or filling in returns. (Even now the Round Game Department is not entirely shaken off.) There is the casualty return, and a report on the doings of the enemy, and another report of one's own doings, and a report on the direction of the wind, and so on. Then there are various indents to fill up—scrawled on a wobbly writing-block with a blunt indelible pencil by the light of a guttering candle—for ammunition, and sandbags, and revetting material.

All this literature has to be sent to Battalion Headquarters by one A.M., either by orderly or telephone. There it is collated and condensed, and forwarded to the Brigade, which submits it to the same process and sends it on, to be served up piping hot and easily digestible at the breakfast-table of the Division, five miles away, at eight o'clock.

You must not imagine, however, that all this night-work is performed in gross darkness. On the contrary. There is abundance of illumination; and by a pretty thought, each side illuminates the other. We perform our nocturnal tasks, in front of and behind the firing trench, amid a perfect hail of star-shells and magnesium lights, topped up at times by a searchlight—all supplied by our obliging friend the Hun. We, on our part, do our best to return these graceful compliments.

The curious and uncanny part of it all is that there is no firing. During these brief hours there exists an informal truce, founded on the principle of live and let live. It would be an easy business to wipe out that working-party, over there by the barbed wire, with a machine-gun. It would be child's play to shell the road behind the enemy's trenches, crowded as it must be with ration-wagons and water-carts, into a blood-stained wilderness. But so long as each side confines itself to purely defensive and recuperative work, there is little or no interference. That slave of duty, Zacchaeus, keeps on pegging away; and occasionally, if a hostile patrol shows itself too boldly, there is a little exuberance from a machine-gun; but on the whole there is silence. After all, if you prevent your enemy from drawing his rations, his remedy is simple: he will prevent you from drawing yours. Then both parties will have to fight on empty stomachs, and neither of them, tactically, will be a penny the better. So, unless some elaborate scheme of attack is brewing, the early hours of the night are comparatively peaceful. But what is that sudden disturbance in the front-line trench? A British rifle rings out, then another, and another, until there is an agitated fusillade from end to end of the section. Instantly the sleepless host across the way replies, and for three minutes or so a hurricane rages. The working parties out in front lie flat on their faces, cursing patiently. Suddenly the storm dies away, and perfect silence reigns once more. It was a false alarm. Some watchman, deceived by the whispers of the night breeze, or merely a prey to nerves, has discerned a phantom army approaching through the gloom, and has opened fire thereon. This often occurs when troops are new to trench-work.

It is during these hours, too, that regiments relieve one another in the trenches. The outgoing regiment cannot leave its post until the incoming regiment has "taken over." Consequently you have, for a brief space, two thousand troops packed into a trench calculated to hold one thousand. Then it is that strong men swear themselves faint, and the Rugby football player has reason to be thankful for his previous training in the art of "getting through the scrum." However perfect your organisation may be, congestion is bound to occur here and there; and it is no little consolation to us to feel, as we surge and sway in the darkness, that over there in the German lines a Saxon and a Prussian private, irretrievably jammed together in a narrow communication trench, are consigning one another to perdition in just the same husky whisper as that employed by Private Mucklewame and his "opposite number" in the regiment which has come to relieve him.

These "reliefs" take place every four or five nights. There was a time, not so long ago, when a regiment was relieved, not when it was weary, but when another regiment could be found to replace it. Our own first battalion once remained in the trenches, unrelieved and only securing its supplies with difficulty, for five weeks and three days. During all that time they were subject to most pressing attentions on the part of the Bosches, but they never lost a yard of trench. They received word from Headquarters that to detach another regiment for their relief would seriously weaken other and most important dispositions. The Commander-in-Chief would therefore be greatly obliged if they could hold on. So they held on.

At last they came out, and staggered back to billets. Their old quarters, naturally, had long been appropriated by other troops, and the officers had some difficulty in recovering their kits.

"I don't mind being kept in trenches for several weeks," remarked their commander to the staff officer who received him when he reported, "and I can put up with losing my sleeping-bag; but I do object to having my last box of cigars looted by the blackguards who took over our billets!"

The staff officer expressed sympathy, and the subject dropped. But not many days later, while the battalion were still resting, their commander was roused in the middle of the night from the profound slumber which only the experience of many nights of anxious vigil can induce, by the ominous message:—

"An orderly to see you, from General Headquarters, sir!"

The colonel rolled stoically out of bed, and commanded that the orderly should be brought before him.

The man entered, carrying, not a despatch, but a package, which he proffered with a salute.

"With the Commander-in-Chief's compliments, sir!" he announced.

The package was a box of cigars!

But that was before the days of "K(1)."

But the night is wearing on. It is half-past one—time to knock off work. Tired men, returning from ration-drawing or sap-digging, throw themselves down and fall dead asleep in a moment. Only the sentries, with their elbows on the parapet, maintain their sleepless watch. From behind the enemy's lines comes a deep boom—then another. The big guns are waking up again, and have decided to commence their day's work by speeding our empty ration-wagons upon their homeward way. Let them! So long as they refrain from practising direct hits on our front-line parapet, and disturbing our brief and hardly-earned repose, they may fire where they please. The ration train is well able to look after itself.

"A whiff o' shrapnel will dae nae harrm to thae strawberry-jam pinchers!" observes Private Tosh bitterly, rolling into his dug-out. By this opprobrious term he designates that distinguished body of men, the Army Service Corps. A prolonged diet of plum-and-apple jam has implanted in the breasts of the men in the trenches certain dark and unworthy suspicions concerning the entire altruism of those responsible for the distribution of the Army's rations.

* * * * * * * *

It is close on daybreak, and the customary whispered order runs down the stertorous trench:—

"Stand to arms!"

Straightway the parapets are lined with armed men; the waterproof sheets which have been protecting the machine-guns from the dews of night are cast off; and we stand straining our eyes into the whitening darkness.

This is the favourite hour for attack. At any moment the guns may open fire upon our parapet, or a solid wall of grey-clad figures rise from that strip of corn-land less than a hundred yards away, and descend upon us. Well, we are ready for them. Just by way of signalising the fact, there goes out a ragged volley of rifle fire, and a machine-gun rips off half a dozen bursts into the standing corn. But apparently there is nothing doing this morning. The day grows brighter, but there is no movement upon the part of Brother Bosche.

But—what is that light haze hanging over the enemy's trenches? It is slight, almost impalpable, but it appears to be drifting towards us. Can it be—?

Next moment every man is hurriedly pulling his gas helmet over his head, while Lieutenant Waddell beats a frenzied tocsin upon the instrument provided for the purpose—to wit, an empty eighteen-pounder shell, which, suspended from a bayonet stuck into the *parados* (or back wall) of the trench, makes a most efficient alarm-gong. The sound is repeated all along the trench, and in two minutes every man is in his place, cowled like a member of the Holy Inquisition, glaring through an eyepiece of mica, and firing madly into the approaching wall of vapour.

But the wall approaches very slowly—in fact, it almost stands still—and finally, as the rising sun disentangles itself from a pink horizon and climbs into the sky, it begins to disappear. In half an hour nothing is left, and we take off our helmets, sniffing the morning air dubiously. But all we smell is the old mixture—corpses and chloride of lime.

The incident, however, was duly recorded by Major Kemp in his report of the day's events, as follows:—

4.07 a.m.—*Gas alarm, false. Due either to morning mist, or the fact that enemy found breeze insufficient, and discontinued their attempt.*

"Still, I'm not sure," he continued, slapping his bald head with a bandana handkerchief, "that a whiff of chlorine or bromine wouldn't do these trenches a considerable amount of good. It would tone down some of the deceased a bit, and wipe out these infernal flies. Waddell, if I give you a shilling, will you take it over to the German trenches and ask them to drop it into the meter?"

"I do not think, sir," replied the literal Waddell, "that an English shilling would fit a German meter. Probably a mark would be required, and I have only a franc. Besides, sir, do you think that—"

"Surgical operation at seven-thirty, sharp!" intimated the major to the medical officer, who entered the dug-out at that moment. "For our friend here"—indicating the bewildered Waddell. "Sydney Smith's prescription! Now, what about breakfast?"

* * * * * * * *

About nine o'clock the enemy indulges in what is usually described, most disrespectfully, as "a little morning hate"—in other words, a bombardment. Beginning with a *hors d'oeuvre* of shrapnel along the reserve trench—much to the discomfort of Headquarters, who are shaving—he proceeds to "search" a tract of woodland in our immediate rear, his quarry being a battery of motor machine-guns, which has wisely decamped some hours previously. Then, after scientifically "traversing" our second line, which has rashly advertised its position and range by cooking its breakfast over a smoky fire, he brings the display to a superfluous conclusion by dropping six "Black Marias" into the deserted ruins of a village not far behind us. After that comes silence; and we are able, in our hot, baking trenches, assisted by clouds of bluebottles, to get on with the day's work.

This consists almost entirely in digging. As already stated, these are bad trenches. The parapet is none too strong—at one point it has been knocked down for three days running—the communication trenches are few and narrow, and there are not nearly enough dug-outs. Yesterday three men were wounded; and owing to the impossibility of carrying a stretcher along certain parts of the trench, they had to be conveyed to the rear in their ground-sheets—bumped against projections, bent round sharp corners, and sometimes lifted, perforce, bodily into view of the enemy. So every man toils with a will, knowing full well that in a few hours' time he may prove to have been his own benefactor. Only the sentries remain at the parapets. They no longer expose themselves, as at night, but take advantage of the laws of optical reflection, as exemplified by the trench periscope. (This, in spite of its grand title, is nothing but a tiny mirror clipped on to a bayonet.)

At half-past twelve comes dinner—bully-beef, with biscuit and jam—after which each tired man, coiling himself up in the trench, or crawling underground, according to the accommodation at his disposal, drops off into instant and heavy slumber. The hours from two till five in the afternoon are usually the most uneventful of the twenty-four, and are therefore devoted to hardly-earned repose.

But there is to be little peace this afternoon. About half-past three, Bobby Little, immersed in pleasant dreams—dreams of cool shades and dainty companionship—is brought suddenly to the surface of things by—

"Whoo-oo-*oo*-oo-UMP!"

—followed by a heavy thud upon the roof of his dug-out. Earth and small stones descend in a shower upon him.

"Dirty dogs!" he comments, looking at his watch. Then he puts his head out of the dug-out.

"Lie close, you men!" he cries. "There's more of this coming. Any casualties?"

The answer to the question is obscured by another burst of shrapnel, which explodes a few yards short of the parapet, and showers bullets and fragments of shell into the trench. A third and a fourth follow. Then comes a pause. A message is passed down for the stretcher-bearers. Things are growing serious. Five minutes later Bobby, having despatched his wounded to the dressing-station, proceeds with all haste to Captain Blaikie's dug-out.

"How many, Bobby?"

"Six wounded. Two of them won't last as far as the rear, I'm afraid, sir."

Captain Blaikie looks grave.

"Better ring up the Gunners, I think. Where are the shells coming from?"

"That wood on our left front, I think."

"That's P 27. Telephone orderly, there?"

A figure appears in the doorway.

"Yes, sirr."

"Ring up Major Cavanagh, and say that H 21 is being shelled from P 27. Retaliate!"

"Verra good, sirr."

The telephone orderly disappears, to return in five minutes.

"Major Cavanagh's compliments, sirr, and he is coming up himself for tae observe from the firing trench."

"Good egg!" observes Captain Blaikie. "Now we shall see some shooting, Bobby!"

Presently the Gunner major arrives, accompanied by an orderly, who pays out wire as he goes. The major adjusts his periscope, while the orderly thrusts a metal peg into the ground and fits a telephone receiver to his head.

"Number one gun!" chants the major, peering into his periscope; "three-five-one-nothing—lyddite—fourth charge!"

These mystic observations are repeated into the telephone by the Cockney orderly, in a confidential undertone.

"Report when ready!" continues the major.

"Report when ready!" echoes the orderly. Then—"Number one gun ready, sir!"

"Fire!"

"Fire!" Then, politely—"Number one has fired, sir."

The major stiffens to his periscope, and Bobby Little, deeply interested, wonders what has become of the report of the gun. He forgets that sound does not travel much faster than a thousand feet a second, and that the guns are a mile and a half back. Presently, however, there is a distant boom. Almost simultaneously the lyddite shell passes overhead with a scream. Bobby, having no periscope, cannot see the actual result of the shot, though he tempts Providence (and Zacchaeus) by peering over the top of the parapet.

"Number one, two-nothing minutes more right," commands the major. "Same range and charge."

Once more the orderly goes through his ritual, and presently another shell screams overhead.

Again the major observes the result.

"Repeat!" he says. "Nothing-five seconds more right."

This time he is satisfied.

"Parallel lines on number one," he commands crisply. "One round battery fire—twenty seconds!"

For the last time the order is passed down the wire, and the major hands his periscope to the ever-grateful Bobby, who has hardly got his eyes to the glass when the round of battery fire commences. One—two—three—four—the avenging shells go shrieking on their way, at intervals of twenty seconds. There are four muffled thuds, and four great columns of earth and *debris* spring up before the wood. Answer comes there none. The offending battery has prudently effaced itself.

"Cease fire!" says the major, "and register!" Then he turns to Captain Blaikie. "That'll settle them for a bit," he observes. "By the way, had any more trouble with Minnie?"

"We had Hades from her yesterday," replies Blaikie, in answer to this extremely personal question. "She started at a quarter-past five in the morning, and went on till about ten."

(Perhaps, at this point, it would be as well to introduce Minnie a little more formally. She is the most unpleasant of her sex, and her full name is *Minenwerfer*, or German trench-mortar. She resides, spasmodically, in Unter den Linden. Her extreme range is about two hundred yards, so she confines her attentions to front-line trenches. Her *modus operandi* is to discharge a large cylindrical bomb into the air. The bomb, which is about fifteen inches long and some eight inches in diameter, describes a leisurely parabola, performing grotesque somersaults on the way, and finally falls with a soft thud into the trench, or against the parapet. There, after an interval of ten seconds, Minnie's offspring explodes; and as she contains about thirty pounds of dynamite, no dug-out or parapet can stand against her.)

"Did she do much damage?" inquires the Gunner.

"Killed two men and buried another. They were in a dug-out."

The Gunner shakes his head.

"No good taking cover against Minnie," he says. "The only way is to come out into the open trench, and dodge her."

"So we found," replies Blaikie. "But they pulled our legs badly the first time. They started off with three 'whizz-bangs'"—a whizz-bang is a particularly offensive form of shell which bursts two or three times over, like a Chinese cracker—"so we all took cover and lay low. The consequence was that Minnie was able to send her little contribution along unobserved. The filthy thing fell short of the trench, and exploded just as we were all getting up again. It smashed up three or four yards of parapet, and scuppered the three poor chaps I mentioned."

"Have you located her?"

"Yes. Just behind that stunted willow, on our left front. I fancy they bring her along there to do her bit, and then trot her back to billets, out of harm's way. She is their two o'clock turn—two a.m. and two p.m."

"Two o 'clock turn—h'm!" says the Gunner major meditatively. "What about our chipping in with a one-fifty-five turn—half a dozen H E shells into Minnie's dressing-room—eh? I must think this over."

"Do!" said Blaikie cordially. "Minnie is Willie's Worst Werfer, and the sooner she is put out of action the better for all of us. To-day, for some reason, she failed to appear, but previous to that she has not failed for five mornings in succession to batter down the same bit of our parapet."

"Where's that?" asks the major, getting out a trench-map.

"P 7—a most unhealthy spot. Minnie pushes it over about two every morning. The result is that we have to mount guard over the breach all day. We build everything up again at night, and Minnie sits there as good as gold, and never dreams of interfering. You can almost hear her cooing over us. Then, as I say, at two o'clock, just as the working party comes in and gets under cover, she lets slip one of her disgusting bombs, and undoes the work of about four hours. It was a joke at first, but we are getting fed up now. That's the worst of the Bosche. He starts by being playful; but if not suppressed at once, he gets rough; and that, of course, spoils all the harmony of the proceedings. So I cordially commend your idea of the one-fifty-five turn, sir."

"I'll see what can be done," says the major. "I think the best plan would be a couple of hours' solid frightfulness, from every battery we can switch on. To-morrow afternoon, perhaps, but I'll let you know. You'll have to clear out of this bit of trench altogether, as we shall shoot pretty low. So long!"

* * * * * * * *

It is six o'clock next evening, and peace reigns over our trench. This is the hour at which one usually shells aeroplanes—or rather, at which the Germans shell ours, for their own seldom venture out in broad daylight. But this evening, although two or three are up in the blue, buzzing inquisitively over the enemy's lines, their attendant escort of white shrapnel puffs is entirely lacking. Far away behind the German lines a house is burning fiercely.

"The Hun is a bit *piano* tonight," observes Captain Blaikie, attacking his tea.

"The Hun has been rather firmly handled this afternoon," replies Captain Wagstaffe. "I think he has had an eye-opener. There are no flies on our Divisional Artillery."

Bobby Little heaved a contented sigh. For two hours that afternoon he had sat, half-deafened, while six-inch shells skimmed the parapet in both directions, a few feet above his head. The Gunner major had been as good as his word. Punctually at one-fifty-five "Minnie's" two o'clock turn had been anticipated by a round of high-explosive shells directed into her suspected place of residence. What the actual result had been nobody knew, but Minnie had made no attempt to raise her voice since. Thereafter the German front-line trenches had been "plastered" from end to end, while the trenches farther back were attended to with methodical thoroughness. The German guns had replied vigorously, but directing only a passing fire at the trenches, had devoted their efforts chiefly to the silencing of the British artillery. In this enterprise they had been remarkably unsuccessful.

"Any casualties?" asked Blaikie.

"None here," replied Wagstaffe. "There may be some back in the support trenches."

"We might telephone and inquire."

"No good at present. The wires are all cut to pieces. The signallers are repairing them now."

"*I* was nearly a casualty," confessed Bobby modestly.

"How?"

"That first shell of ours nearly knocked my head off! I was standing up at the time, and it rather took me by surprise. It just cleared the *parados*. In fact, it kicked a lot of gravel into the back of my neck."

"Most people get it in the neck here, sooner or later," remarked Captain Blaikie sententiously. "Personally, I don't much mind being killed, but I do bar being buried alive. That is why I dislike Minnie so." He rose, and stretched himself. "Heigho! I suppose it's about time we detailed patrols and working parties for to-night. What a lovely sky! A truly peaceful atmosphere—what? It gives one a sort of Sunday-evening feeling, somehow."

"May I suggest an explanation?" said Wagstaffe.

"By all means."

"It *is* Sunday evening!"

Captain Blaikie whistled gently, and said—

"By Jove, so it is." Then, after a pause: "This time last Sunday—"

Last Sunday had been an off-day—a day of cloudless summer beauty. Tired men had slept; tidy men had washed their clothes; restless men had wandered at ease about the countryside, careless of the guns which grumbled everlastingly a few miles away. There had been impromptu Church Parades for each denomination, in the corner of a wood which was part of the demesne of a shell-torn chateau.

It is a sadly transformed wood. The open space before the chateau, once a smooth expanse of tennis-lawn, is now a dusty picketing-ground for transport mules, destitute of a single blade of grass. The ornamental lake is full of broken bottles and empty jam-tins. The pagoda-like summer-house, so inevitable to French chateau gardens, is a quartermaster's store. Half the trees have been cut down for fuel. Still, the July sun streams very pleasantly through the remainder, and the Psalms of David float up from beneath their shade quite as sweetly as they usually do from the neighbourhood of the precentor's desk in the kirk at home—perhaps sweeter.

The wood itself is a *point d'appui*, or fortified post. One has to take precautions, even two or three miles behind the main firing line. A series of trenches zigzags in and out among the trees, and barbed wire is interlaced with the undergrowth. In the farthermost corner lies an improvised cemetery. Some of the inscriptions on the little wooden crosses are only three days old. Merely to read a few of these touches the imagination and stirs the blood. Here you may see the names of English Tommies and Highland Jocks, side by side with their Canadian kith and kin. A little apart lie more graves, surmounted by epitaphs written in strange characters, such as few white men can read. These are the Indian troops. There they lie, side by side—the mute wastage of war, but a living testimony, even in their last sleep, to the breadth and unity of the British Empire. The great, machine-made Empire of Germany can show no such graves: when her soldiers die, they sleep alone.

The Church of England service had come last of all. Late in the afternoon a youthful and red-faced chaplain had arrived on a bicycle, to find a party of officers and men lying in the shade of a broad oak waiting for him. (They were a small party: naturally, the great majority of the regiment are what the identity-discs call "Pres" or "R.C.")

"Sorry to be late, sir," he said to the senior officer, saluting. "This is my sixth sh—service to-day, and I have come seven miles for it."

He mopped his brow cheerfully; and having produced innumerable hymn-books from a saddle-bag and set his congregation in array, read them the service, in a particularly pleasing and well-modulated voice. After that he preached a modest and manly little sermon, containing references which carried Bobby Little, for one, back across the Channel to other scenes and other company. After the sermon came a hymn, sung with great vigour. Tommy loves singing hymns—when he happens to know and like the tune.

"I know you chaps like hymns," said the padre, when they had finished. "Let's have another before you go. What do you want?"

A most unlikely-looking person suggested "Abide with Me." When it was over, and the party, standing as rigid as their own rifles, had sung "God Save the King," the preacher announced, awkwardly—almost apologetically—

"If any of you would like to—er—communicate, I shall be very glad. May not have another opportunity for some time, you know. I think over there"—he indicated a quiet corner of the wood, not far from the little cemetery—"would be a good place."

He pronounced the benediction, and then, after further recurrence to his saddle-bag, retired to his improvised sanctuary. Here, with a ration-box for altar, and strands of barbed wire for choir-stalls, he made his simple preparations.

Half a dozen of the men, and all the officers, followed him. That was just a week ago.

* * * * * * * *

Captain Wagstaffe broke the silence at last.

"It's a rotten business, war," he said pensively—"when you come to think of it. Hallo, there goes the first star-shell! Come along, Bobby!"

Dusk had fallen. From the German trenches a thin luminous thread stole up into the darkening sky, leaned over, drooped, and burst into dazzling brilliance over the British parapet. Simultaneously a desultory rifle fire crackled down the lines. The night's work had begun.

CHAPTER 19

The Trivial Round

We have been occupying trenches, off and on, for a matter of two months, and have settled down to an unexhilarating but salutary routine. Each dawn we "stand to arms," and peer morosely over the parapet, watching the grey grass turn slowly to green, while snipers' bullets buzz over our heads. Each forenoon we cleanse our dew-rusted weapons, and build up with sandbags what the persevering Teuton has thrown down. Each afternoon we creep unostentatiously into subterranean burrows, while our respective gunners, from a safe position in the rear, indulge in what they humorously describe as "an artillery duel." The humour arises from the fact that they fire, not at one another, but at us. It is as if two big boys, having declared a vendetta, were to assuage their hatred and satisfy their honour by going out every afternoon and throwing stones at one another's little brothers. Each evening we go on sentry duty; or go out with patrols, or working parties, or ration parties. Our losses in killed and wounded are not heavy, but they are regular. We would not grudge the lives thus spent if only we could advance, even a little. But there is nothing doing. Sometimes a trench is rushed here, or recaptured there, but the net result is—stalemate.

The campaign upon which we find ourselves at present embarked offers few opportunities for brilliancy. One wonders how Napoleon would have handled it. His favourite device, we remember, was to dash rapidly about the chessboard, insert himself between two hostile armies, and defeat them severally. But how can you insert yourself between two armies when you are faced by only one army—an army stretching from Ostend to the Alps?

One of the first elements of successful strategy is surprise. In the old days, a general of genius could outflank his foe by a forced march, or lay some ingenious trap or ambush. But how can you outflank a foe who has no flanks? How can you lay an ambush for the modern Intelligence Department, with its aeroplane reconnaissance and telephonic nervous system? Do you mass half a million men at a chosen point in the enemy's line? Straightway the enemy knows all about it, and does likewise. Each morning General Headquarters of each side finds upon its breakfast-table a concise summary of the movements of all hostile troops, the disposition of railway rolling-stock—yea, even aeroplane photographs of it all. What could Napoleon himself have done under the circumstances? One is inclined to suspect that that volcanic megalomaniac would have perished of spontaneous combustion of the brain.

However, trench life has its alleviations. There is The Day's Work, for instance. Each of us has his own particular "stunt," in which he takes that personal and rather egotistical pride which only increasing proficiency can bestow.

The happiest—or at least, the busiest—people just now are the "Specialists." If you are engaged in ordinary Company work, your energies are limited to keeping watch, dodging shells, and improving trenches. But if you are what is invidiously termed an "employed" man, life is full of variety.

Do you observe that young officer sitting on a ration-box at his dug-out door, with his head tied up in a bandage? That is Second Lieutenant Lochgair, whom I hope to make better known to you in time. He is a chieftain of high renown in his own inaccessible but extensive fastness; but out here, where every man stands on his own legs, and not his grandfather's, he is known simply as "Othello." This is due to the fact that Major Kemp once likened him to the earnest young actor of tradition, who blacked himself all over to ensure proficiency in the playing of that part. For he is above all things an enthusiast in his profession. Last night he volunteered to go out and "listen" for a suspected mine some fifty yards from the German trenches. He set out as soon as darkness fell, taking with him a biscuit-tin full of water. A circular from Headquarters—one of those circulars which no one but Othello would have treated with proper reverence—had suggested this device. The idea was that, since liquids convey sound better than air, the listener should place his tin of water on the ground, lie down beside it, immerse one ear therein, and so draw secrets from the earth. Othello failed to locate the mine, but kept his head in the biscuit-tin long enough to contract a severe attack of earache.

But he is not discouraged. At present he is meditating a design for painting himself grass-green and climbing a tree—thence to take a comprehensive and unobserved survey of the enemy's dispositions. He will do it, too, if he gets a chance!

The machine-gunners, also, contrive to chase monotony by methods of their own. Listen to Ayling, concocting his diurnal scheme of frightfulness with a colleague. Unrolled upon his knee is a large-scale map.

"I think we might touch up those cross-roads to-night," he says, laying the point of his dividers upon a spot situated some hundreds of yards in rear of the German trenches.

"I expect they'll have lots of transport there about ration-time—eh?"

"Sound scheme," assents his coadjutor, a bloodthirsty stripling named Ainslie. "Got the bearings?"

"Hand me that protractor. Seventy-one, nineteen, true. That comes to"—Ayling performs a mental calculation—"almost exactly eighty-five, magnetic. We'll go out about nine, with two guns, to the corner of this dry ditch here—the range is two thousand five hundred, exactly"—

"Our lightning calculator!" murmurs his admiring colleague. "No elastic up the sleeve, or anything! All done by simple *ledger-de-mang*? Proceed!"

"And loose off a belt or two. What say?"

"Application forwarded, and strongly recommended," announced Ainslie. He examined the map. "Cross-roads—eh? That means at least one estaminet. One estaminet, with Bosches inside, complete! Think of our little bullets all popping in through the open door, five hundred a minute! Think of the rush to crawl under the counter! It might be a Headquarters? We might get Von Kluck or Rupy of Bavaria, splitting a half litre together. We shall earn Military Crosses over this, my boy," concluded the imaginative youth. "Wow, wow!"

"The worst of indirect fire," mused the less gifted Ayling, "is that you never can tell whether you have hit your target or not. In fact, you can't even tell whether there was a target there to hit."

"Never mind; we'll chance it," replied Ainslie. "And if the Bosche artillery suddenly wakes up and begins retaliating on the wrong spot with whizz-bangs—well, we shall know we've tickled up *somebody*, anyhow! Nine o'clock, you say?"

* * * * * * * *

Here, again, is a bombing party, prepared to steal out under cover of night. They are in charge of one Simson, recently promoted to Captain, supported by that hoary fire-eater, Sergeant Carfrae. The party numbers seven all told, the only other member thereof with whom we are personally acquainted being Lance-Corporal M'Snape, the ex-Boy Scout. Every man wears a broad canvas belt full of pockets: each pocket contains a bomb.

Simson briefly outlines the situation. Our fire-trench here runs round the angle of an orchard, which brings it uncomfortably close to the Germans. The Germans are quite as uncomfortable about the fact as we are—some of us are rather inclined to overlook this important feature of the case—and they have run a sap out towards the nearest point of the Orchard Trench (so our aeroplane observers report), in order to supervise our movements more closely.

"It may only be a listening-post," explains Simson to his bombers, "with one or two men in it. On the other hand, they may be collecting a party to rush us. There are some big shell-craters there, and they may be using one of them as a saphead. Anyhow, our orders are to go out to-night and see. If we find the sap, with any Germans in it, we are to bomb them out of it, and break up the sap as far as possible. Advance, and follow me."

The party steals out. The night is very still, and a young and inexperienced moon is making a somewhat premature appearance behind the Bosche trenches. The ground is covered with weedy grass—disappointed hay—which makes silent progress a fairly simple matter. The bombers move forward in extended order searching for the saphead. Simson, in the centre, pauses occasionally to listen, and his well-drilled line pauses with him. Sergeant Carfrae calls stertorously upon the left. Out on the right is young M'Snape, tingling.

They are half-way across now, and the moon is marking time behind a cloud.

Suddenly there steals to the ears of M'Snape—apparently from the recesses of the earth just in front of him—a deep, hollow sound, the sound of men talking in some cavernous space. He stops dead, and signals to his companions to do likewise. Then he listens again. Yes, he can distinctly hear guttural voices, and an occasional *clink, clink*. The saphead has been reached, and digging operations are in progress.

A whispered order comes down the line that M'Snape is to "investigate." He wriggles forward until his progress is arrested by a stunted bush. Very stealthily he rises to his knees and peers over. As he does so, a chance star-shell bursts squarely over him, and comes sizzling officiously down almost on to his back. His head drops like a stone into the bush, but not before the ghostly magnesium flare has shown him what he came out to see—a deep shell-crater. The crater is full of

Germans. They look like grey beetles in a trap, and are busy with pick and shovel, apparently "improving" the crater and connecting it with their own fire-trenches. They have no sentry out. *Dormitat Homerus.*

M'Snape worms his way back, and reports. Then, in accordance with an oft-rehearsed scheme, the bombing party forms itself into an arc of a circle at a radius of some twenty yards from the stunted bush. (Not the least of the arts of bomb-throwing is to keep out of range of your own bombs.) Every man's hand steals to his pocketed belt. Next moment Simson flings the first bomb. It flies fairly into the middle of the crater.

Half a dozen more go swirling after it. There is a shattering roar; a cloud of smoke; a muffled rush, of feet; silence; some groans. Almost simultaneously the German trenches are in an uproar. A dozen star-shells leap to the sky; there is a hurried outburst of rifle fire; a machine-gun begins to patter out a stuttering malediction.

Meanwhile our friends, who have exhibited no pedantic anxiety to remain and behold the result of their labours, are lying upon their stomachs in a convenient fold in the ground, waiting patiently until such time as it shall be feasible to complete their homeward journey.

Half an hour later they do so, and roll one by one over the parapet into the trench. Casualties are slight. Private Nimmo has a bullet-wound in the calf of his leg, and Sergeant Carfrae, whom Nature does not permit to lie as flat as the others, will require some repairs to the pleats of his kilt.

"All present?" inquires Simson.

It is discovered that M'Snape has not returned. Anxious eyes peer over the parapet. The moon is stronger now, but it is barely possible to distinguish objects clearly for more than a few yards.

A star-shell bursts, and heads sink below the parapet. A German bullet passes overhead, with a sound exactly like the crack of a whip. Silence and comparative darkness return. The heads go up again.

"I'll give him five minutes more, and then go and look for him," says Simson. "Hallo!"

A small bush, growing just outside the barbed wire, rises suddenly to its feet; and, picking its way with incredible skill through the nearest opening, runs at full speed for the parapet. Next moment it tumbles over into the trench.

Willing hands extracted M'Snape from his arboreal envelope—he could probably have got home quite well without it, but once a Boy Scout, always a Boy Scout—and he made his report.

"I went back to have a look-see into the crater, sirr."

"Well?"

"It's fair blown in, sirr, and a good piece of the sap too. I tried could I find a prisoner to bring in"—our Colonel has promised a reward of fifty francs to the man who can round up a whole live Bosche—"but there were nane. They had got their wounded away, I doubt."

"Never mind," says Simson. "Sergeant, see these men get some sleep now. Stand-to at two-thirty, as usual. I must go and pitch in a report, and I shall say you all did splendidly. Good-night!"

This morning, the official Intelligence Summary of our Division—published daily and known to the unregenerate as "Comic Cuts"—announced, with solemn relish, among other items of news:—

Last night a small party bombed a suspected saphead at—here followed the exact bearings of the crater on the large-scale map. *Loud groans were heard, so it is probable that the bombs took effect.*

For the moment, life has nothing more to offer to our seven friends.

* * * * * * * *

As already noted, our enthusiasm for our own sphere of activity is not always shared by our colleagues. For instance, we in the trenches frequently find the artillery of both sides unduly obtrusive; and we are of opinion that in trench warfare artillery practice should be limited by mutual consent to twelve rounds per gun per day, fired by the gunners *at* the gunners. "Except, of course, when the Big Push comes." The Big Push is seldom absent from our thoughts in these days.

"That," observed Captain Wagstaffe to Bobby Little, "would leave us foot-sloggers to settle our own differences. My opinion is that we should do so with much greater satisfaction to ourselves if we weren't constantly interfered with by coal-boxes and Black Marias."

"Still, you can't blame them for loosing off their big guns," contended the fair-minded Bobby. "It must be great sport."

"They tell me it's a greatly overrated amusement," replied Wagstaffe—"like posting an insulting letter to some one you dislike. You see, you aren't there when he opens it at breakfast next morning! The only man of them who gets any fun is the Forward Observing Officer. And he," concluded Wagstaffe in an unusual vein of pessimism, "does not live long enough to enjoy it!"

The grievances of the Infantry, however, are not limited to those supplied by the Royal Artillery. There are the machine-guns and the trench-mortars.

The machine-gunner is a more or less accepted nuisance by this time. He has his own emplacements in the line, but he never appears to use them. Instead, he adopts the peculiar expedient of removing his weapon from a snug and well-fortified position, and either taking it away somewhere behind the trenches and firing salvoes over your head (which is reprehensible), or planting it upon the parapet in your particular preserve, and firing it from there (which is criminal). Machine-gun fire always provokes retaliation.

"Why in thunder can't you keep your filthy tea-kettle in its own place, instead of bringing it here to draw fire?" inquired Mr. Cockerell, not altogether unreasonably, as Ayling and his satellites passed along the trench bearing the offending weapon, with water-jacket aboil, back to its official residence.

"It is all for your good, my little man," explained Ayling loftily. "It would never do to give away one's real gun positions. If we did, the Bosches would sit tight and say nothing at the time, but just make a note of the occurrence. Then, one fine morning, when they *really* meant business, they would begin by dropping a Black Maria on top of each emplacement; and where would you and your platoon be then, with an attack coming on and *us* out of action? So long!"

But the most unpopular man in the trenches is undoubtedly the Trench Mortar Officer. His apparatus consists of what looks like a section of rain-pipe, standing on legs. Upon its upturned muzzle is poised a bomb, having the appearance of a plum-pudding on a stick. This he discharges over the parapet into the German trenches, where it causes a comforting explosion. He then walks rapidly away.

For obvious reasons, it is not advisable to fire a trench-mortar too often—at any rate from the same place. But the whole weight of public opinion in our trench is directed against it being fired from anywhere at all. Behold the Trench Mortar Officer and his gang of pariahs creeping stealthily along in the lee of the parados, just as dawn breaks, in the section of trench occupied by No. 10 Platoon. For the moment they are unheeded, for the platoon are "standing-to," and the men are lined along the firing-step, with their backs to the conspirators.

On reaching a suitable spot, the mortar party proceed to erect their apparatus with as little ostentation as possible. But they are soon discovered. The platoon subaltern hurries up.

"Awfully sorry, old man," he says breathlessly, "but the C.O. gave particular orders that this part of the trench was on no account to be used for trench-mortar fire. You see, we are only about seventy yards from the Bosche trenches here—"

"I know," explains the T.M.O.; "that is why I came."

"But it is most important," continues the platoon commander, still quoting glibly from an entirely imaginary mandate of the C.O., "that no retaliatory shell fire should be attracted here. Most serious for the whole Brigade, if this bit of parapet got pushed over. Now, there's a topping place about ten traverses away. You can lob them over from there beautifully. Come along."

And with fair words and honeyed phrases he elbows the dispirited band to a position—for his platoon—of comparative inoffensiveness.

The Trench Mortar Officer drifts on, and presently, with the uneasy assurance of the proprietor of a Punch-and-Judy show who has inadvertently strayed into Park Lane, attempts once more to give his unpopular entertainment. This time his shrift is even shorter, for he encounters Major Kemp—never at his sunniest in the small hours of the morning.

Field officers have no need to employ the language of diplomacy when dealing with subalterns.

"No, you *don't*, my lad!" announces the Major. "Not if I can help it! Take it away! Take your darned liver-pill out of this! Burn, it! Bury it! Eat it! But not here! Creep away!"

The abashed procession complies. This time they find a section of trench in charge of a mere corporal. Here, before any one of sufficient standing can be summoned to deal with the situation, the Trench Mortar Officer seizes his opportunity, and discharges three bombs over the parapet. He then retires defiantly to his dug-out.

But it is an Ishmaelitish existence.

* * * * * * * *

So much for the alleviations which professional enthusiasm bestows. Now for a few alleviations proper. These are Sleep, Food, and Literature.

Sleep is the rarest of these. We seldom get more than a few hours at a time; but it is astonishing how readily one learns to slumber in unlikely surroundings—upon damp earth, in cramped positions, amid ceaseless noise, in clothes and boots that have not been removed for days. One also acquires the priceless faculty of losing no time in dropping off.

As for food, we grumble at times, just as people at home are grumbling at the Savoy, or Lockhart's. It is the Briton's habit so to do. But in moments of repletion we are fain to confess that the organisation of our commissariat is wonderful. Of course the quality of the *menu* varies, according to the immunity of the communication-trenches from shell fire, or the benevolence of the Quartermaster and the mysterious powers behind him, or the facilities for cooking offered by the time and place in which we find ourselves. No large fires are permitted: the smoke would give too good a ranging-mark to Minnie and her relatives. Still, it is surprising how quickly you can boil a canteen over a few chips. There is also, for those who can afford half-a-crown, that invaluable contrivance, "Tommy's Cooker"; and occasionally we get a ration of coke. When times are bad, we live on bully, biscuit, cheese, and water, strongly impregnated with chloride of lime. The water is conveyed to us in petrol-tins—the old familiar friends, Shell and Pratt—hundreds of them. Motorists at home must be feeling the shortage. In normal times we can reckon on plenty of hot, strong tea; possibly some bread; probably an allowance of bacon and jam. And sometimes, when the ration parties arrive, mud-stained and weary, in the dead of night, and throw down their bursting sacks, our eyes feast upon such revelations as tinned butter, condensed milk, raisins, and a consignment of that great chieftain of the ration race, The Maconochie of Maconochie. On these occasions Private Mucklewame collects his share, retires to his kennel, and has a gala-day.

Thirdly, the blessings of literature. Our letters arrive at night, with the rations. The mail of our battalion alone amounts to eight or ten mail-bags a day; from which you may gather some faint idea of the labours of our Field Post Offices. There are letters, and parcels, and newspapers. Letters we may pass over. They are featureless things, except to their recipient. Parcels have more individuality. Ours are of all shapes and sizes, and most of them are astonishingly badly tied. It is quite heartrending to behold a kilted exile endeavouring to gather up a heterogeneous mess of socks, cigarettes, chocolate, soap, shortbread, and Edinburgh rock, from the ruins of what was once a flabby and unstable parcel, but is now a few skimpy rags of brown paper, which have long escaped the control of a most inadequate piece of string—a monument of maternal lavishness and feminine economy.

Then there are the newspapers. We read them right through, beginning at the advertisements and not skipping even the leading articles. Then, when we have finished, we frequently read them right through again. They serve three purposes. They give us information as to how the War is progressing—we get none here, the rank and file, that is; they serve to pass the time; and they afford us topics for conversation. For instance, they enable us to follow and discuss the trend of home politics. And in this connection, I think it is time you were introduced to Captain Achille Petitpois. (That is not his real name, but it is as near to it as most of us are likely to get.) He is one of that most efficient body, the French *liaison* officers, who act as connecting-link between the Allied Forces, and naturally is an accomplished linguist. He is an ardent admirer of British institutions, but is occasionally not a little puzzled by their complexity. So he very sensibly comes to people like Captain Wagstaffe for enlightenment, and they enlighten him.

Behold Achille—a guest in A Company's billet—drinking whisky-and-sparklet out of an aluminium mug, and discussing the news of the day.

"And your people at home," he said, "you think they are taking the War seriously?" (Achille is addicted to reading the English newspapers without discrimination.)

"So seriously," replied Wagstaffe instantly, "that it has become necessary for the Government to take steps to cheer them up."

"Comment?" inquired Achille politely.

For answer Wagstaffe picked up a three-day-old London newspaper, and read aloud an extract from the Parliamentary report. The report dealt faithfully with the latest antics of the troupe of eccentric comedians which appears (to us), since the formation of the Coalition Government, to have taken possession of the front Opposition Bench.

"Who are these assassins—these imbeciles—these *cretins*," inquired Petitpois, "who would endanger the ship of the State?" (Achille prides himself upon his knowledge of English idiom.)

"Nobody knows!" replied Wagstaffe solemnly. "They are children of mystery. Before the War, nobody had ever heard of them. They—"

"But they should be shot!" explained that free-born Republican, Petitpois.

"Not a bit, old son! That is where you fail to grasp the subtleties of British statesmanship. I tell you there are no flies on our Cabinet!"

"Flies?"

"Yes: *mouches*, you know. The agility of our Cabinet Ministers is such that these little insects find it impossible to alight upon them."

"Your Ministers are athletes—yes," agreed Achille comprehendingly. "But the—"

"Only intellectually. What I mean is that they are a very downy collection of old gentlemen—"

Achille, murmuring something hazy about "Downing Street," nodded his head.

"—And when they came into power, they knew as well as anything that after three weeks or so the country would begin to grouse—"

"Grouse? A sporting bird?" interpolated Achille.

"Exactly. They knew that the country would soon start giving them the bird—"

"What bird? The grouse?"

"Oh, dry up, Wagger!" interposed Blaikie. "He means, Petitpois, that the Government, knowing that the electorate would begin to grow impatient if the War did not immediately take a favourable turn—"

Achille smiled.

"I see now," he said. "Proceed, Ouagstaffe, my old!"

"In other words," continued the officer so addressed, "the Government decided that if they gave the Opposition half a chance to get together, and find leaders, and consolidate their new trenches, they might turn them out."

"*Bien*," assented Achille. Every one was listening now, for Wagstaffe as a politician usually had something original to say.

"Well," proceeded Wagstaffe, "they saw that the great thing to do was to prevent the Opposition from making an impression on the country—from being taken too seriously, in fact. So what did they do? They said: 'Let's arrange for a *comic* Opposition—an Opposition *pour rire*, you know. They will make the country either laugh or cry. Anyhow, the country will be much too busy deciding which to do to have any time to worry about *us*; so we shall have a splendid chance to get on with the War.' So they sent down the Strand—that's where the Variety agents foregather, I believe—what you call *entrepreneurs*, Achille—and booked this troupe, complete, for the run of the War. They did the thing in style; spared no expense; and got a comic newspaper proprietor to write the troupe up, and themselves down. The scheme worked beautifully—what you would call a *succes fou*, Achille."

"I am desolated, my good Ouagstaffe," observed Petitpois after a pregnant silence; "but I cannot believe all you say."

"I *may* be wrong," admitted Wagstaffe handsomely, "but that's my reading of the situation. At any rate, Achille, you will admit that my theory squares with the known facts of the case."

Petitpois bowed politely.

"Perhaps it is I who am wrong, my dear Ouagger. There is such a difference of point of view between your politics and ours."

The deep voice of Captain Blaikie broke in.

"If Lancashire," he said grimly, "were occupied by a German army, as the Lille district is to-day, I fancy there would be a considerable levelling up of political points of view all round. No limelight for a comic opposition then, Achille, old son!"

* * * * * * * *

Besides receiving letters, we write them. And this brings us to that mysterious and impalpable despot, the Censor.

There is not much mystery about him really. Like a good many other highly placed individuals, he deputes as much of his work as possible to someone else—in this case that long-suffering maid-of-all-work, the company officer. Let us track Bobby Little to his dug-out, during one of those numerous periods of enforced retirement which occur between the hours of three and six, "Pip Emma"—as our friends the "buzzers" call the afternoon. On the floor of this retreat (which looks like a dog-kennel and smells like a vault) he finds a small heap of letters, deposited there for purposes of what the platoon-sergeant calls "censure." These have to be read (which is bad); licked up (which is far worse); signed on the outside by the officer, and forwarded to Headquarters. Here they are stamped with the familiar red triangle and forwarded to the Base, where they are supposed to be scrutinised by the real Censor—i.e., the gentleman who is paid for the job—and are finally despatched to their destination.

Bobby, drawing his legs well inside the kennel, out of the way of stray shrapnel bullets, begins his task.

The heap resolves itself into three parts. First come the post-cards, which give no trouble, as their secrets are written plain for all to see. There are half a dozen or so of the British Army official issue, which are designed for the benefit of those who lack the epistolatory gift—what would a woman say if you offered such things to her?—and bear upon the back the following printed statements:—

I am quite well.
I have been admitted to hospital.
I am sick ☐ *and am going on well. Wounded* ☐ *and hope to be discharged soon.*
I have received your ☐ *letter, dated ....,* ☐ *telegram,* ☐ *parcel.*
Letter follows at first opportunity.
I have received no letter from you ☐ *lately.* ☐ *for a long time.*

(The gentleman who designed this postcard must have been a descendant of Sydney Smith. You remember that great man's criticism of the Books of Euclid? He preferred the Second Book, on the ground that it was more "impassioned" than the others!)

All the sender of this impassioned missive has to do is to delete such clauses as strike him as untruthful or over-demonstrative, and sign his name. He is not allowed to add any comments of his own. On this occasion, however, one indignant gentleman has pencilled the ironical phrase, "I don't think!" opposite the line which acknowledges the receipt of a parcel. Bobby lays this aside, to be returned to the sender.

Then come some French picture post-cards. Most of these present soldiers—soldiers posing, soldiers exchanging international handgrips, soldiers grouped round a massive and *decolletee* lady in flowing robes, and declaring that *La patrie sera libre!* Underneath this last, Private Ogg has written: "Dear Lizzie,—I hope this finds you well as it leaves me so. I send you a French p.c. The writing means long live the Queen of France."

The next heap consists of letters in official-looking green envelopes. These are already sealed up, and the sender has signed the following attestation, printed on the flap: *I certify on my honour that the contents of this envelope refer to nothing but private and family matters.* Setting aside a rather bulky epistle addressed to The Editor of a popular London weekly, which advertises a circulation of over a million copies—a singularly unsuitable recipient for correspondence of a private and family nature—Bobby turns to the third heap, and sets to work upon his daily task of detecting items of information, "which if intercepted or published might prove of value to the enemy."

It is not a pleasant task to pry into another person's correspondence, but Bobby's scruples are considerably abated by the consciousness that on this occasion he is doing so with the writer's full knowledge. Consequently it is a clear case of *caveat scriptor.* Not that Bobby's flock show any embarrassment at the prospect of his scrutiny. Most of them write with the utmost frankness, whether they are conducting a love affair, or are involved in a domestic broil of the most personal nature. In fact, they seem rather to enjoy having an official audience. Others cheerfully avail themselves of this opportunity of conveying advice or reproof to those above them, by means of what the Royal Artillery call "indirect fire." Private Dunshie remarks: "We have been getting no pay these three weeks, but I doubt the officer will know what has become of the money." It is the firm conviction of every private soldier in "K(1)" that all fines and deductions go straight into the pocket of the officer who levies them. Private Hogg, always an optimist, opines: "The officers should know better how to treat us now, for they all get a read of our letters."

But, as recorded above, the outstanding feature of this correspondence is an engaging frankness. For instance, Private Cosh, who under an undemonstrative, not to say wooden, exterior evidently conceals a heart as inflammable as flannelette, is conducting single-handed no less than four parallel love affairs. One lady resides in his native Coatbridge, the second is in service in South Kensington, the third serves in a shop in Kelvinside, and the fourth moth appears to have been attracted to this most unlikely candle during our sojourn in winter billets in Hampshire. Cosh writes to them all most ardently every week—sometimes oftener—and Bobby Little, as he ploughs wearily through repeated demands for photographs, and touching protestations of lifelong affection, curses the verbose and susceptible youth with all his heart.

But this mail brings him a gleam of comfort.

So you tell me, Chrissie, writes Cosh to the lady in South Kensington, *that you are engaged to be married on a milkman....*

("Thank heaven!" murmurs Bobby piously.)

No, no, Chrissie, you need not trouble yourself. It is nothing to me.

("He's as sick as muck!" comments Bobby.)

All I did before was in friendship's name.

("Liar!")

Bobby, thankfully realising that his daily labours will be materially lightened by the withdrawal of the fickle Chrissie from the postal arena, ploughs steadily through the letters. Most of them begin in accordance with some approved formula, such as—

It is with the greatest of pleasure that I take up my pen—

It is invariably a pencil, and a blunt one at that.

Crosses are ubiquitous, and the flap of the envelope usually bears the mystic formula, S.W.A.K. This apparently means "Sealed with a kiss," which, considering that the sealing is done not by the writer but by the Censor, seems to take a good deal for granted.

Most of the letters acknowledge the receipt of a "parcle"; many give a guarded summary of the military situation.

We are not allowed to tell you about the War, but I may say that we are now in the trenches. We are all in the pink, and not many of the boys has gotten a dose of lead-poisoning yet.

It is a pity that the names of places have to be left blank. Otherwise we should get some fine phonetic spelling. Our pronunciation is founded on no pedantic rules. Armentieres is *Armentears*, *Busnes* is Business, Bailleul is *Booloo*, and Vieille Chapelle is *Veal Chapel.*

The chief difficulty of the writers appears to be to round off their letters gracefully. *Having no more to say, I will now draw to a close*, is the accepted formula. Private Burke, never a tactician, concludes a most ardent love-letter thus: "*Well, Kate, I will now close, as I have to write to another of the girls.*"

But to Private Mucklewame literary composition presents no difficulties. Here is a single example of his terse and masterly style:—

> *Dere wife, if you could make the next postal order a trifle stronger, I might get getting an egg to my tea.—Your loving husband,*
> Jas. Mucklewame, *No.* 74077.

But there are features of this multifarious correspondence over which one has no inclination to smile. There are wistful references to old days; tender inquiries after bairns and weans; assurances to anxious wives and mothers that the dangers of modern warfare are merely nominal. There is an almost entire absence of boasting or lying, and very little complaining. There is a general and obvious desire to allay anxiety. We are all "fine"; we are all "in the pink." "This is a grand life."

Listen to Lance-Corporal M'Snape: *Well, mother, I got your parcel, and the things was most welcome; but you must not send any more. I seen a shilling stamp on the parcel: that is too much for you to afford.* How many officers take the trouble to examine the stamp on their parcels?

And there is a wealth of homely sentiment and honest affection which holds up its head without shame even in the presence of the Censor. One rather pathetic screed, beginning: *Well, wife, I doubt this will be a poor letter, for I canna get one of they green envelopes to-day, but I'll try my best*—Bobby Little sealed and signed without further scrutiny.

* * * * * * * *

One more picture, to close the record of our trivial round.

It is a dark, moist, and most unpleasant dawn. Captain Blaikie stands leaning against a traverse in the fire-trench, superintending the return of a party from picket duty. They file in, sleepy and dishevelled, through an archway in the parapet, on their way to dug-outs and repose. The last man in the procession is Bobby Little, who has been in charge all night.

Our line here makes a sharp bend round the corner of an orchard, and for security's sake a second trench has been cut behind, making, as it were, the cross-bar of a capital A. The apex of the A is no health resort. Brother Bosche, as already explained, is only fifty yards away, and his trench-mortars make excellent practice with the parapet. So the Orchard Trench is only occupied at night, and the alternative route, which is well constructed and comparatively safe, is used by all careful persons who desire to proceed from one arm of the A to the other.

The present party are the night picket, thankfully relinquishing their vigil round the apex.

Bobby Little remained to bid his company-commander good-morning at the junction of the two trenches.

"Any casualties?" An invariable question at this spot. "No, sir. We were lucky. There was a lot of sniping."

"It's a rum profession," mused Captain Blaikie, who was in a wakeful mood.

"In what way, sir?" inquired the sleepy but respectful Bobby.

"Well"—Captain Blaikie began to fill his pipe—"who takes about nine-tenths of the risk, and does practically all the hard work in the Army? The private and the subaltern—you and your picket, in fact. Now, here is the problem which has puzzled me ever since I joined the Army, and I've had nineteen years' service. The farther away you remove the British soldier from the risk of personal injury, the higher you pay him. Out here, a private of the line gets about a shilling a day. For that he digs, saps, marches, and fights like a hero. The motor-transport driver gets six shillings a day, no danger, and lives like a fighting cock. The Army Service Corps drive about in motors, pinch our rations, and draw princely incomes. Staff Officers are compensated for their comparative security by extra cash, and first chop at the war medals. Now—why?"

"I dare say they would sooner be here, in the trenches, with us," was Bobby's characteristic reply.

Blaikie lit his pipe—it was almost broad daylight now—and considered.

"Yes," he agreed—"perhaps. Still, my son, I can't say I have ever noticed Staff Officers crowding into the trenches (as they have a perfect right to do) at four o'clock in the morning. And I can't say I altogether blame them. In fact, if ever I do meet one performing such a feat, I shall say: 'There goes a sahib—and a soldier!' and I shall take off my hat to him."

"Well, get ready now," said Bobby. "Look!"

They were still standing at the trench junction. Two figures, in the uniform of the Staff, were visible in Orchard Trench, working their way down from the apex—picking their steps amid the tumbled sandbags, and stooping low to avoid gaps in the ruined parapet. The sun was just rising behind the German trenches. One of the officers was burly and middle-aged; he did not appear to enjoy bending double. His companion was slight, fair-haired, and looked incredibly young. Once or twice he glanced over his shoulder, and smiled encouragingly at his senior.

The pair emerged through the archway into the main trench, and straightened their backs with obvious relief. The younger officer—he was a lieutenant—noticed Captain Blaikie, saluted him gravely, and turned to follow his companion.

Captain Blaikie did not take his hat off, as he had promised. Instead, he stood suddenly to attention, and saluted in return, keeping his hand uplifted until the slim, childish figure had disappeared round the corner of a traverse.

It was the Prince of Wales.

Chapter 20
The Gathering of the Eagles

When this war is over, and the glory and the praise are duly assigned, particularly honourable mention should be made of the inhabitants of a certain ancient French town with a Scottish name, which lies not far behind a particularly sultry stretch of the trenches. The town is subject to shell fire, as splintered walls and shattered windows testify; yet every shop stands open. The town, moreover, is the only considerable place in the district, and enjoys a monopoly of patronage from all the surrounding billeting areas; yet the keepers of the shops have heroically refrained from putting up their prices to any appreciable extent. This combination of courage and fair-dealing has had its reward. The town has become a local Mecca. British soldiers with an afternoon to spare and a few francs to spend come in from miles around. Mess presidents send in their mess-sergeants, and fearful and wonderful is the marketing which ensues.

In remote and rural billets catering is a simple matter. We take what we can get, and leave it at that. The following business-card, which Bobby Little once found attached to an outhouse door in one of his billets, puts the resources of a French hamlet into a nutshell:

HERE SMOKING ROM BEER WINE WITHE RAID COFFE EGS

But in town the shopper has a wider range. Behold Sergeant Goffin, a true-born Londoner, with the Londoner's faculty of never being at a loss for a word, at the grocer's, purchasing comforts for our officers' mess.

"*Bong jooer*, Mrs. Pankhurst!" he observes breezily to the plump *epiciere*. This is his invariable greeting to French ladies who display any tendency to volubility—and they are many.

"Bon jour, M'sieu le Caporal!" replies the *epiciere*, smiling. *«M'sieu le Caporal desire?»*

The sergeant allows his reduction in rank to pass unnoticed. He does not understand the French tongue, though he speaks it with great fluency and incredible success. He holds up a warning hand.

"Now, keep your 'and off the tap of the gas-meter for one minute *if* you please," he rejoins, "and let me get a word in edgeways. I want"—with great emphasis—"*vinblank* one, *vinrooge* two, *bogeys* six, *Dom* one. *Compree*?"

By some miracle the smiling lady does *compree*, and produces white wine, red wine, candles, and—a bottle of Benedictine! (Sergeant Goffin always names wines after the most boldly printed word upon the label. He once handed round some champagne, which he insisted on calling "a bottle of brute.")

"Combine?" is the next observation.

The *epiciere* utters the series of short sharp sibilants of which all French numerals appear to be composed. It sounds like *"song-song-song."* The resourceful Goffin lays down a twenty-franc note.

"Take it out of that," he says grandly.

He receives his change, and counts it with a great air of wisdom. The *epiciere* breaks into a rapid recital—it sounds rather like our curate at home getting to work on *When the wicked man*—of the beauty and succulence of her other wares. Up goes Goffin's hand again.

"Na pooh!" he exclaims.. "Bong jooer!" And he stumps out to the mess-cart.

"Na pooh!" is a mysterious but invaluable expression. Possibly it is derived from *"Il n'y a plus."* It means, "All over!" You say "Na pooh!" when you push your plate away after dinner. It also means, "Not likely!" or "Nothing doing!" By a further development it has come to mean "done for," "finished," and in extreme cases, "dead." "Poor Bill got na-poohed by a rifle-grenade yesterday," says one mourner to another. The Oxford Dictionary of the English Language will have to be revised and enlarged when this war is over.

* * * * * * * *

Meanwhile, a few doors away, a host of officers is sitting in the Cafe de la Terre. Cafes are as plentiful as blackberries in this, as in most other French provincial towns, and they are usually filled to overflowing with privates of the British Army heroically drinking beer upon which they know it is impossible to get intoxicated. But the proprietor of the Cafe de la Terre is a long-headed citizen. By the simple expedient of labelling his premises "Officers Only," and making a minimum charge of one franc per drink, he has at a single stroke ensured the presence of the *elite* and increased his profits tenfold.

Many arms of the Service are grouped round the little marble-topped tables, for the district is stiff with British troops, and promises to grow stiffer. In fact, so persistently are the eagles gathering together upon this, the edge of the fighting line, that rumour is busier than ever. The Big Push holds redoubled sway in our thoughts. The First Hundred Thousand are well represented, for the whole Scottish Division is in the neighbourhood. Beside the glengarries there are countless flat caps—line regiments, territorials, gunners, and sappers. The Army Service Corps is there in force, recruiting exhausted nature from the strain of dashing about the countryside in motor-cars. The R.A.M.C. is strongly represented, doubtless to test the purity of the refreshment provided. Even the Staff has torn itself away from its arduous duties for the moment, as sundry red tabs testify. In one corner sit four stout French civilians, playing a mysterious card-game.

At the very next table we find ourselves among friends. Here are Major Kemp, also Captain Blaikie. They are accompanied by Ayling, Bobby Little, and Mr. Waddell. The battalion came out of trenches yesterday, and for the first time found itself in urban billets. For the moment haylofts and wash-houses are things of the dim past. We are living in real houses, sleeping in real beds, some with sheets.

To this group enters unexpectedly Captain Wagstaffe.

"Hallo, Wagger!" says Blaikie. "Back already?"

"Your surmise is correct," replies Wagstaffe, who has been home on leave. "I got a wire yesterday at lunch-time—in the Savoy, of all places! Every one on leave has been recalled. We were packed like herrings on the boat. *Garcon, biere*—the *brunette* kind!"

"Tell us all about London," says Ayling hungrily. "What does it look like? Tell us!"

We have been out here for the best part of five months now. Leave opened a fortnight ago, amid acclamations—only to be closed again within a few days. Wagstaffe was one of the lucky few who slipped through the blessed portals. He now sips his beer and delivers his report.

"London is much as usual. A bit rattled over Zeppelins—they have turned out even more street lamps—but nothing to signify. Country districts crawling with troops. All the officers appear to be colonels. Promotion at home is more rapid than out here. Chin, chin!" Wagstaffe buries his face in his glass mug.

"What is the general attitude," asked Mr. Waddell, "towards the war?"

"Well, one's own friends are down in the dumps. Of course it's only natural, because most of them are in mourning. Our losses are much more noticeable at home than abroad, somehow. People seemed quite surprised when I told them that things out here are as right as rain, and that our troops are simply tumbling over one another, and that we don't require any comic M.P.'s sent out to cheer us up. The fact is, some people read the papers too much. At the present moment the London press is, not to put too fine a point on it, making a holy show of itself. I suppose there's some low-down political rig at the back of it all, but the whole business must be perfect jam for the Bosches in Berlin."

"What's the trouble?" inquired Major Kemp.

"Conscription, mostly. (Though why they should worry their little heads about it, I don't know. If K. wants it we'll have it: if not, we won't; so that's that!) Both sides are trying to drag the great British Public into the scrap by the back of the neck. The Conscription crowd, with whom one would naturally side if they would play the game, seem to be out to unseat the Government as a preliminary. They support their arguments by stating that the British Army on the Western front is reduced to a few platoons, and that they are allowed to fire one shell per day. At least, that's what I gathered."

"What do the other side say?" inquired Kemp.

"Oh, theirs is a very simple line of argument. They state, quite simply, that if the personal liberty of Britain's workers—that doesn't mean you and me, as you might think: we are the Overbearing Militarist Oligarchy: a worker is a man who goes on strike,—they say that if the personal liberty of these sacred perishers is interfered with by the Overbearing Militarist Oligarchy aforesaid, there will be a Revolution. That's all! Oh, they're a sweet lot, the British newspaper bosses!"

"But what," inquired that earnest seeker after knowledge, Mr. Waddell, "is the general attitude of the country at large upon this grave question?"

Captain Wagstaffe chuckled.

"The dear old country at large," he replied, "is its dear old self, as usual. It is not worrying one jot about Conscription, or us, or anything like that. The one topic of conversation at present is—Charlie Chaplin."

"Who is Charlie Chaplin?" inquired several voices.

Wagstaffe shook his head.

"I haven't the faintest idea," he said. "All I know is that you can't go anywhere in London without running up against him. He is It. The mention of his name in a *revue* is greeted with thunders of applause. At one place I went to, twenty young men came upon the stage at once, all got up as Charlie Chaplin."

"But who *is* he?"

"That I can't tell you. I made several attempts to find out; but whenever I asked the question people simply stared at me in amazement. I felt quite ashamed: it was plain that I ought to have known. I have a vague idea that he is some tremendous new boss whom the Government have appointed to make shells, or something. Anyhow, the great British Nation is far too much engrossed with Charles to worry about a little thing like Conscription. Still, I should like to know. I feel I have been rather unpatriotic about it all."

"I can tell you," said Bobby Little. "My servant is a great admirer of his. He is the latest cinema star. Falls off roofs, and gets run over by motors—"

"And keeps the police at bay with a fire-hose," added Wagstaffe. "That's him! I know the type. Thank you, Bobby!"

Major Kemp put down his glass with a gentle sigh, and rose to go.

"We are a great nation," he remarked contentedly. "I was a bit anxious about things at home, but I see now there was nothing to worry about. We shall win all right. Well, I am off to the Mess. See you later, everybody!"

"Meanwhile," inquired Wagstaffe, as the party settled down again, "what is brewing here! I haven't seen the adjutant yet."

"You'll see him soon enough," replied Blaikie grimly. He glanced over his shoulder towards the four civilian card-players. They looked bourgeois enough and patriotic enough, but it is wise to take no risks in a cafe, as a printed notice upon the war, signed by the Provost-Marshal, was careful to point out. "Come for a stroll," he said.

Presently the two captains found themselves in a shady boulevard leading to the outskirts of the town. Darkness was falling, and soon would be intense; for lights are taboo in the neighbourhood of the firing line.

"Have we finished that new trench in front of our wire?" asked Wagstaffe.

"Yes. It is the best thing we have done yet. Divisional Headquarters are rightly pleased about it."

Blaikie gave details. The order had gone forth that a new trench was to be constructed in front of our present line—a hundred yards in front. Accordingly, when night fell, two hundred unconcerned heroes went forth, under their subalterns, and, squatting down in line along a white tape (laid earlier in the evening by our imperturbable friends, Lieutenants Box and Cox, of the Royal Engineers), proceeded to dig the trench. Thirty yards ahead of them, facing the curious eyes of countless Bosches, lay a covering party in extended order, ready to repel a rush. Hour by hour the work went on—skilfully, silently. On these occasions it is impossible to say what will happen. The enemy knows we are there: he can see us quite plainly. But he has his own night-work to do, and if he interferes with us he knows that our machine-guns will interfere with him. So, provided that our labours are conducted in a manner which is neither ostentatious nor contemptuous—that is to say, provided we do not talk, whistle, or smoke—he leaves us more or less alone.

But this particular task was not accomplished without loss: it was too obviously important. Several times the German machine-guns sputtered into flame, and each time the stretcher-bearers were called upon to do their duty. Yet the work went on to its accomplishment, without question, without slackening. The men were nearly all experts: they had handled pick and shovel from boyhood. Soldiers of the line would have worked quite as hard, maybe, but they would have taken twice as long. But these dour sons of Scotland worked like giants—trained giants. In four nights the trench, with traverses and approaches, was complete. The men who had made it fell back to their dug-outs, and shortly afterwards to their billets—there to spend the few odd francs which their separation allotments had left them, upon extremely hard-earned glasses of extremely small beer.

At home, several thousand patriotic Welshmen, fellows of the same craft, were upholding the dignity of Labour, and the reputation of the British Nation, by going out on strike for a further increase of pay—an increase which they knew a helpless Government would grant them. It was one of the strangest contrasts that the world has ever seen. But the explanation thereof, as proffered by Private Mucklewame, was quite simple and eminently sound.

"All the decent lads," he observed briefly, "are oot here."

"Good work!" said Wagstaffe, when Blaikie's tale was told. "What is the new trench for, exactly?"

Blaikie told him.

"Tell me more!" urged Wagstaffe, deeply interested.

Blaikie's statement cannot be set down here, though the substance of it may be common property to-day. When he had finished Wagstaffe whistled softly.

"And it's to be the day after tomorrow?" he said.

"Yes, if all goes well."

It was quite dark now. The horizon was brilliantly lit by the flashes of big guns, and a continuous roar came throbbing through the soft autumn darkness.

"If this thing goes with a click, as it ought to do," said Wagstaffe, "it will be the biggest thing that ever happened—bigger even than Charlie Chaplin."

"Yes—*if!*" assented the cautious Blaikie.

"It's a tremendous opportunity for our section of 'K(1),'" continued Wagstaffe. "We shall have a chance of making history over this, old man."

"Whatever we make—history or a bloomer—we'll do our level best," replied Blaikie. "At least, I hope 'A' Company will."

Then suddenly his reserved, undemonstrative Scottish tongue found utterance.

"Scotland for Ever!" he cried softly.

Chapter 21

The Battle of the Slag-Heaps

"Half-past two, and a cold morning, sir."

Thus Bobby Little's servant, rousing his employer from uneasy slumber under the open sky, in a newly-constructed trench running parallel to and in rear of the permanent trench line.

Bobby sat up, and peering at his luminous wrist-watch, morosely acquiesced in his menial's gruesome statement. But he cheered up at the next intimation.

"Breakfast is ready, sir."

Tea and bacon are always tea and bacon, even in the gross darkness and mental tension which precede a Big Push. Presently various humped figures in greatcoats, having gathered in the open ditch which did duty for Officers' Mess, broke into spasmodic conversation—conversation rendered even more spasmodic by the almost ceaseless roar of guns. There were guns all round us—rank upon rank: to judge by the noise, you would have said tier upon tier as well. Half a mile ahead, upon the face of a gentle slope, a sequence of flames would spout from the ground, and a storm of shells go whistling on their way. No sooner had this happened than there would come a shattering roar from the ground beneath our feet, and a heavy battery, concealed in a hedge fifty yards to our front, would launch its contribution. Farther back lay heavier batteries still, and beyond that batteries so powerful and so distant that one heard the shell pass before the report arrived. One of these monsters, coming apparently from infinity and bound for the back of beyond, lumbered wearily over the heads of "A" Company, partaking of breakfast.

Private Mucklewame paused in the act of raising his canteen to his lips.

"There's Wullie awa' for a walk!" he observed.

Considering that they were upon the eve of an epoch-making combat, the regiment were disappointingly placid.

In the Officers' Mess the prevailing note was neither lust of battle nor fear of death: it was merely that ordinary snappishness which is induced by early rising and uncomfortable surroundings.

"It's going to rain, too," grumbled Major Kemp.

At this moment the Colonel arrived, with final instructions from the Brigadier.

"We move off at a quarter to four," he said, "up Fountain Alley and Scottish Trench, into Central Boyau"—"boyau" is the name which is given to a communication-trench in trenches which, like those in front of us, are of French extraction—"and so over the parapet. There we extend, as arranged, into lines of half-companies, and go at 'em, making Douvrin our objective, and keeping the Hohenzollern and Fosse Eight upon our left."

Fosse Eight is a mighty waste-heap, such as you may behold anywhere along the railway in the colliery districts between Glasgow and Edinburgh. The official map calls such an eminence a Fosse; the Royal Engineers call it a Dump; Operation Orders call it a Slag-Heap; experts like Ogg and Hogg (who ought to know if any one does) call it a Bing. From this distance, two miles away, the Fosse looks as big as North Berwick Law. It is one of the many scattered about this district, all carefully numbered by the Ordnance. There are others, again, towards Hulluch and Loos. Number Eight has been the object of pressing attentions on the part of our big guns ever since the bombardment began, three weeks ago; but it still stands up—gaunt, grim, and defiant—against the eastern sky. Whether any one is left alive upon it, or in it, is another question. We shall have cause to remember Fosse Eight before this fight is over.

The Hohenzollern Redoubt, on the other hand, is a most inconspicuous object, but a very important factor in the present situation. It has been thrust forward from the Bosche lines to within a hundred yards of our own—a great promontory, a maze of trenches, machine-gun emplacements, and barbed wire, all flush with or under the ground, and terribly difficult to cripple by shell fire. It has been a source of great exasperation to us—a starting-point for saps, mines, and bombing parties. As already stated, this mighty fortress has been christened by its constructors, the Hohenzollern. It is attached to its parent trench-line by two communicating trenches, which the British Army, not to be outdone in reverence to the most august of dynasties, have named Big and Little Willie respectively.

A struggling dawn breaks, bringing with it promise of rain, and the regiment begins to marshal in the trench called Fountain Alley, along which it is to wind, snake-like, in the wake of the preceding troops, until it debouches over the parapet, a full mile away, and extends into line.

Presently the order is given to move off, and the snake begins to writhe. Progress is steady, but not exhilarating. We have several battalions of the Division in front of us (which Bobby Little resents as a personal affront), but have been assured that we shall see all the fighting we want. The situation appears to be that owing to the terrific artillery bombardment the attacking force will meet with little or no opposition in the German front-line trenches; or second line, for that matter.

"The whole Division," explains Captain Wagstaffe to Bobby Little, "should be able to get up into some sort of formation about the Bosche third line before any real fighting begins; so it does not very much matter whether we start first or fiftieth in the procession."

Captain Wagstaffe showed himself an accurate prophet.

We move on. At one point we pass through a howitzer battery, where dishevelled gentlemen give us a friendly wave of the hand. Others, not professionally engaged for the moment, sit unconcernedly in the ditch with their backs to the proceedings, frying bacon. This is their busy hour.

Presently the pace grows even slower, and finally we stop altogether. Another battalion has cut in ahead of us, and we must perforce wait, snapping our fingers with impatience, like theatre-goers in a Piccadilly block, whose taxis have been held up by the traffic debouching from Berkeley Street.

"Luckily the curtain doesn't rise till five-fifty," observes Captain Wagstaffe.

We move on again at last, and find ourselves in Central Boyau, getting near the heart of things. Suddenly we are conscious of an overpowering sense of relief. Our guns have ceased firing. For the first time for three days and nights there is peace.

Captain Wagstaffe looks at his watch.

"That means that our first line are going over the parapet," he says. "Punctual, too! The gunners have stopped to put up their sights and lengthen their fuses. We ought to be fairly in it in half an hour."

But this proves to be an under-estimate. There are mysterious and maddening stoppages—maddening, because in communication-trench stoppages it is quite impossible to find out what is the matter.

Furious messages begin to arrive from the rear. The original form of inquiry was probably something like this: "Major Kemp would like to know the cause of the delay." As transmitted sonorously from mouth to mouth by the rank and file it finally arrives (if it ever arrives at all) in some such words as: "Pass doon; what for is this (asterisk, obelus) wait?" But as no answer is ever passed back it does not much matter.

The righteous indignation of Major Kemp, who is situated somewhere about the middle of the procession, reaches its culminating point when, with much struggling and pushing and hopeless jamming, a stretcher carrying a wounded man is borne down the crowded trench on its way to the rear. The Major delivers himself.

"This is perfectly monstrous! You stretcher-bearers will kill that poor chap if you try to drag him down here. There is a specially constructed road to the dressing-station over there—Bart's Alley, it is called. We cannot have up-and-down traffic jumbled together like this. For heaven's sake, Waddell, pass up word to the C.O. that it is mistaken kindness to allow these fellows down here. He *must* send them back."

Waddell volunteers to climb out of the trench and go forward with a message. But this the Major will not allow. "Your platoon will require a leader presently," he mentions. "We'll try the effect of a note."

The note is passed up, and anon an answer comes back to the effect that no wounded have been allowed down from the head of the column. They must be getting in by a sidetrack somewhere. The Major groans, but can do nothing.

Presently there is a fresh block.

"What is it this time?" inquires the afflicted Kemp. "More wounded, or are we being photographed?"

The answer races joyously down the line—"Gairman prisoners, sirr—seeventy of them!"

This time the Major acts with promptness and decision.

"Prisoners? No, they *don't*! Pass up word from me that the whole boiling are to be hoisted on to the parapet, with their escort, and made to walk above ground."

The order goes forward. Presently our hearts are rejoiced by an exhilarating sight. Across the field through which our trench winds comes a body of men, running rapidly, encouraged to further fleetness of foot by desultory shrapnel and stray bullets. They wear grey-green uniform, and flat, muffin-shaped caps. They have no arms or equipment: some are slightly wounded. In front of this contingent, running even more rapidly, are their escort—some dozen brawny Highlanders, armed to the teeth. But the prisoners exhibit no desire to take advantage of this unusual order of things. Their one ambition in life appears to be to put as large a space as possible between themselves and their late comrades-in-arms, and, if possible, overtake their captors.

Some of them find time to grin, and wave their hands to us. One addresses the scandalised M'Slattery as *"Kamarad!"* "No more dis war for me!" cries another, with unfeigned satisfaction.

After this our progress is more rapid. As we near the front line, the enemy's shrapnel reaps its harvest even in our deep trench. More than once we pass a wounded man, hoisted on to the parapet to wait for first-aid. More than once we step over some poor fellow for whom no first-aid will avail.

Five minutes later we reach the parapet—that immovable rampart over which we have peeped so often and so cautiously with our periscopes—and clamber up a sandbag staircase on to the summit. We note that our barbed wire has all been cut away, and that another battalion, already extended into line, is advancing fifty yards ahead of us. Bullets are pinging through the air, but the guns are once more silent. Possibly they are altering their position. Dotted about upon the flat ground before us lie many kilted figures, strangely still, in uncomfortable attitudes.

A mile or so upon our right we can see two towers—pit-head towers—standing side by side. They mark the village of Loos, where another Scottish Division is leading the attack. To the right of Loos again, for miles and miles and miles, we know that wave upon wave of impetuous French soldiers is breaking in a tempest over the shattered German trenches. Indeed, we conjecture that down there, upon our right, is where the Biggest Push of all is taking place. Our duty is to get forward if we can, but before everything to engage as many German troops and guns as possible. Even if we fight for a week or more, and only hold our own, we shall have done the greater part of what was required of us. But we hope to do more than that.

Upon our left lies the Hohenzollern. It is silent; so we know that it has been captured. Beyond that, upon our left front, looms Fosse Eight, still surmounted by its battered shaft-tower. Right ahead, peeping over a low ridge, is a church steeple, with a clock-face in it. That is our objective.

Next moment we have deployed into extended order, and step out, to play our little part in the great Battle of the Slag-Heaps.

* * * * * * * *

Twenty-four hours later, a little group of officers sat in a roomy dug-out. Major Kemp was there, with his head upon the plank table, fast asleep. Bobby Little, who had neither eaten nor slept since the previous dawn, was nibbling chocolate, and shaking as if with ague. He had gone through a good deal. Waddell sat opposite to him, stolidly devouring bully-beef out of a tin with his fingers. Ayling reclined upon the floor, mechanically adjusting a machine-gun lock, which he had taken from his haversack. Captain Wagstaffe was making cocoa over a Tommy's Cooker. He looked less the worse for wear than the others, but could hardly have been described as spruce in appearance. The whole party were splashed with mud and soaked to the skin, for it had rained hard during the greater part of the night. They were all sick for want of food and sleep. Moreover, all had seen unusual sights. It was Sunday morning.

Presently Wagstaffe completed his culinary arrangements, and poured out the cocoa into some aluminium cups. He touched Major Kemp on the shoulder.

"Have some of this, Major," he said.

The burly Kemp roused himself and took the proffered cup gratefully. Then, looking round, he said—

"Hallo, Ayling! You arrived? Whereabouts in the line were you?"

"I got cut off from the Battalion in the advance up Central Boyau, sir," said Ayling. "Everybody had disappeared by the time I got the machine-guns over the parapet. However, knowing the objective, I pushed on towards the Church Tower."

"How did you enjoy yourself passing Fosse Eight?" inquired Captain Wagstaffe.

"Thank you, we got a dose of our own medicine—machine-gun fire, in enfilade. It was beastly."

"We also noticed it," Wagstaffe intimated. "That was where poor Sinclair got knocked out. What did you do?"

"I signalled to the men to lie flat for a bit, and I did the same. I did not know that it was possible for a human being to lie as flat as I lay during that quarter of an hour. But it was no good. The guns must have been high up on the Fosse: they had excellent command. The bullets simply greased all round us. I could feel them combing out my hair, and digging into the ground underneath me."

"What were your sensations, *exactly*?" asked Kemp.

"I felt just as if an invisible person were tickling me," replied Ayling, with feeling.

"So did I," said Kemp. "Go on."

"I heard one of my men cry out that he was hit," continued Ayling, "and I came to the conclusion that we would have a better chance as moving targets than as fixed; so I passed the word to get up and move forward steadily, in single file. Ultimately we struck a stray communication-trench, into which we descended with as much dignity as possible. It led us into some quarries."

"Off our line altogether."

"So I learned from two Companies of an English regiment which were there, acting as reserve to a Brigade which was scrapping somewhere in the direction of Hulluch; so I realised that we had worked too far to the right. We moved out of the quarries and struck over half-left, and ultimately found the Battalion, a very long way ahead, in what I took to be a Bosche third-line trench, facing east."

"Right! Fosse Alley," said Kemp. "You remember it on the map?"

"Yes, I do now," said Ayling. "Well, I planted myself on the right flank of the Battalion with-two guns, and sent Sergeant Killick along with the other two to the left. You know the rest."

"I'm not sure that I do," said the Major. "We were packed so tight in that blooming trench that it was quite impossible to move about, and I only saw what was going on close around me. Did you get much machine-gun practice?"

"A fair amount, sir," replied Ayling, with professional satisfaction. "There was a lot of firing from our right front, so I combed out all the bushes and house-fronts I could see; and presently the firing died down, but not before I had had one gun put out of action with a bullet through the barrel-casing. After dark things were fairly quiet, except for constant alarms, until the order came to move back to the next trench."

Major Kemp's fist came down upon the plank table.

"Move back!" he exclaimed angrily. "Just so! To capture Fosse Alley, hold it all day and half the night, and then be compelled to move back, simply because we had pushed so far ahead of any other Division that we had no support on either flank! It was tough—rotten—hellish! Excuse my exuberance. 'You all right, Wagstaffe?"

"Wonderful, considering," replied Wagstaffe. "I was mildly gassed by a lachrymose shell about two o'clock this morning, but nothing to signify."

"Did your respirator work?"

"I found that in the heat of the moment I had mislaid it."

"What did you do?"

"I climbed on to the parapet and sat there. It seemed the healthiest spot under the circumstance: anyhow, the air was pure. When I recovered I got down. What happened to 'A,' Bobby? I heard rumours, but hoped—"

He hesitated.

"Go on," he said abruptly; and Bobby, more composed now, told his tale.

"A" Company, it appeared, had found themselves clinging grimly to the section of Fosse Alley which they had captured, with their left flank entirely in the air. Presently came an order. Further forward still, half-right, another isolated trench was being held by a portion of the Highland Brigade. These were suffering cruelly, for the German artillery had the range to a nicety, and convenient sapheads gave the German bombers easy access to their flanks. It is more than likely that this very trench had been constructed expressly for the inveiglement of a too successful attacking party. Certainly no troops could live in it for long. "A" Company were to go forward and support.

Captain Blaikie, passing word to his men to be ready, turned to Bobby.

"I'm a morose, dour, monosyllabic Scot, Bobbie," he said; "but this sort of thing bucks me up."

Next moment he was over the parapet and away, followed by his Company. In that long, steadily-advancing line were many of our friends. Mucklewame was there, panting heavily, and cannily commending his soul to Providence. Messrs. Ogg and Hogg were there, shoulder to shoulder. M'Ostrich, the Ulster visionary, was there, six paces ahead of any other man, crooning some Ironside canticle to himself. Next behind him came the reformed revolutionary, M'Slattery.

Straightway the enemy observed the oncoming reinforcements, and shrapnel began to fly. The men pressed on, at a steady double now. M'Ostrich was the first to go down. Game to the last, he waved encouragement to his mates with a failing arm as they passed over his body.

"Come along, boys!" cried Captain Blaikie, suddenly eloquent. "There is the trench! The other lads are waiting for you. Come along! Charge!"

The men needed no further bidding. They came on—with a ragged cheer—and assuredly would have arrived, but for one thing. Suddenly they faltered, and stopped dead.

Captain Blaikie turned to his faithful subaltern panting behind him.

"We are done in, Bobby," he said. "Look! Wire!"

He was right. This particular trench, it was true, was occupied by our friends; but it had been constructed in the first instance for the use of our enemies. Consequently it was wired, and heavily wired, upon the side facing the British advance.

Captain Blaikie, directing operations with a walking-stick as if the whole affair were an Aldershot field-day, signalled to the Company to lie down, and began to unbutton a leather pouch in his belt.

"You too, Bobby," he said; "and don't dare to move a muscle until you get the order!"

He strolled forward, pliers in hand, and began methodically to cut a passage, strand by strand, through the forest of wire.

Then it was that invisible machine-guns opened, and a very gallant officer and Scotsman fell dead upon the field of honour.

Half an hour later, "A" Company, having expended all their ammunition and gained never a yard, fell back upon the rest of the Battalion. Including Bobby Little (who seemed to bear a charmed life), they did not represent the strength of a platoon.

"I wonder what they will do with us next," remarked Mr. Waddell, who had finished his bully.

"If they have any sense of decency," said Major Kemp, "they will send us back to rest a bit, and put another Division in. We have opened the ball and done a lot of dirty work for them, and have lost a lot of men and officers. Bed for me, please!"

"I should be more inclined to agree with you, Major," said Wagstaffe, "if only we had a bit more to show for our losses."

"We haven't done so badly," replied Kemp, who was growing more cheerful under the influence of hot cocoa. "We have got the Hohenzollern, and the Bosche first line at least, and probably Fosse Eight. On the right I hear we have taken Loos. That's not so dusty for a start. I have not the slightest doubt that there will be a heavy counter-attack, which we shall repel. After that we shall attack again, and gain more ground, or at least keep the Bosche exceedingly busy holding on. That is our allotted task in this entertainment—to go on hammering the Hun, occupying his attention and using up his reserves, regardless of whether we gain ground or lose it, while our French pals on the right are pushing him off the map. At least, that is my theory: I don't pretend to be in touch with the official mind. This battle will probably go on for a week or more, over practically the same ground. It will be dreadful for the wounded, but even if we only hold on to what we have gained already, we are the winners. Still, I wish we could have consolidated Fosse Alley before going to bed."

At this moment the Colonel, stooping low in the tiny doorway, entered the dug-out, followed by the Adjutant. He bade his supporters good-morning.

"I am glad to find that you fellows have been able to give your men a meal," he said. "It was capital work getting the ration-carts up so far last night."

"Any news, Colonel?" asked Major Kemp.

"Most decidedly. It seems that the enemy have evacuated Fosse Alley again. Nobody quite knows why: a sudden attack of cold feet, probably. Our people command their position from Fosse Eight, on their left rear, so I don't altogether blame them. Whoever holds Fosse Eight holds Fosse Alley. However, the long and short of it all is that the Brigade are to go forward again this evening, and reoccupy Fosse Alley. Meanwhile, we consolidate things here."

Major Kemp sighed.

"Bed indefinitely postponed!" he remarked resignedly.

* * * * * * * *

By midnight on the same Sunday the Battalion, now far under its original strength, had re-entered the scene of yesterday's long struggle, filing thither under the stars, by a deserted and ghostly German *boyau* nearly ten feet deep. Fosse Alley erred in the opposite direction. It was not much more than four feet in depth; the chalky parapet could by no stretch of imagination be described as bullet-proof; dug-outs and communication-trenches were non-existent. On our left the trench-line was continued by the troops of another Division: on our right lay another battalion of our own brigade.

"If the line has been made really continuous this time," observed the Colonel, "we should be as safe as houses. Wonderful fellows, these sappers! They have wired almost our whole front already. I wish they had had time to do it on our left as well."

Within the next few hours all defensive preparations possible in the time had been completed; and our attendant angels, most effectively disguised as Royal Engineers, had flitted away, leaving us to wait for Monday morning—and Brother Bosche.

With the dawn, our eyes, which had known no sleep since Friday night, peered rheumily out over the whitening landscape.

To our front the ground stretched smooth and level for two hundred yards, then fell gently away, leaving a clearly denned skyline. Beyond the skyline rose houses, of which we could descry only the roofs and upper windows.

"That must be either Haisnes or Douvrin," said Major Kemp. "We are much farther to the left than we were yesterday. By the way, *was* it yesterday?"

"The day before yesterday, sir," the ever-ready Waddell informed him.

"Never mind; to-day's the day, anyhow. And it's going to be a busy day, too. The fact is, we are in a tight place, and all through doing too well. We have again penetrated so much farther forward than any one else in our neighbourhood that we *may* have to fall back a bit. But I hope not. We have a big stake, Waddell. If we can hold on to this position until the others make good upon our right and left, we shall have reclaimed a clear two miles of the soil of France, my son." The Major swept the horizon with his glasses. "Let me see: that is probably Hulluch away on our right front: the Loos towers must be in line with us on our extreme right, but we can't see them for those hillocks. There is our old friend Fosse Eight towering over us on our left rear. I don't know anything about the ground on our absolute left, but so long as that flathead regiment hold on to their trench, we can't go far wrong. Waddell, I don't like those cottages on our left front. They block the view, and also spell machine-guns. I see one or two very suggestive loopholes in those red-tiled roofs. Go and draw Ayling's attention to them. A little preliminary *strafing* will do them no harm."

Five minutes later one of Ayling's machine-guns spoke out, and a cascade of tiles came sliding down the roofs of the offending cottages.

"That will tickle them up, if they have any guns set up on those rafters," observed the Major, with ghoulish satisfaction. "I wonder if Brer Bosche is going to attack. I hope he does. There is only one thing I am afraid of, and that is that there may be some odd saps running out towards us, especially on our flanks. If so, we shall have some close work with bombs—a most ungentlemanly method of warfare. Let us pray for a straightforward frontal attack."

But Brer Bosche had other cards to play first. Suddenly, out of nowhere, the air was filled with "whizz-bang" shells, moving in a lightning procession which lasted nearly half an hour. Most of these plastered the already scarred countenance of Fosse Eight: others fell shorter and demolished our parapet. When the tempest ceased, as suddenly as it began, the number of casualties in the crowded trench was considerable. But there was little time to attend to the wounded. Already the word was running down, the line—

"Look out to your front!"

Sure enough, over the skyline, two hundred yards away, grey figures were appearing—not in battalions, but tentatively, in twos and threes. Next moment a storm of rapid rifle fire broke from the trench. The grey figures turned and ran. Some disappeared over the horizon, others dropped flat, others simply curled up and withered. In three minutes solitude reigned again, and the firing ceased.

"Well, that's that!" observed Captain Wagstaffe to Bobby Little, upon the right of the Battalion line. "The Bosche has 'bethought himself and went,' as the poet says. Now he knows we are here, and have brought our arquebuses with us. He will try something more ikey next time. Talking of time, what about breakfast? When was our last meal, Bobby?"

"Haven't the vaguest notion," said Bobby sleepily.

"Well, it's about breakfast-time now. Have a bit of chocolate? It is all I have."

It was eight o'clock, and perfect silence reigned. All down the line men, infinitely grubby, were producing still grubbier fragments of bully-beef and biscuits from their persons. For an hour, squatting upon the sodden floor of the trench—it was raining yet again—the unappetising, intermittent meal proceeded.

Then—

"Hallo!" exclaimed Bobby with a jerk (for he was beginning to nod), "what was that on our right?"

"I'm afraid," replied Wagstaffe, "that it was bombs. It was right in this trench, too, about a hundred yards long. There must be a sap leading up there, for the bombers certainly have not advanced overground. I've been looking out for them since stand-to. Who is this anxious gentleman?"

A subaltern of the battalion on our right was forcing his way along the trench. He addressed Wagstaffe.

"We are having a pretty bad time with Bosche bombers on our right, sir," he said. "Will you send us down all the bombs you can spare?"

Wagstaffe hoisted himself upon the parapet.

"I will see our C.O. at once," he replied, and departed at the double. It was a risky proceeding, for German bullets promptly appeared in close attendance; but he saved a good five minutes on his journey to Battalion Headquarters at the other end of the trench.

Presently the bombs began to arrive, passed from hand to hand. Wagstaffe returned, this time along the trench.

"We shall have a tough fight for it," he said. "The Bosche bombers know their business, and probably have more bombs than we have. But those boys on our right seem to be keeping their end up."

"Can't *we* do anything?" asked Bobby feverishly.

"Nothing—unless the enemy succeed in working right down here; in which case we shall take our turn of getting it in the neck—or giving it! I fancy old Ayling and his popgun will have a word to say, if he can find a nice straight bit of trench. All we can do for the present is to keep a sharp look-out in front. I have no doubt they will attack in force when the right moment comes."

For close on three hours the bomb-fight went on. Little could be seen, for the struggle was all taking place upon the extreme right; but the sounds of conflict were plain enough. More bombs were passed up, and yet more; men, some cruelly torn, were passed down.

Then a signal-sergeant doubled up across country from somewhere in rear, paying out wire, and presently the word went forth that we were in touch with the Artillery. Directly after, sure enough, came the blessed sound and sight of British shrapnel bursting over our right front.

"That won't stop the present crowd," said Wagstaffe, "but it may prevent their reinforcements from coming up. We are holding our own, Bobby. What's that, Sergeant?"

"The Commanding Officer, sirr," announced Sergeant Carfrae, "has just passed up that we are to keep a sharp look-out to our left. They've commenced for to bomb the English regiment now."

"Golly, both flanks! This is getting a trifle steep," remarked Wagstaffe.

Detonations could now be distinctly heard upon the left.

"If they succeed in getting round behind us," said Wagstaffe in a low voice to Bobby, "we shall have to fall back a bit, into line with the rest of the advance. Only a few hundred yards, but it means a lot to *us*!"

"It hasn't happened yet," said Bobby stoutly.

Captain Wagstaffe knew better. His more experienced eye and ear had detected the fact that the position of the regiment upon the left was already turned. But he said nothing.

Presently the tall figure of the Colonel was seen, advancing in leisurely fashion along the trench, stopping here and there to exchange a word with a private or a sergeant.

"The regiment on the left may have to fall back, men," he was saying. "We, of course, will stand fast, and cover their retirement."

This most characteristic announcement was received with a matter-of-fact "Varra good, sir," from its recipients, and the Colonel passed on to where the two officers were standing.

"Hallo, Wagstaffe," he said; "good-morning! We shall get some very pretty shooting presently. The enemy are massing on our left front, down behind those cottages. How are things going on our right?"

"They are holding their own, sir."

"Good! Just tell Ayling to get his guns trained. But doubtless he has done so already. I must get back to the other flank."

And back to the danger-spot our C.O. passed—an upright, gallant figure, saying little, exhorting not at all, but instilling confidence and cheerfulness by his very presence.

Half-way along the trench he encountered Major Kemp.

"How are things on the left, sir?" was the Major's *sotto voce* inquiry.

"Not too good. Our position is turned. We have been promised reinforcements, but I doubt if they can get up in time. Of course, when it comes to falling back, this regiment goes last."

"Of course, sir."

* * * * * * * *

Highlanders! Four hundred yards! At the enemy advancing half-left, rapid fire!

Twenty minutes had passed. The regiment still stood immovable, though its left flank was now utterly exposed. All eyes and rifles were fixed upon the cluster of cottages. Through the gaps that lay between these could be discerned the advance of the German infantry—line upon line, moving towards the trench upon our left. The ground to our front was clear. Each time one of these lines passed a gap the rifles rang out and Ayling's remaining machine-gun uttered joyous barks. Still the enemy advanced. His shrapnel was bursting overhead; bullets were whistling from nowhere, for the attack in force was now being pressed home in earnest.

The deserted trench upon our left ran right through the cottages, and this restricted our view. No hostile bombers could be seen; it was evident that they had done their bit and handed on the conduct of affairs to others. Behind the shelter of the cottages the infantry were making a safe detour, and were bound, unless something unexpected happened, to get round behind us.

"They'll be firing from our rear in a minute," said Kemp between his teeth. "Lochgair, order your platoon to face about and be ready to fire over the parados."

Young Lochgair's method of executing this command was characteristically thorough. He climbed in leisurely fashion upon the parados; and standing there, with all his six-foot-three in full view, issued his orders.

"Face this way, boys! Keep your eyes on that group of buildings just behind the empty trench, in below the Fosse. You'll get some target practice presently. Don't go and forget that you are the straightest-shooting platoon in the Company. There they are"—he pointed with his stick—"lots of them—coming through that gap in the wall! Now then, rapid fire, and let them have it! Oh, well done, boys! Good shooting! Very good! Very good ind—"

He stopped suddenly, swayed, and toppled back into the trench. Major Kemp caught him in his arms, and laid him gently upon the chalky floor. There was nothing more to be done. Young Lochgair had given his platoon their target, and the platoon were now firing steadily upon the same. He closed his eyes and sighed, like a tired child.

"Carry on, Major!" he murmured faintly. "I'm all right."

So died the simple-hearted, valiant enthusiast whom we had christened Othello.

The entire regiment—what was left of it—was now firing over the back of the trench; for the wily Teuton had risked no frontal attack, seeing that he could gain all his ends from the left flank. Despite vigorous rifle fire and the continuous maledictions of the machine-gun, the enemy were now pouring through the cottages behind the trench. Many grey figures began to climb up the face of Fosse Eight, where apparently there was none to say them nay.

"We shall have a cheery walk back, I *don't* think!" murmured Wagstaffe.

He was right. Presently a withering fire was opened from the summit of the Fosse, which soon began to take effect in the exiguous and ill-protected trench.

"The Colonel is wounded, sir," reported the Sergeant-Major to Major Kemp.

"Badly?"

"Yes, sir."

Kemp looked round him. The regiment was now alone in the trench, for the gallant company upon their right had been battered almost out of existence.

"We can do no more good by staying here any longer," said the Major. "We have done our little bit. I think it is a case of 'Home, John!' Tell off a party to bring in the C.O., Sergeant-Major."

Then he passed the order.

"Highlanders, retire to the trenches behind, by Companies, beginning from the right."

"Whatever we may think of the Bosche as a gentleman," mused that indomitable philosopher, Captain Wagstaffe, as he doubled stolidly rearward behind his Company, "there is no denying his bravery as a soldier or his skill in co-ordinating an attack. It's positively uncanny, the way his artillery supports his infantry. (Hallo, that was a near one!) This enfilade fire from the Fosse is most unpleasant. (I fancy that one went through my kilt.) Steady there, on the left: don't bunch, whatever you do! Thank heaven, there's the next line of trenches, fully manned. And thank God, there's that boy Bobby tumbling in unhurt!"

* * * * * * * *

So ended our share in the Big Push. It was a very small episode, spread over quite a short period, in one of the biggest and longest battles in the history of the world. It would have been easy to select a more showy episode, but hard to find a better illustration of the character of the men who took part in it. The battle which began upon that grey September morning has been raging, as I write, for nearly three weeks. It still surges backwards and forwards over the same stricken mile of ground; and the end is not yet. But the Hun is being steadily beaten to earth. (Only yesterday, in one brief furious counter-attack, he lost eight thousand killed.) When the final advance comes, as come it must, and our victorious line sweeps forward, it will pass over two narrow, ill-constructed, shell-torn trenches. In and around those trenches will be found the earthly remains of men—Jocks and Jimmies, and Sandies and Andies—clad in the uniform of almost every Scottish regiment. That assemblage of mute, glorious witnesses marks the point reached, during the first few hours of the first day's fighting, by the Scottish Division of "K(1)." *Molliter ossa cubent.*

There is little more to add to the record of those three days. For yet another night we carried on—repelling counter-attacks, securing the Hohenzollern, making sorties out of Big Willie, or manning the original front line parapet against eventualities. As is inevitable in a fight of these proportions, whole brigades were mingled together, and unexpected leaders arose to take the place of those who had fallen. Many a stout piece of work was done that night by mixed bands of kilties, flat-heads, and even cyclists, marshalled in a captured German trench and shepherded by a junior subaltern.

Finally, about midnight, came the blessed order that fresh troops were coming up to continue the attack, and that we were to be extricated from the *melee* and sent back to rest. And so, after a participation in the battle of some seventy-two hours, our battered Division came out—to sleep the sleep of utter exhaustion in dug-outs behind the railway line, and to receive, upon waking, the thanks of its Corps Commander.

* * * * * * * *

And here I propose (for a time, at least) to take leave of The First Hundred Thousand. Some day, if Providence wills, the tale shall be resumed; and you shall hear how Major Kemp, Captain Wagstaffe, Ayling, and Bobby Little, assisted by such veterans as Corporal Mucklewame, built up the regiment, with copious drafts and a fresh batch of subalterns, to its former strength.

But the title of the story will have to be changed. In the hearts of those who drilled them, reasoned with them, sometimes almost wept over them, and ultimately fought shoulder to shoulder with them, the sturdy, valiant legions, whose humorously-pathetic career you have followed so patiently for fifteen months, will always be First; but alas! they are no longer The Hundred Thousand.

So we will leave them, as is most justly due, in sole possession of their proud title.

To All Second Lieutenants

And In Particular To The Memory Of

One Second Lieutenant

Author's Note

The First Hundred Thousand closed with the Battle of Loos. The present narrative follows certain friends of ours from the scene of that costly but valuable experience, through a winter campaign in the neighbourhood of Ypres and Ploegsteert, to profitable participation in the Battle of the Somme.

Much has happened since then. The initiative has passed once and for all into our hands; so has the command of the air. Russia has been reborn, and, like most healthy infants, is passing through an uproarious period of teething trouble; but now America has stepped in, and promises to do more than redress the balance. All along the Western Front we have begun to move forward, without haste or flurry, but in such wise that during the past twelve months no position, once fairly captured and consolidated, has ever been regained by the enemy. To-day you can stand upon certain recently won eminences—Wytchaete Ridge, Messines Ridge, Vimy Ridge, and Monchy—looking down into the enemy's lines, and looking forward to the territory which yet remains to be restored to France.

You can also look back—not merely from these ridges, but from certain moral ridges as well—over the ground which has been successfully traversed, and you can marvel for the hundredth time, not that the thing was well or badly done, but that it was ever done at all.

But while this narrative was being written, none of these things had happened. We were still struggling uphill, with inadequate resources. So, since the incidents of the story were set down, in the main, as they occurred and when they occurred, the reader will find very little perspective, a great deal of the mood of the moment, and none at all of that profound wisdom which comes after the event. For the latter he must look home—to the lower walks of journalism and the back benches of the House of Commons.

It is not proposed to carry this story to a third volume. The First Hundred Thousand, as such, are no more. Like the "Old Contemptibles," they are now merged in a greater and more victorious army—in an armed nation, in fact. And, as Sergeant Mucklewame once observed to me, "There's no that mony of us left now, onyways." So with all reverence—remembering how, when they were needed most, these men did not pause to reason why or count the cost, but came at once—we bid them good-bye.

CHAPTER 1
Winter Quarters

We are getting into our stride again. Two months ago we trudged into Bethune, gaunt, dirty, soaked to the skin, and reduced to a comparative handful. None of us had had his clothes off for a week. Our ankle-puttees had long dropped to pieces, and our hose-tops, having worked under the soles of our boots, had been cut away and discarded. The result was a bare and mud-splashed expanse of leg from boot to kilt, except in the case of the enterprising few who had devised artistic spat-puttees out of an old sandbag. Our headgear consisted in a few cases of the regulation Balmoral bonnet, usually minus "toorie" and badge; in a few more, of the battered remains of a gas helmet; and in the great majority, of a woollen cap-comforter. We were bearded like that incomparable fighter, the *poilu*, and we were separated by an abyss of years, so our stomachs told us, from our last square meal.

But we were wonderfully placid about it all. Our regimental pipers, who had come out to play us in, were making what the Psalmist calls "a joyful noise" in front; and behind us lay the recollection of a battle, still raging, in which we had struck the first blow, and borne our full share for three days and nights. Moreover, our particular blow had bitten deeper into the enemy's line than any other blow in the neighbourhood. And, most blessed thought of all, everything was over, and we were going back to rest. For the moment, the memory of the sights we had seen, and the tax we had levied upon our bodies and souls, together with the picture of the countless sturdy lads whom we had left lying beneath the sinister shade of Fosse Eight, were beneficently obscured by the prospect of food, sleep, and comparative cleanliness.

After restoring ourselves to our personal comforts, we should doubtless go somewhere to refit. Drafts were already waiting at the Base to fill up the great gaps in our ranks. Our companies having been brought up to strength, a spate of promotions would follow. We had no Colonel, and only our Company Commander. Subalterns—what was left of them—would come by their own. N.C.O.'s, again, would have to be created by the dozen. While all this was going on, and the old names were being weeded out of the muster-roll to make way for the new, the Quartermaster would be drawing fresh equipment—packs, mess-tins, water-bottles, and the hundred oddments which always go astray in times of stress. There would be a good deal of dialogue of this sort:—

"Private M'Sumph, I see you are down for a new pack. Where is your old one?"

"Blawn off ma back, sirr!"

"Where are your puttees?"

"Blawn off ma feet, sirr!"

"Where is your iron ration?"

"Blawn oot o' ma pooch, sirr!"

"Where is your head?"

"Blawn—I beg your pardon, sirr!"—followed by generous reissues all round.

After a month or so our beloved regiment, once more at full strength, with traditions and morale annealed by the fires of experience, would take its rightful place in the forefront of "K (1)."

Such was the immediate future, as it presented itself to the wearied but optimistic brain of Lieutenant Bobby Little. He communicated his theories to Captain Wagstaffe.

"I wonder!" replied that experienced officer.

II

The chief penalty of doing a job of work well is that you are promptly put on to another. This is supposed to be a compliment.

The authorities allowed us exactly two days' rest, and then packed us off by train, with the new draft, to a particularly hot sector of the trench-line in Belgium—there to carry on with the operation known in nautical circles as "executing repairs while under steam."

Well, we have been in Belgium for two months now, and, as already stated, are getting into our stride again.

There are new faces everywhere, and some of the old faces are not quite the same. They are finer-drawn; one is conscious of less chubbiness all round. War is a great maturing agent. There is, moreover, an air of seasoned authority abroad. Many who were second lieutenants or lance corporals three months ago are now commanding companies and platoons. Bobby Little is in command of "A" Company: if he can cling to this precarious eminence for thirty days—that is, if no one is sent out to supersede him—he becomes an "automatic" captain, aged twenty! Major Kemp commands the battalion; Wagstaffe is his senior major. Ayling has departed from our midst, and rumour says that he is leading a sort of Pooh Bah existence at Brigade Headquarters.

There are sad gaps among our old friends of the rank and file. Ogg and Hogg, M'Slattery and M'Ostrich, have gone to the happy hunting-grounds. Private Dunshie, the General Specialist (who, you may remember, found his true vocation, after many days, as battalion chiropodist), is reported "missing." But his comrades are positive that no harm has befallen him. Long experience has convinced them that in the art of landing on his feet their departed friend has no equal.

"I doot he'll be a prisoner," suggests the faithful Mucklewame to the Transport Sergeant.

"Aye," assents the Transport Sergeant bitterly; "he'll be a prisoner. No doot he'll try to pass himself off as an officer, for to get better quarters!"

(The Transport Sergeant, in whose memory certain enormities of Dunshie had rankled ever since that versatile individual had abandoned the veterinary profession, owing to the most excusable intervention of a pack-mule's off hind leg, was not far out in his surmise, as subsequent history may some day reveal. But the telling of that story is still a long way off.)

Company Sergeant-Major Pumpherston is now Sergeant-Major of the Battalion. Mucklewame is a corporal in his old company. Private Tosh was "offered a stripe," too, but declined, because the invitation did not include Private Cosh, who, owing to a regrettable lapse not unconnected with the rum ration, had been omitted from the Honours' List. Consequently these two grim veterans remain undecorated, but they are objects of great veneration among the recently joined for all that.

So you see us once more in harness, falling into the collar with energy, if not fervour. We no longer regard War with the least enthusiasm: we have seen It, face to face. Our sole purpose now is to screw our sturdy followers up to the requisite pitch of efficiency, and keep them remorselessly at that standard until the dawn of triumphant and abiding peace.

We have one thing upon our side—youth.

"Most of our regular senior officers are gone, sir," remarked Colonel Kemp one day to the Brigadier—"dead, or wounded, or promoted to other commands; and I have something like twenty new subalterns. When you subtract a centenarian like myself, the average age of our Battalion Mess, including Company Commanders, works out at something under twenty-three. But I am not exchanging any of them, thanks!"

III

Trench-life in Belgium is an entirely different proposition from trench-life in France. The undulating country in which we now find ourselves offers an infinite choice of unpleasant surroundings.

Down south, Vermelles way, the trenches stretch in a comparatively straight line for miles, facing one another squarely, and giving little opportunity for tactical enterprise. The infantry blaze and sputter at one another in front; the guns roar behind; and that is all there is to be said about it. But here, the line follows the curve of each little hill. At one place you are in a salient, in a trench which runs round the face of a bulging "knowe"—a tempting target for shells of every kind. A few hundred yards farther north, or south, the ground is much lower, and the trench-line runs back into a re-entrant, seeking for a position which shall not be commanded from higher ground in front.

The line is pierced at intervals by railway-cuttings, which have to be barricaded, and canals, which require special defences. Almost every spot in either line is overlooked by some adjacent ridge, or enfiladed from some adjacent trench. It is disconcerting for a methodical young officer, after cautiously scrutinising the trench upon his front through a periscope, to find that the entire performance has been visible (and his entire person exposed) to the view of a Boche trench situated on a hill-slope upon his immediate left.

And our trench-line, with its infinity of salients and re-entrants, is itself only part of the great salient of "Wipers." You may imagine with what methodical solemnity the Boche "crumps" the interior of that constricted area. Looking round at night, when the star-shells float up over the skyline, one could almost imagine one's self inside a complete circle, instead of a horseshoe.

The machine-gunners of both sides are extremely busy. In the plains of France the pursuit of their nefarious trade was practically limited to front-line work. When they did venture to indulge in what they called "overhead" fire, their friends in the forefront used to summon them after the performance, and reproachfully point out sundry ominous rents and abrasions in the back of the front-line parapet. But here they can withdraw behind a convenient ridge, and *strafe* Boches a mile and a half away, without causing any complaints. Needless to say, Brother Boche is not backward in returning the compliment. He has one gun in particular which never tires in its efforts to rouse us from *ennui*. It must be a long way off, for we can only just hear the report. Moreover, its contribution to our liveliness, when it does arrive, falls at an extremely steep angle—so steep, indeed, that it only just clears the embankment under which we live, and falls upon the very doorsteps of the dug-outs with which that sanctuary is honeycombed.

This invigorating shower is turned on regularly for ten minutes, at three, six, nine, and twelve o'clock daily. Its area of activity includes our tiny but, alas! steadily growing cemetery. One evening a regiment which had recently "taken over" selected 6 P.M. as a suitable hour for a funeral. The result was a grimly humorous spectacle—the mourners, including the Commanding Officer and officiating clergy, taking hasty cover in a truly novel trench; while the central figure of the obsequies, sublimely indifferent to the Hun and all his frightfulness, lay on the grass outside, calm and impassive amid the whispering hail of bullets.

As for the trenches themselves—well, as the immortal costermonger observed, "there ain't no word in the blooming language" for them.

In the first place, there is no settled trench-line at all. The Salient has been a battlefield for twelve months past. No one has ever had the time, or opportunity, to construct anything in the shape of permanent defences. A shallow trench, trimmed with an untidy parapet of sandbags, and there is your stronghold! For rest and meditation, a hole in the ground, half-full of water and roofed with a sheet of galvanised iron; or possibly a glorified rabbit-burrow in a canal-bank. These things, as a modern poet has observed, are all right in the summer-time. But winter here is a disintegrating season. It rains heavily for, say, three days. Two days of sharp frost succeed, and the rain-soaked earth is reduced to the necessary degree of friability. Another day's rain, and trenches and dug-outs come sliding down like melted butter. Even if you revet the trenches, it is not easy to drain them. The only difference is that if your line is situated on the forward slope of a hill the support trench drains into the firing-trench; if they are on the reverse slope, the firing-trench drains into the support trench. Our indefatigable friends Box and Cox, of the Royal Engineers, assisted by sturdy Pioneer Battalions, labour like heroes; but the utmost they can achieve, in a low-lying country like this, is to divert as much water as possible into some other Brigade's area. Which they do, right cunningly.

In addition to the Boche, we wage continuous warfare with the elements, and the various departments of Olympus render us characteristic assistance. The Round Game Department has issued a set of rules for the correct method of massaging and greasing the feet. (Major Wagstaffe refers to this as, "Sole-slapping; or What to do in the Children's Hour; complete in Twelve Fortnightly Parts.") The Fairy Godmother Department presents us with what the Quartermaster describes as "Boots, gum, thigh"; and there has also been an issue of so-called fur jackets, in which the Practical Joke Department has plainly taken a hand. Most of these garments appear to have been contributed by animals unknown to zoology, or more probably by a syndicate thereof. Corporal Mucklewame's costume gives him the appearance of a St. Bernard dog with Astrakhan fore legs. Sergeant Carfrae is attired in what looks like the skin of Nana, the dog-nurse in "Peter Pan." Private Nigg, an undersized youth of bashful disposition, creeps forlornly about his duties disguised as an imitation leopard. As he passes by, facetious persons pull what is left of his tail. Private Tosh, on being confronted with his winter *trousseau*, observed bitterly—

"I jined the Airmy for tae be a sojer; but I doot they must have pit me doon as a mountain goat!"

Still, though our variegated pelts cause us to resemble an unsuccessful compromise between Esau and an Eskimo, they keep our bodies warm. We wish we could say the same for our feet. On good days we stand ankle-deep; on bad, we are occasionally over the knees. Thrice blessed then are our Boots, Gum, Thigh, though even these cannot altogether ward off frost-bite and chilblains.

Over the way, Brother Boche is having a bad time of it: his trenches are in a worse state than ours. Last night a plaintive voice cried out—

"Are you dere, Jock? Haf you whiskey? We haf plenty water!"

Not bad for a Boche, the platoon decided.

There is no doubt that whatever the German General Staff may think about the war and the future, the German Infantry soldier is "fed-up." His satiety takes the form of a craving for social intercourse with the foe. In the small hours, when the vigilance of the German N.C.O.'s is relaxed, and the officers are probably in their dug-outs, he makes rather pathetic overtures. We are frequently invited to come out and shake hands. "Dis war will be ober the nineteen of nex' month!" (Evidently the Kaiser has had another revelation.) The other morning a German soldier, with a wisp of something white in his hand, actually clambered out of the firing-trench and advanced towards our lines.

The distance was barely seventy yards. No shot was fired, but you may be sure that safety-catches were hastily released. Suddenly, in the tense silence, the ambassador's nerve failed him. He bolted back, followed by a few desultory bullets. The reason for his sudden panic was never rightly ascertained, but the weight of public opinion inclined to the view that Mucklewame, who had momentarily exposed himself above the parapet, was responsible.

"I doot he thocht ye were a lion escapit from the Scottish Zoo!" explained a brother corporal, referring to his indignant colleague's new winter coat.

Here is another incident, with a different ending. At one point our line approaches to within fifteen yards of the Boche trenches. One wet and dismal dawn, as the battalion stood to arms in the neighbourhood of this delectable spot, there came a sudden shout from the enemy, and an outburst of rapid rifle fire. Almost simultaneously two breathless and unkempt figures tumbled over our parapet into the firing-trench. The fusillade died away.

To the extreme discomfort and shame of a respectable citizen of Bannockburn, one Private Buncle, the more hairy of the two visitors, upon recovering his feet, promptly flung his arms around his neck and kissed him on both cheeks. The outrage was repeated, by his companion, upon Private Nigg. At the same time both visitors broke into a joyous chant of *"Russky! Russky!"* They were escaped Russian prisoners.

When taken to Headquarters they explained that they had been brought up to perform fatigue work near the German trenches, and had seized upon a quiet moment to slip into some convenient undergrowth. Later, under cover of night, they had made their way in the direction of the firing-line, arriving just in time to make a dash before daylight discovered them. You may imagine their triumphal departure from our trenches—loaded with cigarettes, chocolate, bully beef, and other imperishable souvenirs.

We have had other visitors. One bright day a Boche aeroplane made a reconnaissance of our lines. It was a beautiful thing, white and birdlike. But as its occupants were probably taking photographs of our most secret fastnesses, artistic appreciation was dimmed by righteous wrath—wrath which turned to profound gratification when a philistine British plane appeared in the blue and engaged the glittering stranger in battle. There was some very pretty aerial manoeuvring, right over our heads, as the combatants swooped and circled for position. We could hear their machine-guns pattering away; and the volume of sound was increased by the distant contributions of "Coughing Clara"—our latest anti-aircraft gun, which appears to suffer from chronic irritation of the mucous membrane.

Suddenly the German aeroplane gave a lurch; then righted herself; then began to circle down, making desperate efforts to cross the neutral line. But the British airman headed her off. Next moment she lurched again, and then took a "nosedive" straight into the British trenches. She fell on open ground, a few hundred yards behind our second line. The place had been a wilderness a moment before; but the crowd which instantaneously sprang up round the wreck could not have been less than two hundred strong. (One observes the same uncanny phenomenon in London, when a cab-horse falls down in a deserted street.) However, it melted away at the rebuke of the first officer who hurried to the spot, the process of dissolution being accelerated by several bursts of German shrapnel.

Both pilot and observer were dead. They had made a gallant fight, and were buried the same evening, with all honour, in the little cemetery, alongside many who had once been their foes, but were now peacefully neutral.

IV

The housing question in Belgium confronts us with several novel problems. It is not so easy to billet troops here, especially in the Salient, as in France. Some of us live in huts, others in tents, others in dug-outs. Others, more fortunate, are loaded on to a fleet of motor-buses and whisked off to more civilised dwellings many miles away. These buses once plied for hire upon the streets of London. Each bus is in charge of the identical pair of cross-talk comedians who controlled its destinies in more peaceful days. Strangely attired in khaki and sheepskin, they salute officers with cheerful *bonhomie*, and bellow to one another throughout the journey the simple and primitive jests of their previous incarnation, to the huge delight of their fares. The destination-boards and advertisements are no more, for the buses are painted a neutral green all over; but the conductor is always ready and willing to tell you what his previous route was.

"That Daimler behind you, sir," he informs you, "is one of the Number Nineteens. Set you down at the top of Sloane Street many a time, I'll be bound. Ernie"—this to the driver, along the side of the bus—"you oughter have slowed down when thet copper waved his little flag: he wasn't pleased with yer, ole son!" (The "copper" is a military mounted policeman, controlling the traffic of a little town which lies on our way to the trenches.) "This is a Number Eight, sir. No, that dent in the staircase wasn't done by no shell. The ole girl got that through a skid up against a lamp-post, one wet Saturday night in the Vauxhall Bridge Road. Dangerous place, London!"

We rattle through a brave little town, which is "carrying on" in the face of paralysed trade and periodical shelling. Soldiers abound. All are muddy, but some are muddier than others. The latter are going up to the trenches, the former are coming back. Upon the walls, here and there, we notice a gay poster advertising an entertainment organised by certain Divisional troops, which is to be given nightly throughout the week. At the foot of the bill is printed in large capitals, A HOOGE SUCCESS! We should like to send a copy of that plucky document to Brother Boche. He would not understand it, but it would annoy him greatly.

Now we leave the town behind, and quicken up along the open road—an interminable ribbon of *pave*, absolutely straight, and bordered upon either side by what was once macadam, but is now a quagmire a foot deep. Occasionally there is a warning cry of "Wire!" and the outside fares hurriedly bow from the waist, in order to avoid having their throats cut by a telephone wire—"Gunners for a dollar!" surmises a strangled voice—tightly stretched across the road between two poplars. Occasionally, too, that indefatigable humorist, Ernie, directs his course beneath some low-spreading branches, through which the upper part of the bus crashes remorselessly, while the passengers, lying sardine-wise upon the roof uplift their voices in profane and bloodthirsty chorus.

"Nothing like a bit o' fun on the way to the trenches, boys! It may be the last you'll get!" is the only apology which Ernie offers.

* * * * * * * *

Presently our vehicle bumps across a nubbly bridge, and enters what was once a fair city. It is a walled city, like Chester, and is separated from the surrounding country by a moat as wide as the upper Thames. In days gone by those ramparts and that moat could have held an army at bay—and probably did, more than once. They have done so yet again; but at what a cost!

We glide through the ancient gateway and along the ghostly streets, and survey the crowning achievement of the cultured Boche. The great buildings—the Cathedral, the Cloth Hall—are jagged ruins. The fronts of the houses have long disappeared, leaving the interiors exposed to view, like a doll's house. Here is a street full of shops.

That heap of splintered wardrobes and legless tables was once a furniture warehouse. That snug little corner house, with the tottering zinc counter and the twisted beer engine, is an obvious estaminet. You may observe the sign, "Aux Deux Amis," in dingy lettering over the doorway. Here is an oil-and-colour shop: you can still see the red ochre and white lead splashed about among the ruins.

In almost every house the ceilings of the upper floors have fallen in. Chairs, tables, and bedsteads hang precariously into the room below. Here and there a picture still adheres to the wall. From one of the bedposts flutters a tattered and diminutive garment of blue and white check—some little girl's frock. Where is that little girl now, we wonder; and has she got another frock?

One is struck above all things with the minute detail of the damage. You would say that a party of lunatics had been let loose on the city with coal-hammers: there is hardly a square yard of any surface which is not pierced, or splintered, or dented. The whole fabric of the place lies prostrate, under a shroud of broken bricks and broken plaster. The Hun has said in his majesty: "If you will not yield me this, the last city in the last corner of Belgium, I can at least see to it that not one stone thereof remains upon another.—So yah!"

Such is the appearance presented by the venerable and historic city of Ypres, after fifteen months of personal contact with the apostles of the new civilisation. Only the methodical and painstaking Boche could have reduced a town of such a size to such a state. Imagine Chester in a similar condition, and you may realise the number of shells which have fallen, and are still falling, into the stricken city.

But—the main point to observe is this. We are inside, and the Boche is outside! Fenced by a mighty crescent of prosaic trenches, themselves manned by paladins of an almost incredible stolidity, Ypres still points her broken fingers to the sky—shattered, silent, but inviolate still; and all owing to the obstinacy of a dull and unready nation which merely keeps faith and stands by its friends. Such an attitude of mind is incomprehensible to the Boche, and we are well content that it should be so.

CHAPTER 2

Shell Out!

This, according to our latest subaltern from home, is the title of a *revue* which is running in Town; but that is a mere coincidence. The entertainment to which I am now referring took place in Flanders, and the leading parts were assigned to distinguished members of "K (1)."

The scene was the Chateau de Grandbois, or some other kind of Bois; possibly Vert. Not that we called it that: we invariably referred to it afterwards as Hush Hall, for reasons which will be set forth in due course.

One morning, while sojourning in what Olympus humorously calls a rest-camp,—a collection of antiquated wigwams half submerged in a mud-flat,—we received the intelligence that we were to extricate ourselves forthwith, and take over a fresh sector of trenches. The news was doubly unwelcome, because, in the first place, it is always unpleasant to face the prospect of trenches of any kind; and secondly, to take over strange trenches in the dead of a winter night is an experience which borders upon nightmare—the hot-lobster-and-toasted-cheese variety.

The opening stages of this enterprise are almost ritualistic in their formality. First of all, the Brigade Staff which is coming in visits the Headquarters of the Brigade which is going out—usually a chateau or farm somewhere in rear of the trenches—and makes the preliminary arrangements. After that the Commanding Officers and Company Commanders of the incoming battalions visit their own particular section of the line. They are shown over the premises by the outgoing tenants, who make little or no attempt to conceal their satisfaction at the expiration of their lease. The Colonels and the Captains then return to camp, with depressing tales of crumbling parapets, noisome dug-outs, and positions open to enfilade.

On the day of the relief various advance parties go up, keeping under the lee of hedges and embankments, and marching in single file. (At least, that is what they are supposed to do. If not ruthlessly shepherded, they will advance in fours along the skyline.) Having arrived, they take over such positions as can be relieved by daylight in comparative safety. They also take over trench-stores, and exchange trench-gossip. The latter is a fearsome and uncanny thing. It usually begins life at the "refilling point," where the A.S.C. motor-lorries dump down next day's rations, and the regimental transport picks them up.

An A.S.C. Sergeant mentions casually to a regimental Quartermaster that he has heard it said at the Supply Depot that heavy firing has been going on in the Channel. The Quartermaster, on returning to the Transport Lines, observes to his Quartermaster-Sergeant that the German Fleet has come out at last. The Quartermaster-Sergeant, when he meets the ration parties behind the lines that night, announces to a platoon Sergeant that we have won a great naval victory. The platoon Sergeant, who is suffering from trench feet and is a constant reader of a certain pessimistic halfpenny journal, replies gloomily: "We'll have had heavy losses oorselves, too, I doot!" This observation is overheard by various members of the ration party. By midnight several hundred yards of the firing-line know for a fact that there has been a naval disaster of the first magnitude off the coast of a place which every one calls Gally Polly, and that the whole of our Division are to be transferred forthwith to the Near East to stem the tide of calamity.

Still, we must have *something* to chat about.

* * * * * * * *

Meanwhile Brigade Majors and Adjutants, holding a stumpy pencil in one hand and a burning brow in the other, are composing Operation Orders which shall effect the relief, without—

(1) Leaving some detail—the bombers, or the snipers, or the sock-driers, or the pea-soup experts—unrelieved altogether.

(2) Causing relievers and relieved to meet violently together in some constricted fairway.

(3) Trespassing into some other Brigade Area. (This is far more foolhardy than to wander into the German lines.)

(4) Getting shelled.

Pitfall Number One is avoided by keeping a permanent and handy list of "all the people who do funny things on their own" (as the vulgar throng call the "specialists"), and checking it carefully before issuing Orders.

Number Two is dealt with by issuing a strict time-table, which might possibly be adhered to by a well-drilled flock of archangels, in broad daylight, upon good roads, and under peace conditions.

Number Three is provided for by copious and complicated map references.

Number Four is left to Providence—and is usually the best-conducted feature of the excursion.

Under cover of night the Battalion sets out, in comparatively small parties. They form a strange procession. The men wear their trench-costume—thigh-boots (which do not go well with a kilt), variegated coats of skins, and woollen nightcaps. Stuffed under their belts and through their packs they carry newspapers, broken staves for firewood, parcels from home, and sandbags loaded with mysterious comforts. A dilapidated parrot and a few goats are all that is required to complete the picture of Robinson Crusoe changing camp.

Progress is not easy. It is a pitch-black night. By day, this road (and all the countryside) is a wilderness: nothing more innocent ever presented itself to the eye of an inquisitive aeroplane. But after nightfall it is packed with troops and transport, and not a light is shown. If you can imagine what the Mansion House crossing would be like if called upon to sustain its midday traffic at midnight—the Mansion House crossing entirely unilluminated, paved with twelve inches of liquid mud, intersected by narrow strips of *pave*, and liberally pitted with "crump-holes"—you may derive some faint idea of the state of things at a busy road-junction lying behind the trenches.

Until reaching what is facetiously termed "the shell area"—as if any spot in this benighted district were not a shell area—the troops plod along in fours at the right of the road. If they can achieve two miles an hour, they do well. At any moment they may be called upon to halt, and crowd into the roadside, while a transport-train passes carrying rations, and coke, and what is called "R.E. material"—this may be anything from a bag of nails to steel girders nine feet long—up to the firing-line. When this procession, consisting of a dozen limbered wagons, drawn by four mules and headed by a profane person on horseback—the Transport Officer—has rumbled past, the Company, which has been standing respectfully in the ditch, enjoying a refreshing shower-bath of mud and hoping that none of the steel girders are projecting from the limber more than a yard or two, sets out once more upon its way—only to take hasty cover again as sounds of fresh and more animated traffic are heard approaching from the opposite direction. There is no mistaking the nature of this cavalcade: the long vista of glowing cigarette-ends tells an unmistakable tale. These are artillery wagons, returning empty from replenishing the batteries; scattering homely jests like hail, and proceeding, wherever possible, at a hand-gallop. He is a cheery soul, the R.A. driver, but his interpretation of the rules of the road requires drastic revision.

Sometimes an axle breaks, or a wagon side-slips off the *pave* into the morass reserved for infantry, and overturns. The result is a block, which promptly extends forward and back for a couple of miles. A peculiarly British chorus of inquiry and remonstrance—a blend of biting sarcasm and blasphemous humour—surges up and down the line; until plunging mules are unyoked, and the offending vehicle man-handled out of sight into the inky blackness by the roadside; or, in extreme cases, is annihilated with axes. Everything has to make way for a ration train. To crown all, it is more than likely that the calmness and smooth working of the proceedings will be assisted by a burst of shrapnel overhead. It is a most amazing scrimmage altogether. One of those members of His Majesty's Opposition who are doing so much at present to save our country from destruction, by kindly pointing out the mistakes of the British Government and the British Army, would refer to the whole scene as a pandemonium of mismanagement and ineptitude. And yet, though the scene is enacted night after night without a break, there is hardly a case on record of the transport being surprised upon these roads by the coming of daylight, and none whatever of the rations and ammunition failing to get through.

It is difficult to imagine that Brother Boche, who on the other side of that ring of star-shells is conducting a precisely similar undertaking, is able, with all his perfect organisation and cast-iron methods, to achieve a result in any way superior to that which Thomas Atkins reaches by rule of thumb and sheer force of character.

* * * * * * * *

At length the draggled Company worms its way through the press to the fringe of the shell-area, beyond which no transport may pass. The distance of this point from the trenches varies considerably, and depends largely upon the caprice of the Boche. On this occasion, however, we still have a mile or two to go—across country now, in single file, at the heels of a guide from the battalion which we are relieving.

Guides may be divided into two classes—

(1) Guides who do not know the way, and say so at the outset.

(2) Guides who do not know the way, but leave it to you to discover the fact.

There are no other kinds of guides.

The pace is down to a mile an hour now, except in the case of men in the tail of the line, who are running rapidly. It is a curious but quite inexplicable fact that if you set a hundred men to march in single file in the dark, though the leading man may be crawling like a tortoise, the last man is compelled to proceed at a profane double if he is to avoid being left behind and lost.

Still, everybody gets there somehow, and in due course the various Company Commanders are enabled to telephone to their respective Battalion Headquarters the information that the Relief is completed. For this relief, much thanks!

After that the outgoing Battalion files slowly out, and the newcomers are left gloomily contemplating their new abiding-place, and observing—

"I wonder if there is *any* Division in the whole blessed Expeditionary Force, besides ours, which ever does a single damn thing to keep its trenches in repair!"

II

All of which brings us back to Hush Hall, where the Headquarters of the outgoing Brigade are handing over to their successors.

Hush Hall, or the Chateau de Quelquechose, is a modern country house, and once stood up white and gleaming in all its brave finery of stucco, conservatories, and ornamental lake, amid a pleasant wood not far from a main road. It is such a house as you might find round about Guildford or Hindhead. There are many in this fair countryside, but few are inhabited now, and none by their rightful owners. They are all marked on the map, and the Boche gunners are assiduous map-readers. Hush Hall has got off comparatively lightly. It is still habitable, and well furnished. The roof is demolished upon the side most exposed to the enemy, and many of the trees in the surrounding wood are broken and splintered by shrapnel. Still, provided the weather remains passable, one can live there. Upon the danger-side the windows are closed and shuttered. Weeds grow apace in the garden. No smoke emerges from the chimneys. (If it does, the Mess Corporal hears about it from the Staff Captain.) A few strands of barbed wire obstruct the passage of those careless or adventurous persons who may desire to explore the forbidden side of the house. The front door is bolted and barred: visitors, after approaching stealthily along the lee of a hedge, like travellers of dubious *bona fides* on a Sunday afternoon, enter unobtrusively by the back door, which is situated on the blind side of the chateau. Their path thereto is beset by imploring notices like the following:—

The Slightest Movement Draws Shell Fire.
Keep Close To The Hedge

A later hand has added the following moving postscript:—

We Live Here. You Don't!

It was the Staff Captain who was responsible for the rechristening of the establishment.

"What sort of place is this new palace we are going to doss in?" inquired the Machine-Gun Officer, when the Staff Captain returned from his preliminary visit.

The Staff Captain, who was a man of a few words, replied—

"It's the sort of shanty where everybody goes about in felt slippers, saying 'Hush!'"

* * * * * * * *

Brigade Headquarters—this means the Brigadier, the Brigade Major, the Staff Captain, the Machine-Gun Officer, the Signal Officer, mayhap a Padre and a Liaison Officer, accompanied by a mixed multitude of clerks, telegraphists, and scullions—arrived safely at their new quarters under cover of night, and were hospitably received by the outgoing tenants, who had finished their evening meal and were girded up for departure. In fact, the Machine-Gun Officer, Liaison Officer, and Padre had already gone, leaving their seniors to hold the fort till the last. The Signal Officer was down in the cellar, handing over ohms, amperes, short-circuits, and other mysterious trench-stores to his "opposite number."

Upon these occasions there is usually a good deal of time to fill in between the arrival of the new brooms and the departure of the old. This period of waiting may be likened to that somewhat anxious interval with which frequenters of race-courses are familiar, between the finish of the race and the announcement of the "All Right!" The outgoing Headquarters are waiting for the magic words—"Relief Complete!" Until that message comes over the buzzer, the period of tension endures. The main point of difference is that the gentleman who has staked his fortune on the legs of a horse has only to wait a few minutes for the confirmation of his hopes; while a Brigadier, whose bedtime (or even breakfast-time) is at the mercy of an errant platoon, may have to sit up all night.

"Sit down and make yourselves comfortable," said A Brigade to X Brigade.

X Brigade complied, and having been furnished with refreshment, led off with the inevitable question—

"Does one—er—get shelled much here?"

There was a reassuring coo from A Brigade.

"Oh, no. This is a very healthy spot. One has to be careful, of course. No movement, or fires, or anything of that kind. A sentry or two, to warn people against approaching over the open by day, and you'll be as cooshie as anything!" ("Cooshie" is the latest word here. That and "crump.")

"I ought to warn you of one thing," said the Brigadier. "Owing to the surrounding woods, sound is most deceptive here. You will hear shell-bursts which appear quite close, when in reality they are quite a distance away. That, for instance!"—as a shell exploded apparently just outside the window. "That little fellow is a couple of hundred yards away, in the corner of the wood. The Boche has been groping about there for a battery for the last two days."

"Is the battery there?" inquired a voice.

"No; it is farther east. But there is a Gunner's Mess about two hundred yards from here, in that house which you passed on the way up."

"Oh!" observed X Brigade.

Gunners are peculiar people. When professionally engaged, no men could be more retiring. They screen their operations from the public gaze with the utmost severity, shrouding batteries in screens of foliage and other rustic disguises. If a layman strays anywhere near one of these arboreal retreats, a gunner thrusts out a visage enflamed with righteous wrath, and curses him for giving the position away. But in his hours of relaxation the gunner is a different being. He billets himself in a house with plenty of windows: he illuminates all these by night, and hangs washing therefrom by day. When inclined for exercise, he goes for a promenade across an open space labelled—"Not to be used by troops by daylight." Therefore, despite his technical excellence and superb courage, he is an uncomfortable neighbour for establishments like Hush Hall.

In this respect he offers a curious contrast to the Sapper. Off duty, the Sapper is the most unobtrusive of men—a cave-man, in fact. He burrows deep into the earth, or the side of a hill, and having secured the roof of this cavern against direct hits by ingenious contrivances of his own manufacture, constructs a suite of furniture of a solid and enduring pattern, and lives the life of a comfortable recluse. But when engaged in the pursuit of his calling, the Sapper is the least retiring of men. The immemorial tradition of the great Corps to which he belongs has ordained that no fire, however fierce, must be allowed to interfere with a Sapper in the execution of his duty. This rule is usually interpreted by the Sapper to mean that you must not perform your allotted task under cover when it is possible to do so under fire. To this is added, as a rider, that in the absence of an adequate supply of fire, you must draw fire. So the Sapper walks cheerfully about on the tops of parapets, hugging large and conspicuous pieces of timber, or clashing together sheets of corrugated iron, as happy as a king.

"You will find this house quite snug," continued the Brigadier. "The eastern suite is to be avoided, because there is no roof there; and if it rains outside for a day, it rains in the best bedroom for a week. There is a big kitchen in the basement, with a capital range. That's all, I think. The chief thing to avoid is movement of any kind. The leaves are coming off the trees now—"

At this moment an orderly entered the room with a pink telegraph message.

"Relief complete, sir!" announced the Brigade Major, reading it.

"Good work!" replied both Brigadiers, looking at their watches simultaneously, "considering the state of the country." The Brigadier of "A" rose to his feet.

"Now we can pass along quietly," he said. "Good luck to you. By the way, take care of Edgar, won't you? Any little attention which you can show him will be greatly appreciated."

"Who is Edgar?"

"Oh, I thought the Staff Captain would have told you. Edgar is the swan—the last of his race, I'm afraid, so far as this place is concerned. He lives on the lake, and usually comes ashore to draw his rations about lunch-time. He is inclined to be stand-offish on one side, as he has only one eye; but he is most affable on the other. Well, now to find our horses!"

As the three officers departed down the backdoor steps, a hesitating voice followed them—"H'm! Is there any place where one can go—a cellar, or any old spot of that kind—just in case we are—"

"Bless you, you'll be all right!" was the cheery reply. (The outgoing Brigade is always excessively cheery.) "But there are dug-outs over there—in the garden. They haven't been occupied for some months, so you may find them a bit ratty. You won't require them, though. Good-night!"

III

Whizz! Boom! Bang! Crash! Wump!

"It's just as well," mused the Brigade Major, turning in his sleep about three o'clock the following morning, "that they warned us about the deceptive sound of the shelling here. One would almost imagine that it was quite close.... That last one was heavy stuff: it shook the whole place!... This is a topping mattress: it would be rotten having to take to the woods again after getting into really cooshie quarters at last.... There they go again!" as a renewed tempest of shells rent the silence of night. "That old battery must be getting it in the neck!... Hallo, I could have sworn something hit the roof that time! A loose slate, I expect! Anyhow ..."

The Brigade Major, who had had a very long day, turned over and went to sleep again.

IV

The next morning, a Sunday, broke bright and clear. Contrary to his usual habit, the Brigade Major took a stroll in the garden before breakfast. The first object which caught his eye, as he came down the back-door steps, was the figure of the Staff Captain, brooding pensively over a large crater, close to the hedge. The Brigade Major joined him.

"I wonder if that was there yesterday!" he observed, referring to the crater.

"Couldn't have been," growled the Staff Captain. "We walked to the house along this very hedge. No craters then!"

"True!" agreed the Brigade Major amiably. He turned and surveyed the garden. "That lawn looks a bit of a golf course. What lovely bunkers!"

"They appear to be quite new, too," remarked the Staff Captain thoughtfully. "Come to breakfast!"

On their way back they found the Brigadier, the Machine-Gun Officer, and the Padre, gazing silently upward.

"I wonder when that corner of the house got knocked off," the M.G.O. was observing.

"Fairly recently, I should say," replied the Brigadier.

"Those marks beside your bedroom window, sir,—they look pretty fresh!" interpolated the Padre, a sincere but somewhat tactless Christian.

Brigade Headquarters regarded one another with dubious smiles.

"I *wonder*," began a tentative voice, "if those fellows last night were indulging in a leg-pull—what is called in this country a *lire-jambe*—when they assured us—"

Whoo-oo-*oo*-oo-ump!

A shell came shrieking over the tree-tops, and fell with a tremendous splash into the geometrical centre of the lake, fifty yards away.

* * * * * * * *

For the next two hours, shrapnel, "whizz-bangs," "Silent Susies," and other explosive wildfowl raged round the walls of Hush Hall. The inhabitants thereof, some twenty persons in all, were gathered in various apartments on the lee side.

"It is still possible," remarked the Brigadier, lighting his pipe, "that they are not aiming at us. However, it is just as inconvenient to be buried by accident as by design. As soon as the first direct hit is registered upon this imposing fabric, we will retire to the dug-outs. Send word to the kitchen that every one is to be ready to clear out of the house when necessary."

Next moment there came a resounding crash, easily audible above the tornado raging in the garden, followed by the sound of splintering glass. Hush Hall rocked. The Mess waiter appeared.

"A shell has just came in through the dining-room window, sirr," he informed the Mess President, "and broke three of they new cups!"

"How tiresome!" said the Brigadier. "Dug-outs, everybody!"

V

There were no casualties, which was rather miraculous. Late in the afternoon Brigade Headquarters ventured upon another stroll in the garden. The tumult had ceased, and the setting Sabbath sun glowed peacefully upon the battered countenance of Hush Hall. The damage was not very extensive, for the house was stoutly built. Still, two bedrooms, recently occupied, were a wreck of broken glass and splintered plaster, while the gravel outside was littered with lead sheeting and twisted chimney-cans. The shell which had aroused the indignation of the Mess waiter by entering the dining-room window, had in reality hit the ground directly beneath it. Six feet higher, and the Brigadier's order to clear the house would have been entirely superfluous.

The Brigade Major and the Staff Captain surveyed the unruffled surface of the lake—a haunt of ancient peace in the rays of the setting sun. Upon the bosom thereof floated a single, majestic, one-eyed swan, performing intricate toilet exercises. It was Edgar.

"He must have a darned good dug-out somewhere!" observed the Brigade Major enviously.

CHAPTER 3
Winter Sports: Various

Hush Hall having become an even less desirable place of residence than had hitherto been thought possible, Headquarters very sensibly sent for their invaluable friends, Box and Cox, of the Royal Engineers, and requested that they would proceed to make the place proof against shells and weather, forthwith, if not sooner.

Those phlegmatic experts made a thorough investigation of the resources of the establishment, and departed mysteriously, after the fashion of the common plumber of civilisation, into space. Three days later they returned, accompanied by a horde of acolytes, who, with characteristic contempt for the pathetic appeals upon the notice-boards, proceeded to dump down lumber, sandbags, and corrugated iron roofing in the most exposed portions of the garden.

This done, some set out to shore up the ceilings of the basement with mighty battens of wood, and to convert that region into a nest of cunningly devised bedrooms. Others reinforced the flooring above with a layer of earth and brick rubble three feet deep. On the top of all this they relaid not only the original floor, but eke the carpet.

"The only difference from before, sir," explained Box to the admiring Staff Captain, "is that people will have to walk up three steps to get into the dining-room now, instead of going in on the level."

"I wonder what the Marquise de Chilquichose will think of it all when she returns to her ancestral home," mused the Staff Captain.

"If anything," maintained the invincible Box, "we have improved it for her. For example, she can now light the chandelier without standing on a chair—without getting up from table, in fact! However, to resume. The fireplace, you will observe, has not been touched. I have left a sort of well in the floor all round it, lined with some stuff I found in Mademoiselle's room. At least," added Box coyly,

"I think it must have been Mademoiselle's room! You can sit in the well every evening after supper. The walls of this room"—prodding the same—"are lined with sandbags, covered with tapestry. Pretty artistic—what?"

"Extremely," agreed the Staff Captain. "You will excuse my raising the point, I know, but can the apartment now be regarded as shell-proof?"

"Against everything but a direct hit. I wouldn't advise you to sleep on this floor much, but you could have your meals here all right. Then, if the Boche starts putting over heavy stuff, you can pop down into the basement and have your dessert in bed. You'll be absolutely safe there. In fact, the more the house tumbles down the safer you will be. It will only make your protection shell thicker. So if you hear heavy thuds overhead, don't be alarmed!"

"I won't," promised the Staff Captain. "I shall lie in bed, drinking a nice hot cup of tea, and wondering whether the last crash was the kitchen chimney, or only the drawing-room piano coming down another storey. Now show me my room."

"We have had to put you in the larder," explained Box apologetically, as he steered his guest through a forest of struts with an electric torch. "At least, I think it's the larder: it has a sort of meaty smell. The General is in the dairy—a lovely little suite, with white tiles. The Brigade Major has the scullery: it has a sink, so is practically as good as a flat in Park Place. I have run up cubicles for the others in the kitchen. Here is your little cot. It is only six feet by four, but you can dress in the garden."

"It's a *sweet* little nest, dear!" replied the Staff Captain, quite hypnotised by this time. "I'll just get my maid to put me into something loose, and then I'll run along to your room, and we'll have a nice cosy gossip together before dinner!"

* * * * * * * *

In due course we removed our effects from the tottering and rat-ridden dug-outs in which we had taken sanctuary during the shelling, and prepared to settle down for the winter in our new quarters.

"We might be *very* much worse off!" we observed the first evening, listening to the comfortably muffled sounds of shells overhead.

And we were right. Three days later we received an intimation from the Practical Joke Department that we were to evacuate our present sector of trenches (including Hush Hall) forthwith, and occupy another part of the line.

In all Sports, Winter and Summer, the supremacy of the Practical Joke Department is unchallenged.

II

Meanwhile, up in the trenches, the combatants are beguiling the time in their several ways.

Let us take the reserve line first—the lair of Battalion Headquarters and its appurtenances. Much of our time here, as elsewhere, is occupied in unostentatious retirement to our dug-outs, to avoid the effects of a bombardment. But a good amount—an increasing amount—of it is devoted to the contemplation of our own shells bursting over the Boche trenches. Gone are the days during which we used to sit close and "stick it out," consoling ourselves with the vague hope that by the end of the week our gunners might possibly have garnered sufficient ammunition to justify a few brief hours' retaliation. The boot is on the other leg now. For every Boche battery that opens on us, two or three of ours thunder back a reply—and that without any delays other than those incidental to the use of that maddening instrument, the field-telephone. During the past six months neither side has been able to boast much in the way of ground actually gained; but the moral ascendancy—the initiative—the offensive—call it what you will—has changed hands; and no one knows it better than the Boche. We are the attacking party now.

The trenches in this country are not arranged with such geometric precision as in France. For instance, the reserve line is not always connected with the firing-lines by a communication-trench. Those persons whose duty it is to pay daily visits to the fire-trenches—Battalion Commanders, Gunner and Sapper officers, an occasional Staff Officer, and an occasional most devoted Padre—perform the journey as best they may. Sometimes they skirt a wood or hedge, sometimes they keep under the lee of an embankment, sometimes they proceed across the open, with the stealthy caution of persons playing musical chairs, ready to sit down in the nearest shell-crater the moment the music—in the form of a visitation of "whizz-bangs"—strikes up.

It is difficult to say which kind of weather is least favourable to this enterprise. On sunny days one's movements are visible to Boche observers upon distant summits; while on foggy days the Boche gunners, being able to see nothing at all, amuse themselves by generous and unexpected contributions of shrapnel in all directions. Stormy weather is particularly unpleasant, for the noise of the wind in the trees makes it difficult to hear the shell approaching. Days of heavy rain are the most desirable on the whole, for then the gunners are too busy bailing out their gun-pits to worry their heads over adventurous pedestrians.

One learns, also, to mark down and avoid particular danger-spots. For instance, the southeast corner of that wood, where a reserve company are dug in, is visited by "Silent Susans" for about five minutes each noontide: it is therefore advisable to select some other hour for one's daily visit. (Silent Susan, by the way, is not a desirable member of the sex. Owing to her intensely high velocity she arrives overhead without a sound, and then bursts with a perfectly stunning detonation and a shower of small shrapnel bullets.) There is a fixed rifle-battery, too, which fires all day long, a shot at a time, down the main street of the ruined and deserted village named Vrjoozlehem, through which one must pass on the way to the front-line trenches. Therefore in negotiating this delectable spot, one shapes a laborious course through a series of back yards and garden-plots, littered with broken furniture and brick rubble, allowing the rifle-bullets the undisputed use of the street. The mention of Vrjoozlehem—that is not its real name, but a simplified form of it—brings to our notice the wholesale and whole-hearted fashion in which the British Army has taken Belgian institutions under its wing. Nomenclature, for instance. In France we make no attempt to interfere with this: we content ourselves with devising a pronounceable variation of the existing name. For example, if a road is called La Rue de Bois, we simply call it "Roodiboys," and leave it at that. On the same principle, Etaples is modified to "Eatables," and Sailly-la-Bourse to "Sally Booze." But in Belgium more drastic procedure is required. A Scotsman is accustomed to pronouncing difficult names, but even he is unable to contend with words composed almost entirely of the letters *j, z,* and *v*. So our resourceful Ordnance Department has issued maps—admirable maps—upon which the outstanding features of the landscape are marked in plain figures. But instead of printing the original place-names, they put MOATED GRANGE, or CLAPHAM JUNCTION, or DEAD DOG FARM, which simplifies matters beyond all possibility of error. (The system was once responsible, though, for an unjust if unintentional aspersion upon the character of a worthy man. The C.O. of a certain battalion had occasion to complain to those above him of the remissness of one of his chaplains. "He's a lazy beggar, sir," he said. "Over and over again I have told him to come up and show himself in the front-line trenches, but he never seems to be able to get past LEICESTER SQUARE!")

The naming of the trenches themselves has been left largely to local enterprise. An observant person can tell, by a study of the numerous name-boards, which of his countrymen have been occupying the line during the past six months. GRAINGER STREET and JESMOND

DENE give direct evidence of "Canny N'castle." SHERWOOD AVENUE and NOTTS FOREST have a Midland flavour. Lastly, no great mental effort is required to decide who labelled two communication trenches THE GORBALS and COOCADDENS respectively!

Some names have obviously been bestowed by officers, as SACKVILLE STREET, THE ALBANY, and BURLINGTON ARCADE denote. PINCH-GUT and CRAB-CRAWL speak for themselves. So does VERMIN VILLA. Other localities, again, have obviously been labelled by persons endowed with a nice gift of irony. SANCTUARY WOOD is the last place on earth where any one would dream of taking sanctuary; while LOVERS' WALK, which bounds it, is the scene of almost daily expositions of the choicest brand of Boche "hate."

And so on. But one day, when the War is over, and this mighty trench-line is thrown open to the disciples of the excellent Mr. Cook—as undoubtedly it will be—care should be taken that these street-names are preserved and perpetuated. It would be impossible to select a more characteristic and fitting memorial to the brave hearts who constructed them—too many of whom are sleeping their last sleep within a few yards of their own cheerful handiwork.

III

After this digression we at length reach the firing-line. It is quite unlike anything of its kind that we have hitherto encountered. It is situated in what was once a thick wood. Two fairly well-defined trenches run through the undergrowth, from which the sentries of either side have been keeping relentless watch upon one another, night and day, for many months. The wood itself is a mere forest of poles: hardly a branch, and not a twig, has been spared by the shrapnel. In the no-man's-land between the trenches the poles have been reduced to mere stumps a few inches high.

It is behind the firing-trench that the most unconventional scene presents itself. Strictly speaking, there ought to be—and generally is—a support-line some seventy yards in rear of the first. This should be occupied by all troops not required in the firing-trench. But the trench is empty—which is not altogether surprising, considering that it is half-full of water. Its rightful occupants are scattered through the wood behind—in dug-outs, in redoubts, or *en plein air*—cooking, washing, or repairing their residences. The whole scene suggests a gipsy encampment rather than a fortified post. A hundred yards away, through the trees, you can plainly discern the Boche firing-trench, and the Boche in that trench can discern you: yet never a shot comes. It is true that bullets are humming through the air and glancing off trees, but these are mostly due to the enterprise of distant machine-guns and rifle-batteries, firing from some position well adapted for enfilade. Frontal fire there is little or none. In the front-line trenches, at least, Brother Boche has had enough of it. His motto now is, "Live and let live!" In fact, he frequently makes plaintive statements to that effect in the silence of night.

You might think, then, that life in Willow Grove would be a tranquil affair. But if you look up among the few remaining branches of that tall tree in the centre of the wood, you may notice shreds of some material flapping in the breeze. Those are sandbags—or were. Last night, within the space of one hour, seventy-three shells fell into this wood, and the first of them registered a direct hit upon the dug-out of which those sandbags formed part. There were eight men in that dug-out. The telephone-wires were broken in the first few minutes, and there was some delay before word could be transmitted back to Head-quarters. Then our big guns far in rear spoke out, until the enemy's batteries (probably in response to an urgent appeal from their own front line) ceased firing. Thereupon "A" Company, who at Bobby Little's behest had taken immediate cover in the water-logged support-trench, returned stolidly to their dug-outs in Willow Grove. Death, when he makes the mistake of raiding your premises every day, loses most of his terrors and becomes a bit of a bore.

This morning the Company presents its normal appearance: its numbers have been reduced by eight—*c'est tout*! It may be some one else's turn to-morrow, but after all, that is what we are here for. Anyhow, we are keeping the Boches out of "Wipers," and a bit over. So we stretch our legs in the wood, and keep the flooded trench for the next emergency.

Let us approach a group of four which is squatting sociably round a small and inadequate fire of twigs, upon which four mess-tins are simmering. The quartet consists of Privates Cosh and Tosh, together with Privates Buncle and Nigg, preparing their midday meal.

"Tak' off your damp chup, Jimmy," suggested Tosh to Buncle, who was officiating as stoker. "Ye mind what the Captain said aboot smoke?"

"It wasna the Captain: it was the Officer," rejoined Buncle cantankerously.

(It may here be explained, at the risk of another digression, that no length of association or degree of intimacy will render the average

British soldier familiar with the names of his officers. The Colonel is "The C.O."; the Second in Command is "The Major"; your Company Commander is "The Captain," and your Platoon Commander "The Officer." As for all others of commissioned rank in the regiment, some twenty-four in all, they are as nought. With the exception of the Quartermaster, in whose shoes each member of the rank and file hopes one day to stand, they simply do not exist.)

"Onyway," pursued the careful Tosh, "he said that if any smoke was shown, all fires was tae be pitten oot. So mind and see no' to get a cauld dinner for us all, Jimmy!"

"Cauld or het," retorted the gentleman addressed, "it's little dinner I'll be gettin' this day! And ye ken fine why!" he added darkly.

Private Tosh removed a cigarette from his lower lip and sighed patiently.

"For the last time," he announced, with the air of a righteous man suffering long, "I did not lay ma hand on your dirrty wee bit ham!"

"Maybe," countered the bereaved Buncle swiftly, "you did not lay your hand upon it; but you had it tae your breakfast for all that, Davie!"

"I never pit ma hand on it!" repeated Tosh doggedly.

"No? Then I doot you gave it a bit kick with your foot," replied the inflexible Buncle.

"Or got some other body tae luft it for him!" suggested Private Nigg, looking hard at Tosh's habitual accomplice, Cosh.

"I had it pitten in an auld envelope from hame, addressed with my name," continued the mourner. "It couldna hae got oot o' that by accident!"

"Weel," interposed Cosh, with forced geniality, "it's no a thing tae argie-bargie aboot. Whatever body lufted it, it's awa' by this time. It's a fine day, boys!"

This flagrant attempt to raise the conversation to a less controversial plane met with no encouragement. Private Buncle, refusing to be appeased, replied sarcastically—

"Aye, is it? And it was a fine nicht last nicht, especially when the shellin' was gaun on! Especially in number seeven dug-oot!"

There was a short silence. Number seven dug-out was no more, and five of its late occupants were now lying under their waterproof sheets, not a hundred yards away, waiting for a Padre. Presently, however, the pacific Cosh, who in his hours of leisure was addicted to mild philosophical rumination, gave a fresh turn to the conversation.

"Mphm!" he observed thoughtfully. "They say that in a war every man has a bullet waiting for him some place or other, with his name on it! Sooner or later, he gets it. Aye! Mphm!" He sucked his teeth reflectively, and glanced towards the Field Ambulance. "Sooner or later!"

"What for would he pit his name on it, Wully?" inquired Nigg, who was not very quick at grasping allusions.

"He wouldna pit on the name himself," explained the philosopher. "What I mean is, there's a bullet for each one of us somewhere over there"—he jerked his head eastward—"in a Gairman pooch."

"What way could a Gairman pit my name on a bullet?" demanded Nigg triumphantly. "He doesna ken it!"

"Man," exclaimed Cosh, shedding some of his philosophic calm, "can ye no unnerstand that what I telled ye was jist a mainner of speakin'? When I said that a man's name was on a bullet, I didna mean that it was *written* there."

"Then what the hell *did* ye mean?" inquired the mystified disciple—not altogether unreasonably.

Private Tosh made a misguided but well-meaning attempt to straighten out the conversation.

"He means, Sandy," he explained in a soothing voice, "that the name was just stampit on the bullet. Like—like—like an identity disc!" he added brilliantly.

The philosopher clutched his temples with both hands.

"I dinna mean onything o' the kind," he roared. "What I intend tae imply is *this*, Sandy Nigg. Some place over there there is a bullet in a Gairman's pooch, and one day that bullet will find its way intil your insides as sure as if your name was written on it! *That's* what I meant. Jist a mainner of speakin'. Dae ye unnerstand me the noo?"

But it was the injured Buncle who replied—like a lightning-flash.

"Never you fear, Sandy, boy!" he proclaimed to his perturbed ally. "That bullet has no' gotten your length yet. Maybe it never wull. There's mony a thing in this worrld with one man's name on it that finds its way intil the inside of some other man." He fixed Tosh with a relentless eye. "A bit ham, for instance!"

It was a knock-out blow.

"For ony sake," muttered the now demoralised Tosh, "drop the subject, and I'll gie ye a bit ham o' ma ain! There's just time tae cook it—"

"What kin' o' a fire is this?"

A cold shadow fell upon the group as a substantial presence inserted itself between the debaters and the wintry sunshine. Corporal Mucklewame was speaking, in his new and awful official voice, pointing an accusing finger at the fire, which, neglected in the ardour of discussion, was smoking furiously.

"Did you wish the hale wood tae be shelled?" continued Mucklewame sarcastically. "Put oot the fire at once, or I'll need tae bring ye all before the Officer. It is a cauld dinner ye'll get, and ye'll deserve it!"

IV

In the fire-trench—or perhaps it would be more correct to call it the water-trench—life may be short, and is seldom merry; but it is not often dull. For one thing, we are never idle.

A Boche trench-mortar knocks down several yards of your parapet. Straightway your machine-gunners are called up, to cover the gap until darkness falls and the gaping wound can be stanched with fresh sandbags. A mine has been exploded upon your front, leaving a crater into which predatory Boches will certainly creep at night. You summon a *posse* of bombers to occupy the cavity and discourage any such enterprise. The heavens open, and there is a sudden deluge. Immediately it is a case of all hands to the trench-pump! A better plan, if you have the advantage of ground, is to cut a culvert under the parapet and pass the inundation on to a more deserving quarter. In any case you need never lack healthful exercise.

While upon the subject of mines, we may note that this branch of military industry has expanded of late to most unpleasant dimensions. The Boche began it, of course—he always initiates these undesirable pastimes,—and now we have followed his lead and caught him up.

To the ordinary mortal, to become a blind groper amid the dark places of the earth, in search of a foe whom it is almost certain death to encounter there, seems perhaps the most idiotic of all the idiotic careers open to those who are idiotic enough to engage in modern warfare. However, many of us are as much at home below ground as above it. In most peaceful times we were accustomed to spend eight hours a day there, lying up against the "face" in a tunnel perhaps four feet high, and wielding a pick in an attitude which would have convulsed any ordinary man with cramp. But there are few ordinary men in "K(1)" There is never any difficulty in obtaining volunteers for the Tunnelling Company.

So far as the amateur can penetrate its mysteries, mining, viewed under our present heading—namely, Winter Sports—offers the following advantages to its participants:—

(1) In winter it is much warmer below the earth than upon its surface, and Thomas Atkins is the most confirmed "frowster" in the world.

(2) Critics seldom descend into mines.

(3) There is extra pay.

The disadvantages are so obvious that they need not be enumerated here.

In these trenches we have been engaged upon a very pretty game of subterranean chess for some weeks past, and we are very much on our mettle. We have some small leeway to make up. When we took over these trenches, a German mine, which had been maturing (apparently unheeded) during the tenancy of our predecessors, was exploded two days after our arrival, inflicting heavy casualties upon "D" Company. Curiously enough, the damage to the trench was comparatively slight; but the tremendous shock of the explosion killed more than one man by concussion, and brought down the roofs of several dug-outs upon their sleeping occupants. Altogether it was a sad business, and the Battalion swore to be avenged.

So they called upon Lieutenant Duff-Bertram—usually called Bertie the Badger, in reference to his rodent disposition—to make the first move in the return match. So Bertie and his troglodyte assistants sank a shaft in a retired spot of their own selecting, and proceeded to burrow forward towards the Boche lines.

After certain days Bertie presented himself, covered in clay, before Colonel Kemp, and made a report.

Colonel Kemp considered.

"You say you can hear the enemy working?" he said.

"Yes, sir."

"Near?"

"Pretty near, sir."

"How near?"

"A few yards."

"What do you propose to do?"

Bertie the Badger—in private life he was a consulting mining engineer with a beautiful office in Victoria Street and a nice taste in spats—scratched an earthy nose with a muddy forefinger.

"I think they are making a defensive gallery, sir," he announced.

"Let us have your statement in the simplest possible language, please," said Colonel Kemp. "Some of my younger officers," he added rather ingeniously, "are not very expert in these matters."

Bertie the Badger thereupon expounded the situation with solemn relish. By a defensive gallery, it appeared that he meant a lateral tunnel running parallel with the trench-line, in such a manner as to intercept any tunnel pushed out by the British miners.

"And what do you suggest doing to this Piccadilly Tube of theirs?" inquired the Colonel.

"I could dig forward and break into it, sir," suggested Bertie.

"That seems a move in the right direction," said the Colonel. "But won't the Boche try to prevent you?"

"Yes, sir."

"How?"

"He will wait until the head of my tunnel gets near enough, and then blow it in."

"That would be very tiresome of him. What other alternatives are open to you?"

"I could get as near as possible, sir," replied Bertie calmly, "and then blow up *his* gallery."

"That sounds better. Well, exercise your own discretion, and don't get blown up unless you particularly want to. And above all, be quite sure that while you are amusing yourself with the Piccadilly Tube, the wily Boche isn't burrowing past *you*, and under my parapet, by the Bakerloo! Good luck! Report any fresh development at once."

So Bertie the Badger returned once more to his native element and proceeded to exercise his discretion. This took the form of continuing his aggressive tunnel in the direction of the Boche defensive gallery. Next morning, encouraged by the absolute silence of the enemy's miners, he made a farther and final push, which actually landed him in the "Piccadilly Tube" itself.

"This is a rum go, Howie!" he observed in a low voice to his corporal. "A long, beautiful gallery, five by four, lined with wood, electrically lighted, with every modern convenience—and not a Boche in it!"

"Varra bad discipline, sir!" replied Corporal Howie severely.

"Are you sure it isn't a trap?"

"It may be, sirr; but I doot the oversman is awa' to his dinner, and the men are back in the shaft, doing naething." Corporal Howie had been an "oversman" himself, and knew something of subterranean labour problems.

"Well, if you are right, the Boche must be getting demoralised. It is not like him to present us with openings like this. However, the first thing to do is to distribute a few souvenirs along the gallery. Pass the word back for the stuff. Meanwhile I shall endeavour to test your theory about the oversman's dinner-hour. I am going to creep along and have a look at the Boche entrance to the Tube. It's down there, at the south end, I think. I can see a break in the wood lining. If you hear any shooting, you will know that the dinner-hour is over!"

At the end of half an hour the Piccadilly Tube was lined with sufficient explosive material—securely rammed and tamped—to ensure the permanent closing of the line. Still no Boche had been seen or heard.

"Now, Howie," said Bertie the Badger, fingering the fuse, "what about it?"

"About what, sirr?" inquired Howie, who was not quite *au fait* with current catch-phrases.

"Are we going to touch off all this stuff now, and clear out, or are we going to wait and see?"

"I would like fine—" began the Corporal wistfully.

"So would I," said Bertie. "Tell the men to get back and out; and you and I will hold on until the guests return from the banquet."

"Varra good, sirr."

For another half-hour the pair waited—Bertie the Badger like a dog in its kennel, with his head protruding into the hostile gallery, while his faithful henchman crouched close behind him. Deathly stillness reigned, relieved only by an occasional thud, as a shell or trench-mortar bomb exploded upon the ground above their heads.

"I'm going to have another look round the corner," said Bertie at last. "Hold on to the fuse."

He handed the end of the fuse to his subordinate, and having wormed his way out of the tunnel, proceeded cautiously on all-fours along the gallery. On his way he passed the electric light. He twisted off the bulb and crawled on in the dark.

Feeling his way by the east wall of the gallery, he came presently to the break in the woodwork. Very slowly, lying flat on his stomach now, he wriggled forward until his head came opposite the opening. A low passage ran away to his left, obviously leading back to the Boche trenches. Three yards from the entrance the passage bent sharply to the right, thus interrupting the line of sight.

"There's a light burning just round that bend," said Bertie the Badger to himself. "I wonder if it would be rash to go on and have a look at it!"

He was still straining at this gnat, when suddenly his elbow encountered a shovel which was leaning against the wall of the gallery. It tumbled down with a clatter almost stunning. Next moment a hand came round the bend of the tunnel and fired a revolver almost into the explorer's face.

Another shot rang out directly after.

The devoted Howie, hastening to the rescue, collided sharply with a solid body crawling towards him in the darkness.

"Curse you, Howie!" said the voice of Bertie the Badger, with refreshing earnestness. "Get back out of this! Where's your fuse?"

The pair scrambled back into their own tunnel, and the end of the fuse was soon recovered. Almost simultaneously three more revolver-shots rang out.

"I thought I had fixed that Boche," murmured Bertie in a disappointed voice. "I heard him grunt when my bullet hit him. Perhaps this is another one—or several. Keep back in the tunnel, Howie, confound you, and don't breathe up my sleeve! They are firing straight along the gallery now. I will return the compliment. Ouch!"

"What's the matter, sirr?" inquired the anxious voice of Howie, as his officer, who had tried to fire round the corner with his left hand, gave a sudden exclamation and rolled over upon his side.

"I must have been hit the first time," he explained. "Collar-bone, I think. I didn't know, till I rested my weight on my left elbow.... Howie, I am going to exercise my discretion again. Somebody in this gallery is going to be blown up presently, and if you and I don't get a move on, p.d.q., it will be us! Give me the fuse-lighter, and wait for me at the foot of the shaft. Quick!"

Very reluctantly the Corporal obeyed. However, he was in due course joined at the foot of the shaft by Bertie the Badger, groaning profanely; and the pair made their way to the upper regions with all possible speed. After a short interval, a sudden rumbling, followed by a heavy explosion, announced that the fuse had done its work, and that the Piccadilly Tube, the fruit of many toilsome weeks of Boche calculation and labour, had been permanently closed to traffic of all descriptions.

Bertie the Badger received a Military Cross, and his abettor the D.C.M.

V

But the newest and most fashionable form of winter sport this season is The Flying Matinee.

This entertainment takes place during the small hours of the morning, and is strictly limited to a duration of ten minutes—quite long enough for most matinees, too. The actors are furnished by a unit of "K(1)" and the role of audience is assigned to the inhabitants of the Boche trenches immediately opposite. These matinees have proved an enormous success, but require most careful rehearsal.

It is two A.M., and comparative peace reigns up and down the line. The rain of star-shells, always prodigal in the early evening, has died down to a mere drizzle. Working and fatigue parties, which have been busy since darkness set in at five o'clock,—rebuilding parapets, repairing wire, carrying up rations, and patrolling debatable areas,—have ceased their labours, and are sleeping heavily until the coming of the wintry dawn shall rouse them, grimy and shivering, to another day's unpleasantness.

Private Hans Dumpkopf, on sentry duty in the Boche firing-trench, gazes mechanically over the parapet; but the night is so dark and the wind so high that it is difficult to see and quite impossible to hear anything. He shelters himself beside a traverse, and waits patiently for his relief. It begins to rain, and Hans, after cautiously reconnoitring the other side of the traverse, to guard against prowling sergeants, sidles a few yards to his right beneath the friendly cover of an improvised roof of corrugated iron sheeting, laid across the trench from parapet to *parados*. It is quite dry here, and comparatively warm. Hans closes his eyes for a moment, and heaves a gentle sigh.

Next moment there comes a rush of feet in the darkness, followed by a metallic clang, as of hobnailed boots on metal. Hans, lying prostrate and half-stunned beneath the galvanised iron sheeting, which, dislodged from its former position by the impact of a heavy body descending from above, now forms part of the flooring of the trench, is suddenly aware that this same trench is full of men—rough, uncultured men, clad in short petticoats and the skins of wild animals, and armed with knobkerries. The Flying Matinee has begun, and Hans Dumpkopf has got in by the early door.

Each of the performers—there are fifty of them all told—has his part to play, and plays it with commendable aplomb. One, having disarmed an unresisting prisoner, assists him over the parapet and escorts him affectionately to his new home. Another clubs a recalcitrant foeman over the head with a knobkerry, and having thus reduced him to a more amenable frame of mind, hoists him over the parapet and drags him after his *"kamarad."*

Other parties are told off to deal with the dug-outs. As a rule, the occupants of these are too dazed to make any resistance,—to be quite frank, the individual Boche in these days seems rather to welcome captivity than otherwise,—and presently more of the "bag" are on their way to the British lines.

But by this time the performance is drawing to a close. The alarm has been communicated to the adjacent sections of the trench, and preparations for the ejection of the intruders are being hurried forward. That is to say, German bombers are collecting upon either flank, with the intention of bombing "inwards" until the impudent foe has been destroyed or evicted. As we are not here to precipitate a general action, but merely to round up a few prisoners and do as much damage as possible in ten minutes, we hasten to the finale. As in most finales, one's actions now become less restrained—but, from a brutal point of view, more effective. A couple of hand-grenades are thrown into any dug-out which has not yet surrendered. (The Canadians, who make quite a speciality of flying matinees, are accustomed, we understand, as an artistic variant to this practice, to fasten an electric torch along the barrel of a rifle, and so illuminate their lurking targets while they shoot.) A sharp order passes along the line; every one scrambles out of the trench; and the troupe makes its way back, before the enemy in the adjacent trenches have really wakened up, to the place from which it came. The matinee, so far as the actors are concerned, is over.

Not so the audience. The avenging host is just getting busy. The bombing-parties are now marshalled and proceed with awful solemnity and Teutonic thoroughness to clear the violated trench. The procedure of a bombing-party is stereotyped. They begin by lobbing hand-grenades over the first traverse into the first bay. After the ensuing explosion, they trot round the traverse in single file and occupy the bay. This manoeuvre is then repeated until the entire trench is cleared. The whole operation requires good discipline, considerable courage, and carefully timed co-operation with the other bombing-party. In all these attributes the Boche excels. But one thing is essential to the complete success of his efforts, and that is the presence of the enemy. When, after methodically desolating each bay in turn (and incidentally killing their own wounded in the process), the two parties meet midway—practically on top of the unfortunate Hans Dumpkopf, who is still giving an imitation of a tortoise in a corrugated shell—it is discovered that the beautifully executed counter-attack has achieved nothing but the recapture of an entirely empty trench. The birds have flown, taking their prey with them. Hans is the sole survivor, and after hearing what his officer has to say to him upon the subject, bitterly regrets the fact.

Meanwhile, in the British trenches a few yards away, the box-office returns are being made up. These take the form, firstly, of some twenty-five prisoners, including one indignant officer—he had been pulled from his dug-out half asleep and frog-marched across the British lines by two private soldiers well qualified to appreciate the richness of his language—together with various souvenirs in the way of arms and accoutrements; and secondly, of the knowledge that at least as many more of the enemy had been left permanently incapacitated for further warfare in the dug-outs. A grim and grisly drama when you come to criticise it in cold blood, but not without a certain humour of its own—and most educative for Brother Boche!

But he is a slow pupil. He regards the profession of arms and the pursuit of war with such intense and solemn reverence that he *cannot* conceive how any one calling himself a soldier can be so criminally frivolous as to write a farce round the subject—much less present the farce at a Flying Matinee. That possibly explains why the following stately paragraph appeared a few days later in the periodical communiqué which keeps the German nation in touch with its Army's latest exploits:—

During the night of Jan. 4th-5th attempts were made by strong detachments of the enemy to penetrate our line near Sloozleschump, S.E. of Ypres. The attack failed utterly.

"And they don't even realise that it was only a leg-pull!" commented the Company Commander who had stage-managed the affair. "These people simply don't deserve to have entertainments arranged for them at all. Well, we must pull the limb again, that's all!"

And it was so.

Chapter 4
The Push that Failed

"I wonder if they really mean business this time," surmised that youthful Company Commander, Temporary Captain Bobby Little, to Major Wagstaffe.

"It sounds like it," said Wagstaffe, as another salvo of "whizz-bangs" broke like inflammatory surf upon the front-line trenches. "Intermittent *strafes* we are used to, but this all-day performance seems to indicate that the Boche is really getting down to it for once. The whole proceeding reminds me of nothing so much as our own 'artillery preparation' before the big push at Loos."

"Then you think the Boches are going to make a push of their own?"

"I do; and I hope it will be a good fat one. When it comes, I fancy we shall be able to put up something rather pretty in the way of a defence. The Salient is stiff with guns—I don't think the Boche quite realises *how* stiff! And we owe the swine something!" he added through his teeth.

There was a pause in the conversation. You cannot hold the Salient for three months without paying for the distinction; and the regiment had paid its full share. Not so much in numbers, perhaps, as in quality. Stray bullets, whistling up and down the trenches, coming even obliquely from the rear, had exacted most grievous toll. Shells and trench-mortar bombs, taking us in flank, had extinguished many valuable lives. At this time nothing but the best seemed to satisfy the Fates. One day it would be a trusted colour-sergeant, on another a couple of particularly promising young corporals. Only last week the Adjutant—athlete, scholar, born soldier, and very lovable schoolboy, all most perfectly blended—had fallen mortally wounded, on his morning round of the fire-trenches, by a bullet which came from nowhere. He was the subject of Wagstaffe's reference.

"Is it not possible," suggested Mr. Waddell, who habitually considered all questions from every possible point of view, "that this bombardment has been specially initiated by the German authorities, in order to impress upon their own troops a warning that there must be no Christmas truce this year?"

"If that is the Kaiser's Christmas greeting to his loving followers," observed Wagstaffe dryly, "I think he might safely have left it to us to deliver it!"

"They say," interposed Bobby Little, "that the Kaiser is here himself."

"How do you know?"

"It was rumoured in 'Comic Cuts.'" ("Comic Cuts" is the stately Summary of War Intelligence issued daily from Olympus.)

"If that is true," said Wagstaffe, "they probably will attack. All this fuss and bobbery suggest something of the kind. They remind me of the commotion which used to precede Arthur Roberts's entrance in the old days of Gaiety burlesque. Before your time, I fancy, Bobby?"

"Yes," said Bobby modestly. "I first found touch with the Gaiety over 'Our Miss Gibbs.' And I was quite a kid even then," he added, with characteristic honesty. "But what about Arthur Roberts?"

"Some forty or fifty years ago," explained Wagstaffe, "when I was in the habit of frequenting places of amusement, Arthur Roberts was leading man at the establishment to which I have referred. He usually came on about half-past eight, just as the show was beginning to lose its first wind. His entrance was a most tremendous affair. First of all the entire chorus blew in from the wings—about sixty of them in ten seconds—saying "Hurrah, hurrah, girls!" or something rather subtle of that kind; after which minor characters rushed on from opposite sides and told one another that Arthur Roberts was coming. Then the band played, and everybody began to tell the audience about it in song. When everything was in full blast, the great man would appear—stepping out of a bathing-machine, or falling out of a hansom-cab, or sliding down a chute on a toboggan. He was assisted to his feet by the chorus, and then proceeded to ginger the show up. Well, that's how this present entertainment impresses me. All this noise and obstreperousness are leading up to one thing—Kaiser Bill's entrance. Preliminary bombardment—that's the chorus getting to work! Minor characters—the trench-mortars—spread the glad news! Band *and* chorus—that's the grand attack working up to boiling-point! Finally, preceded by clouds of gas, the Arch-Comedian in person, supported by spectacled coryphees in brass hats! How's that for a Christmas pantomime?"

"Rotten!" said Bobby, as a shell sang over the parapet and burst in the wood behind.

II

Kaiser or no Kaiser, Major Wagstaffe's extravagant analogy held good. As Christmas drew nearer, the band played louder and faster; the chorus swelled higher and shriller; and it became finally apparent that something (or somebody) of portentous importance was directing the storm.

Between six and seven next morning, the Battalion, which had stood to arms all night, lifted up its heavy head and sniffed the misty dawn-wind—an east wind—dubiously. Next moment gongs were clanging up and down the trench, and men were tearing open the satchels which contained their anti-gas helmets.

Major Wagstaffe, who had been sent up from Battalion Headquarters to take general charge of affairs in the firing-trench, buttoned the bottom edge of his helmet well inside his collar and clambered up on the firing-step to take stock of the position. He crouched low, for a terrific bombardment was in progress, and shells were almost grazing the parapet.

Presently he was joined by a slim young officer similarly disguised. It was the Commander of "A" Company. Wagstaffe placed his head close to Bobby's left ear, and shouted through the cloth—

"We shan't feel this gas much. They're letting it off higher up the line. Look!"

Bobby, laboriously inhaling the tainted air inside his helmet,—being preserved from a gas attack is only one degree less unpleasant than being gassed,—turned his goggles northward.

In the dim light of the breaking day he could discern a greenish-yellow cloud rolling across from the Boche trenches on his left.

"Will they attack?" he bellowed.

Wagstaffe nodded his head, and then cautiously unbuttoned his collar and rolled up the front of his helmet. Then, after delicately sampling the atmosphere by a cautious sniff, he removed his helmet altogether. Bobby followed his example. The air was not by any means so pure as might have been desired, but it was infinitely preferable to that inside a gas-helmet.

"Nothing to signify," pronounced Wagstaffe. "We're only getting the edge of it. Sergeant, pass down that men may roll up their helmets, but must keep them on their heads. Now, Bobby, things are getting interesting. Will they attack, or will they not?"

"What do you think?" asked Bobby.

"They are certainly going to attack farther north. The Boche does not waste gas as a rule—not this sort of gas! And I think he'll attack here too. The only reason why he has not switched on our anaesthetic is that the wind isn't quite right for this bit of the line. I think it is going to be a general push. Bobby, have a look through this sniper's loophole. Can you see any bayonets twinkling in the Boche trenches?"

Bobby applied an eye to the loophole.

"Yes," he said, "I can see them. Those trenches must be packed with men."

"Absolutely stiff with them," agreed Wagstaffe, getting out his revolver. "We shall be in for it presently. Are your fellows all ready, Bobby?"

The youthful Captain ran his eye along the trench, where his Company, with magazines loaded and bayonets fixed, were grimly awaiting the onset. There had been an onset similar to this, with the same green, nauseous accompaniment, in precisely the same spot eight months before, which had broken the line and penetrated for four miles. There it had been stayed by a forlorn hope of cooks, brakesmen, and officers' servants, and disaster had been most gloriously retrieved. What was going to happen this time? One thing was certain: the day of stink-pots was over.

"When do you think they'll attack?" shouted Bobby to Wagstaffe, battling against the noise of bursting shells.

"Quite soon—in a minute or two. Their guns will stop directly—to lift their sights and set up a barrage behind us. Then, perhaps the Boche will step over his parapet. Perhaps not!"

The last sentence rang out with uncanny distinctness, for the German guns with one accord had ceased firing. For a full two minutes there was absolute silence, while the bayonets in the opposite trenches twinkled with tenfold intent.

Then, from every point in the great Salient of Ypres, the British guns replied.

Possibly the Imperial General Staff at Berlin had been misinformed as to the exact strength of the British Artillery. Possibly they had been informed by their Intelligence Department that Trades Unionism, had ensured that a thoroughly inadequate supply of shells was to hand in the Salient. Or possibly they had merely decided, after the playful habit of General Staffs, to let the infantry in the trenches take their chance of any retaliation that might be forthcoming.

Whatever these great men were expecting, it is highly improbable that they expected that which arrived. Suddenly the British batteries spoke out, and they all spoke together. In the space of four minutes they deposited *thirty thousand* high-explosive shells in the Boche front-line trenches—yea, distributed the same accurately and evenly along all that crowded arc. Then they paused, as suddenly as they began, while British riflemen and machine-gunners bent to their work.

But few received the order to fire. Here and there a wave of men broke over the German parapet and rolled towards the British lines—only to be rolled back crumpled up by machine-guns. Never once was the goal reached. The great Christmas attack was over. After months of weary waiting and foolish recrimination, that exasperating race of bad starters but great stayers, the British people, had delivered "the goods," and made it possible for their soldiers to speak with the enemy in the gate upon equal—nay, superior, terms.

"Is that all?" asked Bobby Little, peering out over the parapet, a little awe-struck, at the devastation over the way.

"That is all," said Wagstaffe, "or I'm a Boche! There will be much noise and some irregular scrapping for days, but the tin lid has been placed upon the grand attack. The great Christmas Victory is off!"

Then he added, thoughtfully, referring apparently to the star performer:—

"We *have* been and spoiled his entrance for him, haven't we?"

CHAPTER 5
Unbending the Bow

There is a certain type of English country-house female who is said to "live in her boxes." That is to say, she appears to possess no home of her own, but flits from one indulgent roof-tree to another; and owing to the fact that she is invariably put into a bedroom whose wardrobe is full of her hostess's superannuated ball-frocks and winter furs, never knows what it is to have all her "things" unpacked at once.

Well, we out here cannot be said to live in our boxes, for we do not possess any; but we do most undoubtedly live in our haversacks and packs. And this brings us to the matter in hand—namely, so-called "Rest-Billets." The whole of the hinterland of this great trench-line is full of tired men, seeking for a place to lie down in, and living in their boxes when they find one.

At present we are indulging in such a period of repose; and we venture to think that on the whole we have earned it. Our last rest was in high summer, when we lay about under an August sun in the district round Bethune, and called down curses upon all flying and creeping insects. Since then we have undergone certain so-called "operations" in the neighbourhood of Loos, and have put in three months in the Salient of Ypres. As that devout adherent of the Roman faith, Private Reilly, of "B" Company, put it to his spiritual adviser—

"I doot we'll get excused a good slice of Purgatory for this, father!"

We came out of the Salient just before Christmas, in the midst of the mutual unpleasantness arising out of the grand attack upon the British line which was to have done so much to restore the waning confidence of the Hun. It was meant to be a big affair—a most majestic victory, in fact; but our new gas-helmets nullified the gas, and our new shells paralysed the attack; so the Third Battle of Ypres was not yet. Still, as I say, there was considerable unpleasantness all round;

and we were escorted upon our homeward way, from Sanctuary Wood to Zillebeke, and from Zillebeke to Dickebusche, by a swarm of angry and disappointed shells.

Next day we found ourselves many miles behind the firing-line, once more in France, with a whole month's holiday in prospect, comfortably conscious that one could walk round a corner or look over a wall without preliminary reconnaissance or subsequent extirpation.

As for the holiday itself, unreasonable persons are not lacking to point out that it is of the busman's variety. It is true that we are no longer face to face with the foe, but we—or rather, the authorities—make believe that we are. We wage mimic warfare in full marching order; we fire rifles and machine-guns upon improvised ranges; we perform hazardous feats with bombs and a dummy trench. More galling still, we are back in the region of squad-drill, physical exercises, and handling of arms—horrors of our childhood which we thought had been left safely interned at Aldershot.

But the authorities are wise. The regiment is stiff and out of condition: it is suffering from moral and intellectual "trench-feet." Heavy drafts have introduced a large and untempered element into our composition. Many of the subalterns are obviously "new-jined"—as the shrewd old lady of Ayr once observed of the rubicund gentleman at the temperance meeting. Their men hardly know them or one another by sight. The regiment must be moulded anew, and its lustre restored by the beneficent process vulgarly known as "spit and polish." So every morning we apply ourselves with thoroughness, if not enthusiasm, to tasks which remind us of last winter's training upon the Hampshire chalk.

But the afternoon and evening are a different story altogether. If we were busy in the morning, we are busier still for the rest of the day. There is football galore, for we have to get through a complete series of Divisional cup-ties in four weeks. There is also a Brigade boxing-tournament. (No, that was not where Private Tosh got his black eye: that is a souvenir of New Year's Eve.) There are entertainments of various kinds in the recreation-tent. This whistling platoon, with towels round their necks, are on their way to the nearest convent, or asylum, or Ecole des Jeunes Filles—have no fear; these establishments are untenanted!—for a bath. There, in addition to the pleasures of ablution, they will receive a partial change of raiment.

Other signs of regeneration are visible. That mysterious-looking vehicle, rather resembling one of the early locomotives exhibited in the South Kensington Museum, standing in the mud outside a farm-billet, its superheated interior stuffed with "C" Company's blankets, is performing an unmentionable but beneficent work.

Buttons are resuming their polish; the pattern of our kilts is emerging from its superficial crust; and Church Parade is once more becoming quite a show affair.

Away to the east the guns still thunder, and at night the star-shells float tremblingly up over the distant horizon. But not for us. Not yet, that is. In a few weeks' time we shall be back in another part of the line. Till then—Company drill and Cup-Ties! *Carpe diem!*

II

It all seemed very strange and unreal to Second-Lieutenant Angus M'Lachlan, as he alighted from the train at railhead, and supervised the efforts of his solitary N.C.O. to arrange the members of his draft in a straight line. There were some thirty of them in all. Some were old hands—men from the First and Second Battalions, who had been home wounded, and had now been sent out to leaven "K(1)." Others were Special Reservists from the Third Battalion. These had been at the Depot for a long time, and some of them stood badly in need of a little active service. Others, again, were new hands altogether—the product of "K to the *nth*." Among these Angus M'Lachlan numbered himself, and he made no attempt to conceal the fact. The novelty of the sights around him was almost too much for his *insouciant* dignity as a commissioned officer.

Angus M'Lachlan was a son of the Manse, and incidentally a child of Nature. The Manse was a Highland Manse; and until a few months ago Angus had never, save for a rare visit to distant Edinburgh, penetrated beyond the small town which lay four miles from his native glen, and of whose local Academy he had been "dux." When the War broke out he had been upon the point of proceeding to Edinburgh University, where he had already laid siege to a bursary, and captured the same; but all these plans, together with the plans of countless more distinguished persons, had been swept to the winds by the invasion of Belgium. On that date Angus summoned up his entire stock of physical and moral courage and informed his reverend parent of his intention to enlist for a soldier. Permission was granted with quite stunning readiness. Neil M'Lachlan believed in straight hitting both in theology and war, and was by no means displeased at the martial aspirations of his only son. If he quitted himself like a man in the forefront of battle, the boy could safely look forward to being cock of his own Kirk-Session in the years that came afterwards. One reservation the old man made. His son, as a Highland gentleman, would lead men to battle, and not merely accompany them. So the impatient Angus was bidden to apply for a Commission—his attention during the period of waiting being directed by his parent to the study of the campaigns of Joshua, and the methods employed by that singular but successful strategist in dealing with the Philistine.

Angus had a long while to wait, for all the youth of England—and Scotland too—was on fire, and others nearer the fountain of honour had to be served first. But his turn came at last; and we now behold him, as typical a product of "K to the *nth*" as Bobby Little had been of "K(1)," standing at last upon the soil of France, and inquiring in a soft Highland voice for the Headquarters of our own particular Battalion.

He had half expected, half hoped, to alight from the train amidst a shower of shells, as he knew the Old Regiment had done many months before, just after the War broke out. But all he saw upon his arrival was an untidy goods yard, littered with military stores, and peopled by British privates in the *deshabille* affected by the British Army when engaged in menial tasks.

Being quite ignorant of the whereabouts of his regiment—when last heard of they had been in trenches near Ypres—and failing to recollect the existence of that autocratic but indispensable *genius loci*, the R.T.O., Angus took uneasy stock of his surroundings and wondered what to do next.

Suddenly a friendly voice at his elbow remarked—

"There's a queer lot o' bodies hereaboot, sirr."

Angus turned, to find that he was being addressed by a short, stout private of the draft, in a kilt much too big for him.

"Indeed, that is so," he replied politely. "What is your name?"

"Peter Bogle, sirr. I am frae oot of Kirkintilloch." Evidently gratified by the success of his conversational opening, the little man continued—

"I would like fine for tae get a contrack oot here after the War. This country is in a terrible state o' disrepair." Then he added confidentially—

"I'm a hoose-painter tae a trade."

"I should not like to be that myself," replied Angus, whose early training as a minister's son was always causing him to forget the social gulf which is fixed between officers and the rank-and-file. "Climbing ladders makes me dizzy."

"Och, it's naething! A body gets used tae it," Mr. Bogle assured him.

Angus was about to proceed further with the discussion, when the cold and disapproving voice of the Draft-Sergeant announced in his ear—

"An officer wishes to speak to you, sir."

Second-Lieutenant M'Lachlan, suddenly awake to the enormity of his conduct, turned guiltily to greet the officer, while the Sergeant abruptly hunted the genial Private Bogle back into the ranks.

Angus found himself confronted by an immaculate young gentleman wearing two stars. Angus, who only wore one, saluted hurriedly.

"Morning," observed the stranger. "You in charge of this draft?"

"Yes, sir," said Angus respectfully.

"Right-o! You are to march them to 'A' Company billets. I'll show you the way. My name's Cockerell. Your train is late. What time did you leave the Base?"

"Indeed," replied Angus meekly, "I am not quite sure. We had barely landed when they told me the train would start at seventeen-forty. What time would that be—sir?"

"About a quarter to ten: more likely about midnight! Well, get your bunch on to the road, and—Hallo, what's the matter? Let go!"

The new officer was gripping him excitedly by the arm, and as the new officer stood six-foot-four and was brawny in proportion, Master Cockerell's appeal was uttered in a tone of unusual sincerity.

"Look!" cried Angus excitedly. "The dogs, the dogs!"

A small cart was passing swiftly by, towed by two sturdy hounds of unknown degree. They were pulling with the feverish enthusiasm which distinguishes the Dog in the service of Man, and were being urged to further efforts by a small hatless girl carrying the inevitable large umbrella.

"All right!" explained Cockerell curtly. "Custom of the country, and all that."

The impulsive Angus apologised; and the draft, having been safely manoeuvred on to the road, formed fours and set out upon its march.

"Are the Battalion in the trenches at present, sir?" inquired Angus.

"No. Rest-billets two miles from here. About time, too! You'll get lots of work to do, though."

"I shall welcome that," said Angus simply. "In the depot at home we were terribly idle. There is a windmill!"

"Yes; one sees them occasionally out here," replied Cockerell dryly.

"Everything is so strange!" confessed the open-hearted Angus. "Those dogs we saw just now—the people with their sabots—the country carts, like wheelbarrows with three wheels—the little shrines at the cross-roads—the very children talking French so glibly—"

"Wonderful how they pick it up!" agreed Cockerell. But the sarcasm was lost on his companion, whose attention was now riveted upon an approaching body of infantry, about fifty strong.

"What troops are those, please?"

Cockerell knitted his brows sardonically.

"It's rather hard to tell at this distance," he said; "but I rather think they are the Grenadier Guards."

Two minutes later the procession had been met and passed. It consisted entirely of elderly gentlemen in ill-fitting khaki, clumping along upon their flat feet and smoking clay pipes. They carried shovels on their shoulders, and made not the slightest response when called upon by the soldierly old corporal who led them to give Mr. Cockerell "eyes left!" On the contrary, engaged as they were in heated controversy or amiable conversation with one another, they cut him dead.

Angus M'Lachlan said nothing for quite five minutes. Then—

"I suppose," he said almost timidly, "that those were members of a *Reserve* Regiment of the Guards?"

Cockerell, who had never outgrown certain characteristics which most of us shed upon emerging from the Lower Fourth, laughed long and loud.

"That crowd? They belong to one of the Labour Battalions. They make roads, and dig support trenches, and sling mud about generally. Wonderful old sportsmen! Pleased as Punch when a shell falls within half a mile of them. Something to write home about. What? I say, I pulled your leg that time! Here we are at Headquarters. Come and report to the C.O. Grenadier Guards! My aunt!"

* * * * * * * *

Angus, although his Celtic enthusiasm sometimes led him into traps, was no fool. He soon settled down in his new surroundings, and found favour with Colonel Kemp, which was no light achievement.

"You won't find that the War, in its present stage, calls for any display of genius," the Colonel explained to Angus at their first interview. "I don't expect my officers to exhibit any quality but the avoidance of *sloppiness*. If I detail you to be at a certain spot, at a certain hour, with a certain number of men—a ration-party, or a working-party, or a burial-party, or anything you like,—all I ask is that you will be *there*, at the appointed hour, with the whole of your following. That may not sound a very difficult feat, but experience has taught me that if a man can achieve it, and can be *relied* upon to achieve it, say, nine times out of ten—well, he is a pearl of price; and there is not a C.O. in the British Army who wouldn't scramble to get him! That's all, M'Lachlan. Good morning!"

By punctilious attention to this sound advice Angus soon began to build up a reputation. He treated war-worn veterans like Bobby Little with immense respect, and this, too, was counted to him for righteousness. He exercised his platoon with appalling vigour. Upon Company route-marches he had to be embedded in some safe place in the middle of the column; in fact, his enormous stride and pedestrian enthusiasm would have reduced his followers to pulp. At Mess he was mute: like a wise man, he was feeling for his feet.

But being, like Moses, slow of tongue, he provided himself with an Aaron. Quite inadvertently, be it said. Bidden to obtain a servant for his personal needs, he selected the only man in the Battalion whose name he knew—Private Bogle, the *ci-devant* painter of houses. That friendly creature obeyed the call with alacrity. If his house-painting was no better than his valeting, then his prospects of a "contrack" after the War were poor indeed; but as a Mess waiter he was a joy for ever. Despite the blood-curdling whispers of the Mess Corporal, his natural urbanity of disposition could not be stemmed. Of the comfort of others he was solicitous to the point of oppressiveness. A Mess waiter's idea of efficiency as a rule is to stand woodenly at attention in an obscure corner of the room. When called upon, he starts forward with a jerk, and usually trips over something—probably his own feet. Not so Private Bogle.

"Wull you try another cup o' tea, Major?" he would suggest at breakfast to Major Wagstaffe, leaning affectionately over the back of his chair.

"No, thank you, Bogle," Major Wagstaffe would reply gravely.

"Weel, it's cauld onyway," Bogle would rejoin, anxious to endorse his superior's decision.

Or—in the same spirit—

"Wull I luft the soup now, sir?"

"*No!*"

"Varra weel: I'll jist let it bide the way it is."

****

Lastly, Angus M'Lachlan proved himself a useful acquisition—especially in rest-billets—as an athlete. He arrived just in time to take part—no mean part, either—in a Rugby Football match played between the officers of two Brigades. Thanks very largely to his masterly leading of the forwards, our Brigade were preserved from defeat at the hands of their opponents, who on paper had appeared to be irresistible.

Rugby Football "oot here" is a rarity, though Association, being essentially the game of the rank-and-file, flourishes in every green field. But an Inverleith or Queen's Club crowd would have recognised more than one old friend among the thirty who took the field that day. There were those participating whose last game had been one of the spring "Internationals" in 1914, and who had been engaged in a prolonged and strenuous version of an even greater International ever since August of that fateful year. Every public school in Scotland was represented—sometimes three or four times over—and there were numerous doughty contributions from establishments south of the Tweed.

The lookers-on were in different case. They were to a man devoted—nay, frenzied—adherents of the rival code. In less spacious days they had surged in their thousands every Saturday afternoon to Ibrox, or Tynecastle, or Parkhead, there to yell themselves into convulsions—now exhorting a friend to hit some one a kick on the nose, now recommending the foe to play the game, now hoarsely consigning the referee to perdition. To these, Rugby Football—the greatest of all manly games—was a mere name. Their attitude when the officers appeared upon the field was one of indulgent superiority—the sort of superiority that a brawny pitman exhibits when his Platoon Commander steps down into a trench to lend a hand with the digging.

But in five minutes their mouths were agape with scandalised astonishment; in ten, the heavens were rent with their protesting cries. Accustomed to see football played with the feet, and to demand with one voice the instant execution of any player (on the other side) who laid so much as a finger upon the ball or the man who was playing it, the exhibition of savage and promiscuous brutality to which their superior officers now treated them shocked the assembled spectators to the roots of their sensitive souls. Howls of virtuous indignation burst forth upon all sides.

When the three-quarter-backs brought off a brilliant passing run, there were stern cries of "Haands, there, referee!" When Bobby Little stopped an ugly rush by hurling himself on the ball, the supporters of the other Brigade greeted his heroic devotion with yells of execration. When Angus M'Lachlan saved a certain try by tackling a speedy wing three-quarter low and bringing him down with a crash, a hundred voices demanded his removal from the field. And, when Mr. Waddell, playing a stuffy but useful game at half, gained fifty yards for his side by a series of judicious little kicks into touch, the spectators groaned aloud, and remarked caustically—

"This maun be a Cup-Tie, boys! They are playin' for a draw, for tae get a second gate!"

Altogether a thoroughly enjoyable afternoon, both for players and spectators. And so home to tea, domesticity, and social intercourse. In this connection it may be noted that our relations with the inhabitants are of the friendliest. On the stroke of six—oh yes, we have our licensing restrictions out here too!—half a dozen kilted warriors stroll into the farm-kitchen, and mumble affably to Madame—

"*Bone sworr!* Beer?"

France boasts one enormous advantage over Scotland. At home, you have at least to walk to the corner of the street to obtain a drink: "oot here" you can purchase beer in practically every house in a village. The French licensing laws are a thing of mystery, but the system appears roughly to be this. Either you possess a license, or you do not. If you do you may sell beer, and nothing else. If you do not, you may—or at any rate do—sell anything you like, including beer.

However, we have left our friends thirsty.

Their wants are supplied with cheerful alacrity, and, having been accommodated with seats round the stove, they converse with the family. Heaven only knows what they talk about, but talk they do—in the throaty unintelligible Doric of the Clydeside, with an occasional Gallicism, like, *"Allyman no bon!"* or *"Compree?"* thrown in as a sop to foreign idiosyncrasies. Madame and family respond, chattering French (or Flemish) at enormous speed. The amazing part of it all is that neither side appears to experience the slightest difficulty in understanding the other. One day Mr. Waddell, in the course of a friendly chat with his hostess of the moment—she was unable to speak a word of English—received her warm congratulations upon his contemplated union with a certain fair one of St. Andrew (to whom reference has previously been made in these pages). Mr. Waddell, a very fair linguist, replied in suitable but embarrassed terms, and asked for the source of the good lady's information.

"Mais votre ordonnance, m'sieur!" was the reply.

Tackled upon the subject, the "ordonnance" in question, Waddell's servant—a shock-headed youth from Dundee—admitted having communicated the information; and added—

"She's a decent body, sirr, the lady o' the hoose. She lost her husband, she was tellin' me, three years ago. She has twa sons in the Airmy. Her auld Auntie is up at the top o' the hoose—lyin' badly, and no expectin' tae rise."

And yet some people study Esperanto!

We also make ourselves useful. "K(1)" contains members of every craft. If the pig-sty door is broken, a carpenter is forthcoming to mend it. Somebody's elbow goes through a pane of glass in the farm-kitchen: straightway a glazier materialises from the nearest platoon, and puts in another. The ancestral eight-day clock of the household develops internal complications; and is forthwith dismembered and reassembled, "with punctuality, civility, and despatch," by a gentleman who until a few short months ago had done nothing else for fifteen years.

And it was in this connection that Corporal Mucklewame stumbled on to a rare and congenial job, and incidentally made the one joke of his life.

One afternoon a cow, the property of Madame *la fermiere*, developed symptoms of some serious disorder. A period of dolorous bellowing was followed by an outburst of homicidal mania, during which "A" Company prudently barricaded itself into the barn, the sufferer having taken entire possession of the farmyard. Next, and finally—so rapidly did the malady run its course—a state of coma intervened; and finally the cow, collapsing upon the doorstep of the Officers' Mess, breathed her last before any one could be found to point out to her the liberty she was taking.

It was decided to hold a *post-mortem*—firstly, to ascertain the cause of death; secondly, because it is easier to remove a dead cow after dissection than before. Madame therefore announced her intention of sending for the butcher, and was upon the point of doing so when Corporal Mucklewame, in whose heart, at the spectacle of the stark and lifeless corpse, ancient and romantic memories were stirring—it may be remembered that before answering to the call of "K(1)" Mucklewame had followed the calling of butcher's assistant at Wishaw—volunteered for the job. His services were cordially accepted by thrifty Madame; and the Corporal, surrounded by a silent and admiring crowd, set to work.

The officers, leaving the Junior Subaltern in charge, went with one accord for a long country walk.

Half an hour later Mucklewame arrived at the seat of the deceased animal's trouble—the seat of most of the troubles of mankind—its stomach. After a brief investigation, he produced therefrom a small bag of nails, recently missed from the vicinity of a cook-house in course of construction in the corner of the yard.

Abandoning the role of surgical expert for that of coroner, Mucklewame held the trophy aloft, and delivered his verdict—

"There, boys! That's what comes of eating your iron ration without authority!"

III

Here is an average billet, and its personnel.

The central feature of our residence is the refuse-pit, which fills practically the whole of the rectangular farmyard, and resembles (in size and shape *only*) an open-air swimming bath. Its abundant contents are apparently the sole asset of the household; for if you proceed, in the interests of health, to spread a decent mantle of honest earth thereover, you do so to the accompaniment of a harmonised chorus of lamentation, very creditably rendered by the entire family, who are grouped *en masse* about the spot where the high diving-board ought to be.

Round this perverted place of ablution runs a stone ledge, some four feet wide, and round that again run the farm buildings—the house at the top end, a great barn down one side, and the cowhouse, together with certain darksome piggeries and fowl-houses, down the other. These latter residences are occupied only at night, their tenants preferring to spend the golden hours of day in profitable occupation upon the happy hunting ground in the middle.

Within the precincts of this already overcrowded establishment are lodged some two hundred British soldiers and their officers. The men sleep in the barn, their meals being prepared for them upon the Company cooker, which stands in the muddy road outside, and resembles the humble vehicle employed by Urban District Councils for the preparation of tar for road-mending purposes. The officers occupy any room which may be available within the farmhouse itself. The Company Commander has the best bedroom—a low-roofed, stone-floored apartment, with a very small window and a very large bed. The subalterns sleep where they can—usually in the *grenier*, a loft under the tiles, devoted to the storage of onions and the drying, during the winter months, of the family washing, which is suspended from innumerable strings stretched from wall to wall.

For a Mess, there is usually a spare apartment of some kind. If not, you put your pride in your pocket and take your meals at the kitchen table, at such hours as the family are not sitting humped round the same with their hats on, partaking of soup or coffee. (This appears to be their sole sustenance.) A farm-kitchen in northern France is a scrupulously clean place—the whole family gets up at half-past four in the morning and sees to the matter—and despite the frugality of her own home *menu*, the *fermiere* can produce you a perfect omelette at any hour of the day or night.

This brings us to the kitchen-stove, which is a marvel. No massive and extravagant English ranges here! There is only one kind: we call it the Coffin and Flower-pot. The coffin—small, black, and highly polished—projects from the wall about four feet, the further end being supported by what looks like an ornamental black flower-pot standing on a pedestal. The coffin is the oven, and the flower-pot is the stove. Given a handful of small coal or charcoal, Madame appears capable of keeping it at work all day, and of boiling, baking, or roasting you innumerable dishes.

Then there is the family. Who or what they all are, and where they all sleep, is a profound mystery. The family tree is usually headed by a decrepit and ruminant old gentleman in a species of yachting-cap. He sits behind the stove—not exactly with one foot in the grave, but with both knees well up against the coffin—and occasionally offers a mumbled observation of which no one takes the slightest notice. Sometimes, too, there is an old, a very old, lady. Probably she is some one's grandmother, or great-grandmother, but she does not appear to be related to the old gentleman. At least, they never recognise one another's existence in any way.

There are also vague people who possess the power of becoming invisible at will. They fade in and out of the house like wraiths: their one object in life appears to be to efface themselves as much as possible. Madame refers to them as "*refugies*"; this the sophisticated Mr. Cockerell translates, "German spies."

Next in order come one or two farmhands—usually addressed as "'Nri!" and "'Seph!" They are not as a rule either attractive in appearance or desirable in character. Every man in this country, who *is* a man, is away, as a matter of course, doing a man's only possible duty under the circumstances. This leaves 'Nri and 'Seph, who through physical or mental shortcomings are denied the proud privilege, and shamble about in the muck and mud of the farm, leering or grumbling, while Madame exhorts them to further activity from the kitchen door. They take their meals with the family: where they sleep no one knows. External evidence suggests the cow-house.

Then, the family. First, Angele. She may be twenty-five, but is more probably fifteen. She acts as Adjutant to Madame, and rivals her mother as deliverer of sustained and rapid recitative. She milks the cows, feeds the pigs, and dragoons her young brothers and sisters. But though she works from morning till night, she has always time for a smiling salutation to all ranks. She also speaks English quite creditably—a fact of which Madame is justly proud. "College!" explains the mother, full of appreciation for an education which she herself has never known, and taps her learned daughter affectionately upon the head.

Next in order comes Emile. He must be about fourteen, but War has forced manhood on him. All day long he is at work, bullying very large horses, digging, hoeing, even ploughing. He is very much a boy, for all that. He whistles excruciatingly—usually English music-hall melodies—grins sheepishly at the officers, and is prepared at any moment to abandon the most important tasks, in order to watch a man cleaning a rifle or oiling a machine-gun. We seem to have encountered Emile in other countries than this.

After Emile, Gabrielle. Her age is probably seven. If you were to give her a wash and brush-up, dress her in a gauzy frock, and exchange her thick woollen stockings and wooden sabots for silk and dancing slippers, she would make a very smart little fairy. Even in her native state she is a most attractive young person, of an engaging coyness. If you say: *"Bonjour, Gabrielle!"* she whispers: *"B'jour M'sieur le Capitaine"*—or, *"M'sieur le Caporal"*; for she knows all badges of rank—and hangs her head demurely. But presently, if you stand quite still and look the other way, Gabrielle will sidle up to you and squeeze your hand. This is gratifying, but a little subversive of strict discipline if you happen to be inspecting your platoon at the moment.

Gabrielle is a firm favourite with the rank and file. Her particular crony is one Private Mackay, an amorphous youth with flaming red hair. He and Gabrielle engage in lengthy conversations, which appear to be perfectly intelligible to both, though Mackay speaks with the solemn unction of the Aberdonian, and Gabrielle prattles at express speed in a *patois* of her own. Last week some unknown humorist, evidently considering that Gabrielle was not making sufficient progress in her knowledge of English, took upon himself to give her a private lesson. Next morning Mackay, on sentry duty at the farm gate, espied his little friend peeping round a corner.

"Hey, Garibell!" he observed cheerfully. (No Scottish private ever yet mastered a French name quite completely.)

Gabrielle, anxious to exhibit her new accomplishment, drew nearer, smiled seraphically, and replied—

"'Ello, Gingeair!"

Last of the bunch comes Petit Jean, a chubby and close-cropped youth of about six. Petit Jean is not his real name, as he himself indignantly explained when so addressed by Major Wagstaffe.

"Moi, z'ne suis pas Petit Jean; z'suis Maurrrice!"

Major Wagstaffe apologised most humbly, but the name stuck.

Petit Jean is an enthusiast upon matters military. He possesses a little wooden rifle, the gift of a friendly "Ecossais," tipped with a flashing bayonet cut from a biscuit-tin; and spends most of his time out upon the road, waiting for some one to salute. At one time he used to stand by the sentry, with an ancient Glengarry crammed over his bullet head, and conform meticulously to his comrade's slightest movement. This procedure was soon banned, as being calculated to bring contempt and ridicule upon the King's uniform, and Petit Jean was assigned a beat of his own. Behold him upon sentry-go.

A figure upon horseback swings round the bend in the road.

"Here's an officer, Johnny!" cries a friendly voice from the farm gate.

Petit Jean, as upright as a post, brings his rifle from stand-at-ease to the order, and from the order to the slope, with the epileptic jerkiness of a marionette, and scrutinises the approaching officer for stars and crowns. If he can discern nothing but a star or two, he slaps the small of his butt with ferocious solemnity; but if a crown, or a red hatband, reveals itself, he blows out his small chest to its fullest extent and presents arms. If the salute is acknowledged—as it nearly always is—Petit Jean is crimson with gratification. Once, when a friendly subaltern called his platoon to attention, and gave the order, "Eyes right!" upon passing the motionless little figure at the side of the road, Petit Jean was so uplifted that he committed the military crime of deserting his post while on duty—in order to run home and tell his mother about it.

* * * * * * * *

Last of all we arrive at the keystone of the whole fabric—Madame herself. She is one of the most wonderful women in the world. Consider. Her husband and her eldest son are away—fighting, she knows not where, amid dangers and privations which can only be imagined. During their absence she has to manage a considerable farm, with the help of her children and one or two hired labourers of more than doubtful use or reliability. In addition to her ordinary duties as a parent and *fermiere*, she finds herself called upon, for months on end, to maintain her premises as a combination of barracks and almshouse. Yet she is seldom cross—except possibly when the *soldats* steal her apples and pelt the pigs with the cores—and no accumulations of labour can sap her energy. She is up by half-past four every morning; yet she never appears anxious to go to bed at night. The last sound which sleepy subalterns hear is Madame's voice, uplifted in steady discourse to the circle round the stove, sustained by an occasional guttural chord from 'Nri and 'Seph. She has been doing this, day in, day out, since the combatants settled down to trench-warfare. Every few weeks brings a fresh crop of tenants, with fresh peculiarities and unknown proclivities; and she assimilates them all.

The only approach to a breakdown comes when, after paying her little bill—you may be sure that not an omelette nor a broken window will be missing from the account—and wishing her "Bonne chance!" ere you depart, you venture on a reference, in a few awkward, stumbling sentences, to the absent husband and son. Then she weeps, copiously, and it seems to do her a world of good. All hail to you, Madame—the finest exponent, in all this War, of the art of Carrying On! We know now why France is such a great country.

Chapter 6
Ye Merrie Buzzers

Practically all the business of an Army in the field is transacted by telephone. If the telephone breaks down, whether by the Act of God or of the King's Enemies, that business is at a standstill until the telephone is put right again.

The importance of the disaster varies with the nature of the business. For instance, if the wire leading to the Round Game Department is blown down by a March gale, and your weekly return of Men Recommended for False Teeth is delayed in transit, nobody minds very much—except possibly the Deputy Assistant Director of Auxiliary Dental Appliances. But if you are engaged in battle, and the wires which link up the driving force in front with the directing force behind are devastated by a storm of shrapnel, the matter assumes a more—nay, a most—serious aspect. Hence the superlative importance in modern warfare of the Signal Sections of the Royal Engineers—tersely described by the rank-and-file as the "Buzzers," or the "Iddy-Umpties."

During peace-training, the Buzzer on the whole has a very pleasant time of it. Once he has mastered the mysteries of the Semaphore and Morse codes, the most laborious part of his education is over. Henceforth he spends his days upon some sheltered hillside, in company with one or two congenial spirits, flapping cryptic messages out of a blue-and-white flag at a similar party across the valley.

A year ago, for instance, you might have encountered an old friend, Private M'Micking,—one of the original "Buzzers" of "A" Company, and ultimately Battalion Signal Sergeant—under the lee of a pine wood near Hindhead, accompanied by Lance-Corporal Greig and Private Wamphray, regarding with languid interest the frenzied efforts of three of their colleagues to convey a message from a sunny hillside three quarters of a mile away.

"Here a message comin' through, boys," announces the Lance-Corporal. "They're in a sair hurry: I doot the officer will be there. Jeams, tak' it doon while Sandy reads it."

Mr. James M'Micking seats himself upon a convenient log. In order not to confuse his faculties by endeavouring to read and write simultaneously, he turns his back upon the fluttering flag, and bends low over his field message-pad. Private Wamphray stands facing him, and solemnly spells out the message over his head.

"Tae g-o-c—I dinna ken what that means—r-e-d, *reid*—a-r-m-y, *airmy*—h-a-z—"

"All richt; that'll be Haslemere," says Private M'Micking, scribbling down the word. "Go on, Sandy!"

Private Wamphray, pausing to expectorate, continues—

"R-e-c-o-n-n-o-i-t-r—Cricky, what a worrd! Let's hae it repeatit."

Wamphray flaps his flag vigorously,—he knows this particular signal only too well,—and the word comes through again. The distant signaller, slowing down a little, continues,—

"'Reconnoitring patrol reports hostile cavalry scou—'"

"That'll be 'scouts,'" says the ever-ready M'Micking. "Carry on!"

Wamphray continues obediently,—"'Country'; stop; 'Have thrown out flank guns'; stop; 'Shall I advance or re—'"

"—tire," gabbles M'Micking, writing it down.

"—'where I am'; stop; 'From O C Advance Guard'; stop; message ends."

"And aboot time, too!" observes the scribe severely. "Haw, Johnny!"

The Lance-Corporal, who has been indulging in a pleasant reverie upon a bank of bracken, wakes up and reads the proffered message.

* * * * * * * *

"Tae G O C, Reid Airmy, Hazlemere. Reconnoitring patrol reports hostile cavalry scouts country. Have thrown oot flank guns. Shall I advance or retire where I am? From O C Advance Guard."

"This message doesna sound altogether sense," he observes mildly. "That 'shall' should be 'wull,' onyway. Would it no' be better to get it repeatit? The officer—"

"I've given the 'message-read' signal now," objects the indolent Wamphray.

"How would it be," suggests the Lance-Corporal, whose besetting sin is a *penchant* for emendation, "if we were tae transfair yon stop, and say: 'Reconnoitring patrol reports hostile cavalry scouts. Country has thrown oot flank guns'?"

"What does that mean?" inquires M'Micking scornfully.

"I dinna ken; but these messages about Generals and sic'-like bodies—"

At this moment, as ill-luck will have it, the Signal Sergeant appears breasting the hillside. He arrives puffing—he has seen twenty years' service—and scrutinises the message.

"You boys," he says reproachfully, "are an aggravate altogether. Here you are, jumping at your conclusions again! After all I have been telling you! See! That worrd in the address should no' be Haslemere at all. It's just a catch! It's Hazebroucke—a Gairman city that we'll be capturing this time next year. 'Scouts' is no 'scouts,' but 'scouring'—meaning 'sooping up.' 'Guns' should be 'guarrd,' and 'retire' should be 'remain.' Mind me, now; next time, you'll be up before the Captain for neglect of duty. Wamphray, give the 'C.I.,' and let's get hame to oor dinners!"

II

But "oot here" there is no flag-wagging. The Buzzer's first proceeding upon entering the field of active hostilities is to get underground, and stay there.

He is a seasoned vessel, the Buzzer of to-day, and a person of marked individuality. He is above all things a man of the world. Sitting day and night in a dug-out, or a cellar, with a telephone receiver clamped to his ear, he sees little; but he hears much, and overhears more. He also speaks a language of his own. His one task in life is to prevent the letter B from sounding like C, or D, or P, or T, or V, over the telephone; so he has perverted the English language to his own uses. He calls B "Beer," and D "Don," and so on. He salutes the rosy dawn as "Akk Emma," and eventide as "Pip Emma." He refers to the letter S as "Esses," in order to distinguish it from F. He has no respect for the most majestic military titles. To him the Deputy Assistant Director of the Mobile Veterinary Section is merely a lifeless formula, entitled Don Akk Don Emma Vic Esses.

He is also a man of detached mind. The tactical situation does not interest him. His business is to disseminate news, not to write leading articles about it. (*O si sic omnes!*) You may be engaged in a life-and-death struggle for the possession of your own parapet with a Boche bombing-party; but this does not render you immune from a pink slip from the Signal Section, asking you to state your reasons in writing for having mislaid fourteen pairs of "boots, gum, thigh," lately the property of Number Seven Platoon. A famous British soldier tells a story somewhere in his reminiscences of an occasion upon which, in some long-forgotten bush campaign, he had to defend a *zareba* against a heavy attack. For a time the situation was critical. Help was badly needed, but the telegraph wire had been cut. Ultimately the attack withered away, and the situation was saved. Almost simultaneously the victorious commander was informed that telegraphic communication with the Base had been restored. A message was already coming through.

"News of reinforcements, I hope!" he remarked to his subordinate.

But his surmise was incorrect. The message said, quite simply:—

"Your monthly return of men wishing to change their religion is twenty-four hours overdue. Please expedite."

There was a time when one laughed at that anecdote as a playful invention. But we know now that it is true, and we feel a sort of pride in the truly British imperturbability of our official machinery.

Thirdly, the Buzzer is a humorist, of the sardonic variety. The constant clash of wits over the wires, and the necessity of framing words quickly, sharpens his faculties and acidulates his tongue. Incidentally, he is an awkward person to quarrel with. One black night, Bobby Little, making his second round of the trenches about an hour before "stand-to," felt constrained to send a telephone message to Battalion Headquarters. Taking a good breath,—you always do this before entering a trench dug-out,—he plunged into the noisome cavern where his Company Signallers kept everlasting vigil. The place was in total darkness, except for the illumination supplied by a strip of rifle-rag burning in a tin of rifle-oil. The air, what there was of it, was thick with large, fat, floating particles of free carbon. The telephone was buzzing plaintively to itself, in unsuccessful competition with a well-modulated quartet for four nasal organs, contributed by Bobby's entire signalling staff, who, locked in the inextricable embrace peculiar to Thomas Atkins in search of warmth, were snoring harmoniously upon the earthen floor.

The signaller "on duty"—one M'Gurk—was extracted from the heap and put under arrest for sleeping at his post. The enormity of his crime was heightened by the fact that two undelivered messages were found upon his person.

Divers pains and penalties followed. Bobby supplemented the sentence with a homily on the importance of vigilance and despatch. M'Gurk, deeply aggrieved at forfeiting seven days' pay, said nothing, but bided his time. Two nights later the Battalion came out of trenches for a week's rest, and Bobby, weary and thankful, retired to bed in his hut at 9 P.M., in comfortable anticipation of a full night's repose.

His anticipations were doomed to disappointment. He was roused from slumber—not without difficulty—by Signaller M'Gurk, who appeared standing by his bedside with a guttering candle-end in one hand and a pink despatch-form in the other. The message said:—

"Prevailing wind for next twenty-four hours probably S.W., with some rain."

Mindful of his own recent admonitions, Bobby thanked M'Gurk politely, and went to sleep again.

M'Gurk called again at half-past two in the morning, with another message, which announced:—

"Baths will be available for your Company from 2 to 3 P.M. to-morrow."

Bobby stuffed the missive under his air-pillow, and rolled over without a word. M'Gurk withdrew, leaving the door of the hut open.

His next visit was about four o'clock. This time the message said:—

"A Zeppelin is reported to have passed over Dunkirk at 5 P.M. yesterday afternoon, proceeding in a northerly direction."

Bobby informed M'Gurk that he was a fool and a dotard, and cast him forth.

M'Gurk returned at five-thirty, bearing written evidence that the Zeppelin had been traced as far as Ostend.

This time his Company Commander promised him that if he appeared again that night he would be awarded fourteen days' Field Punishment Number One.

The result was that upon sitting down to breakfast at nine next morning, Bobby found upon his plate yet another message—from his Commanding Officer—summoning him to the Orderly-room on urgent matters at eight-thirty.

But Bobby scored the final and winning trick. Sending for M'Gurk and Sergeant M'Micking, he said:—

"This man, Sergeant, appears to be unable to decide when a message is urgent and when it is not. In future, whenever M'Gurk is on night duty, and is in doubt as to whether a message should be delivered at once or put aside till morning, he will come to you and ask for your guidance in the matter. Do you understand?"

"Perrfectly, sirr!" replied the Sergeant, outwardly calm.

"M'Gurk, do *you* understand?"

M'Gurk looked at Bobby, and then round at Sergeant M'Micking. He received a glance which shrivelled his marrow. The game was up. He grinned sheepishly, and answered,—

"Yis, sirr!"

III

Having briefly set forth the character and habits of the Buzzer, we will next proceed to visit the creature in his lair. This is an easy feat. We have only to walk up the communication-trench which leads from the reserve line to the firing-line. Upon either side of the trench, neatly tacked to the muddy wall by a device of the hairpin variety, run countless insulated wires, clad in coats of various colours and all duly ticketed. These radiate from various Headquarters in the rear to numerous signal stations in the front, and were laid by the Signallers themselves. (It is perhaps unnecessary to mention that that single wire running, in defiance of all regulations, across the top of the trench, which neatly tipped your cap off just now, was laid by those playful humorists, the Royal Artillery.) It follows that if we accompany these wires far enough we shall ultimately find ourselves in a signalling station.

Our only difficulty lies in judicious choice, for the wires soon begin to diverge up numerous byways. Some go to the fire-trench, others to the machine-guns, others again to observation posts—or O.P.'s—whence a hawk-eyed Forward Observing Officer, peering all day through a chink in a tumble-down chimney or sandbagged loophole, is sometimes enabled to flash back the intelligence that he can discern transport upon such a road in rear of the Boche trenches, and will such a battery kindly attend to the matter at once?

However, chance guides us to the Signal dug-out of "A" Company, where, by the best fortune in the world, Private M'Gurk in person is installed as officiating sprite. Let us render ourselves invisible, sit down beside him, and "tap" his wire.

In the dim and distant days before such phrases as "Boche," and "T.N.T.," and "munitions," and "economy" were invented; when we lived in houses which possessed roofs, and never dreamed of lying down motionless by the roadside when we heard a taxi-whistle blown thrice, in order to escape the notice of approaching aeroplanes,—in short, in the days immediately preceding the war,—some of us said in our haste that the London Telephone Service was The Limit! Since then we have made the acquaintance of the military field-telephone, and we feel distinctly softened towards the young woman at home who, from her dug-out in "Gerrard," or "Vic.," or "Hop.," used to goad us to impotent frenzy. She was at least terse and decided. If you rang her up and asked for a number, she merely replied,—

(a) "Number engaged";

(b) "No reply";

(c) "Out of order"—

as the case might be, and switched you off. After that you took a taxi to the place with which you wished to communicate, and there was an end of the matter. Above all, she never explained, she never wrangled, she spoke tolerably good English, and there was only one of her—or at least she was of a uniform type.

Now, if you put your ear to the receiver of a field-telephone, you find yourself, as it were, suddenly thrust into a vast subterranean cavern, filled with the wailings of the lost, the babblings of the feeble-minded, and the profanity of the exasperated. If you ask a high-caste Buzzer—say, an R.E. Signalling Officer—why this should be so, he will look intensely wise and recite some solemn gibberish about earthed wires and induced currents.

The noises are of two kinds, and one supplements the other. The human voice supplies the libretto, while the accompaniment is provided by a syncopated and tympanum-piercing *ping-ping*, suggestive of a giant mosquito singing to its young.

The instrument with which we are contending is capable (in theory) of transmitting a message either telephonically or telegraphically. In practice, this means that the signaller, having wasted ten sulphurous minutes in a useless attempt to convey information through the medium of the human voice, next proceeds, upon the urgent advice of the gentleman at the other end, and to the confusion of all other inhabitants of the cavern, to "buzz" it, employing the dots and dashes of the Morse code for the purpose.

It is believed that the wily Boche, by means of ingenious and delicate instruments, is able to "tap" a certain number of our trench telephone messages. If he does, his daily Intelligence Report must contain some surprising items of information. At the moment when we attach our invisible apparatus to Mr. M'Gurk's wire, the Divisional Telephone system appears to be fairly evenly divided between—

(1) A Regimental Headquarters endeavouring to ring up its Brigade.

(2) A glee-party of Harmonious Blacksmiths, indulging in the Anvil Chorus.

(3) A choleric Adjutant on the track of a peccant Company Commander.

(4) Two Company Signallers, engaged in a friendly chat from different ends of the trench line.

(5) An Artillery F.O.O., endeavouring to convey pressing and momentous information to his Battery, two miles in rear.

(6) The Giant Mosquito aforesaid.

The consolidated result is something like this:—

REGIMENTAL HEADQUARTERS (*affably*). Hallo, Brigade! Hallo, Brigade! HALLO, BRIGADE!

THE MOSQUITO. *Ping!*

THE ADJUTANT (*from somewhere in the Support Line, fiercely*). Give me B Company!

THE FORWARD OBSERVING OFFICER (*from his eyrie*). Is that C Battery? There's an enemy working-party—

FIRST CHATTY SIGNALLER (*from B Company's Station*). Is that yoursel', Jock? How's a' wi' you?

SECOND CHATTY SIGNALLER (*from D Company's Station*). I'm daen fine! How's your—

REGIMENTAL HEADQUARTERS. HALLO, BRIGADE!

THE ADJUTANT. Is that B Company?

A MYSTERIOUS AND DISTANT VOICE (*politely*.) No, sir; this is Akk and Esses Aitch.

THE ADJUTANT (*furiously*). Then for the Lord's sake get off the line!

THE MOSQUITO. *Ping! Ping!*

THE ADJUTANT. And stop that——————buzzing!

THE MOSQUITO. *Ping! Ping! PING*!

THE F.O.O. Is that C Battery? There's—

FIRST CHATTY SIGNALLER (*peevishly*). What's that you're sayin'?

THE F.O.O. (*perseveringly*). Is that C Battery? There's an enemy working-party in a coppice at—

FIRST CHATTY SIGNALLER. This is Beer Company, sir. Weel, Jock, did ye get a quiet nicht?

SECOND CHATTY SIGNALLER. Oh, aye. There was a wee—

THE F.O.O. Is that C Battery? There's—

SECOND CHATTY SIGNALLER. No, sir. This is Don Company. Weel, Jimmy, there was a couple whish-bangs came intil—

REGIMENTAL HEADQUARTERS. HALLO, BRIGADE!

A CHEERFUL COCKNEY VOICE. Well, my lad, what abaht it?

REGIMENTAL HEADQUARTERS (*getting to work at once*). Hold the line, Brigade. Message to Staff Captain. "Ref. your S.C. fourr stroke seeven eight six, the worrking-parrty in question—"

THE F.O.O. (*seeing a gleam of hope*). Working-party? Is that C Battery? I want to speak to—

THE ADJUTANT—BRIGADE HEADQUARTERS. Get off the line! REGIMENTAL HEADQUARTERS.

FIRST CHATTY SIGNALLER. Haw, Jock, was ye hearin' aboot Andra?

SECOND CHATTY SIGNALLER. No. Whit was that?

FIRST CHATTY SIGNALLER. Weel—

THE F.O.O. (*doggedly*). Is that C Battery?

REGIMENTAL HEADQUARTERS (*resolutely*). "The wor-rking-parrty in question was duly detailed for tae proceed to the rendiss vowse at"—

THE ADJUTANT. Is that B Company, curse you?

REGIMENTAL HEADQUARTERS (*quite impervious to this sort of thing*),—"the *rendiss vowse*, at seeven thirrty Akk Emma, at point H two B eight nine, near the cross-roads by the *Estamint Repose dee Bicyclistees*, for tae"—*honk! honkle! honk!*

BRIGADE HEADQUARTERS (*compassionately*). You're makin' a 'orrible mess of this message, ain't you? Shake your transmitter, do!

REGIMENTAL HEADQUARTERS (*after dutifully performing this operation*). *Honkle, honkle, honk. Yang!*

BRIGADE HEADQUARTERS. Buzz it, my lad, buzz it!

REGIMENTAL HEADQUARTERS (*dutifully*). *Ping, ping! Ping, ping! Ping, ping, ping! Ping*—

GENERAL CHORUS. Stop that —, ——, ——, —— *buzzing*!

FIRST CHATTY SIGNALLER. Weel, Andra says tae the Sergeant-Major of Beer Company, says he—

THE ADJUTANT. Is that B Company?

FIRST CHATTY SIGNALLER. No, sir; this is Beer Company.

THE ADJUTANT (*fortissimo*). I *said* Beer Company!

FIRST CHATTY SIGNALLER. Oh! I thocht ye meant Don Company, sir.

THE ADJUTANT. Why the blazes haven't you answered me sooner?

FIRST CHATTY SIGNALLER (*tactfully*). There was other messages comin' through, sir.

THE ADJUTANT. Well, get me the Company Commander.

FIRST CHATTY SIGNALLER. Varra good, sirr.

A pause. Regimental Headquarters being engaged in laboriously "buzzing" its message through to the Brigade, all other conversation is at a standstill. The Harmonious Blacksmiths seize the opportunity to give a short selection. Presently, as the din dies down—

THE F.O.O. (*faint, yet pursuing*). Is that C Battery?

A JOVIAL VOICE. Yes.

THE F.O.O. What a shock! I thought you were all dead. Is that you, Chumps?

THE JOVIAL VOICE. It is. What can I do for you this morning?

THE F.O.O. You can boil your signal sentry's head!

THE JOVIAL VOICE. What for?

THE F.O.O. For keeping me waiting.

THE JOVIAL VOICE. Righto! And the next article?

THE F.O.O. There's a Boche working-party in a coppice two hundred yards west of a point—

THE MOSQUITO (*with renewed vigour*). *Ping, ping!*

THE F.O.O. (*savagely*). Shut up!

THE JOVIAL VOICE. Working-party? I'll settle them. What's the map reference?

THE F.O.O. They are in Square number—

THE HARMONIOUS BLACKSMITHS (*suddenly and stunningly*). *Whang!*

THE F.O.O. Shut up! They are in Square—

FIRST CHATTY SIGNALLER. Hallo, Headquarters! Is the Adjutant there? Here's the Captain tae speak with him.

AN EAGER VOICE. Is that the Adjutant?

REGIMENTAL HEADQUARTERS. No, sirr. He's away tae his office. Hold the line while I'll—

THE EAGER VOICE. No you don't! Put me straight through to C Battery—quick! Then get off the line, and stay there! (*Much buzzing.*) Is that C Battery?

THE JOVIAL VOICE. Yes, sir.

THE EAGER VOICE. I am O.C. Beer Company. They are shelling my front parapet, at L8, with pretty heavy stuff. I want retaliation, please.

THE JOVIAL VOICE. Very good, sir. (*The voice dies away.*)

A SOUND OVER OUR HEADS (*thirty seconds later*). *Whish! Whish! Whish!*

SECOND CHATTY SIGNALLER. Did ye hear that, Jimmy?

FIRST CHATTY SIGNALLER (*with relish*). Mphm! That'll sorrt them!

THE F.O.O. Is that C Battery?

THE JOVIAL VOICE. Yes. What luck, old son?

THE F.O.O. You have obtained two direct hits on the Boche parapet. Will you have a cocoanut or a ci—

THE JOVIAL VOICE. A little less lip, my lad! Now tell me all about your industrious friends in the Coppice, and we will see what we can do for *them!*

* * * * * * * *

And so on. Apropos of Adjutants and Company Commanders, Private Wamphray, whose acquaintance we made a few pages back, was ultimately relieved of his position as a Company Signaller, and returned ignominiously to duty, for tactless if justifiable interposition in one of these very dialogues.

It was a dark and cheerless night in mid-winter. Ominous noises in front of the Boche wire had raised apprehensive surmises in the breast of Brigade Headquarters. A forward sap was suspected in the region opposite the sector of trenches held by "A" Company. The trenches at this point were barely forty yards apart, and there was a very real danger that Brother Boche might creep under his own wire, and possibly under ours too, and come tumbling over our parapet.

To Bobby Little came instructions to send a specially selected patrol out to investigate the matter. Three months ago he would have led the expedition himself. Now, as a full-blown Company Commander, he was officially precluded from exposing his own most responsible person to gratuitous risks. So he chose out that recently-joined enthusiast, Angus M'Lachlan, and put him over the parapet on the dark night in question, accompanied by Corporal M'Snape and two scouts, with orders to probe the mystery to its depth and bring back a full report.

It was a ticklish enterprise. As is frequently the case upon these occasions, nervous tension manifested itself much more seriously at Headquarters than in the front-line trenches. The man on the spot is, as a rule, much too busy with the actual execution of the enterprise in hand to distress himself by speculation upon its ultimate outcome. It may as well be stated at once that Angus duly returned from his quest, with an admirable and reassuring report. But he was a long time absent. Hence this anecdote.

Bobby had strict orders to report all "developments," as they occurred, to Headquarters by telephone. At half-past eleven that night, as Angus M'Lachlan's colossal form disappeared, crawling, into the blackness of night, his superior officer dutifully rang up Battalion Headquarters, and announced that the venture was launched. It is possible that the Powers Behind were in possession of information as to the enemy's intentions unrevealed to Bobby; for as soon as his opening announcement was received, he was switched right through to a very august Headquarters indeed, and commanded to report direct.

Long-distance telephony in the field involves a considerable amount of "linking-up." Among other slaves of the Buzzer who assisted in establishing the necessary communications upon this occasion was Private Wamphray. For the next hour and a half it was his privilege in his subterranean exchange, to sit, with his receiver clamped to his ear, an unappreciative auditor of dialogues like the following:—

"Is that 'A' Company?"

"Yes, sir."

"Any news of your patrol?"

"No, sir."

Again, five minutes later:—

"Is that 'A' Company?"

"Yes, sir."

"Has your officer returned yet?"

"No, sir. I will notify you when he does."

This sort of thing went on until nearly one o'clock in the morning. Towards that hour, Bobby, who was growing really concerned over Angus's prolonged absence, cut short his august interlocutor's fifteenth inquiry and joined his Sergeant-Major on the firing-step. The two had hardly exchanged a few low-pitched sentences when Bobby was summoned back to the telephone.

"Is that Captain Little?"

"Yes, sir."

"Has your patrol come in?"

"No, sir."

Captain's Little's last answer was delivered in a distinctly insubordinate manner. Feeling slightly relieved, he returned to the firing-step. Two minutes later Angus M'Lachlan and his posse rolled over the parapet, safe and sound, and Bobby was able, to his own great content and that of the weary operators along the line, to announce,—

"The patrol has returned, sir, and reports everything quite satisfactory. I am forwarding a detailed statement."

Then he laid down the receiver with a happy sigh, and crawled out of the dug-out on to the duck-board.

"Now we'll have a look round the sentries, Sergeant-Major," he said.

But the pair had hardly rounded three traverses when Bobby was haled back to the Signal Station.

"Why did you leave the telephone just now?" inquired a cold voice.

"I was going to visit my sentries, sir."

"But *I* was speaking to you."

"I thought you had finished, sir."

"I had *not* finished. If I had finished, I should have informed you of the fact, and would have said' Good-night!'"

"How *does* one choke off a tripe-merchant of this type?" wondered the exhausted officer.

From the bowels of the earth came the answer to his unspoken question—delivered in a strong Paisley accent—

"For Goad's sake, kiss him, and say 'Good-Nicht,' and hae done with it!"

As already stated, Private Wamphray was returned to his platoon next morning.

IV

But to regard the Buzzer simply and solely as a troglodyte, of sedentary habits and caustic temperament, is not merely hopelessly wrong: it is grossly unjust. Sometimes he goes for a walk—under some such circumstances as the following.

The night is as black as Tartarus, and it is raining heavily. Brother Boche, a prey to nervous qualms, is keeping his courage up by distributing shrapnel along our communication-trenches. Signal-wires are peculiarly vulnerable to shrapnel. Consequently no one in the Battalion Signal Station is particularly surprised when the line to "Akk" Company suddenly ceases to perform its functions.

Signal-Sergeant M'Micking tests the instrument, glances over his shoulder, and observes,—

"Line BX is gone, some place or other. Away you, Duncan, and sorrt it!"

Mr. Duncan, who has been sitting hunched over a telephone, temporarily quiescent, smoking a woodbine, heaves a resigned sigh, extinguishes the woodbine and places it behind his ear; hitches his repairing-wallet nonchalantly over his shoulder, and departs into the night—there to grope in several inches of mud for the two broken ends of the wire, which may be lying fifty yards apart. Having found them, he proceeds to effect a junction, his progress being impeded from time to time by further bursts of shrapnel. This done, he tests the new connection, relights his woodbine, and splashes his way back to Headquarters. That is a Buzzer's normal method of obtaining fresh air and exercise.

More than that. He is the one man in the Army who can fairly describe himself as indispensable.

In these days, when whole nations are deployed against one another, no commander, however eminent, can ride the whirlwind single-handed. There are limits to individual capacity. There are limits to direct control. There are limits to personal magnetism. We fight upon a collective plan nowadays. If we propose to engage in battle, we begin by welding a hundred thousand men into one composite giant. We weld a hundred thousand rifles, a million bombs, a thousand machine-guns, and as many pieces of artillery, into one huge weapon of offence, with which we arm our giant. Having done this, we provide him with a brain—a blend of all the experience and wisdom and military genius at our disposal. But still there is one thing lacking—a nervous system. Unless our giant have that,—unless his brain be able to transmit its desires to his mighty limbs,—he has nothing. He is of no account; the enemy can make butcher's-meat of him. And that is why I say that the purveyor of this nervous system—our friend the Buzzer—is indispensable. You can always create a body of sorts and a brain of sorts. But unless you can produce a nervous system of the highest excellence, you are foredoomed to failure.

Take a small instance. Supposing a battalion advances to the attack, and storms an isolated, exposed position. Can they hold on, or can they not? That question can only be answered by the Artillery behind them. If the curtain of shell-fire which has preceded the advancing battalion to its objective can be "lifted" at the right moment and put down again, with precision, upon a certain vital zone beyond the captured line, counter-attacks can be broken up and the line held. But the Artillery lives a long way—sometimes miles—in rear. Without continuous and accurate information it will be more than useless; it will be dangerous. (A successful attacking party has been shelled out of its hardly won position by its own artillery before now—on both sides!) Sometimes a little visual signalling is possible: sometimes a despatch-runner may get back through the enemy's curtain of fire; but in the main your one hope of salvation hangs upon a slender thread of insulated wire. And round that wire are strung some of the purest gems of heroism that the War has produced.

At the Battle of Loos, half a battalion of "K(1)" pushed forward into a very advanced hostile position. There they hung, by their teeth. Their achievement was great; but unless Headquarters could be informed of their exact position and needs, they were all dead men. So Corporal Greig set out to find them, unreeling wire as he went. He was blown to pieces by an eight-inch shell, but another signaller was never lacking to take his place. They pressed forward, these lackadaisical non-combatants, until the position was reached and communication established. Again and again the wire was cut by shrapnel, and again and again a Buzzer crawled out to find the broken ends and piece them together. And ultimately, the tiny, exposed limb in front having been enabled to explain its exact requirements to the brain behind, the necessary help was forthcoming and the Fort was held.

Next time you pass a Signaller's Dug-out peep inside. You will find it occupied by a coke brazier, emitting large quantities of carbon monoxide, and an untidy gentleman in khaki, with a blue-and-white device upon his shoulder-straps, who is humped over a small black instrument, luxuriating in a "frowst" most indescribable. He is reading a back number of a rural Scottish newspaper which you never heard of. Occasionally, in response to a faint buzz, he takes up his transmitter and indulges in an unintelligible altercation with a person unseen. You need feel no surprise if he is wearing the ribbon of the Distinguished Conduct Medal.

CHAPTER 7

Pastures New

The outstanding feature of to-day's intelligence is that spring is coming—has come, in fact.

It arrived with a bump. March entered upon its second week with seven degrees of frost and four inches of snow. We said what was natural and inevitable to the occasion, wrapped our coats of skins more firmly round us, and made a point of attending punctually when the rum ration was issued.

Forty-eight hours later winter had disappeared. The sun was blazing in a cloudless sky. Aeroplanes were battling for photographic rights overhead; the brown earth beneath our feet was putting forth its first blades of tender green. The muck-heap outside our rest-billet displayed unmistakable signs of upheaval from its winter sleep. Primroses appeared in Bunghole Wood; larks soared up into the sky above No Man's Land, making music for the just and the unjust. Snipers, smiling cheerfully over the improved atmospheric conditions, polished up their telescopic sights. The artillery on each side hailed the birth of yet another season of fruitfulness and natural increase with some more than usually enthusiastic essays in mutual extermination. Half the Mess caught colds in their heads.

Frankly, we are not sorry to see the end of winter. Caesar, when he had concluded his summer campaign, went into winter quarters. Caesar, as Colonel Kemp once huskily remarked, knew something!

Still, each man to his taste. Corporal Mucklewame, for one, greatly prefers winter to summer.

"In the winter," he points out to Sergeant M'Snape, "a body can breathe withoot swallowing a wheen bluebottles and bum-bees. A body can aye streitch himself doon under a tree for a bit sleep withoot getting wasps and wee beasties crawling up inside his kilt, and puddocks craw-crawing in his ear! A body can keep himself frae sweitin'—"

"He can that!" assents M'Snape, whose spare frame is more vulnerable to the icy breeze than that of the stout corporal.

However, the balance of public opinion is against Mucklewame. Most of us are unfeignedly glad to feel the warmth of the sun again. That working-party, filling sandbags just behind the machine-gun emplacement, are actually singing. Spring gets into the blood, even in this stricken land. The Boche over the way resents our efforts at harmony.

Sing us a song, a song of Bonnie Scotland! Any old song will do. By the old camp-fire, the rough-and-ready choir Join in the chorus too. "You'll tak' the high road and I'll tak' the low road"—'Tis a song that we all know, To bring back the days in Bonnie Scotland, Where the heather and the bluebells—

Whang!

The Boche, a Wagnerian by birth and upbringing, cannot stand any more of this, so he has fired a rifle-grenade at the glee-party—on the whole a much more honest and direct method of condemnation than that practiced by musical critics in time of peace. But he only elicits an encore. Private Nigg perches a steel helmet on the point of a bayonet, and patronisingly bobs the same up and down above the parapet.

These steel helmets have not previously been introduced to the reader's notice. They are modelled upon those worn in the French Army—and bear about as much resemblance to the original pattern as a Thames barge to a racing yacht. When first issued, they were greeted with profound suspicion. Though undoubtedly serviceable,—they saved many a crown from cracking round The Bluff the other day,—they were undeniably heavy, and they were certainly not becoming to the peculiar type of beauty rampant in "K(1)." On issue, then, their recipients elected to regard the wearing of them as a peculiarly noxious form of "fatigue." Private M'A. deposited his upon the parapet, like a foundling on a doorstep, and departed stealthily round the nearest traverse, to report his new headpiece "lost through the exigencies of military service." Private M'B. wore his insecurely perched upon the top of his tam-o'-shanter bonnet, where it looked like a very large ostrich egg in a very small khaki nest. Private M'C. set his up on a convenient post, and opened rapid fire upon it at a range of six yards, surveying the resulting holes with the gloomy satisfaction of the vindicated pessimist. Private M'D. removed the lining from his, and performed his ablutions in the inverted crown.

"This," said Colonel Kemp, "will never do. We must start wearing the dashed things ourselves."

And it was so. Next day, to the joy of the Battalion, their officers appeared in the trenches self-consciously wearing what looked like small sky-blue wash-hand basins balanced upon their heads. But discipline was excellent. No one even smiled. In fact, there was a slight reaction in favour of the helmets. Conversations like the following were overheard:—

"I'm tellin' you, Jimmy, the C.O. is no the man for tae mak' a show of himself like that for naething. These tin bunnets must be some use. Wull we pit oors on?"

"Awa' hame, and bile your held!" replied the unresponsive James.

"They'll no stop a whish-bang," conceded the apostle of progress, "but they would keep off splunters, and a wheen bullets, and—and—"

"And the rain!" supplied Jimmy sarcastically.

This gibe suddenly roused the temper of the other participant in the debate.

"I tell you," he exclaimed, in a voice shrill with indignation, "that these—helmets are some—use!"

"And I tell *you*," retorted James earnestly, "that these—helmets are no—use!"

When two reasonable persons arrive at a controversial *impasse*, they usually agree to differ and go their several ways. But in "K(1)" we prefer practical solutions. The upholder of helmets hastily thrust his upon his head.

"I'll show you, Jimmy!" he announced, and clambered up on the firing-step.

"And I'll—well show *you*, Wullie!" screamed James, doing likewise.

Simultaneously the two zealots thrust their heads over the parapet, and awaited results. These came. The rifles of two Boche snipers rang out, and both demonstrators fell heavily backwards into the arms of their supporters.

By all rights they ought to have been killed. But they were both very much alive. Each turned to the other triumphantly, and exclaimed,—

"I tellt ye so!"

There was a hole right through the helmet of Jimmy, the unbeliever. The fact that there was not also a hole through his head was due to his forethought in having put on a tam-o'-shanter underneath. The net result was a truncated "toorie." Wullie's bullet had struck his helmet at a more obtuse angle, and had glanced off, as the designer of the smooth exterior had intended it to do.

At first glance, the contest was a draw. But subsequent investigation elicited the fact that Jimmy in his backward fall had bitten his tongue to the effusion of blood. The verdict was therefore awarded, on points, to Wullie, and the spectators dispersed in an orderly manner just as the platoon sergeant came round the traverse to change the sentry.

II

We have occupied our own present trenches since January. There was a time when this sector of the line was regarded as a Vale of Rest. Bishops were conducted round with impunity. Members of Parliament came out for the week-end, and returned to their constituents with first-hand information about the horrors of war. Foreign journalists, and sight-seeing parties of munitions-workers, picnicked in Bunghole Wood. In the village behind the line, if a chance shell removed tiles from the roof of a house, the owner, greatly incensed, mounted a ladder and put in some fresh ones.

But that is all over now. "K(1)"—hard-headed men of business, bountifully endowed with munitions—have arrived upon the scene, and the sylvan peace of the surrounding district is gone. Pan has dug himself in.

The trouble began two months ago, when our Divisional Artillery arrived. Unversed in local etiquette, they commenced operations by "sending up"—to employ a vulgar but convenient catch-phrase—a strongly fortified farmhouse in the enemy's support line. The Boche, by way of gentle reproof, deposited four or five small "whizz-bangs" in our front-line trenches. The tenants thereof promptly telephoned to "Mother," and Mother came to the assistance of her offspring with a salvo of twelve-inch shells. After that. Brother Boche, realising that the golden age was past, sent north to the Salient for a couple of heavy batteries, and settled down to shell Bunghole village to pieces. Within a week he had brought down the church tower: within a fortnight the population had migrated farther back, leaving behind a few patriots, too deeply interested in the sale of small beer and picture postcards to uproot themselves. Company Headquarters in Bunghole Wood ceased to grow primroses and began to fill sandbags.

A month ago the village was practically intact. The face of the church tower was badly scarred, but the houses were undamaged. The little shops were open; children played in the streets. Now, if you stand at the cross-roads where the church rears its roofless walls, you will understand what the Abomination of Desolation means. Occasionally a body of troops, moving in small detachments at generous intervals, trudges by, on its way to or from the trenches. Occasionally a big howitzer shell swings lazily out of the blue and drops with a crash or a dull thud—according to the degree of resistance encountered—among the crumbling cottages. All is solitude.

But stay! Right on the cross-roads, in the centre of the village, just below the fingers of a sign-post which indicates the distance to four French townships, whose names you never heard of until a year ago, and now will never forget, there hangs a large, white, newly painted board, bearing a notice in black letters six inches high. Exactly underneath the board, rubbing their noses appreciatively against the sign-post, stand two mules, attached to a limbered wagon, the property of the A.S.C. Their charioteers are sitting adjacent, in a convenient shell-hole, partaking of luncheon.

"That was a rotten place we' ad to wait in yesterday, Sammy," observes Number One. "The draught was somethink cruel."

The recumbent Samuel agrees. "This little 'oiler is a bit of all right," he remarks. "When you've done strarfin' that bully-beef, 'and it over, ole man!"

He leans his head back upon the lip of the shell-hole, and gazes pensively at the notice-board six feet away. It says:—

VERY DANGEROUS.
DO NOT LOITER HERE.

III

Here is another cross-roads, a good mile farther forward—and less than a hundred yards behind the fire-trench. It is dawn.

The roads themselves are not so distinct as they were. They are becoming grass-grown: for more than a year—in daylight at least—no human foot has trodden them. The place is like hundreds of others that you may see scattered up and down this countryside—two straight, flat, metalled country roads, running north and south and east and west, crossing one another at a faultless right angle.

Of the four corners thus created, one is—or was—occupied by an estaminet: you can still see the sign, *Estaminet au Commerce*, over the door. Two others contain cottages,—the remains of cottages. At the fourth, facing south and east, stands what is locally known as a "Calvaire,"—bank of stone, a lofty cross, and a life-size figure of Christ, facing east, towards the German lines.

This spot is shelled every day—has been shelled every day for months. Possibly the enemy suspects a machine-gun or an observation post amid the tumble-down buildings. Hardly one brick remains upon another. And yet—the sorrowful Figure is unbroken. The Body is riddled with bullets—in the glowing dawn you may Count not five but fifty wounds—but the Face is untouched. It is the standing miracle of this most materialistic war. Throughout the length of France you will see the same thing.

Agnostics ought to come out here, for a "cure."

IV

With spring comes also the thought of the Next Push.

But we do not talk quite so glibly of pushes as we did. Neither, for that matter, does Brother Boche. He has just completed six weeks' pushing at Verdun, and is beginning to be a little uncertain as to which direction the pushing is coming from.

No; once more the military textbooks are being rewritten. We started this war under one or two rather fallacious premises. One was that Artillery was more noisy than dangerous. When Antwerp fell, we rescinded that theory. Then the Boche set out to demonstrate that an Attack, provided your Artillery preparation is sufficiently thorough, and you are prepared to set *no* limit to your expenditure of Infantry, must ultimately succeed. To do him justice, the Boche supported his assertions very plausibly. His phalanx bundled the Russians all the way from Tannenburg to Riga. The Austrians adopted similar tactics, with similar results.

We were duly impressed. The world last summer did not quite realize how far the results of the campaign were due to German efficiency and how far to Russian unpreparedness. (Russia, we realise now, found herself in the position of the historic Mrs. Partington, who endeavoured to repel the Atlantic with a mop. This year, we understand, she is in a position to discard the mop in favour of something far, far better.)

Then came—Verdun. Military science turned over yet another page, and noted that against consummate generalship, unlimited munitions, and selfless devotion on the part of the defence, the most spectacular and highly-doped phalanx can spend itself in vain. Military science also noted that, under modern conditions, the capture of this position or that signifies nothing: the only method of computing victory is to count the dead on either side. On that reckoning, the French at Verdun have already gained one of the great victories of all time.

"In fact," said Colonel Kemp, "this war will end when the Boche has lost so many men as to be unable to man his present trench-line, and not before."

"You don't think, sir, that we shall make another Push?" suggested Angus M'Lachlan eagerly. The others were silent: they had experienced a Push already.

"Not so long as the Boche continues to play our game for us, by attacking. If he tumbles to the error he is making, and digs himself in again—well, it may become necessary to draw him. In that case, M'Lachlan, you shall have first chop at the Victoria Crosses. Afraid I can't recommend you for your last exploit, though I admit it must have required some nerve!"

There was unseemly laughter at this allusion. Four nights previously Angus had been sent out in charge of a wiring-party. He had duly crawled forth with his satellites, under cover of darkness, on to No Man's Land; and, there selecting a row of "knife-rests" which struck him as being badly in need of repair, had well and truly reinforced the same with many strands of the most barbarous brand of barbed wire. This, despite more than usually fractious behaviour upon the part of the Boche.

Next morning, through a sniper's loophole, he exhibited the result of his labours to Major Wagstaffe. The Major gazed long and silently upon his subordinate's handiwork. There was no mistaking it. It stood out bright and gleaming in the rays of the rising sun, amid its dingy surroundings of rusty ironmongery. Angus M'Lachlan waited anxiously for a little praise.

"Jolly good piece of work," said Major Wagstaffe at last. "But tell me, why have you repaired the Boche wire instead of your own?"

"The only enemy we have to fear," continued Colonel Kemp, rubbing his spectacles savagely, "is the free and independent British voter—I mean, the variety of the species that we have left at home. Like the gentleman in Jack Point's song, 'He likes to get value for money'; and he is quite capable of asking us, about June or July, 'if we know that we are paid to be funny?'—before we are ready. What's your view of the situation at home, Wagstaffe? You're the last off leave."

Wagstaffe shook his head.

"The British Nation," he said, "is quite mad. That fact, of course, has been common property on the Continent of Europe ever since Cook's Tours were invented. But what irritates the orderly Boche is that there is no method in its madness. Nothing you can go upon, or take hold of, or wring any advantage from."

"As how?"

"Well, take compulsory service. For generations the electorate of our country has been trained by a certain breed of politician—the

Bandar-log of the British Constitution—to howl down such a low and degrading business as National Defence. A nasty Continental custom, they called it. Then came the War, and the glorious Voluntary System got to work."

"Aided," the Colonel interpolated, "by a campaign of mural advertisement which a cinema star's press agent would have boggled at!"

"Quite so," agreed Wagstaffe. "Next, when the Voluntary System had done its damnedest—in other words, when the willing horse had been worked to his last ounce—we tried the Derby Scheme. The manhood of the nation was divided into groups, and a fresh method of touting for troops was adopted. Married shysters, knowing that at least twenty groups stood between them and a job of work, attested in comparatively large numbers. The single shysters were less reckless—so much less reckless, in fact, that compulsion began to materialise at last."

"But only for single shysters," said Bobby Little regretfully.

"Yes; and the married shyster rejoiced accordingly. But the single shyster is a most subtle reptile. On examination, it was found that the single members of this noble army of martyrs were all 'starred,' or 'reserved', or 'ear-marked'—or whatever it is that they do to these careful fellows. So the poor old married shyster, who had only attested to show his blooming patriotism and encourage the others, suddenly found himself confronted with the awful prospect of having to defend his country personally, instead of by letter to the halfpenny press. Then the fat was fairly in the fire! The married martyr—"

"Come, come, old man! Not all of them!" said Colonel Kemp. "I have a married brother of my own, a solicitor of thirty-eight, who is simply clamouring for active service!"

"I know that, sir," admitted Wagstaffe quickly. "Thank God, these fellows are only a minority, and a freak minority at that; but freak minorities seem to get the monopoly of the limelight in our unhappy country."

"The whole affair," mused the Colonel, "can hardly be described as a frenzied rally round the Old Flag. By God," he broke out suddenly, "it fairly makes one's blood boil! When I think of the countless good fellows, married and single, but mainly married, who left *all* and followed the call of common decency and duty the moment the War broke out—most of them now dead or crippled; and when I see this miserable handful of shirkers, holding up vital public business while the pros and cons of their wretched claims to exemption are considered—well, I almost wish I had been born a Boche!"

"I don't think you need apply for naturalisation papers yet, Colonel," said Wagstaffe. "The country is perfectly sound at heart over this question, and always was. The present agitation, as I say, is being engineered by the more verminous section of our incomparable daily Press, for its own ends. It makes our Allies lift their eyebrows a bit; but they are sensible people, and they realise that although we are a nation of lunatics, we usually deliver the goods in the end. As for the Boche, poor fellow, the whole business makes him perfectly rabid. Here he is, with all his splendid organisation and brutal efficiency, and he can't even knock a dent into our undisciplined, back-chatting, fool-ridden, self-depreciating old country! I, for one, sympathise with the Boche profoundly. On paper, we don't *deserve* to win!"

"But we shall!" remarked that single-minded paladin, Bobby Little.

"Of course we shall! And what's more, we are going to derive a national benefit out of this war which will in itself be worth the price of admission!"

"How?" asked several voices.

Wagstaffe looked round the table. The Battalion were for the moment in Divisional Reserve, and consequently out of the trenches. Some one had received a box of Coronas from home, and the mess president had achieved a bottle of port. Hence the present symposium at Headquarters Mess. Wagstaffe's eyes twinkled.

"Will each officer present," he said, "kindly name his pet aversion among his fellow-creatures?"

"A person or a type?" asked Mr. Waddell cautiously.

"A type."

Colonel Kemp led off.

"Male ballet-dancers," he said.

"Fat, shiny men," said Bobby Little, "with walrus moustaches!"

"All conscientious objectors, passive resisters, pacifists, and other cranks!" continued the orthodox Waddell.

"All people who go on strike during war-time," said the Adjutant. There was an approving murmur—then silence.

"Your contribution, M'Lachlan?" said Wagstaffe.

Angus, who had kept silence from shyness, suddenly blazed out:—

"I think," he said, "that the most contemptible people in the world to-day are those politicians and others who, in years gone by, systematically cried down anything in the shape of national defence or national inclination to personal service, because they saw there were no *votes* in such a programme; and who *now*"—Angus's passion rose to fever-heat,—"stand up and endeavour to cultivate popular favour by reviling the Ministry and the Army for want of preparedness and initiative. Such men do not deserve to live! Oh, sirs—"

But Angus's peroration was lost in a storm of applause.

"You are adjudged to have hit the bull's-eye, M'Lachlan," said Colonel Kemp. "But tell us, Wagstaffe, your exact object in compiling this horrible catalogue."

"Certainly. It is this. Universal Service is a *fait accompli* at last, or is shortly going to be—and without anything very much in the way of exemption either. When it comes, just think of it! All these delightful people whom we have been enumerating will have to toe the line at last. For the first time in their little lives they will learn the meaning of discipline, and fresh air, and *esprit de corps*. Isn't that worth a war? If the present scrap can only be prolonged for another year, our country will receive a tonic which will carry it on for another century. Think of it! Great Britain, populated by men who have actually been outside their own parish; men who know that the whole is greater than the part; men who are too wide awake to go on doing just what the *Bandar-log* tell them, and allow themselves to be used as stalking-horses for low-down political ramps! When *we*, going round in bath-chairs and on crutches, see that sight—well, I don't think we shall regret our missing arms and legs quite so much, Colonel. War is Hell, and all that; but there is one worse thing than a long war, and that is a long peace!"

"I wonder!" said Colonel Kemp reflectively. He was thinking of his wife and four children in distant Argyllshire.

But the rapt attitude and quickened breath of Temporary Captain Bobby Little endorsed every word that Major Wagstaffe had spoken. As he rolled into his "flea-bag" that night, Bobby requoted to himself, for the hundredth time, a passage from Shakespeare which had recently come to his notice. He was not a Shakespearian scholar, nor indeed a student of literature at all; but these lines had been sent to him, cut out of a daily almanac, by an equally unlettered and very adorable confidante at home:—

"And gentlemen in England now a-bed, Shall think themselves accursed they were not here, And hold their manhoods cheap whiles any speaks That fought with us upon Saint Crispin's day!"

Bobby was the sort of person who would thoroughly have enjoyed the Battle of Agincourt.

CHAPTER 8

"The Non-Combatant"

We will call the village St. Gregoire. That is not its real name; because the one thing you must not do in war-time is to call a thing by its real name. To take a hackneyed example, you do not call a spade a spade: you refer to it, officially, as *Shovels, General Service, One.* This helps to deceive, and ultimately to surprise, the enemy; and as we all know by this time, surprise is the essence of successful warfare. On the same principle, if your troops are forced back from their front-line trenches, you call this "successfully straightening out an awkward salient."

But this by the way. Let us get back to St. Gregoire. Hither, mud-splashed, ragged, hollow-cheeked, came our battalion—they call us the Seventh Hairy Jocks nowadays—after four months' continuous employment in the firing-line. Ypres was a household word to them; Plugstreet was familiar ground; Givenchy they knew intimately; Loos was their wash-pot—or rather, a collection of wash-pots, for in winter all the shell-craters are full to overflowing. In addition to their prolonged and strenuous labours in the trenches, the Hairy Jocks had taken part in a Push—a part not altogether unattended with glory, but prolific in casualties. They had not been "pulled out" to rest and refit for over six months, for Divisions on the Western Front were not at that period too numerous, the voluntary system being at its last gasp, while the legions of Lord Derby had not yet crystallised out of the ocean of public talk which held them in solution. So the Seventh Hairy Jocks were bone tired. But they were as hard as a rigorous winter in the open could make them, and—they were going back to rest at last. Had not their beloved C.O. told them so? And he had added, in a voice not altogether free from emotion, that if ever men deserved a solid rest and a good time, "you boys do!"

So the Hairy Jocks trudged along the long, straight, nubbly French road, well content, speculating with comfortable pessimism as to the character of the billets in which they would find themselves.

Meanwhile, ten miles ahead, the advance party were going round the town in quest of the billets.

Billet-hunting on the Western Front is not quite so desperate an affair as hunting for lodgings at Margate, because in the last extremity you can always compel the inhabitants to take you in—or at least, exert pressure to that end through the *Mairie*. But at the best one's course is strewn with obstacles, and fortunate is the Adjutant who has to his hand a subaltern capable of finding lodgings for a thousand men without making a mess of it.

The billeting officer on this, as on most occasions, was our friend Cockerell,—affectionately known to the entire Battalion as "Sparrow,"—and his qualifications for the post were derived from three well-marked and invaluable characteristics, namely, an imperious disposition, a thick skin, and an attractive *bonhomie* of manner.

Behold him this morning dismounting from his horse in the *place* of St. Gregoire. Around him are grouped his satellites—the Quartermaster-Sergeant, four Company Sergeants, some odd orderlies, and a forlorn little man in a neat drab uniform with light blue facings,—the regimental interpreter. The party have descended, with the delicate care of those who essay to perform acrobatic feats in kilts, from bicycles—serviceable but appallingly heavy machines of Government manufacture, the property of the "Buzzers," but commandeered for the occasion. The Quartermaster-Sergeant, who is not accustomed to strenuous exercise, mops his brow and glances expectantly round the *place*. His eye comes gently to rest upon a small but hospitable-looking *estaminet*.

Lieutenant Cockerell examines his wrist-watch.

"Half-past ten!" he announces. "Quartermaster-Sergeant!"

"Sirr!" The Quartermaster-Sergeant unglues his longing gaze from the *estaminet* and comes woodenly to attention.

"I am going to see the Town Major about a billeting area. I will meet you and the party here in twenty minutes."

Master Cockerell trots off on his mud-splashed steed, followed by the respectful and appreciative salutes of his followers—appreciative, because a less considerate officer would have taken the whole party direct to the Town Major's office and kept them standing in the street, wasting moments which might have been better employed elsewhere, until it was time to proceed with the morning's work.

****

"How strong are you?" inquired the Town Major.

Cockerell told him. The Town Major whistled.

"That all? Been doing some job of work, haven't you?"

Cockerell nodded, and the Town Major proceeded to examine a large-scale plan of St. Gregoire, divided up into different-coloured plots.

"We are rather full up at present," he said; "but the Cemetery Area is vacant. The Seventeenth Geordies moved out yesterday. You can have that." He indicated a triangular section with his pencil.

Master Cockerell gave a deprecatory cough.

"We have come here, sir," he intimated dryly, "for a change of scene."

The stout Town Major—all Town Majors are stout—chuckled.

"Not bad for a Scot!" he conceded. "But it's quite a cheery district, really. You won't have to doss down in the cemetery itself, you know. These two streets here—" he flicked a pencil—"will hold practically all your battalion, at its present strength. There's a capital house in the Rue Jean Jacques Rousseau which will do for Battalion Headquarters. The corporal over there will give you your *billets de logement*."

"Are there any other troops in the area, sir?" asked Cockerell, who, as already indicated, was no child in these matters.

"There ought not to be, of course. But you know what the Heavy Gunners and the A.S.C. are! If you come across any of them, fire them out. If they wear too many stars and crowns for you, let me know, and I will perform the feat myself. You fellows need a good rest and no worries, I know. Good-morning."

At ten minutes to eleven Cockerell found the Quartermaster-Sergeant and party, wiping their moustaches and visibly refreshed, at the exact spot where he had left them; and the hunt for billets began.

"A" Company were easily provided for, a derelict tobacco factory being encountered at the head of the first street. Lieutenant Cockerell accordingly detached a sergeant and a corporal from his train, and passed on. The wants of "B" Company were supplied by commandeering a block of four dilapidated houses farther down the street—all in comparatively good repair except the end house, whose roof had been disarranged by a shell during the open fighting in the early days of the war.

This exhausted the possibilities of the first street, and the party debouched into the second, which was long and straggling, and composed entirely of small houses.

"Now for a bit of the retail business!" said Master Cockerell resignedly. "Sergeant M'Nab, what is the strength of 'C' Company?"

"One hunner and thairty-fower other ranks, sirr," announced Sergeant M'Nab, consulting a much-thumbed roll-book.

"We shall have to put them in twos and threes all down the street," said Cockerell. "Come on; the longer we look at it the less we shall like it. Interpreter!"

The forlorn little man, already described, trotted up, and saluted with open hand, French fashion. His name was Baptiste Bombominet ("or words to that effect," as the Adjutant put it), and may have been so inscribed upon the regimental roll; but throughout the rank and file Baptiste was affectionately known by the generic title of "Alphonso." The previous seven years had been spent by him in the congenial and blameless atmosphere of a Ladies' Tailor's in the west end of London, where he enjoyed the status and emoluments of chief cutter. Now, called back to his native land by the voice of patriotic obligation, he found himself selected, by virtue of a residence of seven years in England, to act as official interpreter between a Scottish Regiment which could not speak English, and Flemish peasants who could not speak French. No wonder that his pathetic brown eyes always appeared full of tears. However, he followed Cockerell down the street, and meekly embarked upon a contest with the lady Inhabitants thereof, in which he was hopelessly outmatched from the start.

At the first door a dame of massive proportions, but keen business instincts, announced her total inability to accommodate *soldats*, but explained that she would be pleased to entertain *officiers* to any number. This is a common gambit. Twenty British privates in your *grenier*, though extraordinarily well-behaved as a class, make a good deal of noise, buy little, and leave mud everywhere. On the other hand, two or three officers give no trouble, and can be relied upon to consume and pay for unlimited omelettes and bowls of coffee.

That seasoned vessel, Lieutenant Cockerell, turned promptly to the Sergeant and Corporal of "C" Company.

"Sergeant M'Nab," he said, "you and Corporal Downie will billet here." He introduced hostess and guests by an expressive wave of the hand. But shrewd Madame was not to be bluffed.

"*Pas de sergents, Monsieur le Capitaine!*" she exclaimed. "*Officiers!*"

"*Ils sont officiers—sous-officiers*," explained Cockerell, rather ingeniously, and moved off down the street.

At the next house the owner—a small, wizened lady of negligible physique but great staying power—entered upon a duet with Alphonso, which soon reduced that very moderate performer to breathlessness. He shrugged his shoulders feebly, and cast an appealing glance towards the Lieutenant.

"What does she say?" inquired Cockerell.

"She say dis' ouse no good, sair! She 'ave seven children, and one *malade*—seek."

"Let me see," commanded the practical officer.

He insinuated himself as politely as possible past his reluctant opponent, and walked down the narrow passage into the kitchen. Here he turned, and inquired—

"Er—*ou est la pauvre petite chose?*"

Madame promptly opened a door, and displayed a little girl in bed—a very flushed and feverish little girl.

Cockerell grinned sympathetically at the patient, to that young lady's obvious gratification; and turned to the mother.

"*Je suis tres—triste,*» he said; «*j'ai grand misericorde. Je ne placerai pas de soldats ici. Bon jour!*"

By this time he was in the street again. He saluted politely and departed, followed by the grateful regards of Madame.

No special difficulties were encountered at the next few houses. The ladies at the house-door were all polite; many of them were most friendly; but naturally each was anxious to get as few men and as many officers as possible—except the proprietess of an *estaminet*, who offered to accommodate the entire regiment. However, with a little tact here and a little firmness there, Master Cockerell succeeded in distributing "C" Company among some dozen houses. One old gentleman, with a black alpaca cap and a six-days beard, proprietor of a lofty establishment at the corner of the street, proved not only recalcitrant, but abusive. With him Cockerell dealt promptly.

"*Ca suffit!*" he announced. "*Montres-moi votre grenier!*"

The old man, grumbling, led the way up numerous rickety staircases to the inevitable loft under the tiles. This proved to be a noble apartment thirty feet long. From wall to wall stretched innumerable strings.

"We can get a whole platoon in here," said Cockerell contentedly. "Tell him, Alphonso. These people," he explained to Sergeant M'Nab, "always dislike giving up their lofts, because they hang their laundry there in winter. However, the old boy must lump it. After all, we are in this country for his health, not ours; and he gets paid for every man who sleeps here. That fixes 'C' Company. Now for 'D'! The other side of the street this time."

Quarters were found in due course for "D" Company; after which Cockerell discovered a vacant building-site which would serve for transport lines. An empty garage was marked down for the Quartermaster's ration store, and the Quartermaster-Sergeant promptly faded into its recesses with a grateful sigh. An empty shop in the Rue Jean Jacques Rousseau, conveniently adjacent to Battalion Headquarters, was appropriated for that gregarious band, the regimental signallers and telephone section; while a suitable home for the Anarchists, or Bombers, together with their stock-in-trade, was found in the basement of a remote dwelling on the outskirts of the area.

After this, Lieutenant Cockerell, left alone with Alphonso and the orderly in charge of his horse, heaved a sigh of exhaustion and transferred his attention from his notebook to his watch.

"That finishes the rank and file," he said. "I breakfasted at four this morning, and the battalion won't arrive for a couple of hours yet. Alphonso, I am going to have an omelette somewhere. I shall want you in half an hour exactly. Don't go wandering off for the rest of the day, pinching soft billets for yourself and the Sergeant-Major and your other pals, as you usually do!"

Alphonso saluted guiltily—evidently the astute Cockerell had "touched the spot"—and was turning away, when suddenly the billeting officer's eye encountered an illegible scrawl at the very foot of his list.

"Stop a moment, Alphonso! I have forgotten those condemned machine-gunners, as usual. *Strafe* them! Come on! Once more into the breach, Alphonso! There is a little side-alley down here that we have not tried."

The indefatigable Cockerell turned down the Rue Gambetta, followed by Alphonso, faint but resigned.

"Here is the very place!" announced Cockerell almost at once. "This house, Number Five. We can put the gunners and their little guns into that stable at the back, and the officer can have a room in the house itself. *Sonnez*, for the last time before lunch!"

The door was opened by a pleasant-faced young woman of about thirty, who greeted Cockerell—tartan is always popular with French ladies—with a beaming smile, but shook her head regretfully upon seeing the *billet de logement* in his hand. The inevitable duet with Alphonso followed. Presently Alphonso turned to his superior.

"Madame is ver' sorry, sair, but an *officier* is here already."

"Show me the *officier*!" replied the prosaic Cockerell.

The duet was resumed.

"Madame say," announced Alphonso presently, "that the *officier* is not here now; but he will return."

"So will Christmas! Meanwhile I am going to put an *Emma Gee* officer in here."

Alphonso's desperate attempt to translate the foregoing idiom into French was interrupted by Madame's retirement into the house, whither she beckoned Cockerell to follow her. In the front room she produced a frayed sheet of paper, which she proffered with an apologetic smile. The paper said:—

This billet is entirely reserved for the Supply Officer of this District. It is not to be occupied by troops passing through the town. By Order.

Lieutenant Cockerell whistled softly and vindictively through his teeth.

"Well," he said, "for consummate and concentrated nerve, give me the underlings of the A.S.C.! This pot-bellied blighter not only butts into an area which doesn't belong to him, but actually leaves a chit to warn people off the grass even when he isn't here! He hasn't signed the document, I observe. That means that he is a newly joined subaltern, trying to get mistaken for a Brass Hat! I'll fix *him*!"

With great stateliness Lieutenant Cockerell tore the offending screed into four portions, to the audible concern of Madame. But the Lieutenant smiled reassuringly upon her.

"*Je vous donnerai un autre, vous savez*," he assured her.

He sat down at the table, tore a leaf from his Field Service Pocket Book, and wrote:—

The Supply Officer of the District is at liberty to occupy this billet only at such times as it is not required by the troops of the Combatant Services.

Signed, F.J. Cockerell, Lieut. & Asst. Adj., 7th B. & W. Highes.

"That's a pretty nasty one!" he observed with relish. Then, having pinned the insulting document conspicuously to the mantelpiece, he observed to the mystified lady of the house:—

"*Voila, Madame. Si l'officier reviendra, je le verrai moi-meme, avec grand plaisir. Bon jour*!"

And with this dark saying Sparrow Cockerell took his departure.

II

The Battalion, headed by their tatterdemalion pipers, stumped into the town in due course, and were met on the outskirts by the billeting party, who led the various companies to their appointed place. After inspecting their new quarters, and announcing with gloomy satisfaction that they were the worst, dirtiest, and most uncomfortable yet encountered, everybody settled down in the best place he could find, and proceeded to make himself remarkably snug.

Battalion Headquarters and the officers of "A" Company were billeted in an imposing mansion which actually boasted a bathroom. It is true that there was no water, but this deficiency was soon made good by a string of officers' servants bearing buckets. Beginning with Colonel Kemp, who was preceded by an orderly bearing a small towel and a large loofah, each officer performed a ceremonial ablution; and it was a collection of what Major Wagstaffe termed "bright and bonny young faces" which collected round the Mess table at seven o'clock.

It was in every sense a gala meal. Firstly, it was weeks since any one (except Second Lieutenant M'Corquodale, newly joined, and addressed, for painfully obvious reasons, as "Tich") had found himself at table in an apartment where it was possible to stand upright. Secondly, the Mess President had coaxed glass tumblers out of the ancient *concierge*; and only those who have drunk from enamelled ironware for weeks on end can appreciate the pure joy of escape from the indeterminate metallic flavour which such vessels impart to all beverages. Thirdly, these same tumblers were filled to the brim with inferior but exhilarating champagne—purchased, as they euphemistically put it in the Supply Column, "locally." Lastly, the battalion had several months of hard fighting behind it, probably a full month's rest before it, and the conscience of duty done and recognition earned floating like a halo above it. For the moment memories of Nightmare Wood and the Kidney Bean Redoubt—more especially the latter—were effaced. Even the sorrowful gaps in the ring round the table seemed less noticeable.

The menu, too, was almost pretentious. First came the *hors d'oeuvres*—a tin of sardines. This was followed by what the Mess Corporal described as a savoury omelette, but which the Second-in-Command condemned as "a regrettable incident."

"It is false economy," he observed dryly to the Mess President, "to employ Mark One[1] eggs as anything but hand-grenades."

However, the tide of popular favour turned with the haggis, contributed by Lieutenant Angus M'Lachlan, from a parcel from home. Even the fact that the Mess cook, an inexperienced aesthete from Islington, had endeavoured to tone down the naked repulsiveness of the dainty with discreet festoons of tinned macaroni, failed to arouse

1: In the British army each issue of arms or equipment receives a distinctive "Mark." Mark I denotes the earliest issue.

the resentment of a purely Scottish Mess. The next course—the beef ration, hacked into the inevitable gobbets and thinly disguised by a sprinkling of curry powder—aroused no enthusiasm; but the unexpected production of a large tin of Devonshire cream, contributed by Captain Bobby Little, relieved the canned peaches of their customary monotony. Last of all came a savoury—usually described as *the* savoury—consisting of a raft of toast per person, each raft carrying an abundant cargo of fried potted meat, and provided with a passenger in the shape of a recumbent sausage.

A compound of grounds and dish-water, described by the optimistic Mess Corporal as coffee, next made its appearance, mitigated by a bottle of Cointreau and a box of Panatellas; and the Mess turned itself to more intellectual refreshment. A heavy and long-overdue mail had been found waiting at St. Gregoire. Letters had been devoured long ago. Now, each member of the Mess leaned back in his chair, straightened his weary legs under the table, and settled down, cigar in mouth, to the perusal of the *Spectator* or the *Tatler*, according to rank and literary taste.

Colonel Kemp, unfolding a week-old *Times*, looked over his glasses at his torpid disciples.

"Where is young Sandeman?" he inquired.

Young Sandeman was the Adjutant.

"He went out to the Orderly Room, sir, five minutes ago," replied Bobby Little.

"I only want to give him to-morrow's Orders. No doubt he'll be back presently. I may as well mention to you fellows that I propose to allow the men three clear days' rest, except for bathing and re-clothing. After that we must do Company Drill, good and hard, so as to polish up the new draft, who are due to-morrow. I am going to start a bombing-school, too: at least seventy-five per cent. of the Battalion ought to pass the test before we go back to the line. However, we need not rush things. We should be here in peace for at least a month. We must get up some sports, and I think it would be a sound scheme to have a singsong one Saturday night. I was just saying, Sandeman,"—this to the Adjutant, who re-entered the room at that moment,—"that it would be a sound—"

The Adjutant laid a pink field-telegraph slip before his superior.

"This has just come in from Brigade Headquarters, sir," he said. "I have sent for the Sergeant-Major."

The Colonel adjusted his glasses and read the despatch. A deathly, sickening silence reigned in the room. Then he looked up.

"I am afraid I was a bit previous," he said quietly. "The Royal Stickybacks have lost the Kidney Bean, and we are detailed to go up and retake it. Great compliment to the regiment, but a trifle mis-timed! You young fellows had better go to bed. Parade at 4 a.m., sharp! Good-night! Come along to the Orderly Room, Sandeman."

The door closed, and the Mess, grinding the ends of their cigars into their coffee-cups, heaved themselves resignedly to their aching feet.

"There ain't," quoted Major Wagstaffe, "no word in the blooming language for it!"

III

The Kidney Bean Redoubt is the key to a very considerable sector of trenches.

It lies just behind a low ridge. The two horns of the bean are drawn back out of sight of the enemy, but the middle swells forward over the skyline and commands an extensive view of the country beyond. Direct observation of artillery fire is possible: consequently an armoured observation post has been constructed here, from which gunner officers can direct the fire of their batteries with accuracy and elegance. Lose the Kidney Bean, and the boot is on the other leg. The enemy has the upper ground now: he can bring observed artillery fire to bear upon all our tenderest spots behind the line. He can also enfilade our front-line trenches.

Well, as already stated, the Twenty-Second Royal Stickybacks had lost the Kidney Bean. They were a battalion of recent formation, stout-hearted fellows all, but new to the refinements of intensive trench warfare. When they took over the sector, they proceeded to leave undone various vital things which the Hairy Jocks had always made a point of doing, and to do various unnecessary things which the Hairy Jocks had never done. The observant Hun promptly recognised that he was faced by a fresh batch of opponents, and, having carefully studied the characteristics of the newcomers, prescribed and administered an exemplary dose of frightfulness. He began by tickling up the Stickybacks with an unpleasant engine called the *Minenwerfer*, which despatches a large sausage-shaped projectile in a series of ridiculous somersaults, high over No Man's Land into the enemy's front-line trench, where it explodes and annihilates everything in that particular bay. Upon these occasions one's only chance of salvation is to make a rapid calculation as to the bay into which the sausage is going to fall, and then double speedily round a traverse—or, if possible, two traverses—into another.

It is an exhilarating pastime, but presents complications when played by a large number of persons in a restricted space, especially when the persons aforesaid are not unanimous as to the ultimate landing-place of the projectile.

After a day and a night of these aerial torpedoes the Hun proceeded to an intensive artillery bombardment. He had long coveted the Kidney Bean, and instinct told him that he would never have a better opportunity of capturing it than now. Accordingly, two hours before dawn, the Redoubt was subjected to a sudden, simultaneous, and converging fire from all the German artillery for many miles round, the whole being topped up with a rain of those crowning instruments of demoralisation, gas-shells. At the same time an elaborate curtain of shrapnel and high explosive was let down behind the Redoubt, to serve the double purpose of preventing either the sending up of reinforcements or the temporary withdrawal of the garrison.

At the first streak of dawn the bombardment was switched off, as if by a tap; the curtain fire was redoubled in volume; and a massed attack swept across the disintegrated wire into the shattered and pulverised Redoubt. Other attacks were launched on either flank; but these were obvious blinds, intended to prevent a too concentrated defence of the Kidney Bean. The Royal Stickybacks—what was left of them—put up a tough fight; but half of them were lying dead or buried, or both, before the assault was launched, and the rest were too dazed and stupefied by noise and chlorine gas to withstand—much less to repel—the overwhelming phalanx that was hurled against them. One by one they went down, until the enemy troops, having swamped the Redoubt, gathered themselves up in a fresh wave and surged towards the reserve-line trenches, four hundred yards distant. At this point, however, they met a strong counter-attack, launched from the Brigade Reserve, and after heavy fighting were bundled back into the Redoubt itself. Here the German machine-guns had staked out a defensive line, and the German retirement came to a standstill.

Meanwhile a German digging party, many hundred strong, had been working madly in No Man's Land, striving to link up the newly acquired ground with the German lines. By the afternoon the Kidney Bean was not only "reversed and consolidated," but was actually included in the enemy's front trench system. Altogether a well-planned and admirably executed little operation.

Forty-eight hours later the Kidney Bean Redoubt was recaptured, and remains in British hands to this day. Many arms of the Service took honourable part in the enterprise—heavy guns, field guns, trench-mortars, machine-guns; Sappers and Pioneers; Infantry in various capacities. But this narrative is concerned only with the part played by the Seventh Hairy Jocks.

"Sorry to pull you back from rest, Colonel," said the Brigadier, when the commander of the Hairy Jocks reported; "but the Divisional General considers that the only feasible way to hunt the Boche from the Kidney Bean is to bomb him out of it. That means trench-fighting, pure and simple. I have called you up because you fellows know the ins and outs of the Kidney Bean as no one else does. The Brigade who are in the line just now are quite new to the place. Here is an aeroplane photograph of the Redoubt, as at present constituted. Tell off your own bombing parties; make your own dispositions; send me a copy of your provisional orders; and I will fit my plan in with yours. The Corps Commander has promised to back you with every gun, trench-mortar, culverin, and arquebus in his possession."

In due course Battalion Orders were issued and approved. They dealt with operations most barbarous amid localities of the most homelike sound. Number Nine Platoon, for instance (Commander Lieutenant Cockerell), were to proceed in single file, carrying so many grenades per man, up CHARING CROSS ROAD, until stopped by the barrier which the enemy were understood to have erected in TRAFALGAR SQUARE, where a bombing-post and at least one machine-gun would probably be encountered. At this point they were to wait until Trafalgar Square had been suitably dealt with by a trench-mortar. (Here followed a paragraph addressed exclusively to the Trench-Mortar Officer.) After this the bombers of Number Three Platoon would bomb their way across the Square and up the Strand. Another party would clear NORTHUMBERLAND AVENUE, while a Lewis gun raked WHITEHALL. And so on. Every detail was thought out, down to the composition of the parties which were to "clean up" afterwards—that is, extract the reluctant Boche from various underground fastnesses well known to the extractors. The whole enterprise was then thoroughly rehearsed in some dummy trenches behind the line, until every one knew his exact part. Such is modern warfare.

Next day the Kidney Bean Redoubt was in British hands again. The Hun—what was left of him after an intensive bombardment of twenty-four hours—had betaken himself back over the ridge, *via* the remnants of his two new communication trenches, to his original front line. The two communication trenches themselves were blocked and sandbagged, and were being heavily supervised by a pair of British machine-guns. Fighting in the Redoubt itself had almost ceased, though a humorous sergeant, followed by acolytes bearing bombs, was still "combing out" certain residential districts in the centre of the maze. Ever and anon he would stoop down at the entrance of some deep dug-out, and bawl—

"Ony mair doon there? Come away, Fritz! I'll gie ye five seconds. Yin, Twa, Three—"

Then, with a rush like a bolt of rabbits, two or three close-cropped, grimy Huns would scuttle up from below and project themselves from one of the exits; to be taken in charge by grinning Caledonians wearing "tin hats" very much awry, and escorted back through the barrage to the "prisoners' base" in rear.

All through the day, amidst unremitting shell fire and local counter-attack, the Hairy Jocks reconsolidated the Kidney Bean; and they were so far successful that when they handed over the work to another battalion at dusk, the parapet was restored, the machine-guns were in position, and a number of "knife-rest" barbed-wire entanglements were lying just behind the trench, ready to be hoisted over the parapet and joined together in a continuous defensive line as soon as the night was sufficiently dark.

One by one the members of Number Nine Platoon squelched—for it had rained hard all day—back to the reserve line. They were utterly exhausted, and still inclined to feel a little aggrieved at having been pulled out from rest; but they were well content. They had done the State some service, and they knew it; and they knew that the higher powers knew it too. There would be some very flattering reading in Divisional Orders in a few days' time.

Meanwhile, their most pressing need was for something to eat. To be sure, every man had gone into action that morning carrying his day's rations. But the British soldier, improvident as the grasshopper, carries his day's rations in one place, and one place only—his stomach. The Hairy Jocks had eaten what they required at their extremely early breakfast: the residue thereof they had abandoned.

About midnight Master Cockerell, in obedience to a most welcome order, led the remnants of his command, faint but triumphant, back from the reserve line to a road junction two miles in rear, known as Dead Dog Corner. Here the Battalion was to *rendezvous*, and march back by easy stages to St. Gregoire. Their task was done.

But at the cross-roads Number Nine Platoon found no Battalion: only a solitary subaltern, with his orderly. This young Casabianca informed Cockerell that he, Second Lieutenant Candlish, had been left behind to "bring in stragglers."

"Stragglers?" exclaimed the infuriated Cockerell. "Do we look like stragglers?"

"No," replied the youthful Candlish frankly; "you look more like sweeps. However, you had better push on. The Battalion isn't far ahead. The order is to march straight back to St. Gregoire and re-occupy former billets."

"What about rations?"

"Rations? The Quartermaster was waiting here for us when we *rendezvoused*, and every man had a full ration and a tot of rum." (Number Nine Platoon cleared their parched throats expectantly.) "But I fancy he has gone on with the column. However, if you leg it you should catch them up. They can't be more than two miles ahead. So long!"

IV

But the task was hopeless. Number Nine Platoon had been bombing, hacking, and digging all day. Several of them were slightly wounded—the serious cases had been taken off long ago by the stretcher-bearers—and Cockerell's own head was still dizzy from the fumes of a German gas-shell. He lined up his disreputable paladins in the darkness, and spoke—

"Sergeant M'Nab, how many men are present?"

"Eighteen, sirr." The platoon had gone into action thirty-four strong.

"How many men are deficient of an emergency ration? I can make a good guess, but you had better find out."

Five minutes later the Sergeant reported. Cockerell's guess was correct. The British private has only one point of view about the portable property of the State. To him, as an individual, the sacred emergency ration is an unnecessary encumbrance, and the carrying thereof a "fatigue." Consequently, when engaged in battle, one of the first (of many) things which he jettisons is this very ration. When all is over, he reports with unctuous solemnity that the provender in question has been blown out of his haversack by a shell. The Quartermaster-Sergeant writes it off as "lost owing to the exigencies of military service," and indents for another.

Lieutenant Cockerell's haversack contained a packet of meat-lozenges and about half a pound of chocolate. These were presented to the Sergeant.

"Hand these round as far as they will go, Sergeant," said Cockerell. "They'll make a mouthful a man, anyhow. Tell the platoon to lie down for ten minutes; then we'll push off. It's only fifteen miles. We ought to make it by breakfast-time. . . ."

Slowly, mechanically, all through the winter night the victors hobbled along. Cockerell led the way, carrying the rifle of a man with a wounded arm. Occasionally he checked his bearings with map and electric torch. Sergeant M'Nab, who, under a hirsute and attenuated exterior, concealed a constitution of ferro-concrete and the heart of a lion, brought up the rear, uttering fallacious assurances to the faint-hearted as to the shortness of the distance now to be covered, and carrying two rifles.

The customary halts were observed. At ten minutes to four the men flung themselves down for the third time. They had covered about seven miles, and were still eight or nine from St. Gregoire. The everlasting constellation of Verey lights still rose and fell upon the eastern horizon behind them, but the guns were silent.

"There might be a Heavy Battery dug in somewhere about here," mused Cockerell. "I wonder if we could touch them for a few tins of bully. Hallo, what's that?"

A distant rumble came from the north, and out of the darkness loomed a British motor-lorry, lurching and swaying along the rough cobbles of the *pave*. Some of Cockerell's men were lying dead asleep in the middle of the road, right at the junction. The lorry was going twenty miles an hour.

"Get into the side of the road, you men!" shouted Cockerell, "or they'll run over you. You know what these M.T. drivers are!"

With indignant haste, and at the last possible moment, the kilted figures scattered to either side of the narrow causeway. The usual stereotyped and vitriolic remonstrances were hurled after the great hooded vehicle as it lurched past.

And then a most unusual thing happened. The lorry slowed down, and finally stopped, a hundred yards away. An officer descended, and began to walk back. Cockerell rose to his weary feet and walked to meet him.

The officer wore a major's crown upon the shoulder-straps of his sheepskin-lined "British Warm" and the badge of the Army Service Corps upon his cap. Cockerell, indignant at the manner in which his platoon had been hustled off the road, saluted stiffly, and muttered: "Good-morning, sir!"

"Good-morning!" said the Major. He was a stout man of nearly fifty, with twinkling blue eyes and a short-clipped moustache. Cockerell judged him to be one of the few remnants of the original British Army.

"I stopped," explained the older man, "to apologise for the scandalous way that fellow drove over you. It was perfectly damnable; but you know what these converted taxi-drivers are! This swine forgot for the moment that he had an officer on board, and hogged it as usual. He goes under arrest as soon as we get back to billets."

"Thank you very much, sir," said Master Cockerell, entirely thawed. "I'm afraid my chaps were lying all over the road; but they are pretty well down and out at present."

"Where have you come from?" inquired the Major, turning a curious eye upon Cockerell's prostrate followers. Cockerell explained When he had finished, he added wistfully—

"I suppose you have not got an odd tin or two of bully to give away, sir? My fellows are about—"

For answer, the Major took the Lieutenant by the arm and led him towards the lorry. "You have come," he announced, "to the very man you want. I am practically Mr. Harrod. In fact, I am a Corps Supply Officer. How would a Maconochie apiece suit your boys?"

Cockerell, repressing the ecstatic phrases which crowded to his tongue, replied that that was just what the doctor had ordered.

"Where are you bound for?" continued the Major.

"St. Gregoire."

"Of course. You were pulled out from there, weren't you? I am going to St. Gregoire myself as soon as I have finished my round. Home to bed, in fact. I haven't had any sleep worth writing home about for four nights. It is no joke tearing about a country full of shell-holes, hunting for people who have shifted their ration-dump seven times in four days. However, I suppose things will settle down again, now that you fellows have fired Brother Boche out of the Kidney Bean. Pretty fine work, too! Tell me, what is your strength, here and now?"

"One officer," said Cockerell soberly, "and eighteen other ranks."

"All that's left of your platoon?"

Cockerell nodded. The stout Major began to beat upon the tailboard of the lorry with his stick.

"Sergeant Smurthwaite!" he shouted.

There came a muffled grunt from the recesses of the lorry. Then a round and ruddy face rose like a harvest moon above the tailboard, and a stertorous voice replied respectfully—

"Sir?"

"Let down this tailboard; load this officer's platoon into the lorry; issue them with a Maconochie and a tot of rum apiece; and don't forget to put Smee under arrest for dangerous driving when we get back to billets."

"Very good, sir."

Ten minutes later the survivors of Number Nine Platoon, soaked to the skin, dazed, slightly incredulous, but at peace with all the world, reclined close-packed upon the floor of the swaying lorry. Each man held an open tin of Mr. Maconochie's admirable ration between his knees. Perfect silence reigned: a pleasant aroma of rum mellowed the already vitiated atmosphere.

In front, beside the chastened Mr. Smee, sat the Major and Master Cockerell. The latter had just partaken of his share of refreshment, and was now endeavouring, with lifeless fingers, to light a cigarette.

The Major scrutinised his guest intently. Then he stripped off his British Warm coat—incidentally revealing the fact that he wore upon his tunic the ribbons of both South African Medals and the Distinguished Service Order—and threw it round Cockerell's shoulders.

"I'm sorry, boy!" he said. "I never noticed. You are chilled to the bone. Button this round you."

Cockerell made a feeble protest, but was cut short.

"Nonsense! There's no sense in taking risks after you've done your job."

Cockerell assented, a little sleepily. His allowance of rum was bringing its usual vulgar but comforting influence to bear upon an exhausted system.

"I see you have been wounded, sir," he observed, noting with a little surprise two gold stripes upon his host's left sleeve—the sleeve of a "non-combatant."

"Yes," said the Major. "I got the first one at Le Gateau. He was only a little fellow; but the second, which arrived at the Second Show at Ypres, gave me such a stiff leg that I am only an old crock now. I was second-in-command of an Infantry Battalion in those days. In these, I am only a peripatetic Lipton. However, I am lucky to be here at all: I've had twenty-seven years' service. How old are you?"

"Twenty," replied Cockerell. He was too tired to feel as ashamed as he usually did at having to confess to the tenderness of his years.

The Major nodded thoughtfully.

"Yes," he said; "I judged that would be about the figure. My son would have been twenty this month, only—he was at Neuve Chapelle. He was very like you in appearance—very. His mother would have been interested to meet you. You might as well take a nap for half an hour. I have two more calls to make, and we shan't get home till nearly seven. Lean on me, old man. I'll see you don't tumble overboard ..."

So Lieutenant Cockerell, conqueror of the Kidney Bean, fell asleep, his head resting, with scandalous disregard for military etiquette, upon the shoulder of the stout Major.

V

An hour or two later, Number Nine Platoon, distended with concentrated nourishment and painfully straightening its cramped limbs, decanted itself from the lorry into a little *cul-de-sac* opening off the Rue Jean Jacques Rousseau in St. Gregoire. The name of the *cul-de-sac* was the Rue Gambetta.

Their commander, awake and greatly refreshed, looked round him and realised, with a sudden sense of uneasiness, that he was in familiar surroundings. The lorry had stopped at the door of Number Five.

"I don't suppose your Battalion will get back for some time," said the Major. "Tell your Sergeant to put your men into the stable behind this house—there's plenty of straw there—and—"

"Their own billet is just round the corner, sir," replied Cockerell. "They might as well go there, thank you."

"Very good. But come in with me yourself, and doss here for a few hours. You can report to your C.O. later in the day, when he arrives. This is my *pied-a-terre*,"—rapping on the door. "You won't find many billets like it. As you see, it stands in this little backwater, and is not included in any of the regular billeting areas of the town. The Town Major has allotted it to me permanently. Pretty decent of him, wasn't it? And Madame Vinot is a dear. Here she is! *Bonjour, Madame Vinot! Avez-vous un feu—er—inflamme pour moi dans la chambre?*" Evidently the Major's French was on a par with Cockerell's.

But Madame understood him, bless her!

"*Mais oui, M'sieur le Colonel*!" she exclaimed cheerfully—the rank of Major is not recognised by the French civilian population—and threw open the door of the sitting-room, with a glance of compassion upon the Major's mud-splashed companion, whom she failed to recognise.

A bright fire was burning in the open stove.

Immediately above, pinned to the mantelpiece and fluttering in the draught, hung Cockerell's manifesto upon the subject of noncombatants. He could recognise his own handwriting across the room. The Major saw it too.

"Hallo, what's that hanging up, I wonder?" he exclaimed. "A memorandum for me, I expect; probably from my old friend 'Dados.'[1] Let us get a little more light."

He crossed to the window and drew up the blind. Cockerell moved too. When the Major turned round, his guest was standing by the stove, his face scarlet through its grime.

"I'm awfully sorry, sir," said Cockerell, "but that notice—memorandum—of yours has dropped into the fire."

"If it came from Dados," replied the Major, "thank you very much!"

"I can't tell you, sir," added Cockerell humbly, "what a fool I feel."

But the apology referred to an entirely different matter.

1: D.A.D.O.S. Deputy Assistant Director of Ordnance Stores.

CHAPTER 9

Tuning Up

It is just one year to-day since we "came oot." A year plays havoc with the "establishment" of a battalion in these days of civilised warfare. Of the original band of stout-hearted but inexperienced Crusaders who crossed the Channel in the van of The First Hundred Thousand, in May, 1915,—a regiment close on a thousand strong, with twenty-eight officers,—barely two hundred remain, and most of these are Headquarters or Transport men. Of officers there are five—Colonel Kemp, Major Wagstaffe, Master Cockerell, Bobby Little, and Mr. Waddell, who, by the way, is now Captain Waddell, having succeeded to the command of his old Company.

Of the rest, our old Colonel is in Scotland, essaying ambitious pedestrian and equestrian feats upon his new leg. Others have been drafted to the command of newer units, for every member of "K(1)" is a Nestor now. Others are home, in various stages of convalescence. Others, alas! will never go home again. But the gaps have all been filled up, and once more we are at full strength, comfortably conscious that whereas a year ago we were fighting to hold a line, and play for time, and find our feet, while the people at home behind us were making good, now we are fighting for one thing and one thing only; and that is, to administer the knock-out blow to Brother Boche.

Our last casualty was Ayling, who left us under somewhat unusual circumstances.

Towards the end of our last occupancy of trenches the local Olympus decided that what both sides required, in order to awaken them from their winter lethargy, or spring lassitude (or whatever it is that Olympus considers that we in the firing-line are suffering from for the moment), was a tonic. Accordingly orders were issued for a Flying Matinee, or trench raid. Each battalion in the Division was to submit a scheme, and the battalion whose scheme was adjudged the best was to be accorded the honour—so said the Practical Joke Department—of carrying out the scheme in person. To the modified rapture of the Seventh Hairy Jocks their plan was awarded first prize. Headquarters, after a little excusable recrimination on the subject of unnecessary zeal and misguided ambition, set to work to arrange rehearsals of our highly unpopular production.

Brother Boche has grown "wise" to Flying Matinees nowadays, and to score a real success you have to present him with something comparatively novel and unexpected. However, our scheme had been carefully thought out; and, given sufficient preparation, and an adequate cast, there seemed no reason to doubt that the piece would have a highly successful run of one night.

At one point in the enemy's trenches opposite to us his barbed-wire defences had worn very thin, and steps were taken by means of systematic machine-gun fire to prevent him repairing them. This spot was selected for the raid. A party of twenty-five was detailed. It was to be led by Angus M'Lachlan, and was to slip over the parapet on a given moonless night, crawl across No Man's Land to within striking distance of the German trench, and wait. At a given moment the signal for attack would be given, and the wire demolished by a means which need not be specified here. Thereupon the raiding party were to dash forward and—to quote the Sergeant-Major—"mix themselves up in it."

Two elements are indispensable in a successful trench-raid—surprise and despatch. That is to say, you must deliver your raid when and where it is least expected, and then get home to bed before your victims have had time to set the machinery of retaliation in motion. Steps were therefore taken, firstly, to divert the enemy's attention as far as possible from the true objective of the raid, by a sudden and furious bombardment of a sector of trenches three hundred yards away; and secondly, to ensure as far as possible, that the raid, having commenced at 2 a.m., should conclude at 2.12, sharp.

In order to cover the retirement of the excursionists, Ayling was ordered to arrange for machine-gun fire, which should sweep the enemy's parapet for some hundreds of yards upon either flank, and so encourage the enemy to keep his head down and mind his own business.

The raid itself was a brilliant success. Dug-outs were bombed, emplacements destroyed, and a respectable bag of captives brought over. But the element of surprise, upon which so much insistence was laid above, was visited upon both attackers and attacked. To the former the contribution came from that well-meaning but somewhat addlepated warrior, Private Nigg, who formed one of the raiding party.

Nigg's allotted task upon this occasion was to "comb out" certain German dug-outs. (It may be mentioned that each man had a specific duty to perform, and a specific portion of the trench opposite to perform it in; for the raid had been rehearsed several times in a dummy trench behind the lines constructed exactly to scale from an aeroplane photograph.) For this purpose he was provided with bombs. Shortly before two o'clock in the morning the party, headed by Angus M'Lachlan, crawled over the parapet during a brief lull in the activities of the Verey lights, and crept steadily, on hands and knees, across No Man's Land. Fifty yards from the enemy's wire was a collection of shell-holes, relics of a burst of misdirected energy on the part of a six-inch battery. Here the raiders disposed themselves, and waited for the signal.

Now, it is an undoubted fact, that if you curl yourself up, with two or three preliminary twirls, after the fashion of a dog going to bed, in a perfectly circular shell-hole, on a night as black as the inside of the dog in question, you are extremely likely to lose your sense of direction. This is what happened to Private Nigg. He and his infernal machines lay uneasily in their appointed shell-hole for some ten minutes, surrounded by Verey lights which shot suddenly into the sky with a disconcerting *plop*, described a graceful parabola, burst into dazzling flame, and fluttered sizzling down. One or two of these fell quite near Nigg's party, and continued to burn upon the ground, but the raiders sank closer into their shell-holes, and no alarm resulted. Once or twice a machine-gun had a scolding fit, and bullets whispered overhead. But, on the whole, the night was quiet.

Then suddenly, with a shattering roar, the feint-artillery bombardment broke forth. Simultaneously word was passed along the raiding line to stand by. Next moment Angus M'Lachlan and his followers rose to their feet in the black darkness, scrambled out of their nests, and dashed forward to the accomplishment of their mission.

When Nigg, who had paused a moment to collect his bombs, sprang out of his shell-hole, not a colleague was in sight. At least, Nigg could see no one. However, want of courage was not one of his failings. He bounded blindly forward by himself.

Try as he would he could not overtake the raiding party. However, this mattered little, for suddenly a parapet loomed before him. In this same parapet, low down, Nigg beheld a black and gaping aperture—plainly a loophole of some kind.

Without a moment's hesitation, Nigg hurled a Mills grenade straight through the loophole, and then with one wild screech of "Come away, boys!" took a flying leap over the parapet—and landed in his own trench, in the arms of Corporal Mucklewame.

As already noted, it is difficult, when lying curled up in a circular shell-hole in the dark, to maintain a true sense of direction.

So the first-fruits of the raid was Captain Ayling, of the *Emma Gees.* He had stationed himself in a concrete emplacement in the front line, the better to "observe" the fire of his guns when it should be required. Unfortunately this was the destination selected by the misguided Niggs for his first (and as it proved, last) bomb. The raiders came safely back in due course; but by that time Ayling, liberally (but by a miracle not dangerously) ballasted with assorted scrap-iron, was on his way to the First Aid Post.

II

At the present moment we are right back at rest once more, and are being treated with a consideration, amounting almost to indulgence, which convinces us that we are being "fattened up"—to employ the gruesome but expressive phraseology of the moment—for some particularly strenuous enterprise in the near future.

Well, we are ready. It is nine months since Loos, and nearly six since we scraped the nightmare mud of Ypres from our boots, *gum, thigh*, for the last time. Our recent casualties have been light—our only serious effort of late has been the recapture of the Kidney Bean—the new drafts have settled down, and the young officers have been blooded. And above all, victory is in the air. We are going into our next fight with new-born confidence in the powers behind us. Loos was an experimental affair; and though to the humble instruments with which the experiment was made the proceedings were less hilarious than we had anticipated, the results were enormously valuable to a greatly expanded and entirely untried Staff.

"We shall do better this time," said Major Wagstaffe to Bobby Little, as they stood watching the battalion assemble, in workmanlike fashion, for a route-march. "There are just one or two little points which had not occurred to us then. We have grasped them now, I think."

"Such as?"

"Well, you remember we all went into the Loos show without any very lucid idea as to how far we were to go, and where to knock off for the day, so to speak. The result was that the advance of each Division was regulated by the extent to which the German wire in front of it had been cut by our artillery. Ours was well and truly cut, so we penetrated two or three miles. The people on our left never started at all. Lord knows, they tried hard enough. But how could any troops get through thirty feet of uncut wire, enfiladed by machine-guns? The result was that after forty-eight hours' fighting, our whole attacking front, instead of forming a nice straight line, had bagged out into a series of bays and peninsulas."

"Our crowd wasn't even a peninsula," remarked Bobby with feeling. "For an hour or so it was an island!"

"I think you will find that in the next show we shall go forward, after intensive bombardment, quite a short distance; then consolidate; then wait till the *whole* line has come up to its appointed objective; then bombard again; then go forward another piece; and so on. That will make it impossible for gaps to be created. It will also give our gunners a chance to cover our advance continuously. You remember at Loos they lost us for hours, and dare not fire for fear of hitting us. In fact, I expect that in battle plans of the future, instead of the artillery trying to conform to the movements of the infantry, matters will be reversed. The guns, after preliminary bombardment, will create a continuous Niagara of exploding shells upon a given line, marked in everybody's map, and timed for an exact period, just beyond the objective; and the infantry will stroll up into position a comfortable distance behind, reading the time-table, and dig themselves in. Then the barrage will lift on to the next line, and we shall toddle forward again. That's the new plan, Bobby! Close artillery cooperation, and a series of limited objectives!"

"It sounds all right," agreed Bobby. "We shall want a good many guns, though, shan't we?"

"We shall. But don't let that worry you. It is simply raining guns at the Base now. In fact, my grandmother in the War Office"—this mythical relative was frequently quoted by Major Wagstaffe, and certainly her information had several times proved surprisingly correct—"tells me that by the beginning of next year we shall have enough guns, of various calibres, to make a continuous line, hub to hub, from one end of our front to the other."

"Golly!" observed Captain Little, with respectful relish.

"That means," continued Wagstaffe, "that we shall be able to blow Brother Boche's immediate place of business to bits, and at the same time take on his artillery with counter-battery work. Our shell-supply is practically unlimited now; so when the next push comes, we foot-sloggers ought to have a more gentlemanly time of it than we had at Loos and Wipers. And I'll tell you another thing, Bobby. We shall have command of the air too."

"That will be a pleasant change," remarked Bobby. "I'm getting tired of putting my fellows under arrest for rushing out of carefully concealed positions in order to gape up at Boche planes going over. Angus M'Lachlan is as bad as any of them. The fellow—"

"But you have not seen many Boche planes lately?"

"No. Certainly not so many."

"And the number will grow beautifully less. Our little friends in the R.F.C. are getting fairly numerous now, and their machines have been improved out of all knowledge. They are rapidly assuming the position of top dog. Moreover, the average Boche does not take kindly to flying. It is too—too individualistic a job for him. He likes to work in a bunch with other Boches, where he can keep step, and maintain dressing, and mark time if he gets confused. In the air one cannot mark time, and it worries Fritz to death. I think you will see, in the next unpleasantness, that we shall be able to maintain our aeroplane frontier somewhere over the enemy third line. That means that we shall make our own dispositions with a certain degree of privacy, and the Boche will not. Also, when our big guns get to work, they will not need to fire blindly, as in the days of our youth, but will be directed by one of our R.F.C. lads, humming about in his little bus above the target, perhaps fifteen miles from the gun. Hallo, there go the pipes! Tell your men to fall in."

"The whole business," observed Bobby, as he struggled into his equipment, "sounds so attractive that I am beginning quite to look forward to the next show!"

"Don't forget the Boche machine-guns, my lad," replied Wagstaffe.

"One seldom gets the chance," grumbled Bobby. "Is there no way of knocking them out?"

"Well—" Wagstaffe looked intensely mysterious—"of course one never knows, but—have you heard any rumours on the subject?"

"I have. About—"

"About the Hush! Hush! Brigade?"

Bobby nodded.

"Yes," he said. "Young Osborne, my best subaltern after Angus, disappeared last month to join it. Tell me, what *is* the—"

"Hush! Hush!" said Major Wagstaffe. "*Mefiez vous! Taisez vous!* and so on!"

The battalion moved off.

So much for the war-talk of veterans. Now let us listen to the novices.

"Bogle," said Angus M'Lachlan to his henchman, "I think we shall have to lighten this Wolseley valise of mine. With one thing and another it weighs far more than thirty-five pounds."

"That's a fact, sirr," agreed Mr. Bogle. "It carries ower mony books in the heid of it."

They shook out the contents of the valise upon the floor of Angus's bedroom—a loft over the kitchen in "A" Company's farm billet—and proceeded to prune Angus's personal effects. There were boots, socks, shaving-tackle, maps, packets of chocolate, and books of every size, but chiefly of the ever-blessed sevenpenny type.

"A lot of these things will have to go, Bogle," said Angus regretfully. "The colonel has warned officers about their kits, and it would never do to have mine turned back from the wagon at the last minute."

Mr. Bogle pricked up his ears. "The wagon? Are we for off again, sirr?" he inquired.

"Indeed I could not say," replied the cautious Angus; "but it is well to be ready."

"The boys was saying, sirr," observed Bogle tentatively, "that there was to be another grand battle soon."

"It is more than likely," said Angus, with an air of profound wisdom. "Here we are in June, and we must take the offensive, sooner or later, or summer will be over."

"What kind o' a battle will it be this time, sirr?" inquired Bogle respectfully.

"Oh, our artillery will pound the German trenches for a week or two, and then we shall go over the parapet and drive them back for miles," said Angus simply.

"And what then, sirr?"

"What then? We shall go on pushing them until another Division relieves us."

Bogle nodded comprehendingly. He now had firmly fixed in his mind the essential details of the projected great offensive of 1916. He was not interested to go further in the matter. And it is this very faculty—philosophic trust, coupled with absolute lack of imagination—which makes the British soldier the most invincible person in the world. The Frenchman is inspired to glorious deeds by his great spirit and passionate love of his own sacred soil; the German fights as he thinks, like a machine. But the British Tommy wins through owing to his entire indifference to the pros and cons of the tactical situation. He settles down to war like any other trade, and, as in time of peace, he is chiefly concerned with his holidays and his creature comforts. A battle is a mere incident between one set of billets and another. Consequently he does not allow the grim realities of war to obsess his mind when off duty. One might almost ascribe his success as a soldier to the fact that his domestic instincts are stronger than his military instincts.

Put the average Tommy into a trench under fire how does he comport himself? Does he begin by striking an attitude and hurling defiance at the foe? No, he begins by inquiring, in no uncertain voice, where his—dinner is? He then examines his new quarters. Before him stands a parapet, buttressed mayhap with hurdles or balks of timber, the whole being designed to preserve his life from hostile projectiles. How does he treat this bulwark? Unless closely watched, he will begin to chop it up for firewood. His next proceeding is to construct for himself a place of shelter. This sounds a sensible proceeding, but here again it is a case of "safety second." A British Tommy regards himself as completely protected from the assaults of his enemies if he can lay a sheet of corrugated-iron roofing across his bit of trench and sit underneath it. At any rate it keeps the rain off, and that is all that his instincts demand of him. An ounce of comfort is worth a pound of security.

He looks about him. The parapet here requires fresh sandbags; there the trench needs pumping out. Does he fill sandbags, or pump, of his own volition? Not at all. Unless remorselessly supervised, he will devote the rest of the morning to inventing and chalking up a title for his new dug-out—"Jock's Lodge," or "Burns' Cottage," or "Cyclists' Rest"—supplemented by a cautionary notice, such as—*No Admittance. This Means You.* Thereafter, with shells whistling over his head, he will decorate the parapet in his immediate vicinity with picture postcards and cigarette photographs. Then he leans back with a happy sigh. His work is done. His home from home is furnished. He is now at leisure to think about "they Gairmans" again. That may sound like an exaggeration; but "Comfort First" is the motto of that lovable but imprudent grasshopper, Thomas Atkins, all the time.

A sudden and pertinent thought occurred to Mr. Bogle, who possessed a Martha-like nature.

"What way, sir, will a body get his dinner, if we are to be fighting for twa-three days on end?" "Every man," replied Angus, "will be issued, I expect, with two days' rations. But the Colonel tells me that during hard fighting a man does not feel the desire for food—or sleep either for that matter. Perhaps, during a lull, it may occur to him that he has not eaten since yesterday, and he may pull out a bit of biscuit or chocolate from his pocket, just to nibble. Or he may remember that he has had no sleep for twenty-four hours—so he just drops down and sleeps for ten minutes while there is time. But generally, matters of ordinary routine drop out of a man's thoughts altogether."

"That's a queer-like thing, a body forgetting his dinner!" murmured Bogle.

"Of course," continued Angus, warming to his theme like his own father in his pulpit, "if Nature is expelled with a pitchfork in this manner, for too long, *tamen usque recurret*."

"Is that a fact?" replied Bogle politely. He always adopted the line of least resistance when his master took to audible rumination. "Weel, I'll hae to be steppin', sir. I'll pit these twa blankets oot in the sun, in some place where the dooks frae the pond will no get dandering ower them. And if you'll sorrt your books, I'll hand ower the yins ye dinna require to the Y.M.C.A. hut ayont the village." Bogle cherished a profound admiration for Lieutenant M'Lachlan both as a scholar and a strategist, and absorbed his deliverances with a care and attention which enabled him to misquote the same quite fluently to his own associates. That very evening he set forth the coming plan of campaign, as elucidated to him by his master, to a mixed assemblage at the *Estaminet au Clef des Champs*. Some of the party were duly impressed; but Mr. Spike Johnson, a resident in peaceful times of Stratford-atte-Bow, the recognised humorist of the Sappers' Field Company attached to the Brigade, was pleased to be facetious.

"It won't be no good you Jocks goin' over no parapet to attack no 'Uns," he said, "after what 'appened last week!"

This dark saying had the effect of rousing every Scottish soldier in the *estaminet* to a state of bristling attention.

"And what was it," inquired Private Cosh with heat, "that happened last week?"

"Why," replied Mr. Johnson, who had been compounding this jest for some days, and now saw his opportunity to deliver it with effect at short range, "your trenchès got raided last Wednesday, when you was in' em. By the Brandyburgers, I think it was."

The entire symposium stared at the jester with undisguised amazement.

"Our—trenches," proclaimed Private Tosh with forced calm, "were never raided by no—Brandyburrrgerrs! Was they, Jimmie?"

Mr. Cosh corroborated, with three adjectives which Mr. Tosh had not thought of.

Spike Johnson merely smiled, with the easy assurance of a man who has the ace up his sleeve.

"Oh yes, they was!" he reiterated.

"They werre *not*!" shouted half a dozen voices.

The next stage of the discussion requires no description. It terminated, at the urgent request of Madame from behind the bar, and with the assistance of the Military Police, in the street outside.

"And now, Spike Johnson," inquired Private Cosh, breathing heavily but much refreshed, "can you tell me what way Gairmans could get intil the trenches of a guid Scots regiment withoot bein' *seen*?"

"I can," replied Mr. Johnson with relish, "and I will. They got in all right, but you didn't see them, because they was disguised."

Cosh and Tosh snorted disdainfully, and Private Nigg, who was present with his friend Buncle, inquired—

"What way was they disguised?"

Like lightning came the answer—

"*As a joke!* Oh, you Jocks."

Cosh and Tosh (who had already been warned by the Police sergeant) merely glared and gurgled impotently. Private Nigg, who, as already mentioned, was slightly wanting in quickness of perception, was led away by the faithful Buncle, to have the outrage explained to him at leisure. It was Private Bogle who intervened, and brought the intellectual Goliath crashing to the ground. "Man, Johnson," he remarked, and shook his head mournfully, "youse ought to be varra careful aboot sayin' things like that to the likes of us. 'Deed aye!"

"What for, ole son?" inquired the jester indulgently.

"Naithing," replied Bogle with artistic reticence.

"Come along—aht with it!" insisted Johnson. "Cough it up, duckie!"

"Man, man," cried Bogle with passionate earnestness, "dinna gang ower far!"

"What the 'ell *for*?" inquired Johnson, impressed despite himself.

"What for?" Bogle's voice dropped to a ghostly whisper. "Has it ever occurred to you, my mannie, what would happen tae the English—if Scotland was tae make a separate peace?"

And Mr. Bogle retired, not before it was time, within the sheltering portals of the *estaminet*, where not less than seven inarticulate but appreciative fellow-countrymen offered him refreshment.

Chapter 10
Full Chorus

An Observation Post—or "O Pip," in the mysterious *patois* of the Buzzers—is not exactly the spot that one would select either for spaciousness or accessibility. It may be situated up a chimney or up a tree, or down a tunnel bored through a hill. But it certainly enables you to see something of your enemy; and that, in modern warfare, is a very rare and valuable privilege.

Of late the scene-painter's art—technically known as *camouflage*—has raised the concealment of batteries and their observation posts to the realm of the uncanny. According to Major Wagstaffe, you can now disguise anybody as anything. For instance, you can make up a battery of six-inch guns to look like a flock of sheep, and herd them into action browsing. Or you can despatch a scouting party across No Man's Land dressed up as pillar-boxes, so that the deluded Hun, instead of opening fire with a machine-gun, will merely post letters in them—valuable letters, containing military secrets. Lastly, and more important still, you can disguise yourself to look like nothing at all, and in these days of intensified artillery fire it is very seldom that nothing at all is hit.

The particular O Pip with which we are concerned at present, however, is a German post—or was a fortnight ago, before the opening of the Battle of the Somme.

For nearly two years the British Armies on the Western Front have been playing for time. They have been sticking their toes in and holding their ground, with numerically inferior forces and inadequate artillery support, against a nation in arms which has set out, with forty years of preparation at its back, to sweep the earth. We have held them, and now *der Tag* has come for us. The deal has passed into our hand at last. A fortnight ago, ready for the first time to undertake the offensive on a grand and prolonged scale,—Loos was a mere reconnaissance compared with this,—the New British Army went over the parapet shoulder to shoulder with the most heroic Army in the world—the Army of France—and attacked over a sixteen-mile front in the Valley of the Somme.

It was a critical day for the Allies: certainly it was a most critical day in the history of the British Army. For on that day an answer had to be given to a very big question indeed. Hitherto we had been fighting on the defensive—unready, uphill, against odds. It would have been no particular discredit to us had we failed to hold our line. But we had held it, and more. Now, at last, we were ready—as ready as we were ever likely to be. We had the men, the guns, and the munitions. We were in a position to engage the enemy on equal, and more than equal, terms. And the question that the British Empire had to answer in that day, the First of July 1916, was this: "Are these new amateur armies of ours, raised, trained, and equipped in less than two years, with nothing in the way of military tradition to uphold them—nothing but the steady courage of their race: are they a match for, and more than a match for, that grim machine-made, iron-bound host that lies waiting for them along that line of Picardy hills? Because if they are *not*, we cannot win this war. We can only make a stalemate of it."

We, looking back now over a space of twelve months, know how our boys answered that question. In the greatest and longest battle that the world had yet seen, that Army of city clerks, Midland farm-lads, Lancashire mill-hands, Scottish miners, and Irish corner-boys, side by side with their great-hearted brethren from Overseas, stormed positions which had been held impregnable for two years, captured seventy thousand prisoners, reclaimed several hundred square miles of the sacred soil of France, and smashed once and for all the German-fostered fable of the invincibility of the German Army. It was good to have lived and suffered during those early and lean years, if only to be present at their fulfilment.

But at this moment the battle was only beginning, and the bulk of their astounding achievement was still to come. Nevertheless, in the cautious and modest estimate of their Commander-in-Chief, they had already done something.

After ten days and nights of continuous fighting, said the first official report, *our troops have completed the methodical capture of the whole of the enemy's first system of defence on a front of fourteen thousand yards. This system of defence consisted of numerous and continuous lines of fire trenches, extending to depths of from two thousand to four thousand yards, and included five strongly fortified villages, numerous heavily entrenched woods, and a large number of immensely strong redoubts. The capture of each of these trenches represented an operation of some importance, and the whole of them are now in our hands.*

Quite so. One feels, somehow, that Berlin would have got more out of such a theme.

* * * * * * * *

Now let us get back to our O Pip. If you peep over the shoulder of Captain Leslie, the gunner observing officer, as he directs the fire of his battery, situated some thousands of yards in rear, through the medium of map, field-glass, and telephone, you will obtain an excellent view of to-morrow's field of battle. Present in the O Pip are Colonel Kemp, Wagstaffe, Bobby Little, and Angus M'Lachlan. The latter had been included in the party because, to quote his Commanding Officer, "he would have burst into tears if he had been left out."

Overhead roared British shells of every kind and degree of unpleasantness, for the ground in front was being "prepared" for the coming assault. The undulating landscape, running up to a low ridge on the skyline four miles away, was spouting smoke in all directions—sometimes black, sometimes green, and sometimes, where bursting shell and brick-dust intermingled, blood-red. Beyond the ridge all-conquering British aeroplanes occupied the firmament, observing for "mother" and "granny" and signalling encouragement or reproof to these ponderous but sprightly relatives as their shells hit or missed the target.

"Yes, sir," replied Leslie to Colonel Kemp's question, "that is Longueval, on the slope opposite, with the road running through on the way to Flers, over the skyline. That is Delville Wood on its right. As you see, the guns are concentrating on both places. That is Waterlot Farm, on this side of the wood—a sugar refinery. Regular nest of machine-guns there, I'm told."

"No doubt we shall be able to confirm the rumour to-morrow," said Colonel Kemp dryly. "That is Bernafay Wood on our right, I suppose?"

"Yes, sir. We hold the whole of that. The pear-shaped wood out beyond it—it looks as if it were joined on, but the two are quite separate really—is Trones Wood. It has changed hands several times. Just at present I don't think we hold more than the near end. Further away, half-right, you can see Guillemont."

"In that case," remarked Wagstaffe, "our right flank would appear to be strongly supported by the enemy."

"Yes. We are in a sort of right-angled salient here. We have the enemy on our front and our right. In fact, we form the extreme right of the attacking front. Our left is perfectly secure, as we now hold

Mametz Wood and Contalmaison. There they are." He waved his glass to the northwest. "When the attack takes place, I understand that our Division will go straight ahead, for Longueval and Delville Wood, while the next Division makes a lateral thrust out to the right, to push the Boche out of Trones Wood and cover our flank."

"I believe that is so," said the Colonel. "Bobby, take a good look at the approaches to Longueval. That is the scene of to-morrow's constitutional."

Bobby and Angus obediently scanned the village through their glasses. Probably they did not learn much. One bombarded French village is very like another bombarded French village. A cowering assemblage of battered little houses; a pitiful little main street, with its eviscerated shops and *estaminets*; a shattered church-spire. Beyond that, an enclosure of splintered stumps that was once an orchard. Below all, cellars, reinforced with props and sandbags, and filled with machine-guns. *Voila tout!*

Presently the Gunner Captain passed word down to the telephone operator to order the battery to cease fire.

"Knocking off?" inquired Wagstaffe.

"For the present, yes. We are only registering this morning. Not all our batteries are going at once, either. We don't want Brother Boche to know our strength until we tune up for the final chorus. We calculate that—"

"There is a comfortable sense of decency and order about the way we fight nowadays," said Colonel Kemp. "It is like working out a problem in electrical resistance by a nice convenient algebraical formula. Very different from the state of things last year, when we stuck it out by employing rule of thumb and hanging on by our eyebrows."

"The only problem we can't quite formulate is the machine-gun," said Leslie. The Boche's dug-outs here are thirty feet deep. When crumped by our artillery he withdraws his infantry and leaves his machine-gunners behind, safe underground. Then, when our guns lift and the attack comes over, his machine-gunners appear on the surface, hoist their guns after them with a sort of tackle arrangement, and get to work on a prearranged band of fire. The infantry can't do them in until No Man's Land is crossed, and—well, they don't all get across, that's all! However, *I have* heard rumours—"

"So have we all," said Colonel Kemp.

"I forgot to tell you, Colonel," interposed Wagstaffe, "that I met young Osborne at Divisional Headquarters last night. You remember, he left us some time ago to join the Hush! Hush! Brigade."

"I remember," said the Colonel.

By this time the party, including the Gunner Captain, were filing along a communication trench, lately the property of some German gentlemen, on their way back to headquarters.

"Did he tell you anything, Wagstaffe?" continued Colonel Kemp.

"Not much. Apparently the time of the H.H.B. is not yet. But he made an appointment with me for this evening—in the gloaming, so to speak. He is sending a car. If all he says is true, the Boche *Emma Gee* is booked for an eye-opener in a few weeks' time."

II

That evening a select party of sight-seers were driven to a secluded spot behind the battle line. Here they were met by Master Osborne, obviously inflated with some important matter.

"I've got leave from my C.O. to show you the sights, sir," he announced to Colonel Kemp. "If you will all stand here and watch that wood on the opposite side of this clearing, you may see something. We don't show ourselves much except in late evening, so this is our parade hour."

The little group took up its appointed stand and waited in the gathering dusk. In the east the sky was already twinkling with intermittent Verey lights. All around the British guns were thundering forth their hymns of hate—full-throated now, for the hour for the next great assault was approaching.

Wagstaffe's thoughts went back to a certain soft September night last year, when he and Blaikie had stood on the eastern outskirts of Bethune listening to a similar overture—the prelude to the Battle of Loos. But this overture was ten times more awful, and, from a material British point of view, ten times more inspiring. It would have thrilled old Blaikie's fighting spirit, thought Wagstaffe. But Loos had taken his friend from him, and he, Wagstaffe, only was left. What did fate hold in store for him to-morrow? he wondered. And Bobby? They had both escaped marvellously so far. Well, better men had gone before them. Perhaps—

Fingers of steel bit into his biceps muscle, and the excited whinny of Angus M'Lachlan besought him to look!

Down in the forest something stirred. But it was not the note of a bird, as the song would have us believe. From the depths of the wood opposite came a crackling, crunching sound, as of some prehistoric beast forcing its way through tropical undergrowth. And then, suddenly, out from the thinning edge there loomed a monster—a monstrosity. It did not glide, it did not walk. It wallowed. It lurched, with now and then a laborious heave of its shoulders. It fumbled its way over a low bank matted with scrub. It crossed a ditch, by the simple expedient of rolling the ditch out flat, and waddled forward. In its path stood a young tree. The monster arrived at the tree and laid its chin lovingly against the stem. The tree leaned back, crackled, and assumed a horizontal position. In the middle of the clearing, twenty yards farther on, gaped an enormous shell-crater, a present from the Kaiser. Into this the creature plunged blindly, to emerge, panting and puffing, on the farther side. Then it stopped. A magic opening appeared in its stomach, from which emerged, grinning, a British subaltern and his grimy associates.

And that was our friends' first encounter with a "Tank." The secret—unlike most secrets in this publicity-ridden war—had been faithfully kept; so far the Hush! Hush! Brigade had been little more than a legend even to the men high up. Certainly the omniscient Hun received the surprise of his life when, in the early mist of a September morning some weeks later, a line of these selfsame tanks burst for the first time upon his incredulous vision, waddling grotesquely up the hill to the ridge which had defied the British infantry so long and so bloodily—there to squat complacently down on the top of the enemy's machine-guns, or spout destruction from her own up and down beautiful trenches which had never been intended for capture. In fact, Brother Boche was quite plaintive about the matter. He described the employment of such engines as wicked and brutal, and opposed to the recognised usages of warfare. When one of these low-comedy vehicles (named the *Creme-de-Menthe*) ambled down the main street of the hitherto impregnable village of Flers, with hysterical British Tommies slapping her on the back, he appealed to the civilised world to step in and forbid the combination of vulgarism and barbarity.

"Let us at least fight like gentlemen," said the Hun, with simple dignity. "Let us stick to legitimate military devices—the murder of women and children, and the emission of chlorine gas. But Tanks—no! One must draw the line somewhere!"

But the ill-bred *Creme-de-Menthe* took no notice. None whatever. She simply went waddling on—towards Berlin.

"An experiment, of course," commented Colonel Kemp, as they returned to headquarters—"a fantastic experiment. But I wish they were ready now. I would give something to see one of them leading the way into action to-morrow. It might mean saving the lives of a good many of my boys."

CHAPTER 11
The Last Solo

It was dawn on Saturday morning, and the second phase of the Battle of the Somme was more than twenty-four hours old. The programme had opened with a night attack, always the most difficult and uncertain of enterprises, especially for soldiers who were civilians less than two years ago. But no undertaking is too audacious for men in whose veins the wine of success is beginning to throb. And this undertaking, this hazardous gamble, had succeeded all along the line. During the past day and night, more than three miles of the German second system of defences, from Bazentin le Petit to the edge of Delville Wood, had received their new tenants; and already long streams of not altogether reluctant Hun prisoners were being escorted to the rear by perspiring but cheerful gentlemen with fixed bayonets.

Meanwhile—in case such of the late occupants of the line as were still at large should take a fancy to revisit their previous haunts, working-parties of infantry, pioneers, and sappers were toiling at full pressure to reverse the parapets, run out barbed wire, and bestow machine-guns in such a manner as to produce a continuous lattice-work of fire along the front of the captured position.

All through the night the work had continued. As a result, positions were now tolerably secure, the intrepid "Buzzers" had included the newly grafted territory in the nervous system of the British Expeditionary Force, and Battalion Headquarters and Supply Depots had moved up to their new positions.

To Colonel Kemp and his Adjutant Cockerell, ensconced in a dug-out thirty feet deep, furnished with a real bed, electric-light fittings, and ornaments obviously made in Germany, entered Major Wagstaffe, encrusted with mud, but as imperturbable as ever. He saluted.

"Good-morning, sir. You seem to have struck a cushie little home time."

"Yes. The Boche officer harbours no false modesty about acknowledging his desire for creature comforts. That is where he scores off people like you and me, who pretend we like sleeping in mud. Have you been round the advanced positions?"

"Yes. There is some pretty hard fighting going on in the village itself—the Boche still holds the north-west corner—and in the wood on the right. 'A' Company are holding a line of broken-down cottages on our right front, but they can't make any further move until they get more bombs. The Boche is occupying various buildings opposite, but in no great strength at present. However, he seems to have plenty of machine-guns."

"I have sent up more bombs," said the Colonel. "What about 'B' Company?"

"'B' have reached their objective, and consolidated. 'C' and 'D' are lying close up, ready to go forward in support when required. I think 'A' could do with a little assistance."

"I don't want to send up 'C' and 'D'," replied the Colonel, "until the Divisional Reserve arrives. The Brigade has just telephoned through that reinforcements are on the way. When they get here, we can afford to stuff in the whole battalion. Are 'A' Company capable of handling the situation at present?"

"Yes, I think so. Little is directing his platoons from a convenient cellar. He was in touch with them all when I left. But it is possible that the Boche may make a rush when it grows a bit lighter. At present he is too demoralised to attempt anything beyond intermittent machine-gun fire."

Colonel Kemp turned to Cockerell.

"Get Captain Little on the telephone," he said, "and tell him, if the enemy displays any disposition to counter-attack, to let me know at once." Then he turned to Wagstaffe, and asked the question which always lurks furtively on the tongue of a commanding officer.

"Many—casualties?"

"'A' Company have caught it rather badly crossing the open. 'B' got off lightly. Glen is commanding them now: Waddell was killed leading his men in the rush to the final objective."

Colonel Kemp sighed.

"Another good boy gone—veteran, rather. I must write to his wife. Fairly newly married, I fancy?"

"Four months," said Wagstaffe briefly.

"What was his Christian name, do you know?"

"Walter, I think, sir," said Cockerell.

Colonel Kemp, amid the stress of battle, found time to enter a note in his pocket-diary to that effect.

* * * * * * * *

Meanwhile, up in the line, 'A' Company were holding on grimly to what are usually described as "certain advanced elements" of the village.

Village fighting is a confused and untidy business, but it possesses certain redeeming features. The combatants are usually so inextricably mixed up that the artillery are compelled to refrain from participation. That comes later, when you have cleared the village of the enemy, and his guns are preparing the ground for the inevitable counter-attack.

So far 'A' Company had done nobly. From the moment when they had lined up before Montauban in the gross darkness preceding yesterday's dawn until the moment when Bobby Little led them in one victorious rush into the outskirts of the village, they had never encountered a setback. By sunset they had penetrated some way farther; now creeping stealthily forward under the shelter of a broken wall to hurl bombs into the windows of an occupied cottage; now climbing precariously to some commanding position in order to open fire with a Lewis gun; now making a sudden dash across an open space. Such work offered peculiar opportunities to small and well-handled parties—opportunities of which Bobby Little's veterans availed themselves right readily.

Angus M'Lachlan, for instance, accompanied by a small following of seasoned experts, had twice rounded up parties of the enemy in cellars, and had despatched the same back to Headquarters with his compliments and a promise of more. Mucklewame and four men had bombed their way along a communication trench leading to one of the side streets of the village—a likely avenue for a counter-attack—and having reached the end of the trench, had built up a sandbag barricade, and had held the same against the assaults of hostile bombers until a Vickers machine-gun had arrived in charge of an energetic subaltern of that youthful but thriving organisation, the Suicide Club, or Machine-Gun Corps, and closed the street to further Teutonic traffic.

During the night there had been periods of quiescence, devoted to consolidation, and here and there to snatches of uneasy slumber. Angus M'Lachlan, fairly in his element, had trailed his enormous length in and out of the back-yards and brick-heaps of the village, visiting every point in his irregular line, testing defences; bestowing praise; and ensuring that every man had his share of food and rest. Unutterably grimy but inexpressibly cheerful, he reported progress to Major Wagstaffe when that nocturnal rambler visited him in the small hours.

"Well, Angus, how goes it?" inquired Wagstaffe.

"We have won the match, sir," replied Angus with simple seriousness. "We are just playing the bye now!"

And with that he crawled away, with the unnecessary stealth of a small boy playing robbers, to encourage his dour paladins to further efforts.

"We shall probably be relieved this evening," he explained to them, "and we must make everything secure. It would never do to leave our new positions untenable by other troops. They might not be so reliable"—with a paternal smile—"as you! Now, our right flank is not safe yet. We can improve the position very much if we can secure that *estaminet*, standing up like an island among those ruined houses on our right front. You see the sign, *Aux Bons Fermiers*, over the door. The trouble is that a German machine-gun is sweeping the intervening space—and we cannot see the gun! There it goes again. See the brick-dust fly! Keep down! They are firing mainly across our front, but a stray bullet may come this way."

The platoon crouched low behind their improvised rampart of brick rubble, while machine-gun bullets swept low, with misleading *claquement*, along the space in front of them, from some hidden position on their right. Presently the firing stopped. Brother Boche was merely "loosing off a belt," as a precautionary measure, at commendably regular intervals.

"I cannot locate that gun," said Angus impatiently. "Can you, Corporal M'Snape?"

"It is not in the estamint itself, sirr," replied M'Snape. ("Estamint" is as near as our rank and file ever get to *estaminet.*) "It seems to be mounted some place higher up the street. I doubt they cannot see us themselves—only the ground in front of us."

"If we could reach the *estaminet* itself," said Angus thoughtfully, "we could get a more extended view. Sergeant Mucklewame, select ten men, including three bombers, and follow me. I am going to find a jumping-off place. The Lewis gun too."

Presently the little party were crouching round their officer in a sheltered position on the right of the line—which for the moment appeared to be "in the air." Except for the intermittent streams of machine-gun fire, and an occasional shrapnel-burst overhead, all was quiet. The enemy's counter-attack was not yet ready.

"Now listen carefully," said Angus, who had just finished scribbling a despatch. "First of all, you, Bogle, take this message to the telephone, and get it sent to Company Headquarters. Now you others. We will wait till that machine-gun has fired another belt. Then, the moment it has finished, while they are getting out the next belt, I will dash across to the *estaminet* over there. M'Snape, you will come with me, but no one else—yet. If the *estaminet* seems capable of being held, I will signal to you, Sergeant Mucklewame, and you will send your party across, in driblets, not forgetting the Lewis gun. By that time I may have located the German machine-gun, so we should be able to knock it out with the Lewis."

Further speech was cut short by a punctual fantasia from the gun in question. Angus and M'Snape crouched behind the shattered wall, awaiting their chance. The firing ceased.

"*Now!*" whispered Angus.

Next moment officer and corporal were flying across the open, and before the mechanical Boche gunner could jerk the new belt into position, both had found sanctuary within the open doorway of the half-ruined *estaminet.*

Nay, more than both; for as the panting pair flung themselves into shelter, a third figure, short and stout, in an ill-fitting kilt, tumbled heavily through the doorway after them. Simultaneously a stream of machine-gun bullets went storming past.

"Just in time!" observed Angus, well pleased. "Bogle, what are you doing here?"

"I was given tae unnerstand, sirr," replied Mr. Bogle calmly, "when I jined the regiment, that in action an officer's servant stands by his officer."

"That is true," conceded Angus; "but you had no right to follow me against orders. Did you not hear me say that no one but Corporal M'Snape was to come?"

"No, sirr. I doubt I was away at the 'phone."

"Well, now you are here, wait inside this doorway, where you can see Sergeant Mucklewame's party, and look out for signals. M'Snape, let us find that machine-gun."

The pair made their way to the hitherto blind side of the building, and cautiously peeped through a much-perforated shutter in the living-room.

"Do you see it, sirr?" inquired M'Snape eagerly.

Angus chuckled.

"See it? Fine! It is right in the open, in the middle of the street. Look!"

He relinquished his peep-hole. The German machine-gun was mounted in the street itself, behind an improvised barrier of bricks and sandbags. It was less than a hundred yards away, sited in a position which, though screened from the view of Angus's platoon farther down, enabled it to sweep all the ground in front of the position. This it was now doing with great intensity, for the brief public appearance of Angus and M'Snape had effectually converted intermittent into continuous fire.

"We must get the Lewis gun over at once," muttered Angus. "It can knock that breastwork to pieces."

He crossed the house again, to see if any of Mucklewame's men had arrived.

They had not. The man with the Lewis gun was lying dead halfway across the street, with his precious weapon on the ground beside him. Two other men, both wounded, were crawling back whence they came, taking what cover they could from the storm of bullets which whizzed a few inches over their flinching bodies.

Angus hastily semaphored to Mucklewame to hold his men in check for the present. Then he returned to the other side of the house.

"How many men are serving that gun?" he said to M'Snape. "Can you see?"

"Only two, sirr, I think. I cannot see them, but that wee breastwork will not cover more than a couple of men."

"Mphm," observed Angus thoughtfully. "I expect they have been left behind to hold on. Have you a bomb about you?"

The admirable M'Snape produced from his pocket a Mills grenade, and handed it to his superior.

"Just the one, sirr," he said.

"Go you," commanded Angus, his voice rising to a more than usually Highland inflection, "and semaphore to Mucklewame that when he hears the explosion of *this*"—he pulled out the safety-pin of the grenade and gripped the grenade itself in his enormous paw—"followed, probably, by the temporary cessation of the machine-gun, he is to bring his men over here in a bunch, as hard as they can pelt. Put it as briefly as you can, but make sure he understands. He has a good signaller with him. Send Bogle to report when you have finished. Now repeat what I have said to you. . . . That's right. Carry on!"

M'Snape was gone. Angus, left alone, pensively restored the safety-pin to the grenade, and laid the grenade upon the ground beside him. Then he proceeded to write a brief letter in his field message-book. This he placed in an envelope which he took from his breast pocket. The envelope was already addressed—to the *Reverend Neil M'Lachlan, The Manse*, in a very remote Highland village. (Angus had no mother.) He closed the envelope, initialled it, and buttoned it up in his breast pocket again. After that he took up his grenade and proceeded to make a further examination of the premises. Presently he found what he wanted; and by the time Bogle arrived to announce that Sergeant Mucklewame had signalled "message understood," his arrangements were complete.

"Stay by this small hole in the wall, Bogle," he said, "and the moment the Lewis gun arrives tell them to mount it here and open fire on the enemy gun."

He left the room, leaving Bogle alone, to listen to the melancholy rustle of peeling wall-paper within and the steady crackling of bullets without. But when, peering through the improvised loophole, he next caught sight of his officer, Angus had emerged from the house by the cellar window, and was creeping with infinite caution behind the shelter of what had once been the wall of the *estaminet's* back-yard (but was now an uneven bank of bricks, averaging two feet high), in the direction of the German machine-gun. The gun, oblivious of the danger now threatening its right front, continued to fire steadily and hopefully down the street.

Slowly, painfully, Angus crawled on, until he found himself within the right angle formed by the corner of the yard. He could go no further without being seen. Between him and the German gun lay the cobbled surface of the street, offering no cover whatsoever except one mighty shell-crater, situated midway between Angus and the gun, and full to the brim with rainwater.

A single peep over the wall gave him his bearings. The gun was too far away to be reached by a grenade, even when thrown by Angus M'Lachlan. Still, it would create a diversion. It was a time bomb. He would—

He stretched out his long arm to its full extent behind him, gave one mighty over-arm sweep, and with all the crackling strength of his mighty sinews, hurled the grenade.

It fell into the exact centre of the flooded shell-crater.

Angus said something under his breath which would have shocked a disciple of *Kultur*. Fortunately the two German gunners did not hear him. But they observed the splash fifty yards away, and it relieved them from *ennui*, for they were growing tired of firing at nothing. They had not seen the grenade thrown, and were a little puzzled as to the cause of the phenomenon.

Four seconds later their curiosity was more than satisfied. With a muffled roar, the shell-hole suddenly, spouted its liquid contents and other *debris* straight to the heavens, startling them considerably and entirely obscuring their vision.

A moment later, with an exultant yell, Angus M'Lachlan was upon them. He sprang into their vision out of the descending cascade—a towering, terrible, kilted figure, bare-headed and Berserk mad. He was barely forty yards away.

Initiative is not the *forte* of the Teuton. Number One of the German gun mechanically traversed his weapon four degrees to the right and continued to press the thumb-piece. Mud and splinters of brick sprang up round Angus's feet; but still he came on. He was not twenty yards away now. The gunner, beginning to boggle between waiting and bolting, fumbled at his elevating gear, but Angus was right on him before his thumbs got back to work. Then indeed the gun spoke out with no uncertain voice, for perhaps two seconds. After that it ceased fire altogether.

Almost simultaneously there came a triumphant roar lower down the street, as Mucklewame and his followers dashed obliquely across into the *estaminet.* Mucklewame himself was carrying the derelict Lewis gun. In the doorway stood the watchful M'Snape.

"This way, quick!" he shouted. "We have the Gairman gun spotted, and the officer is needing the Lewis!"

But M'Snape was wrong. The Lewis was not required.

A few moments later, in the face of brisk sniping from the houses higher up the street, James Bogle, officer's servant,—a member of that despised class which, according to the *Bandar-log* at home, spend the whole of its time pressing its master's trousers and smoking his cigarettes somewhere back in billets,—led out a stretcher party to the German gun. Number One had been killed by a shot from Angus's revolver. Number Two had adopted Hindenburg tactics, and was no more to be seen. Angus himself was lying, stone dead, a yard from the muzzle of the gun which he, single-handed, had put out of action.

His men carried him back to the *Estaminet aux Bons Fermiers*, with the German gun, which was afterwards employed to good purpose during the desperate days of attacking and counter-attacking which ensued before the village was finally secured. They laid him in the inner room, and proceeded to put the *estaminet* in a state of defence—ready to hold the same against all comers until such time as the relieving Division should take over, and they themselves be enabled, under the kindly cloak of darkness, to carry back their beloved officer to a more worthy resting-place.

In the left-hand breast pocket of Angus's tunic they found his last letter to his father. Two German machine-gun bullets had passed through it. It was forwarded with a covering letter, by Colonel Kemp. In the letter Angus's commanding officer informed Neil M'Lachlan that his son had been recommended posthumously for the highest honour that the King bestows upon his soldiers.

* * * * * * * *

But for the moment Mucklewame's little band had other work to occupy them. Shelling had recommenced; the enemy were mustering in force behind the village; and presently a series of counter-attacks were launched. They were successfully repelled, in the first instance by the remainder of "A" Company, led in person by Bobby Little, and, when the final struggle came, by the Battalion Reserve under Major Wagstaffe. And throughout the whole grim struggle which ensued, the *Estaminet aux Bons Fermiers*, tenanted by some of our oldest friends, proved itself the head and corner of the successful defence.

CHAPTER 12
Recessional

Two steamers lie at opposite sides of the dock. One is painted a most austere and unobtrusive grey; she is obviously a vessel with no desire to advertise her presence on the high seas. In other words, a transport. The other is dazzling white, ornamented with a good deal of green, supplemented by red. She makes an attractive picture in the early morning sun. Even by night you could not miss her, for she goes about her business with her entire hull outlined in red lights, regatta fashion, with a great luminous Red Cross blazing on either counter. Not even the Commander of a U-boat could mistake her for anything but what she is—a hospital ship.

First, let us walk round to where the grey ship is discharging her cargo. The said cargo consists of about a thousand unwounded German prisoners.

With every desire to be generous to a fallen foe, it is quite impossible to describe them as a prepossessing lot. Not one man walks like a soldier; they shamble. Naturally, they are dirty and unshaven,. So are the wounded men on the white ship: but their outstanding characteristic is an invincible humanity. Beneath the mud and blood they are men—white men. But this strange throng are grey—like their ship. With their shifty eyes and curiously shaped heads, they look like nothing human. They move like overdriven beasts. We realise now why it is that the German Army has to attack in mass.

They pass down the gangway, and are shepherded into form in the dock shed by the Embarkation Staff, with exactly the same silent briskness that characterises the R.A.M.C., over the way. Their guard, with fixed bayonets, exhibit no more or no less concern over them than over half-a-dozen Monday morning malefactors paraded for Orderly Room. Presently they will move off, possibly through the streets of the town; probably they will pass by folk against whose kith and kin they have employed every dirty trick possible in warfare. But there will be no demonstration: there never has been. As a nation we possess a certain number of faults, on which we like to dwell. But we have one virtue at least—we possess a certain sense of proportion; and we are not disposed to make subordinates suffer because we cannot, as yet, get at the principals.

They make a good haul. Fifteen German regiments are here represented—possibly more, for some have torn off their shoulder-straps to avoid identification. Some of the units are thinly represented; others more generously. One famous Prussian regiment appears to have thrown its hand in to the extent of about five hundred.

Still, as they stand there, filthy, forlorn, and dazed, one suddenly realises the extreme appropriateness of a certain reference in the Litany to All Prisoners and Captives.

II

We turn to the hospital ship.

Two great 'brows,' or covered gangways, connect her with her native land. Down these the stretchers are beginning to pass, having been raised from below decks by cunning mechanical devices which cause no jar; and are being conveyed into the cool shade of the dock-shed. Here they are laid in neat rows upon the platform, ready for transfer to the waiting hospital train. Everything is a miracle of quietness and order. The curious public are afar off, held aloof by dock-gates. (They are there in force to-day, partly to cheer the hospital trains as they pass out, partly for reasons connected with the grey-painted ship.) In the dock-shed, organisation and method reign supreme. The work has been going on without intermission for several days and nights; and still the great ships come. The *Austurias* is outside, waiting for a place at the dock. The *Lanfranc* is half-way across the English Channel; and there are rumours that the mighty *Britannic*[1] has selected this, the busiest moment in the opening fortnight of the Somme Battle, to arrive with a miscellaneous and irrelevant cargo of sick and wounded from the Mediterranean. But there is no fuss. The R.A.M.C. Staff Officers, unruffled and cheery, control everything, apparently by a crook of the finger. The stretcher-bearers do their work with silent aplomb.

The occupants of the stretchers possess the almost universal feature of a six days' beard—always excepting those who are of an age which is not troubled by such manly accretions. They lie very still—not with

1: These three hospital ships were all subsequently sunk by German submarines.

the stillness of exhaustion or dejection, but with the comfortable resignation of men who have made good and have suffered in the process; but who now, with their troubles well behind them, are enduring present discomfort under the sustaining prospect of clean beds, chicken diet, and ultimate tea-parties. Such as possess them are wearing Woodbine stumps upon the lower lip.

They are quite ready to compare notes. Let us approach, and listen, to a heavily bandaged gentleman who—so the label attached to him informs us—is Private Blank, of the Manchesters, suffering from three "G.S." machine-gun bullet wounds.

"Did the Fritzes run? Yes—they run all right! The last lot saved us trouble by running towards us—with their 'ands up! But their machine-guns—they gave us fair 'Amlet till we got across No Man's Land. After that we used the baynit, and they didn't give us no more vexatiousness. Where did we go in? Oh, near Albert. Our objective was Mary's Court, or some such place." (It is evident that the Battle of the Somme is going to add some fresh household words to our war vocabulary. 'Wipers' is a veteran by this time: 'Plugstreet,' 'Booloo,' and 'Armintears' are old friends. We must now make room for 'Monty Ban,' 'La Bustle,' 'Mucky Farm,' 'Lousy Wood,' and 'Martinpush.')

"What were your prisoners like?"

"'Alf clemmed," said the man from Manchester.

"No rations for three days," explained a Northumberland Fusilier close by. One of his arms was strapped to his side, but the other still clasped to his bosom a German helmet. A British Tommy will cheerfully shed a limb or two in the execution of his duty, but not all the might and majesty of the Royal Army Medical Corps can force him to relinquish a fairly earned 'souvenir.' In fact, owing to certain unworthy suspicions as to the true significance of the initials, "R.A.M.C.," he has been known to refuse chloroform.

"They couldn't get nothing up to them for four days, on account of our artillery fire," he added contentedly.

"'Barrage,' my lad!" amended a rather superior person with a lance-corporal's stripe and a bandaged foot.

Indeed, all are unanimous in affirming that our artillery preparation was a tremendous affair. Listen to this group of officers sunning themselves upon the upper deck. They are 'walking cases,' and must remain on board, with what patience they may, until all the stretcher cases' have been evacuated.

"Loos was child's play to it," says one—a member of a certain immortal, or at least irrepressible Division which has taken part in every outburst of international unpleasantness since the Marne. "The final hour was absolute pandemonium. And when our new trench-mortar batteries got to work too,—at sixteen to the dozen,—well, it was bad enough for *us*; but what it must have been like at the business end of things, Lord knows! For a few minutes I was almost a pro-Boche!"

Other items of intelligence are gleaned. The weather was 'rotten': mud-caked garments corroborate this statement. The wire, on the whole, was well and truly cut to pieces everywhere; though there were spots at which the enemy contrived to repair it. Finally, ninety per cent. of the casualties during the assault were due to machine-gun fire.

But the fact most clearly elicited by casual conversation is this—that the more closely you engage in a battle, the less you know about its progress. This ship is full of officers and men who were in the thick of things for perhaps forty-eight hours on end, but who are quite likely to be utterly ignorant of what was going on round the next traverse in the trench which they had occupied. The wounded Gunners are able to give them a good deal of information. One F.O.O. saw the French advance.

"It was wonderful to see them go in," he said. "Our Batteries were on the extreme right of the British line, so we were actually touching the French left flank. I had met hundreds of *poilus* back in billets, in *cafes*, and the like. To look at them strolling down a village street in their baggy uniforms, with their hands in their pockets, laughing and chatting to the children, you would never have thought they were such tigers. I remember one big fellow a few weeks ago, home on leave—*permission*—who used to frisk about with a big umbrella under his arm! I suppose that was to keep the rain off his tin hat. But when they went for Maricourt the other day, there weren't many umbrellas about—only bayonets! I tell you, they were marvels!"

It would be interesting to hear the *poilu* on his Allies.

The first train moves off, and another takes its place. The long lines of stretchers are thinning out now. There are perhaps a hundred left. They contain men of all units—English, Scottish, and Irish. There are Gunners, Sappers, and Infantry. Here and there among them you may note bloodstained men in dirty grey uniforms—men with dull, expressionless faces and closely cropped heads. They are tended with exactly the same care as the others. Where wounded men are concerned, the British Medical Service is strictly neutral.

A wounded Corporal of the R.A.M.C. turns his head and gazes thoughtfully at one of those grey men.

"You understand English, Fritz?" he enquires.

Apparently not. Fritz continues to stare woodenly at the roof of the dock-shed.

"I should like to tell 'im a story, Jock," says the Corporal to his other neighbour. "My job is on a hospital train. 'Alf-a-dozen 'Un aeroplanes made a raid behind our lines; and seeing a beautiful Red Cross train—it was a new London and North Western train, chocolate and white, with red crosses as plain as could be—well, they simply couldn't resist such a target as that! One of their machines swooped low down and dropped his bombs on us. Luckily he only got the rear coach; but I happened to be in it! D' yer 'ear that, Fritz?"

"I doot he canna unnerstand onything," remarked the Highlander. "He's fair demoralised, like the rest. D' ye ken what happened tae me? I was gaun' back wounded, with *this*—" he indicates an arm strapped close to his side—"and there was six Fritzes came crawlin' oot o' a dugoot, and gave themselves up tae me—*me*, that was gaun' back wounded, withoot so much as my jack-knife! Demoralised—that's it!"

"Did you 'ear," enquired a Cockney who came next in the line, "that all wounded are going to 'ave a nice little gold stripe to wear—a stripe for every wound?"

There was much interest at this.

"That'll be fine," observed a man of Kent, who had been out since Mons, and been wounded three times. "Folks'll know now that I'm not a Derby recruit."

"Where will us wear it?" enquired a gigantic Yorkshireman, from the next stretcher.

"Wherever you was 'it, lad!" replied the Cockney humorist.

"At that rate," comes the rueful reply, "I shall 'ave to stand oop to show mine!"

III

But now R.A.M.C. orderlies are at hand, and the symposium comes to an end. The stretchers are conveyed one by one into the long open coaches of the train, and each patient is slipped sideways, with gentleness and dispatch, into his appointed cot.

One saloon is entirely filled with officers—the severe cases in the cots, the rest sitting where they can. A newspaper is passed round. There are delighted exclamations, especially from a second lieutenant whose features appear to be held together entirely by strips of plaster. Such parts of the countenance as can be discerned are smiling broadly.

"I *knew* we were doing well," says the bandaged one, devouring the headlines; "but I never knew we were doing as well as this. Official, too! Somme Battle—what? Sorry! I apologise!" as a groan ran round the saloon.

"Never mind," said an unshaven officer, with a twinkling eye, and a major's tunic wrapped loosely around him. "I expect that jest will be overworked by more people than you for the next few weeks. Does anybody happen to know where this train is going to?"

"West of England, somewhere, I believe," replied a voice.

There was an indignant groan from various north countrymen.

"I suppose it is quite impossible to sort us all out at a time like this," remarked a plaintive Caledonian in an upper cot; "but I fail to see why the R.A.M.C. authorities should go through the mockery of *asking* every man in the train where he wants to be taken, when the train can obviously only go to one place—or perhaps two. I was asked. I said 'Edinburgh'; and the medical wallah said, 'Righto! We'll send you to Bath!'"

"I think I can explain," remarked the wounded major. "These trains usually go to two places—one half to Bath, the other, say, to Exeter. Bath is nearer to Edinburgh than Exeter, so they send you there. It is kindly meant, but—"

"I say," croaked a voice from another cot,—its owner was a young officer who must just have escaped being left behind at a Base hospital as too dangerously wounded to move,—"is that a newspaper down there? Would some one have a look, and tell me if we have got Longueval all right? Longueval? Long—I got pipped, and don't quite—"

The wounded major turned his head quickly.

"Hallo, Bobby!" he observed cheerfully. "That you? I didn't notice you before."

Bobby Little's hot eyes turned slowly on Wagstaffe, and he exclaimed feverishly:—

"Hallo, Major! Cheeroh! Did we stick to Longueval all right? I've been dreaming about it a bit, and—"

"We did," replied Wagstaffe—"thanks to 'A' Company."

Bobby Little's head fell back on the pillow, and he remarked contentedly:—"Thanks awfully. I think I can sleep a bit now. So long! See you later!"

His eyes closed, and he sighed happily, as the long train slid out from the platform.

CHAPTER 13

"Two Old Soldiers, Broken in the Wars"

The smoking-room of the Britannia Club used to be exactly like the smoking-room of every other London Club. That is to say, members lounged about in deep chairs, and talked shop, or scandal—or slumbered. At any moment you might touch a convenient bell, and a waiter would appear at your elbow, like a jinnee from a jar, and accept an order with silent deference. You could do this all day, and the jinnee never failed to hear and obey.

That was before the war. Now, those idyllic days are gone. So is the waiter. So is the efficacy of the bell. You may ring, but all that will materialise is a self-righteous little girl, in brass buttons, who will shake her head reprovingly and refer you to certain passages in the Defence of the Realm Act.

Towards the hour of six-thirty, however, something of the old spirit of Liberty asserts itself. A throng of members—chiefly elderly gentlemen in expanded uniforms—assembles in the smoking-room, occupying all the chairs, and even overflowing on to the tables and window-sills. They are not the discursive, argumentative gathering of three years ago. They sit silent, restless, glancing furtively at their wrist-watches.

The clocks of London strike half-past six. Simultaneously the door of the smoking-room is thrown open, and a buxom young woman in cap and apron bounces in. She smiles maternally upon her fainting flock, and announces:—

"The half-hour's gone. Now you can *all* have a drink!"

What would have happened if the waiter of old had done this thing, it is difficult to imagine. But the elderly gentlemen greet their Hebe with a chorus of welcome, and clamour for precedence like children at a school-feast. And yet trusting wives believe that in his club, at least, a man is safe!

Major Wagstaffe, D.S.O., having been absent from London upon urgent public affairs for nearly three years, was not well versed in the newest refinements of club life. He had arrived that morning from his Convalescent Home in the west country, and had already experienced a severe reverse at the hands of the small girl with brass buttons on venturing to order a sherry and bitters at 11.45 A.M. Consequently, at the statutory hour, his voice was not uplifted with the rest; and he was served last. Not least, however; for Hebe, observing his empty sleeve, poured out his soda-water with her own fair hands, and offered to light his cigarette.

This scene of dalliance was interrupted by the arrival of Captain Bobby Little. He wore the ribbon of the Military Cross and walked with a stick—a not unusual combination in these great days. Wagstaffe made room for him upon the leather sofa, and Hebe supplied his modest wants with an indulgent smile.

An autumn and a winter had passed since the attack on Longueval. From July until the December floods, the great battle had raged. The New Armies, supplied at last with abundant munitions, a seasoned Staff, and a concerted plan of action, had answered the question propounded in a previous chapter in no uncertain fashion. Through Longueval and Delville Wood, where the graves of the Highlanders and South Africans now lie thick, through Flers and Martinpuich, through Pozieres and Courcelette, they had fought their way, till they had reached the ridge, with High Wood at its summit, which the Boche, not altogether unreasonably, had regarded as impregnable. The tide had swirled over the crest, down the reverse slope, and up at last to the top of that bloodstained knoll of chalk known as the Butte de Warlencourt. There the Hun threw in his hand. With much loud talk upon the subject of victorious retirements and Hindenburg Lines, he withdrew himself to a region far east of Bapaume; with the result that now some thousand square miles of the soil of France had been restored once and for all to their rightful owners.

But Bobby and Wagstaffe had not been there. All during the autumn and winter they had lain softly in hospital, enjoying their first rest for two years. Wagstaffe had lost his left arm and gained a decoration. Bobby, in addition to his Cross, had incurred a cracked crown and a permanently shortened leg. But both were well content. They had done their bit—and something over; and they had emerged from the din of war with their lives, their health, and their reason. A man who can achieve that feat in this war can count himself fortunate.

Now, passed by a Medical Board as fit for Home Service, they had said farewell to their Convalescent Home and come to London to learn what fate Olympus held in store for them.

"Where have you been all day, Bobby?" enquired Wagstaffe, as they sat down to dinner an hour later.

"Down in Kent," replied Bobby briefly.

"Very well: I will not probe the matter. Been to the War Office?"

"Yes. I was there this morning. I am to be Adjutant of a Cadet school, at Great Snoreham. What sort of a job is that likely to be?"

"On the whole," replied Wagstaffe, "a Fairy Godmother Department job. It might have been very much worse. You are thoroughly up to the Adjutant business, Bobby, and of course the young officers under you will be immensely impressed by your game leg and bit of ribbon. A very sound appointment."

"What are they going to do with you?" asked Bobby in his turn.

"I am to command our Reserve Battalion, with acting rank of Lieutenant-Colonel. Think of that, my lad! They have confirmed you in your rank as Captain, I suppose?"

"Yes."

"Good! The only trouble is that you will be stationed in the South of England and I in the North of Scotland; so we shall not see quite so much of one another as of late. However, we must get together occasionally, and split a tin of bully for old times' sake."

"Bully? By gum!" said Bobby thoughtfully. "I have almost forgotten what it tastes like. (Fried sole, please; then roast lamb.) Eight months in hospital do wash out certain remembrances."

"But not all," said Wagstaffe.

"No, not all. I—I wonder how our chaps are getting on, over there."

"The regiment?"

"Yes. It is so hard to get definite news."

"They were in the Arras show. Did better than ever; but—well, they required a big draft afterwards."

"The third time!" sighed Bobby. "Did any one write to you about it?"

"Yes. Who do you think?"

"Some one in the regiment?"

"Yes."

"I didn't know there were any of the old lot left. Who was it?"

"Mucklewame."

"Mucklewame? You mean to say the Boche hasn't got *him* yet? It's like missing Rheims Cathedral."

"Yes, they got him at Arras. Mucklewame is in hospital. Fortunately his chief wound is in the head, so he's doing nicely. Here is his letter."

Bobby took the pencilled screed, and read:—

Major Wagstaffe,
Sir,—I take up my pen for to inform you that I am now in hospital in Glasgow, having become a casualty on the 18th inst.
I was struck on the head by the nose-cap of a German shell (now in the possession of my guidwife). Unfortunately I was wearing one of they steel helmets at the time, with the result that I sustained a serious scalp-wound, also very bad concussion. I have never had a liking for they helmets anyway.
The old regiment did fine in the last attack. They were specially mentioned in Orders next day. The objective was reached under heavy fire and position consolidated before we were relieved next morning.

"Good boys!" interpolated Bobby softly.

Colonel Carmichael, late of the Second Battn., I think, is now in command. A very nice gentleman, but we have all been missing you and the Captain.
They tell me that I will be for home service after this. My head is doing well, but the muscules of my right leg is badly torn. I should have liked fine for to have stayed out and come home with the other boys when we are through with Berlin.
Having no more to say, sir, I will now draw to a close.
Jas. Mucklewame, C.S.M.

After the perusal of this characteristic *Ave atque Vale!* the two friends adjourned to the balcony, overlooking the Green Park. Here they lit their cigars in reminiscent silence, while neighbouring searchlights raked the horizon for Zeppelins which no longer came. It was a moment for confidences.

"Old Mucklewame is like the rest of us," said Wagstaffe at last.

"How?"

"Wanting to go back, and all that. I do too—just because I'm here, I suppose. A year ago, out there, my chief ambition was to get home, with a comfortable wound and a comfortable conscience."

"Same here," admitted Bobby.

"It was the same with practically every one," said Wagstaffe. "If any man asserts that he really enjoys modern warfare, after, say, six months of it, he is a liar. In the South African show I can honestly say I was perfectly happy. We were fighting in open country, against an adversary who was a gentleman; and although there was plenty of risk, the chances were that one came through all right. At any rate, there was no poison gas, and one did not see a whole platoon blown to pieces, or buried alive, by a single shell. If Brother Boer took you prisoner, he did not stick you in the stomach with a saw-edged bayonet. At the worst he pinched your trousers. But Brother Boche is a different proposition. Since he butted in, war has descended in the social scale. And modern scientific developments have turned a sporting chance of being scuppered into a mathematical certainty. And yet—and yet—old Mucklewame is right. One *hates* to be out of it—especially at the finish. When the regiment comes stumping through London on its way back to Euston—next year, or whenever it's going to be—with their ragged pipers leading the way, you would like to be at the head of 'A' Company, Bobby, and I would give something to be exercising my old function of whipper-in. Eh, boy?"

"Never mind," said practical Bobby. "Perhaps we shall be on somebody's glittering Staff. What I hate to feel at present is that the other fellows, out there, have got to go on sticking it, while we—"

"And by God," exclaimed Wagstaffe, "what stickers they are—and were! Did you ever see anything so splendid, Bobby, as those six-months-old soldiers of ours—in the early days, I mean, when we held our trenches, week by week, under continuous bombardment, and our gunners behind could only help us with four or five rounds a day?"

"I never did," said Bobby, truthfully.

"I admit to you," continued Wagstaffe, "that when I found myself pitchforked into 'K(1)' at the outbreak of the war, instead of getting back to my old line battalion, I was a pretty sick man. I hated everybody. I was one of the old school—or liked to think I was—and the ways of the new school were not my ways. I hated the new officers. Some of them bullied the men; some of them allowed themselves to be bullied by N.C.O.'s. Some never gave or returned salutes, others went about saluting everybody. Some came into Mess in fancy dress of their own design, and elbowed senior officers off the hearthrug. I used to marvel at the Colonel's patience with them. But many of them are dead now, Bobby, and they nearly all made good. Then the men! After ten years in the regular Army I hated them all—the way they lounged, the way they dressed, the way they sat, the way they spat. I wondered how I could ever go on living with them. And now—I find myself wondering how I am ever going to live without them. We shall not see their like again. The new lot—present lot—are splendid fellows.

They are probably better soldiers. Certainly they are more uniformly trained. But there was a piquancy about our old scamps in 'K(1)' that was unique—priceless—something the world will never see again."

"I don't know," said Bobby thoughtfully. "That Cockney regiment which lay beside us at Albert last summer was a pretty priceless lot. Do you remember a pair of fat fellows in their leading platoon? We called them Fortnum and Mason!"

"I do—particularly Fortnum. Go on!"

"Well, their bit of trench was being shelled one day, and Fortnum, who was in number one bay with five other men, kept shouting out to Mason, who was round a traverse and out of sight, to enquire how he was getting on. 'Are you all right, Bill?' 'Are you *sure* you're all right, Bill?' 'Are you *still* all right, Bill?' and so on. At last Bill, getting fed up with this unusual solicitude, yelled back: 'What's all the anxiety abaht, eh?' And Fortnum put his head round the traverse and explained. 'We're getting up a little sweepstake in our bay,' he said, 'abaht the first casuality, and I've drawn you, ole son!'"

Wagstaffe chuckled.

"That must have been the regiment that had the historic poker party," he said.

"What yarn was that?"

"I heard it from the Brigadier—four times, to be exact. Five men off duty were sitting in a dug-out playing poker. A gentleman named 'Erb had just gone to the limit on his hand, when a rifle-grenade came into the dug-out from somewhere and did him in. While they were waiting for the stretcher-bearers, one of the other players picked up 'Erb's hand and examined it. Then he laid it down again, and said: 'It doesn't matter, chaps. Poor 'Erb wouldn't a made it, anyway. I 'ad four queens.'"

"Tommy has his own ideas of fun, I'll admit," said Bobby. "Do you remember those first trenches of ours at Festubert? There was a dead Frenchman buried in the parapet—you know how they used to bury people in those days?"

"I did notice it. Go on."

"Well, this poor chap's hand stuck out, just about four feet from the floor of the trench. My dug-out was only a few yards away, and I never saw a member of my platoon go past that spot without shaking the hand and saying, Good-morning, Alphonse!' I had it built up with sandbags ultimately, and they were quite annoyed!"

"They have some grisly notions about life and death," agreed Wagstaffe, "but they are extraordinarily kind to people in trouble, such as wounded men, or prisoners. You can't better them."

"And now there are five millions of them. We are all in it, at last!"

"We certainly are—men and women. I'm afraid I had hardly realised what our women were doing for us. Being on service all the time, one rather overlooks what is going on at home. But stopping a bullet puts one in the way of a good deal of inside information on that score."

"You mean hospital work, and so on?"

"Yes. One meets a lot of wonderful people that way! Sisters, and ward-maids, and V.A.D.'s—"

"I love all V.A.D.'s!" said Bobby, unexpectedly.

"Why, my youthful Mormon?"

"Because they are the people who do all the hard work and get no limelight—like—like—!"

"Like Second Lieutenants—eh?"

"Yes, that is the idea. They have a pretty hard time, you know," continued Bobby confidentially: "And nothing heroic, either. Giving up all the fun that a girl is entitled to; washing dishes; answering the door-bell; running up and downstairs; eating rotten food. That's the sort of—"

"What is her name?" enquired the accusing voice of Major Wagstaffe. Then, without waiting to extort an answer from the embarrassed Bobby:—

"You are quite right. This war has certainly brought out the best in our women. The South African War brought out the worst. My goodness, you should have seen the Mount Nelson Hotel at Capetown in those days! But they have been wonderful this time—wonderful. I love them all—the bus-conductors, the ticket-punchers, the lift-girls—one of them nearly shot me right through the roof of Harrod's the other day—and the window-cleaners and the page-girls and the railway-portresses! I divide my elderly heart among them. And I met a bunch of munitions girls the other day, Bobby, coming home from work. They were all young, and most of them were pretty. Their faces and hands were stained a bright orange-colour with picric acid, and will be, I suppose, until the Boche is booted back into his stye. In other words, they had deliberately sacrificed their good looks for the duration of the war. That takes a bit of doing, I know, innocent bachelor though I am. But bless you, they weren't worrying. They waved their orange-coloured hands to me, and pointed to their orange-coloured faces, and laughed. They were *proud* of them; they were doing their bit. They nearly made me cry, Bobby. Yes, we are all in it now; and those of us who come out of it are going to find this old island of ours a wonderfully changed place to live in."

"How? Why?" enquired Bobby. Possibly he was interested in Wagstaffe's unusual expansiveness: possibly he hoped to steer the conversation away from the topic of V.A.D.'s—possibly towards it. You never know.

"Well," said Wagstaffe, "we are all going to understand one another a great deal better after this war." "Who? Labour and Capital, and so on?"

"'Labour and Capital' is a meaningless and misleading expression, Bobby. For instance, our men regard people like you and me as Capitalists; the ordinary Brigade Major regards us as Labourers, and pretty common Labourers at that. It is all a question of degree. But what I mean is this. You can't call your employer a tyrant and an extortioner after he has shared his rations with you and never spared himself over your welfare and comfort through weary months of trench-warfare; neither, when you have experienced a working-man's courage and cheerfulness and reliability in the day of battle, can you turn round and call him a loafer and an agitator in time of peace—can you? That is just what the *Bandar-log* overlook, when they jabber about the dreadful industrial upheaval that is coming with peace. Most of all have they overlooked the fact that with the coming of peace this country will be invaded by several million of the wisest men that she has ever produced—the New British Army. That Army will consist of men who have spent three years in getting rid of mutual misapprehensions and assimilating one another's point of view—men who went out to the war ignorant and intolerant and insular, and are coming back wise to all the things that really matter. They will flood this old country, and they will make short work of the agitator, and the alarmist, and the profiteer, and all the nasty creatures that merely make a noise instead of *doing* something, and who crab the work of the Army and Navy—more especially the Navy—because there isn't a circus victory of some kind in the paper every morning. Yes, Bobby, when our boys get back, and begin to ask the *Bandar-log* what they did in the Great War—well, it's going to be a rotten season for *Bandar-log* generally!"

There was silence again. Presently Bobby spoke:—

"When our boys get back! Some of them are never coming back again, worse luck!"

"Still," said Wagstaffe, "what they did was worth doing, and what they died for was worth while. I think their one regret to-day would be that they did not live to see their own fellows taking the offensive—the line going forward on the Somme; the old tanks waddling over the Boche trenches; and the Boche prisoners throwing up their hands and yowling *'Kamerad'*! And the Kut unpleasantness cleaned up, and all the kinks in the old Salient straightened out! And Wytchaete and Messines! You remember how the two ridges used to look down into our lines at Wipers and Plugstreet? And now we're on top of both of them! Some of our friends out there—the friends who are not coming back—would have liked to know about that, Bobby. I wish they could, somehow."

"Perhaps they do," said Bobby simply.

It was close on midnight. Our "two old soldiers, broken in the wars," levered themselves stiffly to their feet, and prepared to depart.

"Heigho!" said Wagstaffe. "It is time for two old wrecks like us to be in bed. That's what we are, Bobby—wrecks, dodderers, has-beens! But we have had the luck to last longer than most. We have dodged the missiles of the Boche to an extent which justifies us in claiming that we have followed the progress of their war with a rather more than average degree of continuity. We were the last of the old crowd, too. Kemp has got his Brigade, young Cockerell has gone to be a Staff Captain, and—you and I are here. Some of the others dropped out far too soon. Young Lochgair, old Blaikie—"

"Waddell, too," said Bobby. "We joined the same day."

"And Angus M'Lachlan. I think he would have made the finest soldier of the lot of us," added Wagstaffe. "You remember his remark to me, that we only had the bye to play now? He was a true prophet: we are dormy, anyhow. (Only cold feet at Home can let us down now.) And he only saw three months' service! Still, he made a great exit from this world, Bobby, and that is the only thing that matters in these days. Ha! H'm! As our new Allies would say, I am beginning to 'pull heart stuff' on you. Let us go to bed. Sleeping here?"

"Yes, till to-morrow. Then off on leave."

"How much have you got?"

"A month. I say?"

"Yes?"

"Are you doing anything on the nineteenth?"

Wagstaffe regarded his young friend suspiciously.

"Is this a catch of some kind?" he enquired.

"Oh, no. Will you be my—" Bobby turned excessively pink, and completed his request.

Wagstaffe surveyed him resignedly.

"We all come to it, I suppose," he observed.

"Only some come to it sooner than others. Are you of age, my lad? Have your parents—"

"I'm twenty-two," said Bobby shortly.

"Will the bridesmaids be pretty?"

"They are all peaches," replied Bobby, with enthusiasm. "But nothing whatever," he added, in a voice of respectful rapture, "compared with the bride!"

ALSO FROM LEONAUR

AVAILABLE IN SOFTCOVER OR HARDCOVER WITH DUST JACKET

SEPOYS, SIEGE & STORM *by Charles John Griffiths*—The Experiences of a young officer of H.M.'s 61st Regiment at Ferozepore, Delhi ridge and at the fall of Delhi during the Indian mutiny 1857.

CAMPAIGNING IN ZULULAND *by W. E. Montague*—Experiences on campaign during the Zulu war of 1879 with the 94th Regiment.

THE STORY OF THE GUIDES *by G. J. Younghusband*—The Exploits of the Soldiers of the famous Indian Army Regiment from the northwest frontier 1847 - 1900..

ZULU: 1879 *by D.C.F. Moodie & the Leonaur Editors*—The Anglo-Zulu War of 1879 from contemporary sources: First Hand Accounts, Interviews, Dispatches, Official Documents & Newspaper Reports.

THE RECOLLECTIONS OF SKINNER OF SKINNER'S HORSE *by James Skinner*—James Skinner and his 'Yellow Boys' Irregular cavalry in the wars of India between the British, Mahratta, Rajput, Mogul, Sikh & Pindarree Forces.

TOMMY ATKINS' WAR STORIES 14 FIRST HAND ACCOUNTS—Fourteen first hand accounts from the ranks of the British Army during Queen Victoria's Empire Original & True Battle Stories Recollections of the Indian Mutiny With the 49th in the Crimea With the Guards in Egypt The Charge of the Six Hundred With Wolseley in Ashanti Alma, Inkermann and Magdala With the Gunners at Tel-el-Kebir Russian Guns and Indian Rebels Rough Work in the Crimea In the Maori Rising Facing the Zulus From Sebastopol to Lucknow Sent to Save Gordon On the March to Chitral Tommy by Rudyard Kipling

CHASSEUR OF 1914 *by Marcel Dupont*—Experiences of the twilight of the French Light Cavalry by a young officer during the early battles of the great war in Europe.

TROOP HORSE & TRENCH *by R. A. Lloyd*—The experiences of a British Lifeguardsman of the household cavalry fighting on the western front during the First World War 1914-18.

THE EAST AFRICAN MOUNTED RIFLES *by C. J. Wilson*—Experiences of the campaign in the East African bush during the First World War.

THE FIGHTING CAMELIERS *by Frank Reid*—The exploits of the Imperial Camel Corps in the desert and Palestine campaigns of the First World War.

ALSO FROM LEONAUR

AVAILABLE IN SOFTCOVER OR HARDCOVER WITH DUST JACKET

THE COMPLEAT RIFLEMAN HARRIS *by Benjamin Harris as told to & transcribed by Captain Henry Curling*—The adventures of a soldier of the 95th (Rifles) during the Peninsular Campaign of the Napoleonic Wars

WITH WELLINGTON'S LIGHT CAVALRY *by William Tomkinson*—The Experiences of an officer of the 16th Light Dragoons in the Peninsular and Waterloo campaigns of the Napoleonic Wars.

SERGEANT BOURGOGNE *by Adrien Bourgogne*—With Napoleon's Imperial Guard in the Russian Campaign and on the Retreat from Moscow 1812 - 13.

SWORDS OF HONOUR *by Henry Newbolt & Stanley L. Wood*—The Careers of Six Outstanding Officers from the Napoleonic Wars, the Wars for India and the American Civil War, with dozens of illustrations by Stanley L. Wood.

SURTEES OF THE RIFLES *by William Surtees*—A Soldier of the 95th (Rifles) in the Peninsular campaign of the Napoleonic Wars.

ENSIGN BELL IN THE PENINSULAR WAR *by George Bell*—The Experiences of a young British Soldier of the 34th Regiment 'The Cumberland Gentlemen' in the Napoleonic wars.

HUSSAR IN WINTER *by Alexander Gordon*—A British Cavalry Officer during the retreat to Corunna in the Peninsular campaign of the Napoleonic Wars.

NAPOLEONIC WAR STORIES *by Sir Arthur Quiller-Couch*—Tales of soldiers, spies, battles & sieges from the Peninsular & Waterloo campaingns.

JOURNALS OF ROBERT ROGERS OF THE RANGERS *by Robert Rogers*—The exploits of Rogers & the Rangers in his own words during 1755-1761 in the French & Indian War.

KERSHAW'S BRIGADE VOLUME 1 *by D. Augustus Dickert*—Manassas, Seven Pines, Sharpsburg (Antietam), Fredricksburg, Chancellorsville, Gettysburg, Chickamauga, Chattanooga, Fort Sanders & Bean Station..

KERSHAW'S BRIGADE VOLUME 2 *by D. Augustus Dickert*—At the wilderness, Cold Harbour, Petersburg, The Shenandoah Valley and Cedar Creek.

A TIGER ON HORSEBACK *by L. March Phillips*—The Experiences of a Trooper & Officer of Rimington's Guides - The Tigers - during the Anglo-Boer war 1899 - 1902.

ALSO FROM LEONAUR

AVAILABLE IN SOFTCOVER OR HARDCOVER WITH DUST JACKET

CAPTAIN OF THE 95th (Rifles) *by Jonathan Leach*—An officer of Wellington's Sharpshooters during the Peninsular, South of France and Waterloo Campaigns of the Napoleonic Wars.

THE KHAKEE RESSALAH *by Robert Henry Wallace Dunlop*—Service & adventure with the Meerut volunteer horse during the Indian mutiny 1857-1858

BUGLER AND OFFICER OF THE RIFLES *by William Green & Harry Smith* With the 95th (Rifles) during the Peninsular & Waterloo Campaigns of the Napoleonic Wars

BAYONETS, BUGLES AND BONNETS by *James 'Thomas' Todd*—Experiences of hard soldiering with the 71st Foot - the Highland Light Infantry - through many battles of the Napoleonic wars including the Peninsular & Waterloo Campaigns

A NORFOLK SOLDIER IN THE FIRST SIKH WAR *by J W Baldwin*—Experiences of a private of H.M. 9th Regiment of Foot in the battles for the Punjab, India 1845-46

A CAVALRY OFFICER DURING THE SEPOY REVOLT *by A.R.D. Mackenzie*—Experiences with the 3rd Bengal Light Cavalry, the Guides and Sikh Irregular Cavalry from the outbreak to Delhi and Lucknow

THE ADVENTURES OF A LIGHT DRAGOON *by George Farmer & G.R. Gleig*—A cavalryman during the Peninsular & Waterloo Campaigns, in captivity & at the siege of Bhurtpore, India

THE COMPLEAT RIFLEMAN HARRIS *by Benjamin Harris as told to & transcribed by Captain Henry Curling*—The adventures of a soldier of the 95th (Rifles) during the Peninsular Campaign of the Napoleonic Wars

THE RED DRAGOON by *W.J. Adams*—With the 7th Dragoon Guards in the Cape of Good Hope against the Boers & the Kaffir tribes during the 'war of the axe' 1843-48

THE LIFE OF THE REAL BRIGADIER GERARD - Volume 1 - THE YOUNG HUSSAR 1782 - 1807 *by Jean-Baptiste De Marbot*—A French Cavalryman Of the Napoleonic Wars at Marengo, Austerlitz, Jena, Eylau & Friedland

THE LIFE OF THE REAL BRIGADIER GERARD Volume 2 IMPERIAL AIDE-DE-CAMP 1807 - 1811 *by Jean-Baptiste De Marbot*—A French Cavalryman of the Napoleonic Wars at Saragossa, Landshut, Eckmuhl, Ratisbon, Aspern-Essling, Wagram, Busaco & Torres Vedras

www.ingramcontent.com/pod-product-compliance
Lightning Source LLC
LaVergne TN
LVHW050929080826
845145LV00001B/262

* 9 7 8 1 8 4 6 7 7 3 1 5 0 *